Women of Influence in Contemporary Music

Nine American Composers

Edited by Michael K. Slayton

The Scarecrow Press, Inc.
Lanham • Toronto • Plymouth, UK
2011

Published by Scarecrow Press, Inc.
A wholly owned subsidiary of The Rowman & Littlefield Publishing Group, Inc.
4501 Forbes Boulevard, Suite 200, Lanham, Maryland 20706
http://www.scarecrowpress.com

Estover Road, Plymouth PL6 7PY, United Kingdom

British Cataloging in Publication Information Available

Library of Congress Cataloging-in-Publication Data
Women of influence in contemporary music : nine American composers / edited by Michael K. Slayton.
   p. cm.
   Includes bibliographical references and index.
   ISBN 978-0-8108-7742-9 (cloth : alk. paper) — ISBN 978-0-8108-7748-1 (ebook)
   1. Women composers—United States—Biography. 2. Women composers—United States—Interviews. 3. Music by women composers—United States—21st century—Analysis, appreciation. 4. Music by women composers—United States—20th century—Analysis, appreciation. I. Slayton, Michael.
   ML82.W676 2011
   780.92'273—dc22
   [B]   2010028110

Printed in the United States of America

And now we who are writing women and strange monsters
Still search our hearts to find the difficult answers,

Still hope that we may learn to lay our hands
More gently and more subtly on the burning sands.

To be through what we make more simply human,
To come to the deep place where poet becomes woman,

Where nothing has to be renounced or given over
In the pure light that shines out from the lover,

In the pure light that brings forth fruit and flower
And that great sanity, that sun, the feminine power.

—May Sarton, from "My Sisters, O My Sisters," *The Lion and the Rose*

CONTENTS

Karin Pendle

FOREWORD:
"WHO ARE THESE WOMEN?"

Who are these women, these "women of influence?" Why have they been chosen to represent not "women composers," but "American composers," and why have they been brought before us as people who have something important to say, something perhaps that we need to hear? Who are these women?

The answer—they are living, active, professional composers whose lives span nearly three generations of music history. Some are the products of musical families, where they were introduced to music making at early ages; some came to music later in life and in ways that might have seemed irregular to even the best-known women composers of the past century. Some have had to deal with sexism in pursuit of their goals, but none was denied advanced professional training because of her gender. They studied at major music schools or at public universities. They learned their craft in New England, in Europe, on the West Coast, in New York, in the south, or in the midwest. They write songs and music for piano; they also write chamber music, operas, symphonies, and concert pieces for major orchestras, concertos for celebrated soloists, works that involve electroacoustic media, and more. They create large forms or miniatures. They draw on European traditions or on the latest idioms from the worlds of jazz or pop. They write on commission; their music is performed. For them, the only boundaries are those set by the requirements of the piece and its performers. Finally, most have an interest in passing on what they have learned, by teaching, coaching, conducting, or serving on local and national committees and boards as advocates for their art.

And yet, how different they are. In Elizabeth Austin we see the clear, gradual development of an individual style over time, grounded in the best elements of the Western musical heritage. Susan Botti emerges from the world of the theater, conveying her ideas in a method of notation that links the compositional process to the desired outcome, the performance. World music comes into play strongly and personally in the music of Gabriela Lena Frank and Tania León, their works presenting a multitude of colors and infinite variety heretofore unrevealed to their American listeners. The amazing and purposeful productivity of Libby Larsen, or Judith Shatin's constant experimentation with sound, and their sense of connection to the world around them—these things mark them as individuals who share a drive to communicate through music. Jennifer Higdon, whose rising career has been marked by an energetic determination, her music by a noteworthy accessibility, seems to have sprung fully formed from Philadelphia's Verizon Hall to performance halls throughout the country. Cindy McTee explores the full sounds of the symphony orchestra, the bright sounds of the symphonic band, and the computer-generated sounds made possible by modern technology. Meanwhile, alongside them, Marga Richter, with supreme art and meticulous craft, creates music in an eclectic idiom that continues to draw new listeners.

That these women have been able to forge successful careers in a field where so many women of the past have failed results not only from their superior talent and hard work. Many of the conditions that once dominated society's perceptions and treatment of women have been altered, gradually in the aftermath of World War II, more quickly with the onset of the women's movement of the later twentieth century. The word that best sums up these developments is *access*.

All the women in these essays were encouraged by their families to pursue their dreams, but unlike many women musicians and composers of the past, none had to depend on these families for their training or initiation into the music world as professionals. In North America, the establishment of public education, from elementary school to the university level, provided the model of access for young people to training in fields they might not otherwise have considered possible. Higdon's youthful exposure to music came in a high school band; she then moved on to a state university. Larsen, Frank, Shatin, and McTee received all or part of their training in composition at state universities. Along with many fine private institutions, public schools and universities gave women access to the profession of composer.

Successful composers need access to performers, not only so that others can hear their music but so that they themselves can hear and learn from it. Academic institutions provided initial access in their performing ensembles or in ad hoc groups of students willing to take part in composition recitals. To this end, Larsen helped found the Minnesota (now American) Composers Forum and remained in the Twin Cities because of the many opportunities she saw to have her music performed. Others have enjoyed similar experiences at schools and in cities where they have studied or taught: Higdon, Botti, Shatin, McTee, and Richter, for example. Access to performers has been important in establishing themselves as professional composers.

Other kinds of access have come with developments in technology. For example, access to the public has been facilitated by means of recordings and published scores. Works by all the women covered in this book have been recorded, making their music available for repeated hearings by listeners outside their own geographical areas. Many have found outlets with major publishers (e.g., Frank, Larsen, León, Richter), but computer technology has made self-publishing a viable option, as it has for Higdon and McTee.

Technology has also affected what were formerly the print media. Online journals, blogs, and music reviews come across the Internet with regularity, bringing reports of new music from across the land. Never before have women composers had better access to the kind of review process that is so necessary to establishing their reputations as professional composers. Finally, women have access to new sounds and means of production that have grown out of computer technology. Shatin, McTee, and Larsen are among those who have made telling and creative use of these media. New sounds have also come from the models of world music, accessed by León and Frank from the roots of their cultures, to become part of the American scene.

Together, these women, both in their commonalities and their differences, represent the current state of our concert music in its many incarnations. Their music is genderless, its worth unquestionable. It deserves to be performed, heard, and studied. The essays collected here provide thorough introductions to their lives, their personalities, and their art. In so many ways, they are indeed women of influence.

Michael K. Slayton

EDITOR'S PREFACE

Women of Influence in Contemporary Music: Nine American Composers has been a collaborative project, a collection of nine chapters contributed by eight authors about nine prominent, living American composers: Elizabeth R. Austin, Susan Botti, Gabriela Lena Frank, Jennifer Higdon, Libby Larsen, Tania León, Cindy McTee, Marga Richter, and Judith Shatin. The idea for this project came eight years ago, stemming from my own work with the music of Elizabeth R. Austin. I had been writing extensively about her harmonic language, her intriguing "windowpane" method, and her penchant for weaving the music of the past into a contemporary tapestry. These scholarly, analytical endeavors inevitably led to a personal friendship with Austin herself, and we began a series of discussions that led to pertinent questions quite outside the realm of theoretical analysis: What exactly *is* the state of American culture concerning women who seek to develop careers as composers? What stories would women tell who had chosen this path, say, in the early 1950s? What about now? How have things changed over the past fifty years? Are there things that *haven't* changed? And how may such issues be addressed without drawing further, undesired attention to gender differences?

The composers selected for this book are representative of several different impulses in American music. While they have much in common, not least of all their dedication to their art, their individual stories reveal some of the paths that any American composer may follow. The women in this book have grown up in various circumstances, made various employment decisions, and faced diverse opportunities and obstacles; they demonstrate a variety of stylistic traits and a wide range of physical ages, experiences, and current levels of public prominence.

The contributing authors were chosen in collaboration with the composers themselves. And because each author brings specific expertise and insights to the life and music of the composer with whom he or she is paired, the chapters are able to take an approach that is, above all, a personal one. Each chapter includes a biography of the composer, an interview, and a detailed theoretical and stylistic analysis of one major work. The composers have been asked to reflect openly on their individual journeys. The authors, like the composers, represent a wide range in the spectrum of contemporary musical scholarship. They are as follows:

Michael K. Slayton—Vanderbilt University
Carson Cooman—Boston, MA
Deborah Hayes—University of Colorado, Boulder, emerita
Donald McKinney—Interlochen Arts Academy
Tina Milhorn Stallard—University of South Carolina
James Spinazzola—University of Indianapolis
Sharon Mirchandani—Westminster Choir College of Rider University
Judith Lochhead—State University of New York, Stony Brook

The nine chapters of *Women of Influence in Contemporary Music* seek to reflect the contexts of the shifting societal landscapes in the United States over the last seven decades, as well as different stylistic approaches to writing music. The chapters benefit from the insights of recent cultural studies approaches that contextualize the creative output of composers rather than understanding it as having a source in genius alone. This book will therefore fill an important gap in the scholarly literature, as its combination of biographical information, interviews, discussion of compositional style, and analysis of a specific work presents a unique approach to the topic of American women in music. Dialogues between composer and author, which led to each contribution, situate the studies of these composers in the grounded reality of the composer's own experience. It is hoped this approach will complement those found in other essential resources and will be a welcome update, helping readers find another path to discovery of the important contributions made by American women through its personal approach and clear focus on theoretical and analytical aspects of each composer's style.

Because gender is crucial to personhood, gender issues arise, particularly in the interviews, and there is little uniformity in our subjects' responses to feminism in its various historical manifestations. Composers themselves resist most kinds of labeling because it takes away from a focus on the music; composers who are women, like composers who are men, want simply to have their music considered as music. This book is intended, then, to provide perspective on these issues from the personal vantage point of the composer; plainly put, this book is about music and the people who create it.

ACKNOWLEDGMENTS

It is my great pleasure to express long-overdue gratitude to colleagues, friends, and family who have helped bring this book from idea to reality.

First, I am deeply grateful to my fellow contributing authors: Carson, Deborah, Don, Tina, James, Sharon, and Judy. Thank you for your enthusiasm for this project and for trusting me with your words. I am proud to count you among my colleagues and friends. I owe special thanks to Deborah Hayes, who has been a vital source of counsel for me during the completion stages; I am indebted to her for allowing me (too) much of her valuable time.

To the composers—Elizabeth, Susan, Gabriela, Jennifer, Libby, Tania, Cindy, Marga, and Judith—thank you for your bravery in embarking on this journey with us and for trusting us to tell your stories. I am personally humbled and honored to have been afforded the opportunity to glean new knowledge and understanding from hearing your stories, studying your music, and pondering the life examples you offer. Thank you for your willingness to share with us authors the intimate details that have shaped your careers and informed your writing. We are all indebted to you for making this book a possibility.

I would like to thank my colleagues at Vanderbilt University: Mark Wait, dean of the Blair School of Music, for granting me research leave to see the book to completion. His encouragement, generosity, and friendship have been essential to this project and to my academic career. To my friend and colleague, Cynthia Cyrus, associate dean and associate professor of musicology, who spent several hours intently listening, offering ideas, and reminding me to take time to breathe, thank you for your friendship and keen insights. And to my student research assistants, Scott Lee and Trey Dayton—guys, I owe you more than coffee. Hold me to it.

Thank you to my family for your endless support and encouragement: Jessica, for having continual patience with a husband who's had a computer seemingly affixed to his lap for the past year—your love means the world to me. And to Finn, who was born six months into the editing process, thanks for keeping me laughing, buddy. Taking a break to stack blocks was just what I needed some days. I love you both.

Finally, I am especially and forever indebted to my dear Elizabeth, whose music has drawn me, whose wisdom has instructed me, and whose life has inspired me for the ten years I have known her.

This book was born of her light, and I dedicate it to her.

Michael K. Slayton

ELIZABETH R. AUSTIN (1938–)

Goethe represents for me an ideal. He is a synthesis, as Bach was; he brings together the threads of what has come before him. And how much verse, how much rhyme—something so enormously intense in such a small space—it's amazing. The "Ginkgo" poem is twelve lines, and there is a world in those twelve lines. The poem started with a leaf—just with a leaf—the division of it and what that could mean. And he realized it in such condensed form. Goethe took natural substances and created his own structure, much as I do with my music. He is incontrovertibly passionate, but it is underground passion; he uses his muse, but he's never condescending. That's what I like.[1]

There are moments in the life of the artist when the need to say something significant outweighs the fear of speaking. For Elizabeth Austin, the need was great enough to generate music which, in an era characterized by slow change, flowed with undomesticated enthusiasm and emotion. The music of this gracious composer is the manifestation of artistic need: rippling with life, flowing with confidence, speaking volumes.

Austin's early musical training began at the Peabody Preparatory Department in her hometown of Baltimore, Maryland; as a teenager, she spent her summers at the Junior Conservatory Camp in Vermont under the tutelage of Grace Newsom Cushman.[2] By the age of sixteen, Austin (then, Elizabeth Rhudy) had won several awards, including first prize in the National Federation of Music Club's Composition Competition for her choral piece, *Christ Being Raised*. But it was during her studies at Goucher College that a fortuitous event would pitch her headlong into the composer's life: when Mlle Nadia Boulanger came to visit the school. Upon hearing Austin's *Rilke Lieder* in an evening student concert, an impressed Boulanger offered the nineteen-year-old a scholarship to study at the *Conservatoire Americain* in Fontainebleau.

> *Since I only recognized and accepted myself as an artist, in the true sense of the word, after forty (considering it too precious prior to this "epiphany"), I kept trying to undermine and devaluate the way my mind conducted itself in comparison with those around me. . . . Excusing this mental behavior as simply artistic was dishonest; I have since come to realize that it's all about priorities. Artists squirm until they find a way to relax into their "time at bat."*

Studying at the piano of Boulanger was incalculably intimidating for any young composer, and for Austin the experience was no less so. Not only was she treading the footsteps of Elliott Carter, Aaron Copland, Louise Talma, and Virgil Thompson, she was also confronting the social stigmas of that era and the remarkable fact that Boulanger herself rather openly discouraged women from pursuing musical careers. Having spent most of her childhood at Peabody Conservatory's Preparatory Department and the Junior Conservatory Camp, Austin felt well equipped to brave the challenges of her lessons with Boulanger, but she soon began to understand that she would be continuously pressed to strive for revelations above her own present cognitive powers. Boulanger was requiring the young composer to stand above her own freshly finished work and eye it scrupulously, to subject it to rigid and demanding criteria.

It was this period of study that served to introduce Austin to what she deems the predominantly European attitude of judicious thought, of healthy skepticism regarding the questioning of premises or the premature rush to conclusion. Although her liberal arts education was grounded in intellectual rigor, she still had to learn to be unflinching in the face of probing criticism and to ply these indispensable and scholarly tools herself. "Boulanger was a leading exponent of the critical mind," says Austin, "and those who realized and accepted this invaluable training were so much the better for it." Austin maintains that she owes much of her understanding of the compositional process to her time at Fontainebleau, as well as the instillation of the cogent thinking that would inform her compositional decisions for the rest of her life.

Notwithstanding the obvious bearing Boulanger had upon the young composer (as indeed such a monumental didactic force would have upon any student), the mature Austin yet points to Grace Newsom Cushman as her most significant mentor. Cushman's teaching was indispensable during the formative years, wherein she asked her students to approach a subject with the same type of thoroughness and authenticity as had Mlle Boulanger.

Both mentors shared a generous tolerance and encouragement of all musical styles, provided the compositional details could be thoroughly justified.

> *[Cushman] was unique in requiring her students to hear, play, sing, and write building blocks of sound—to think in time, to stand outside the sound as well as to inhabit it. I owe this woman the acquisition of a good ear. And at an age where I was beginning to realize the aural images in my mind, she and Mlle Boulanger gave their students the only temporal power worth having: the power to communicate and enhance the measure of beauty on this earth.*

Upon returning from France, Austin finished her diploma at Goucher College,[3] and in the short time before she married, she taught music in the Baltimore City public school system. After her wedding in August of 1961,[4] Austin (at that time Elizabeth Scheidel) and her husband moved to a suburb of Hartford, Connecticut,[5] where she taught in the Hartford public schools until her first pregnancy was evident (an observable pregnancy was disallowed at that time in public school teaching). While raising her family, she served as a teacher of music composition and theory at various music preparatory schools in the Hartford area, developing an eight-semester musicianship curriculum designed to emphasize functional harmonic practice from the eighteenth to the twentieth century—a performance/improvisational program of study based on Cushman's teaching. Achieving the essential balance between family and lifework has proven to be a regular source of complexity for Elizabeth Austin; the birth of twins in June 1962, for instance, was at the same moment a source of joy and, undeniably, a mammoth career yield for the budding composer.

> *Having twins ten months after my wedding, I plunged joyfully into maternity in full bloom! When (my daughter) Susan developed life-threatening asthma at fourteen months of age, however, the only "music" I could hear for the next fifteen years was the pitiable wheezing of this poor child in the bedroom down the hall. I tried to compose during that forlorn period, but I knew instinctively that my inner voice wasn't listening or even fine-tuned for the clarity and mental spaciousness necessary for creativity.*

Austin returned to academia in 1979, a rational decision to ensure her family a means of support. She enrolled in the University of Hartford's Hartt School of Music with the purpose of obtaining her state public teaching certification; in doing so, however, she found she had reopened the veritable Pandora's Box, what she calls "the true self-centering of learning and its accompanying ecstasy." Austin pursued her master's degree, studying with Donald Harris and Edward Diemente, each of whom proved to be a basal source of encouragement and freedom. It was a signal point in time for Austin as a composer, and suddenly an unbounded rush of music began to pour forth. Austin's *Zodiac Suite* for piano solo (1980) was her breakthrough work: a monumental, virtuosic eruption, laden with fifteen years of pent-up power and wonder.

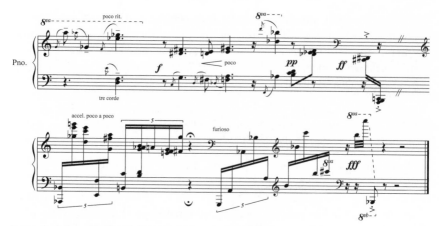

Example 1.1a.   *Zodiac Suite* (1980), "Taurus," ending

Example 1.1b.   *Zodiac Suite*, "Libra," mm. 22–24

Austin candidly acknowledges that during this phase she became absent from the priority of family, succumbing to the lure of the arts—"that fearsome lure which Thomas Mann describes," says the composer, "not romantic, actually quite unpleasant and painful for surrounding and unsuspecting family." Austin realized that she was on a road which would inexorably move her away from family-centeredness. She finished her M.M. in music composition and immediately began the Ph.D. program at the University of Connecticut, where she studied with James Eversole and Jane Brockman. Before long, the rigors of graduate studies, the demands of professional work as organist and teacher, and the challenge and chaos of raising three children unsurprisingly sealed the demise of Austin's first marriage. "Because I was often teaching until very late in the evening, the family rarely enjoyed a dinner meal together," she remembers. "The household became increasingly dysfunctional, and I simply never possessed the alacrity to realize it."

Austin persisted, steadily working and writing, and several pieces were born out of this period of relative reclusion. After the *Zodiac Suite* came the string quartet *Inscapes* (1981),[6] *Christmas the Reason* (1981), for women's choir and amplified piano, and *The Song of Simeon (Nunc Dimittis)* (1983), for mixed choir and organ.[7]

> *I had always considered it a cheap shot to empower myself as artist, having been raised in an "enlightened" but quite middle-class family circle. Bach's image was my guide; he never put on the air of pseudo-artist, but went about his composing as his life's work and calling. . . . The "pearl of great price" is always in the back of my mind as I write music. How many friends and family did I hurt, as I pulled away toward my own center; and how does one ever redeem this act?*

Austin's career has moved steadily forward since this rebirth; she won several awards and honors in the years following, for pieces such as the *Cantata Beatitudines* (1982),[8] *Klavier Double* (1983), and her *Symphony no. 1, "Wilderness,"* which was given a performance by the Hartford Symphony in 1987.[9] As the socio-musical climate grew significantly more tolerant of a variety of musical styles, Austin discovered new opportunities for herself as a composer. The efforts of such organizations as the International Alliance for Women in Music (IAWM) and the Society of Women Artists in German-speaking Countries (GEDOK) began to bring awareness to the dearth of performance opportunities for music written by women, an awareness which has bloomed more fully in the dawning years of this century. "The militancy of that time has been ameliorated today by the same seriousness of purpose on the part of women artists," says Austin, "only now coupled with the realization that composers of both genders must unite to find a way to promote new concert music, especially in America."

Through GEDOK and the *Staatliche Hochschule für Musik Heidelberg-Mannheim* came the truly seminal moments in Austin's career. During the late 1980s and early 1990s, these two institutions sponsored a series of four portrait concerts of her music in Mannheim, and then in 1996, Austin was chosen by GEDOK to represent the Mannheim-Ludwigshafen region in their national seventieth-year anniversary exhibition.[10] Throughout Austin's residency in Mannheim, the *Staatliche Hochschule für Musik* welcomed her by providing her with outstanding performing artists, opportunities to lecture about American composers, and, most importantly, the venue for several of her portrait concerts.[11] During this time, Austin composed some of her most persuasive music, including the harpsichord piece *Lighthouse I* (1989); *To Begin*, for brass quintet (1990); *An die Nachgeborenen*, for SATB chorus, soli, and piano (1992); *Litauische Lieder*, for baritone and piano (1995); *Sans Souci Souvenir*, for viola d'amore and harpsichord (1996); and the highly regarded *Hommage for Hildegard*, for mezzo-soprano, baritone, flute, clarinet, percussion, and piano (1997).[12]

In 1989, Austin married Professor Gerhard Austin, and for many years afterward, the couple spent part of each year in Mannheim and Jena, where Professor Austin directed the Mannheim and Jena Programs for Bilingual Careers.[13] Through these programs, the Austins were given the opportunity to promote an exchange of ideas and peoples through internationally sponsored projects, with an emphasis on cultural activities in Eastern Europe. Frequently being called upon to translate scholarly papers and act as interpreter for German-speaking composers has brought Austin into contact with preeminent musicians both in the United States and abroad. In June 1998, GEDOK sponsored a retrospective concert of Austin's chamber music in Mannheim, and in that same year, performances of her works were presented in Fiuggi, Italy, and Rheinsberg, Germany, as well as in Virginia, Nebraska, and Connecticut. By the turn of the century, Elizabeth Austin had established herself as one of America's distinct compositional voices. In high demand, she currently spends much of her time traveling domestically and internationally for performances of her works, speaking engagements, and teaching residencies.

Hofmannstahl believed in three things, essentially: "Durch das Werk, durch das Kind, durch die Tat" ("Through your work (art), through a child, through action"). Your life can be justified by any one or all of these things. I believe that.

The aural effect of Elizabeth Austin's music upon the listener is one that innately creates a desire to understand it. Found juxtaposed within its walls are the zealous strains of unbridled Romanticism, seemingly impenetrable dissonances, and flashes of sudden lucid tonal clarity. Austin's music is meticulously constructed, and it is no small undertaking to expose the compositional processes which synthesize her works. If any attempt is to be made to understand the composer's stylistic traits, we must come to terms with Austin's music in relation to formal design, as well as her personal affinity for musical nostalgia. But we will begin with the Austinian harmonic language, for it is there that the seeds are planted for future revelations.

The distinct sonorities pervasive to much of Austin's music are born of her penchant for a harmonic system derived from the intertwining of minor sixths and minor thirds. Austin's minor sixth/minor third system rests upon the premise that, beginning at any point, an alternating stacking of these intervals quickly generates an array of harmonies that dutifully struggles to avoid the perfect fifth and especially the perfect octave, thereby promoting major sevenths and major ninths to what Austin calls "the new octave" (see figure 1.1).

This alternate stacking of minor sixths and thirds yields a number of significant observable results, but most important to Austin's purposes is its natural avoidance of tonal center. Beginning with any pitch class (let us use C), we find that stacking alternating minor sixths and thirds creates, quite efficiently, an eight-tone row; and if we continue the process, we

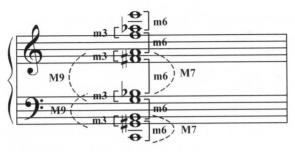

Figure 1.1.

eventually complete the aggregate with minimal pitch class repetition in an alternating pattern of descending semitones (see figure 1.2).[14]

Figure 1.2.

The patent characteristic of this system is its ability to manifest a seemingly infinite collection of nontonal possibilities. Austin's musical passages undulate and twist themselves, shifting from place to place, eluding any sense of centeredness. There exist myriad instances of Austin's employment of the minor sixth/minor third harmonic system in her music; a few notable examples follow:

Example 1.2a.   *Hommage for Hildegard* (1997), mm. 33–35

Example 1.2b. *Capricornus Caribbicus* (1998), mm. 12–14

Example 1.2c. *Rose Sonata* (2002), p. 13

Austin uses the *sheen* of polychordal triadic patterns, but treats them in a non-tonally functional manner. In her vocal writing in particular, the singer is often heartened to work with the tonal and intervallic patterns with which he or she is familiar; the harmonies providing more provocative emotional contrast are typically assigned to the instrumental part(s). One of the more striking examples of this is found in her song cycle *Frauenliebe und -leben,* a contemporary setting of the 1830 Adelbert von Chamisso text. Here we find the implementation of the minor sixth/minor third harmonic system being put to additional task; for in this case, it is the opaqueness of the musical language that ironically serves as a lens through which we may observe the composer wrestling with the modern female condition, even with her own psyche. Austin's musical interpretation of the womanly thoughts embodied in Chamisso's figure may encompass questions, doubts, and objections (particularly in the piano, which is often in starkly dissimilar mood to the voice). It is rather uncomplicated to understand, then, how the preponderance of stacked minor sixths and thirds (and therefore inherent noncenteredness) in *Frauenliebe* lends aid to Austin's effectively communicating this lacking of inner peace inside the woman, the need for stability. This technique, coupled with an interesting array of intertwined triadic polychordal structures, bring to Austin's *Frauenliebe* a sound of constant struggle, a chiaroscuro effect between serenity and chaos, as if the woman, though thoroughly in love and generally happy with her life, could at any moment spin out of control.[15]

Example 1.3a.   Austin, *Frauenliebe und -leben* (1999), I. *Seit ich ihn gesehen*, mm. 7–8

Example 1.3b.   Austin, *Frauenliebe und -leben*, II. *Er, der Herrlichste von allen*, mm. 25–27

Frauenliebe exhibits the rather remarkable level of compositional forethought that further lends character to Elizabeth Austin's music. So much goes into the planning of a piece for her; she is as concerned with the extramusical thematic elements of her work as she is with the notes themselves.

> *I would say in 90 percent of my music I have a literal catalyst. I borrow something from literature; I have a programmatic image.*

From such a vantage point, it is not difficult to recognize the logic in Austin's recent exploration of the botanical world as it correlates to music—of nature's living symbiosis with art. Botanical structures and natural geometric designs have provided Austin with a rich bounty of formal blueprints from which she has constructed several of her more prominent mature works, including the trio piece entitled *Ginkgo Novo* (2001) and the haunting *Rose Sonata* (2002) for solo piano and reciter.

Dieses Baums Blatt, der von Osten	This tree's leaf, that grows entrusted
Meinem Garten anvertraut,	To my garden from the East,
Gibt geheimen Sinn zu kosten,	Yields its secrets that delight us,
Wie's den Wissenden erbaut.	As it pleases those who know.
Ist es ein lebendig Wesen,	Is it living just as *one*,
Das sich in sich selbst getrennt?	Separate within itself?
Sind es zwei, die sich erlesen,	Are there *two*, who chose each other,
Dass man sie als eines kennt?	So that they are known as one?
Solche Frage zu erwidern,	In reply to all these questions
Fand ich wohl den rechten Sinn;	I have found the meaning true:
Fühlst du nicht an meinen Liedern,	Don't you feel in all my singing,
Dass ich eins und doppelt bin?	I am *one* and *double* too?

Figure 1.3. Johann Wolfgang von Goethe, "Ginkgo Biloba"[16]

Johann Wolfgang Goethe's remarkable twelve-line poem about the leaf of the ginkgo tree may be found printed in or around assorted historic sites in Germany, including of course the famous Goethe house in Weimar (see figure 1.3). It is well known that Weimar was and is the Goethe *Stadt*, but less known is that the poet often sought refuge from his official duties in Weimar and traveled to the small town of Jena, some twenty kilometers to the east. He had a ginkgo tree planted there around the turn of the nineteenth century, and so today Jena has the signal honor of having the Goethe ginkgo standing in its botanical garden, calling as muse to Elizabeth Austin, who travels to the site virtually every year.[17]

And so, when commissioned in 2001 to compose a work based on Goethe's celebrated poem for the Weimar Trio PianOVo,[18] Austin turned to the ginkgo tree for inspiration, specifically to its leaf. The leaf of the ginkgo is botanically unique in that it begins, at its inception, as two separate lobes, two parts which then gradually, over the span of their existence, fuse themselves into a singular entity, so that by the time a ginkgo tree is mature, the two parts of its leaves have become one. Focused on Goethe's poetic exploration of the leaf as metaphor for human relationship, Austin composed *Ginkgo Novo* as a musical (and visual) representation of this natural phenomenon. Goethe's poem contains a riddle of sorts;

the reader/observer is left to wonder, does the leaf glory in its double symmetry, or does it yearn to be recognized as one body? *Ginkgo Novo* poses the same question, as Austin asks the performers (English horn and violoncello) to literally separate and rejoin themselves on the stage, following the shape of the ginkgo biloba leaf.

FLOOR DIAGRAM for GINKGO NOVO

If the hornist plays standing up, one will need one chair at each of the three Stations for the cellist (3 chairs in all). Six stands will be needed (with scores in place at each stand!), two at each of the three Stations.

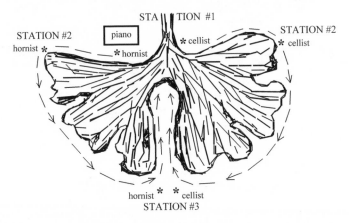

The structural form of the music describes the shape of the ginkgo bilboa leaf. At the beginning, all three players are at Station #1.

At rehearsal letter F (measure 37), the hornist and cellist move in opposite directions to their respective Station #2.

At measure 72, as pianist holds chord, the hornist and cellist move towards each other again (pianist or reciter is reciting lines of poem while they are moving) and stand slightly separated at Station #3.

They remain at Station #3, during 4th recitation, when hornist circles cellist (right after rehearsal letter O).

About 25 seconds after rehearsal letter P, after cellist finishes playing this line, he/she walks back to Station #1. About one minute after rehearsal letter P, after hornist finishes playing this line, he/she walks back to Station #1.

All three players remain there until the end.

Figure 1.4. Austin's *Ginkgo Novo* diagram

The piano is the soil of this garden bed, and the other two instruments describe a "living being which divides within itself."[19] We hear intervallic retrogrades and inversions, melodic mirrors or paradigms, imitative and antiphonal elements, and even a melodic "crab" at one point, as the binary element gradually coalesces into a unified whole. Often separated by extremes of register, there is more or less a proportioned stasis, with little harmonic direction. One hears two or more planes, the "one and double" of Goethe's image; the instruments are distinct entities within an integrated whole. Here it is the fusion of tonal gestures (i.e., triadic constructions) with symmetrical and interlocking intervallic relations (minor sixth/minor third) which further define Austin's harmonic style.

Example 1.4. *Ginkgo Novo* (2001), p. 8, rehearsal K

Near the end, the two begin to make their way to a central point, and the seam—the gap in the biloba leaf—seems to close up. Hand in hand, the instrumentalists return full circle to their original places on stage, having "re-grown together."[20] To further enhance the experience for the audience, Austin has also strategically fused into the work optional recitations of the various lines from the Goethe poem, to be presented by either one of the instrumentalists or a selected reader. The end effect envelops (both musically and literarily) Austin's clear understanding of duplicity.

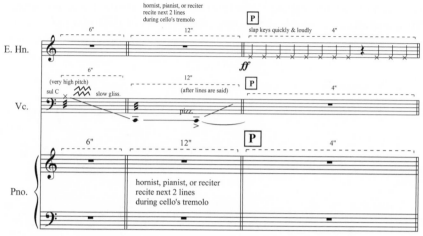

Example 1.5. *Ginkgo Novo,* p. 13, rehearsal P

A faintly contrasting approach to the concept of botanical structure is presented in the *Rose Sonata,* composed the following year. As in *Ginkgo Novo,* Austin brings a literary element into this work, with poetic recitations placed at strategic points in the score. At the "center of the rose," for instance (see figure 1.9), is heard the ennobled poem by Rainer Maria Rilke, *Das Rosen-Innere,* which enlightens Austin's musical form as it delineates the riddle of inner and outer realities, dualism in the face of interconnectedness (something Goethe also addresses in the ginkgo poem). By Rilke's words and Austin's music, the marrow of humanity is revealed: the observer may be observed, the world may become otherworldly, and individual boundaries may become increasingly tenuous.

> *To transform an image into the natural world, perceived through the senses (the "work of eyes"), into musical patterns and phrase-shapes also signals a journey out into your heart, at times a journey of immense loneliness.*

Compositionally speaking, Austin considers the *Rose Sonata* part of "an ongoing exploration of the idea of motivic fragments emerging into a theme, often taken from other composers' works, through an epiphany."[21] The thematic elements embedded within the petals of the rose are wholly derived from Austin's source quote: the first few measures of the Brahms *Intermezzo* no. 2 from op. 118. Motives that burgeoned from this source are carried from the outward petals ever further into the center of the blossom. These motivic elements, however, are well cloaked within Austinian nontonality. For the listener, then, the sonoral path is one of chronoscopic discovery; one is not entirely certain one is hearing a quotation at all until the epiphany, at the center of the rose, where the source quote is at last heard in its entirety.

Example 1.6. *Rose Sonata* (2002), excerpts: motivic fragments from source quote

Austin's utilization of formal structures derived from the natural world intuitively leads toward consideration of her methods concerning proportion and balance. In the following passage, we find one of Austin's hallmark sonorities birthed from the minor sixth/minor third system: specifically, the half-note chords in the second measure, each of which is derived from intertwining two minor sixths a minor third apart (or, conversely, stacking two minor thirds a minor sixth apart). Careful examination of this particular structure will serve as the impetus for discovery and will most concisely speak to the matter at hand.

Example 1.7. *Rose Sonata*, p. 2

This intertwining of minor sixths yields the well-known chord of mixed thirds, a staple of the modern repertoire. When stacked in precisely this manner, however, it has been hailed as the alpha chord of Béla Bartók, mainly due to its sheer prevalence in his works. What is so remarkable about this particular stacking is its resultant intervallic array; precisely, it is that the number of semitones needed to create each interval within corresponds directly to a member of the famed Fibonacci sequence.[22] If we numerically represent each interval by the number of semitones it contains, we quickly recognize the sonority to be wholly derived from Fibonacci intervals.

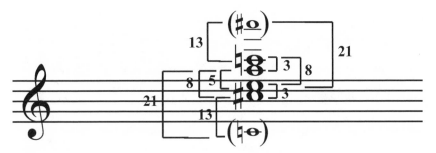

Figure 1.5.

Hypotheses concerning the mathematical properties found in Bartók's music have been supported and refuted for several decades, but regardless of our beliefs regarding Bartók's mathematical intentionality, the idiosyncrasies identified in his music (and specifically in this chord) are irrefutably *present*.[23] And so, if only for the sake of seeking to understand Austin's intentions, we should investigate further. That this particular chordal structure is found littering her scores is no coincidence; it is a natural by-product of the minor sixth/minor third system. But for Austin, the relevancy of its frequent appearance lies at the source of a much higher ideal than mere intervallic intrigue. The crucial trait inherent to the Fibonacci sequence, that being its natural approach toward the "divine proportion" (the golden mean), governs many of Austin's compositional choices regarding form and design.[24]

The golden mean (or golden section) is defined in simplest terms by the mathematical division of any line *AC* by a point *B*, where *BC:AB = AB:AC*. If this ratio holds true, then point *B* lies exactly 0.618 (commonly denoted as *phi*) of the way between *A* and *C* (see figure 1.6).[25]

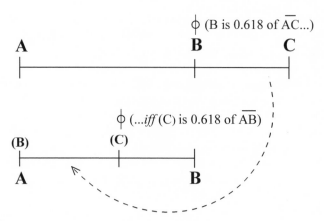

Figure 1.6.

Though many composers have been accused of dividing their musical works into golden sections, such that climactic moments occur at or near the two-thirds point, the position must be proffered that because the divine proportion is innate in nature and inbuilt into human psychology and physiology, in many cases its existence in art and music is more accurately understood as an organic phenomenon than a synthetic one.[26] Some composers and artists have unwittingly created masterworks which adhere to the golden mean precisely; others have made purposeful but unsuccessful attempts. In the end, it is most certainly the *principle* of the golden mean—the core aesthetic of asymmetrical balance in the artistic and natural worlds—more than its exactness that is to be revered.

> *I do believe composers think of patterns, of architecture. I believe in the golden mean; I believe in Fibonacci. This is something that works, obviously, so I plan my work out that way—I and a very large number of other artists! For me this is, again, part of precompositional consciousness—planning your piece, sketching it out, how your time flows.*

Because for Austin the most crucial element of musical infrastructure is its organization according to time and space, it is unsurprising to find her employing the divine proportion in her own works, especially in those pieces purposefully designed around botanical complexes. Her intention is rarely to be rigorous in the endeavor, but simply to embrace the foundational principles of the design; and by tracing the proportional layout of her pieces, one readily uncovers how she engages the golden mean without pursuance of the overtly mathematical. Let us consider the case of Austin's vocal chamber work *Hommage for Hildegard: "Star Equilibrium."*

Clearly this piece is constructed around the golden mean principle. The movements are arranged (temporally) in a perfect arch form, such that

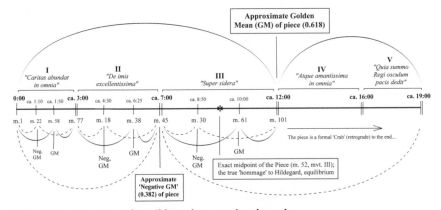

Figure 1.7. *Hommage for Hildegard,* proportional graph

the end of the third movement represents *phi*, while the beginning of the same movement represents the correlative "negative golden mean" (that point which lies at 0.382), an arrangement which necessarily means the work finds its apex, the keystone in the archway, in the exact middle of the third movement. This meticulous construction demonstrates Austin's understanding that true *hommage* to the philosophies of Hildegard must involve a supreme awareness of the mystical properties of balance and proportion. She makes painstaking effort to approach the symbolism of Hildegard's era, to create music which not only honors the sacred feminine equilibrium of the pentacle star, but likewise celebrates the timeless obeisance of *PHI* (*phi*). But Austin is anything but dogged in her approach; although she plans significant events to revolve around the precepts of the golden mean, she plainly understands that time is (and must be) malleable.

In *Wie eine Blume,* another of Austin's botanical works, the design is similar, comparatively proportioned according to golden mean principles. But in this work Austin is quite a bit more precise, as the music seeks to follow the structural path of flower petals in blossom. A rhapsodic, one-movement piece scored for wind sextet and percussion, *Wie eine Blume* utilizes exact patterns from nature, dividing itself into six continuous sections and an expanded center, resulting in an overall hexagonal shape found in certain plants, as well as in wasps' nests and several bacterial forms. The initial section outlines the outer petal of the flower; the next two follow the "scent of the horn"[27] to the center, the inner core. Transformed by the experience of the inner, the music emerges with the final three sections, moving to the outer petal again—now more intense, melodic, and fleeting. One can picture these overlapping petals forming increasingly tighter concentric circles around the inner core or essence of the bloom.

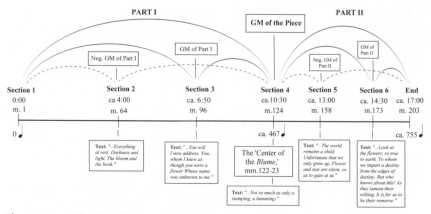

Figure 1.8. *Wie eine Blume,* **proportional graph**

As is often true with Austin's pieces, the music is broken up with various readings or recitations; in this case, we hear texts from Friedrich Hölderlin, Ewald von Kleist, and Rainer Maria Rilke speak to the wonders of the rose, their words marking important breakpoints between sections.[28] Golden mean proportions in this work may be determined by measure numbers ($203 \times 0.618 = 125.4$), quarter note beats ($755 \times 0.618 = 466.5$), or temporal relations ($17{:}00 \times 0.618 = 10{:}50$). In any case, it is clear that Austin intends the "Center of the *Blume*" to position itself at *phi*. And it must not go unnoticed that the two larger parts of the work are further portioned according to the principle; her affinity for denotation of the negative golden mean is again apparent.

Due to the botanical connection between the two pieces, we should be unsurprised to find that a proportional graph of the *Rose Sonata* yields a similar result.

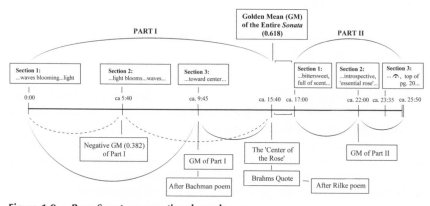

Figure 1.9. *Rose Sonata,* **proportional graph**

In each of these works (and many others), the design is much more than simple mathematical nuance; it is the means to a most essential end. For Austin, the division of her music according to the golden mean is a conduit through which the listener is moving toward impending revelation. It is that particular entity, whatever it may be, waiting at the heart of the piece—in the divine moment of the golden mean—that is of greatest consequence. In *Hildegard*, it is the Delphian sound of the *super sidera* chant melody plucked on the bass strings of the piano, and the soft shimmering of a rising chromatic *tremolo* on the xylophone, swathed on either side with ominous silence. In *Wie eine Blume*, it is a haunting reminiscence of Schumann's *Du bist wie eine Blume* (no. 24 from *Myrthen*, op. 25), played on tuned glasses. And in the *Rose Sonata*, it is the illuminating quote from Brahms resting at the center of the rose; this is the epiphany for which the listener has (perhaps unknowingly) been waiting, and proportionally speaking, Austin places it in the crowning mystical moment.

Example 1.8. *Rose Sonata*, p. 14, the epiphany: the "Center of the Rose"

Austin's transcendent quotation of Brahms in the *Rose Sonata* is an archetypical example of what is perhaps her most relevant trademark, a technique she calls "windowpaning." The importance of this particular procedure to Austin's oeuvre is inestimable, as works such as *A Birthday Bouquet* (1990), *An American Triptych* (2001), and *A Celebration Concerto* (2007) are unanimously constructed around the central focus of incorporating the music of the past into the fabric of the present.[29] With this method, Austin seeks to create a channel through which quoted passages become the alternative sonorities, if due only to their stark relative consonance. As these threads of musical nostalgia are woven in and out of Austin's contemporary tapestry, they create fleeting moments of musical revelation that rise to the ear from the comparative opaqueness of their nontonal substructure.

> *What engages me is to so imbed tonal quotes in a non-tonal or pan-tonal fabric that what has sounded familiar becomes transformed into something regarded as foreign and invasive. It is as though the body allows the cunning invader, wrapped in recognizable guise, to catch it off balance. The musical remembrance exists without expansion, but it is made eccentric through this adjacent pane technique. My aim is for the contemporary sounding fabric to begin to sound "right" to the listener and the tonal quote to sound oddly out of place.*[30]

The zenith illustration of the windowpane method lies with Austin's smallish piano suite, *Puzzle Preludes*, composed in 1994. These five solo piano pieces offer quotations as musical puzzles for the player (and capable audience members), which may be solved through careful listening or analysis of each movement. "Each of the *Preludes* centers around a musical quote from the piano repertoire of the past, cited either directly or 'bent' intentionally," says the composer. "As the harmonic design weaves in and out of the quotational context, the listener is invited to guess the source of each quote."[31] In the end, it is left to the individual to decide how observable or well hidden is each particular quote, but it is the method behind the finished product that is of interest; are Austin's windowpanes simply providing an impetus for musical expansion? Or do they serve both as *hommage* to, and individual commentary on, preexisting themes?

Example 1.9a.   Brahms, *Waltz in A-flat* (op. 39), no. 15, mm. 1–4

Example 1.9b.   Austin, *Puzzle Preludes* (1994), I, mm. 1–3

In this example from the opening of the first prelude, we may readily see that the quote is not a direct one. Not only is the time signature discrepant, but the rhythmic elements within each measure are altered so as to change the placement of accentuation. Austin's opening measures, however, are undeniably derived from Brahms. The rising line from A-flat to D-flat is present in both, as is the centering on C at the end of measure 4 (measure 3 in Austin). What is vastly different about Austin's music is the way the waltz melody is harmonized. Remembering, however, that windowpaning endeavors to imbed the quote in a nontonal or pan-tonal fabric, we should not be surprised by the composer's apparent lack of concern for maintaining Brahmsian sonorities. Austin shepherds her technique in such as way as to create a finished product akin to the original in aesthetic while unique in sonoral effect. The quotes often fit quite agreeably into her preexisting harmonic structure, requiring little preparation and helping the windowpane to remain somewhat indistinct. Such is the case in this prelude, where the Brahms quote enters and departs with ease—as a whisper of the past rather than a glaring aural prominence.

Likewise, in the fifth prelude, where the windowpane stems from the *Impromptu in A-flat Major* of Schubert, we are introduced to the quotation in the opening measures. But here it is aurally masked by the composer's contemporary harmonic scheme to the extent that there exists to the ear only the caress of something familiar. And Austin doesn't allow Schubert's theme to linger; it dissipates as uncertainly as it appeared.

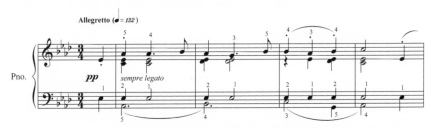

Example 1.10a. **Schubert, *Impromptu in A-flat Major* (op. 142/D. 935), mm. 1–4**

Example 1.10b. **Austin, *Puzzle Preludes*, V, mm. 9–13**

But clever disguise is not always Austin's intention. In the fourth prelude, where the windowpane germinates from the first movement of the *Pathétique Sonata*, the quoted material is treated quite differently. Here, no notes from the original are altered, and the effect is one of startling recognition, as long-cherished passages from Beethoven, fully intact, suddenly rise as the Leviathan from Austin's score for brief moments of aural lucidity, only to resubmerge and disappear into the composer's relatively murky waters. The listener is left pondering, "Did I just hear what I think I heard?"

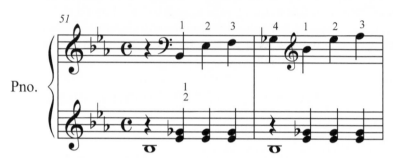

Example 1.11a. Beethoven, *Piano Sonata no. 8* **(op. 13),** *"Pathétique,"* **I, mm. 51–52**

Example 1.11b. Beethoven, *Piano Sonata no. 8* **(op. 13),** *"Pathétique,"* **I, mm. 72–75**

Example 1.11c. Austin, *Puzzle Preludes,* **IV, mm. 26–30**

To bring the past into the present—an intriguing notion for a composer who has spent much of her life rather wrestling *against* the past, against chauvinistic oppression in the 1950s, against the escalating pressures of simultaneous motherhood and studenthood, against societal burdens that confront all women, but it must be understood that Austin's music seeks to do more than simply conjoin the past with the existing world; it means to intertwine them, to make them coexist, to evolve them into something entirely new. This is the imperative understanding of her writing that brings us to the heart of the matter for Austin—the artist as a vessel, "through which the stuff of the cosmos is allowed to flow."[32] And as it flows, we may witness the leaf lobes of the composer's life growing themselves together in time, regenerating past experiences into a new vision of what it is to be one, and double too.

A CONVERSATION WITH ELIZABETH R. AUSTIN

Over the span of the last ten years, it has been my great privilege to convene numerous interviews with this composer; the following is merely a compilation of moments from our ongoing discussion. Some of what is printed here is born from a series of conversations in Austin's Connecticut home between 2002 and the present; the rest stems from my various documentary travels with the composer, including a particular summer evening in 2003, when I found myself sitting with Austin and her husband in the garden of distinguished pianist Ulrich Urban in Droyssig, Germany. On that night I became acquainted with the German Amsel, a European thrush Austin calls her "perfection," one of her "lights." The remarkable quality of this small blackbird is that it literally sings in variations. The Amsel inserts grand pauses between each of its tiny songs, and each song is different from the one before and the one after; it never repeats the same iteration twice. How like my friend Elizabeth, who is ever seeking to forge something new from that which has come before.—Michael Slayton

SLAYTON: Could you comment on your early musical training—your time with Grace Newsom Cushman and Mlle Boulanger?

AUSTIN: I'm old enough now to be simplistic and say that a creative personality usually manifests itself early; I believe it is somewhat inborn. Show me an artist who does not struggle against harmonizing his or her innate compulsion with so-called natural life! I started learning to play the piano at age seven, and then I started to compose at age seven-and-a-half, when I wrote a lullaby for my new baby brother. By age ten, I was attending Peabody Preparatory, and at age thirteen, I was blessed by having Grace Newsom Cushman come into my life. What she did is what I would do with any young composer, and that is to teach him or her to think in time—to think in rhythm. She taught us functional harmony with an emphasis on modality. We learned how to take a chord progression and realize it, thinking in time, improvising on our individual instruments. We were always listening and performing.

SLAYTON: And you went to the Conservatoire Americain in 1958?

AUSTIN: Yes, the year of the Brussels World Fair. I was in Fontainebleau for about six months. I recall Boulanger calling me to the piano on one special occasion, when she had visitors; for some reason she asked me to sit down at the piano and improvise a diminished seventh resolution in all twenty-four keys without stopping. I had been trained to do that, so it was not a problem. Boulanger could be so hard, so discouraging; on this occasion she beamed happily at me! But I will never forget a time in Fontainebleau when my friend Ruth[33] and I strolled along a path, apparently in full view of Boulanger, with a young man whom we had met on board the boat we took to France. Within the very next lesson, the event was brought to the fore. Boulanger said to me, her voice marked with disdain, "My dear, go home and have eight children!" I was crushed (and I naturally thought her prophetic when only a few years later I gave birth to twins). Of course she wasn't actually telling me to leave; she was making a point about priorities. But comments such as that leave their mark.

SLAYTON: Who or what would you say were your primary compositional influences during the time you were a student?

AUSTIN: I was the one of that Peabody circle who was always writing the alternative music. I was the one doing the whole-tone scales—Scriabin, et cetera. I listened to and admired Monteverdi and Messiaen, and though I did not own it, I read the four-hundred-page Partch book.

SLAYTON: You were interested in sound experimentation?

AUSTIN: Oh, yes! I was always an experimental composer. I remember as a younger student concentrating on contemporary usage of the ancient Greek modes, but I did not go through the stages that most composers go through by first writing in an eighteenth-century tonality. I did such exercises later in college. I could do it, but I was experimenting with the octatonic scale and Bartók. I had heard, and was conversant with, all of this. I was fortunate to have heard Carter's quartets when they had just been written, at the Baltimore Museum of Art. It was a beautiful time to be at Peabody; Henry Cowell, for instance, was on the faculty.

SLAYTON: What did you do when you returned from France?

AUSTIN: I had no guidance and absolutely no wherewithal. My widowed mother, despite her pride in me, discouraged a professional career as a composer, and I also felt partially responsible for her well-being. The late fifties was a traditional time. The world had not changed, and we had traditional roles. I lacked the tenacity or the audacity to rise above my middle-class destiny, and I had little means. So I compromised. I realized that my two younger brothers needed the financial attention for their college education, and that I was more or less expected to move on. I had to have employment, so I obtained a provisional public school teaching certificate. I taught school music during the day and took graduate courses toward a teaching certificate at night. Then I was married, and within ten months I had the twins. That really put a stop to my career for a while!

SLAYTON: An escape into marriage?

AUSTIN: Perhaps—if so, I am certainly not proud of this. I had thought to disprove my beloved Mlle Boulanger, and here I was! I already had creative fire burning, but it had to wait until I had raised my precious daughter, one of the twins, who suffered so terribly from debilitating asthma. One cannot write music when listening for the nightly wheezing of a poor asthmatic, struggling for each breath. Of course I have no regrets today; but remember, with three children, I diapered my way through the revolutionary sixties.

SLAYTON: And when your children were older, did you feel yourself to be rebirthed, so to speak?

AUSTIN: Yes, I emerged again on the other side and did not realize, luckily in a way, that the world had changed so. Here I was in my forties, with a glaring hole in my resume, and I became starkly aware for the first time in my life that my primary identity, like it or not, was one of composer. Up until that time, I had consciously and unconsciously devalued my basic raison d'être—having children made this lack of priority so much easier. My generation did not have a Betty Friedan until we were in our mid-twenties and already in maternity clothes. Reading *The Feminine Mystique* in the early sixties was tough to do, between doctor visits and diapering. May I repeat, however, that without the remarkable and rewarding experience of sharing parenthood, I'm not totally certain I would have felt such an irresistible compulsion to return to composing later in life.

SLAYTON: Let me ask you about pedagogy. How do you approach young composers who come to you to study musical composition?

AUSTIN: You meet them where they are—no pontification. Honor the effort and see what they are doing. But as teachers we're looking at process. We are not so much looking at notes on paper, because they are evolving, and it is mystical. But there are two things that I require. One is an ear—and if they don't have an ear, they must develop it. The second thing I require is that they sit down to write every day. Of course there is the tender, tender ego, and though the act of creation may involve ego at first, you must soon realize that you are a vessel, a conduit through which the music flows. We do not teach composition—we teach revelation. And we teach obedience. This obedience has nothing to do with the style you are writing in; it is the fact that to listen, you must be almost Buddhistic, and then the ego calms down.

SLAYTON: One of the things I find interesting in your music is your usage of pitch class cells—the minor sixth/minor third system, and so on.

How do you make your decisions, both tonal and nontonal, as to pitch selection?

AUSTIN: For me, nontonalism is the vehicle through which I explore the tonal as the invader, at times quite humorously, and so my processes surely differ from others. But I believe this is where serialism is wonderfully useful, and although my music has only had the sheen of serialism at times, understanding the serial *process* has taught me to think ahead.

SLAYTON: Yes, this is something else I know about you—your intense dedication to precompositional planning.

AUSTIN: Right, but as far as process is concerned, we are talking about nothing that is original. Everything has roots. When a student initiates self-analysis, one should ask him, "Where are your roots? Your treasures? Where do you come from? Don't think you have anything original. Thank God you do not!" For all of these reasons, I think Berg is going to be the one of the Second Viennese School who endures—for sheer aural beauty coupled with a familiar vernacular use of serial techniques. But of course Webern is one of my big heroes.

SLAYTON: Why is that?

AUSTIN: Economy of means. I think Webern is misunderstood. He is so like a jewel. And in the *"Wilderness,"* there is a place which *is* Webern, practically stolen from Webern.

SLAYTON: A quote? Or the technique?

AUSTIN: It's the technique, and the sound, and the timbre. Listen, if anyone defines himself as being original, be suspicious! We are searching for an answer, a method by which we can generate notes, and Schoenberg's was a marvelous idea. Yes, he was convincing, terribly convincing and dogmatic, because this was a fantastic thing. But if it hadn't been for Schoenberg's op. 23, we would have a more variegated musical landscape, because that brilliant period between 1900 and 1911 would not have been truncated so. I hope we're coming back to that period in our approaches. I think we are. I am always trying to hold on to it in my own music. The irony of our current situation is that this is the healthiest time and place in the American world to be a composer, but with the least audience. American audiences are intimidated and less adventurous when new music is to be performed. I am a romantic, and I am sorry to be so simplistic, but in the end you must put the process aside and *listen* to Schoenberg and say, is this beautiful? Yes, it is beautiful. The musical environment will proliferate richness; it already has.

SLAYTON: Concerning your windowpaning method, to what extent do you expect the listener to be able to discern the quotes upon hearing your pieces, and how much are you leaving for the analyst and performer?

AUSTIN: I never totally hide a quote—because, first, it's paying *hommage,* and second, it is going to be a point of juncture for the listener. When we give the audience obtuse music to listen to, and we expect them to get everything on two hearings (which is what new music gets now), it's not comforting. I do not advocate writing down to garner audience appeal, but it is a responsibility to bring the audience in from the cold, if possible.

SLAYTON: And certainly one will perform a quote much differently if one indeed realizes it is a quote.

AUSTIN: Absolutely. And this speaks to what I feel is the cornerstone of the way I write. I write for the performer; I write for the live person. I believe that if you do not, you are lost, because the performer is a cocreator. Now, I am not necessarily talking about aleatory or giving the performer chances to improvise; I am talking about music coming alive only through this cocreation. A composer has to approach a premiere prepared (and with such a spirit of humility) to have many revelations once you hear the performance—because it is a cocreation. You do not have to be rigid, and you never need be ashamed if you don't have all the answers.

SLAYTON: So you do not believe in the axiom that once the composer puts it on paper, it is no longer hers.

AUSTIN: You take your *ultimate* care to put everything on paper, as much as can go on paper. The score is a template, then, to be enhanced. But how many different interpretations of Debussy are there?—the master craftsman. He put as much on paper as anyone could. And look how he is played—all glorious.

SLAYTON: And all different.

AUSTIN: All different. I am catalyzed by the sound of the performer, or a voice, or a touch at the piano. After a work has had its premiere, I make corrections, usually details of tempo, et cetera. But after a period of six months, it is released. Thank God it is gone! And it becomes part of the real world of art and the imagination.

SLAYTON: You prefer to let the pieces speak for themselves.

AUSTIN: Yes, because *you* are changing. You are going through time yourself, so you are touching this phenomenon as it goes.

SLAYTON: And so through the music, you can follow the evolutionary process of the composer—his or her changing stylistic traits.

AUSTIN: Exactly.

SLAYTON: And are you changing?

AUSTIN: Oh, yes. Actually, I am quite shy with this. I am finding myself in a very mystical stage where I can trust myself, but it is sobering. I am quieting down and becoming rather serious. Composition for me is heading into the inarticulate, outside of the music. I guess it's my age now, where I am finally saying, "My God, I am lucky to be doing what I am doing."

SLAYTON: What you think about current stylistic trends in concert music?

AUSTIN: I think we're at the threshold of breaking into the universal theory of music. If we would welcome and embrace a fusion of all styles—if composers would allow themselves less emphasis on right versus wrong, black versus white, and accept an interesting balance of various approaches—wouldn't we be healthier? For any young composer, the study of world music is irreplaceable. And when you come right down to it, we are really talking about tone colors and how to arrive at them more than stylistic choices.

SLAYTON: There are many reasons composers write, especially in our time. Would you say your music is an expression of the spiritual? Is it for social or political advancement of some kind? Is your music used as protest? Is it just for you?

AUSTIN: To speak for myself and my own impetus, it comes into the spiritual for me. If someone is fortunate enough to hit upon what one is called to do, he or she is darn lucky, and I'm convinced that this is a vocation. You must test the mettle of composition students and ask them, "Are you really ready to forgo monetary gain and take up this lifestyle?" Because you will certainly become monkish. We of course must write music to communicate with the listener, but what happens when my vision of the beautiful clashes with the vision of the listener? Do I then enter the camp of the listener, or do I continue on with my vision?

SLAYTON: So, do you think then that the quality of music is determined by the composer? The audience? The critic?

AUSTIN: This is a difficult question. Music is new wine—the composer doesn't even know its worth. How can she know? My friend, musicologist Imanuel Wilheim, asked the question, "Is it even possible to determine such a thing as quality at any particular time?" For instance, simply because it is increasingly popular to play tonal music in this time, does that mean it is of higher quality? This can become self-imposed censorship for a nontonalist, or even a pan-tonalist.

SLAYTON: This is bringing to mind the expression "serious concert music." I have always puzzled over that particular terminology—isn't it always serious, at least to its maker?

AUSTIN: Of course! I truly believe it all begins with the unfortunate perception that one need know so much before entering the concert hall. This, coupled with the relative absence of musical education in America, is prioritizing pop music and musical theater as our "serious" music and turning concert music into a white elephant. But if the music faculty sells out and stops teaching classical music because it isn't popular, I think they do the entire world a disservice. Is music supposed to be cool? Is it supposed to be accepted? Is it supposed to be smart? Is kitsch the same? Is it only about having a new idea, not necessarily a well-crafted one, or one that will stand the test of time? Are we really going to enter a world where craft isn't important? Now, rock and roll has its master craftsmen, and I in no way devalue that, but to label all styles of music as serious music or to say there is no difference in classical music and rock music is, to me, a bit like the problems we have faced with the gender issue.

SLAYTON: How so?

AUSTIN: Well, gender should never enter into music composition. In music, the difference is in the end product, the quality of the creation; with gender, there is no difference in the end product, only in the processes. But to refuse to admit that there exist differences between the chronology of a male and a female is rather to have one's head in the sand. Life is biological, isn't it? A woman at the end of her life often looks at her supposed creation as her children; for a man, it is typically his work. If the woman looks at her life's work as her important output, does that devalue her devotion to her children? If she doesn't, does that devalue her work? In whose eyes?

SLAYTON: How does one champion women artists and composers without marginalization? Or without becoming such a champion that one loses a correct vision of the art, simply due to the gender of the artist?

AUSTIN: I don't consider that women have ever been crybabies—there has certainly been a difference in the programming of music, but the stride that has been made is the realization that gender has absolutely nothing to do with quality. As we move forward in history, and we get away from solely programming concerts of eighteenth-century music, this understanding will be allowed to germinate and grow. I simply don't honor the attitude that if one is an intelligent woman (composer, scholar), one must be militant and ever on the offensive, seeking to knock male composers down a peg in order to rise as woman. It's not in my nature. Obviously there has been a problem, and hopefully we're on the road to recovery, but there are lingering questions.

SLAYTON: Ageism is an issue for many composers, and I think it is rather linked to those lingering questions.

AUSTIN: At least for me, this is a more difficult problem even than the gender issue. There are many competitions, for instance, for the so-called emerging composer. What does that mean? Shouldn't competitions be searching for the best music, regardless of age? So many composers emerge late in life. I don't want to sound like sour grapes, but this is tough for many of us. We paid our dues; we've devoted ourselves to family, children, and marriage. And now, when there is finally time to get down to the serious business of writing all of this music that has been taking root for years and years, we are told we are too old to emerge. It is, yes, in a way, related to gender, because it is societal that men do not typically stop their careers for children. But men also have ageism issues to face. So it is a problem for everyone, but a particularly knotty one for women.

SLAYTON: How do you think these sorts of issues will affect young women who are studying composition in the twenty-first century? What do you see for their futures?

AUSTIN: Thanks to the fine efforts of the International Alliance for Women in Music, New York Women Composers, GEDOK in Germany, et cetera, women composing today have a broader support system upon which to call for various questions, such as which orchestras are more sympathetic to women composers, which publishers accept music from women more readily, and so on. Online websites offer daily chats regarding practical and scholarly matters related to composing. Frankly, many significant women composers didn't bat an eye at gender issues but simply proceeded to communicate ardently. We hope today, however, that the days of composing in a vacuum for oneself are past—that "room of one's own" should be a foregone conclusion! Certainly the tolerance for music in a variety of styles has increased since I was studying.

SLAYTON: And in what stylistic direction do you see music composition heading in this new century?

AUSTIN: In the air now is this concept of time. How do we approach time? What is it? Is it chronological? Is it collage? Is it windowpane? Is it time machine? I think our direction in music will be preoccupied with what time is all about. Not with the pitches, not with tonality or nontonality, but with this idea of time. And that is why *musique concrète* is so important still. If someone can harness this whole thing, and make different aspects of time, it would be fascinating! I cannot envision it right now; I wish I could. But I would love to have a piece based on how we view time.

SLAYTON: Interesting.

AUSTIN: [laughs] You do it.

ANALYSIS: *SYMPHONY NO. 2,*
"LIGHTHOUSE" (1993, REV. 2002), MOVEMENT I:
LIGHTHOUSE/WATERTOWER MANNHEIM/WATCH HILL

Ich möchte Leuchtturm sein	I wish I were a lighthouse
in Nacht und Wind -	in night and wind -
für Dorsch und Stint,	for cod and smelt,
für jedes Boot -	for every boat -
und bin doch selbst	yet am myself
ein Schiff in Not!	a ship in need!

Figure 1.10. "Ich möchte Leuchtturm sein," from *Laterne, Nacht, und Sterne*, by Wolfgang Borchert[34]

It isn't difficult to imagine Elizabeth Austin in this setting; we may conjure an image of the composer in reflective quiescence, facing a red-orange sunset over the water. In the distance, from the tower on the hill, shines a beacon of light, slowly coming around, closer and closer, then rushing over in a rapid, flashing moment—and gone. But the watcher will wait for the next pass, for the next moment. And as sunlight fades, the beacon becomes the single focus; all else disappears into darkness. Such visual imagery is vivid; we may mentally put ourselves in that moment and see every color and hue, our mind's eye watching the lighthouse, anticipating its unhurried light. But the penetrating question is: can we *hear* it?

> *Naming my first chamber CD* Reflected Light *underlined my lifelong preoccupation with vibrational energy, with one's self as a spiritual vessel through which this divine spark might move. As I spent many summer hours at the ocean, taking in the Watch Hill lighthouse and listening to the bell buoys at close proximity, I was drawn to the power of that arc of light, that beacon which seemed to illuminate the waves. If there were musical snippets in that choppy water, the all-embracing light would pull them toward it—would unify and merge them in the surf!*

The Watch Hill lighthouse sits on a bluff near the east entrance to Fishers Island Sound in Westerly, Rhode Island. The structure was originally erected during the years 1744 to 1748—not to warn ships in the sound, but to warn local residents of naval attacks during the French-Indian and Revolutionary Wars. Reconceived in the mid-nineteenth century, the lighthouse has undergone several renovations in the past two centuries, finally reaching its present status in 1986, when the automated rotating light was installed.[35] This lighthouse, much like the before-mentioned Goethe ginkgo, has been a mecca of sorts for Austin, a place to which she is continually drawn to meditate on its mysteries.

The idea for the "Lighthouse" symphony was undoubtedly birthed from Austin's many hours spent at Watch Hill, but also by a second lighthouse of sorts, the famous *Wasserturm* in Mannheim, which stands as the city's focal landmark and another compelling life image for the composer. Constructed in 1888 and 1889, the sixty-meter Mannheim Water Tower served as the city's potable water source until 2000. Situated on the beautiful *Friedrichsplatz*, and surrounded by lush gardens, the *Wasserturm* accommodates thousands of tourists each year. But for Austin, its call is far more meaningful—coincidence would have this tower crowned with a female figure from Greek mythology: Amphitrite, Poseidon's wife and queen of the sea.[36] By 1993, Austin had been living in Mannheim for five years, had established herself as a composer, and had been honored with two portrait concerts. She felt at home under Amphitrite's watchful eye, experiencing something of a renaissance; her works were asked for, played, reviewed, published, and so forth. So her second symphony was an *hommage*, a way of giving back. And the *Wasserturm* became, for a season, Austin's surrogate lighthouse.

Inspired by these two vestiges, Austin's conception for the "Lighthouse" Symphony was to musically merge the serene imagery of Watch Hill with the urban effigy of Mannheim's city center. She split the time and effort of composing the work between the two cities; much as her life, her second symphony was a transatlantic experience. Austin's immediate task was to tackle the crucial problem of translating a lighthouse beam into a sonic image—the sound that she knew must open the piece, to aurally situate the listener at the water's edge.

Example 1.12. *Symphony no. 2, "Lighthouse"* **(1993), I, mm. 1–8, percussion and strings (score in C)**

As attestation to the composer's talent for musical economy, we find virtually every detail essential to the work embedded within these opening measures. The most significant of these is the falling semitone motive, A to G-sharp, for it is upon the shoulders of this singular entity that the entire movement is constructed. When we first come into sonoral contact with the rotating lighthouse beacon (measures 6–7), we hear the motive in descending motion, progressing downward. The piercing beacon motive arcs upward and outward, emanating from a drone, arising at the expectant moment before the light. As it intensifies to a brilliant sonic beam, we hear the A–G♯ half-step shift in the sound, a light sweep timed precisely with the Watch Hill cycle. That this particular semitone is also central to Debussy's *La Mer* was Austin's genesis for the symphony.

> *Water quotes coming from the sea was the original idea, and the idea of progressing downward came first; it takes less energy to pull one downward. The falling of A to G-sharp in each quote, specifically from* La Mer, *provided the unifying thread. This simulates the Doppler effect (A to G-sharp); it transforms the light into sound. The antithetical rising motives (often half-steps, but also whole steps toward the end) are, for me, a metaphor for hope, for one's being drawn to the light. Life can turn (with suddenness) like the light in the lighthouse; it's either on or off—there is little gray.*

The penetrating ray illuminates various windowpanes in the movement, each with a water theme, and each possessing the same A–G♯ pitch collection, either falling or rising. In typical Austinian fashion, the music from the past is juxtaposed with the contemporary, linked by a succession of mosaic-like harmonies. Our first encounter is with Barber and a quote from *Dover Beach*.

Example 1.13a. Samuel Barber, *Dover Beach* (op. 3), mm. 1–4

Example 1.13b. "Lighthouse" Symphony, I, mm. 46–49, selected instruments

The profusion of descending semitones in the first several pages of the score culminates at this point, where the listener first confronts the past through a nostalgic lens. We should note the subtle discrepancies of pitch class in the accompanying figures between Barber's original music and Austin's windowpane, the composer's intentional bending of the source material. Austin's incentive for these alterations becomes clear when we consider this quote within the greater context of the work. Slight changes in the opening viola figure, for instance (see example 1.13b, m. 47), allow for its lower semitone to be heard more clearly as a *falling* motive (mirroring the A–G♯ above it) from E to D-sharp, rather than as a *rising* motive from D to D-sharp, as is the case in Barber's version. Seeking to offset the rising tones found in other voices—as the importance of the rising motive has not yet surfaced—Austin makes this decisive adjustment while maintaining the aural coherency of the quoted passage (the addition of the cello line beneath the viola makes our case stronger). Here we have a pristine example of how the composer uses the windowpane technique to her distinct advantage, at times purposefully quoting passages indirectly in order to maintain control over the larger vision.

As we make our way through the movement, we begin to realize it is this crucial metamorphosis of the semitone motive—sighing, sinking, descending in the beginning of the work, then rising, turning hopeful, becoming whole, ascending toward the end—that is the basis for understanding the symbolism of the lighthouse. As we pass through the Debussy windowpane near the midpoint of the movement, the opposing versions of the motive begin to contend for supremacy as they intertwine and conflict.

Example 1.14. "Lighthouse" Symphony, I, mm. 70–74, selected instruments

We will recall that this quotation from *La Mer* was Austin's catalyst for the entire movement, and we may now begin to understand why. The quoted material is exact; no alterations are made to Debussy's original (although the violin and piano chords are added). Note the inherent confliction within the passage. The primordial A–G♯ descending semitone dominates the woodwinds, but the horns lie in opposition, accenting G♯–A. The first and second violins directly negate each other; each note in the first violin descends the half step from chord to chord, while the second violins rise by the same interval. As rising tones dominate the lower strings, the overall effect in the orchestra is one of counterbalance.

The motivic equilibrium consummated in these measures, coupled with the opening of the A–G♯ semitone to a whole tone in measure 74 (see example 1.14), signals a dramatic turn in the piece, as the motive now begins to strain upward, stretching itself toward the light. Austin explores this upward expansion as the music progresses, and her next windowpanes seek to illustrate a rising new sense of hope (see examples 1.15a–b and 1.16a–b).

The following examples unquestionably demonstrate a structural change in the general direction of the motive, we must observe that the descending semitone has not been utterly abandoned. In the quote from *Die schöne Müllerin*, the original A–G♯ motive is quite present, sounding against the rising lines of Schubert's dirge. The brook is speaking here, bringing solace and peace to the poor journeyman, who had thrown himself into its waters, his love having been rejected.

As the movement begins to arc toward denouement, Austin invites the listener into the inner sanctum of this music, into her centermost feelings of mysticism surrounding the lighthouse. A darkened passage from Jakob Handl moans through the swirling beacon motive, effecting the spiritual climax of the movement.

Immediately following the Handl quotation, the bells of Mannheim begin to ring underneath the orchestra.[37] Over this recorded sound, Debussy's *L'isle joyeuse* proffers a windowpane of peaceful melancholy, yearning for Watteau's mythical other world, while in the distance is heard the plaintive call of Watch Hill bell buoys.[38]

Example 1.15a.   R. Schumann, *Liederkreis* (op. 39), "Mondnacht," mm. 5–8

Example 1.15b.   **"Lighthouse" Symphony, I, mm. 82–86, selected instruments**

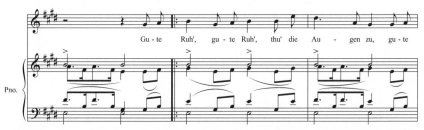

Example 1.16a.   Schubert, *Die schöne Müllerin* (op. 25) XX, "Des Baches Wiegenlied,"
mm. 4–6

As Austin's sonoral waves subsequently begin to surge and crash, covering all traces of nostalgia, the listener is drawn back to the darker waters of the movement's opening measures. And as the final notes die away, we are confronted outright with the significance of the semitone motive and its subsequent transformations. In Austin's final windowpane, which consists of a short passage from the "Lacrimosa" movement of the

Example 1.16b. "Lighthouse" Symphony, I, mm. 93–96, selected instruments

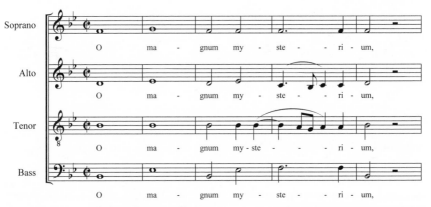

Example 1.17a. Jakob Gallus (Handl), *O magnum mysterium* (ca. 1586), mm. 1–5

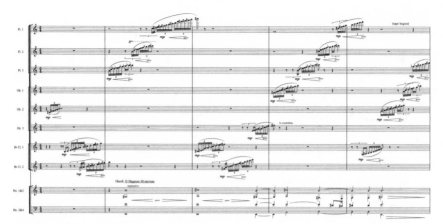

Example 1.17b. "Lighthouse" Symphony, I, mm. 108–112, selected instruments

Mozart *Requiem* (a nod to Mozart's presence in Mannheim as he struggled to acquire permanent employment), we find that the motive has amended itself and returned to its original A–G♯ configuration. But the contrast of relatively hopeful rising lines in the bassoon and second violins creates uncertainty. If the falling semitone represents the doubts, struggles, and

Example 1.18. "Lighthouse" Symphony, I, mm. 113–117, selected instruments

apprehension of Austin's early life, while she waited for the light to turn, the antithetical rising motives must symbolize the successes of middle life, representing the joy of emerging, stretching and growing, living in the light's radiant beam. We are left, then, wondering what questions remain unanswered for Austin as the movement abruptly closes in sudden, unanticipated silence. What is the great mystery of the lighthouse? What secrets does it hold for the composer? Do these windowpanes of the past mirror instead Austin's own reflection, looking out?

Example 1.19. "Lighthouse" Symphony, I, final measures, selected instruments

I don't embrace tonality for its harmonic function, but almost always as imagery, inserted for a sense of the past—both of my symphonies employ this method. J. M. W. Turner, my favorite artist, speaks of "historical memory" in his paintings. I think of what I do as "quotational polyphony"; the layering sharpens associative values of the quotes and heightens their effect.

The comprehensive utilization of quoted materials in this movement certainly provides insight into the composer's impetuses for its composition, as well her spiritual affect concerning the lighthouse as life metaphor. But we would be remiss to neglect the wealth of music *surrounding* the quotes. Indeed, as previously determined, it is Austin's *non*tonality that creates the suitable environment for such tonal passages to seem "oddly out of place." Polychordal structures and planed fifths notwithstanding, it is Austin's minor sixth/minor third harmonic system that governs most of this tapestry, and its role is imperative to the work's success. We will recall the system's natural avoidance of tonal center, as well as its promotion of the major and minor ninth (and their reciprocal sevenths) over the octave. In the *Lighthouse Symphony*, chordal structures derived from such a foundation serve to create the chromatic tension necessary to the composer's task. A few representative passages from this movement will illustrate the countless ways in which the minor sixth/minor third harmonic system is employed to actively create the characteristic Austinian sound (see examples 1.20a–d):

Example 1.20a.   "Lighthouse" Symphony, I, mm. 44–45, selected instruments

Austin's harmonic system isn't atonal in the lasting traditions of the Second Viennese School, but there is virtually no sense of harmonic centering within its walls. Indeed, this music seems strangely balanced unto itself, often relying entirely upon nonharmonic entities to engage the ear. It isn't difficult, therefore, to imagine the aural shock and surprise of suddenly encountering an excerpt from Schubert or Schumann, replete with the strong melodic content and angular harmony orthodox to German Romantic style. Austin's harmonic palette is one where opacity adjoins clarity and the traditional is freely juxtaposed with the unconventional.

> *I use the word nontonal versus tonal because this is, in my music, an agent for contrast. This is the way I approach tonality, to set it against a nontonality. I think we are all looking for this balance, but how do we approach it?*

Example 1.20b. **"Lighthouse" Symphony, I, mm. 53–54, selected instruments**

Focusing our gaze toward the formal design of this piece must begin with a closer inspection of measures 80 and 81 (see example 1.20d), which reveals extensive usage of the before-mentioned chord of mixed thirds, or Fibonacci chord. Austin readily employs this particular sonority in the "Lighthouse," again demonstrating her penchant for the perfect aesthetic asymmetry found within the golden mean. The entire movement, in fact, is tightly constructed around such principles.

Austin's structural arrangement for the movement was conceived through her precise timing of the Watch Hill lighthouse cycle, as she struggled with the concept of a predetermined, periodic, visual image being converted into the energy and lyricism of an aural one. The low drone at the onset of each cycle simulates the attractive power of the light before it sweeps into the viewer-listener's space. The highest pitch represents the "total on"[39] of the light, and the ensuing downward pitches, with added *glissandi*, simulate a muttering Doppler effect as it rushes away (see figure 1.11).

Example 1.20c. "Lighthouse" Symphony, I, mm. 69–70, selected instruments

Example 1.20d. "Lighthouse" Symphony, I, mm. 80–81, selected instruments

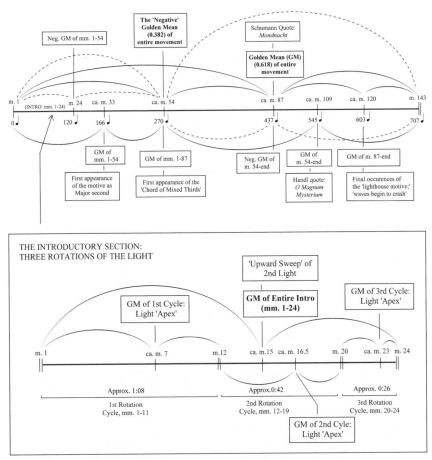

Figure 1.11. *Lighthouse Symphony*, I, proportional graph

From the above graph, we see that the three light cycles in the introduction are golden mean proportioned according to time; that is, the timing of the first light cycle (68 seconds), when multiplied by 0.618, yields the timing of the second light cycle (42 seconds), which is then itself multiplied by 0.618 to arrive at the timing for the third (26 seconds). The timings were precompositionally calculated, but as is always the case with the temporal, each performance will vary. This is a reality that Austin embraces.

I observed the Watch Hill light, now a decade ago, and saw that the light was on for six seconds and off for four seconds. At first, my time grid was in multiples of five—I put in bar lines simply to make the ensemble easier. I tried to give the illusion of time compression by condensing each succeeding appearance of the aural beacon, as well as the silence (off light) between these appearances. The compulsion of the periodic return of this beacon theme is akin to the centrifugal pull one feels upon viewing the light. There is an uneasy or eerie quality portrayed by the bridge music following the last of the upward scalar beacons; it is night and the sea is full of motion.

Beyond the proportional interest of the introduction, it must be noted that the most significant happenings of the movement proper likewise occur at divine moments (see figure 1.11). Of these, the most important are the events delineating the negative and positive sides of the golden mean. The negative mean (0.382) ushers in the previously discussed chord of mixed thirds in measure 54, while the golden mean itself (0.618), which occurs in measure 87, carries with it the weight of Austin's most significant motivic evolution. It is at this moment, initiated by the quote from Schumann, that the A–G♯ motive emphatically bends upward and begins to reach toward the hopeful.

That it is the quote from *Mondnacht* lying at the golden mean of the movement is certainly no accident. This famous Eichendorff poem sees the moonlit panorama (from an elevated standpoint) as a gate through which the soul may enter eternal life. And in Buddhistic reflection, the final stanza speaks of the individual soul uniting with nature. This poetic idea undoubtedly connects with Austin's infusion of the botanical and the natural into her writing, but it is also closely linked to her paradigmatic model of a relationship between lovers—holding hands, but side by side, and gazing out into the world—rather than being turned involutedly to one another, gazing into each other's eyes.

But it could be that the secrets of the lighthouse and its surrounding seas are not meant to be gained. The underlying concept of the work is periodicity set against stasis, and its symbolism doesn't serve to answer our questions as much as to challenge us to consider the human condition. What is life, after all, if not a protracted series of brief, illuminated moments? What happens in the dark while we wait for the light to circle again? For Austin, serenity seems to come in recognizing the unfailing turning of the tide, for she has certainly experienced both the duskish quietude and the sudden, rushing fortuity offered by the steadfast alternation of life's revolving, reflecting light.

CODA

Continuing to compose daily, Elizabeth Austin recently completed *Brainstorm* (for concert double bass and piano) and a clarinet quartet entitled *Weep No More.*[40] She is currently devoting most of her time to her first opera, which is based on Kleist's *The Marquise of O*. Austin maintains her teaching and her service as organist and choir director at St. Paul's

Church, while still finding time for involvement in Connecticut Composers Inc., diligently searching for venues to showcase the talents of the composer membership.

In Elizabeth Austin we find a distinct American voice. Analysis of her works demonstrates unswerving dedication to compositional craftsmanship coupled with artistic passion. Her approach to musical composition is simultaneously simple and complex, austere yet gracefully personal. And her numerous performances, involving artists such as Karl Kramer (horn), Jerome A. Reed (piano), Ieva Jokubaviciute (piano), and Eun-Jung Auh (soprano), as well as a recent featured production of her piano works, performed by distinguished pianist Ulrich Urban and broadcast by MDR (*Mitteldeutscher Rundfunk*, Leipzig, Germany) have helped bestow more than a modicum of recognition.

> *I am grateful, above all, terribly grateful, finally to have arrived at that truly blessed juncture in life where I am being asked to write music, that the feedback seems so positive, that performers enjoy playing or singing the music, and that I never seem to run out of ideas (that was never a problem!). It is clear to me that artists are mere vessels (no room for ego here) through which the stuff of the universe pours in an oddly personalized way. But it is still not I who writes this music—I receive the energy and convert it, merely.*

As Austin's music continues to reach listeners around the world, it is undoubtedly her hope that there may be a positive reaffirmation of artistic goals, and that the lesson found within her writing will make itself evident: that compositional craft and individual personality can and must meld into one entity, enlarging the boundaries of human understanding, to touch the divine.

NOTES

1. Unless otherwise cited, all quotations and personal information are from direct correspondences with the author, and permission for their usage has been granted by the composer. Photo is used by permission, Carole Horwell.

2. This would later become the famous Walden School in Dublin, New Hampshire. The Walden School carries on Mrs. Cushman's legacy to this day.

3. Austin's composition teachers at Goucher were Sherrod Ray Albritton (who became an Episcopal priest, and who taught music at the Virginia Theological Seminary) and Robert Hall Lewis. Although Dr. Albritton was encouraging of Austin's music, Austin credits Bob Lewis and Elliott Galkin (musicology), who turned her direction to the possibility of a profession as composer. She finished her degree in 1960.

4. Elizabeth Matthaei Rhudy married Rolf Scheidel on August 26; Austin composed as Elizabeth Scheidel for the next several years.

5. Manchester, then South Windsor, Connecticut.

6. *Inscapes* was given a reading by the Emerson Quartet.

7. *Song of Simeon (Nunc Dimittis)* was written for and dedicated to Peter Harvey, then director of the St. Joseph Cathedral Choir in Hartford, Connecticut, and voice teacher at the Hartford Conservatory.

8. *Cantata Beatitudines* was awarded honorable mention in the International Alliance for Women in Music (IWAM) "Search for New Music."

9. The *"Wilderness" Symphony* was Austin's doctoral dissertation piece; the performance by the symphony was in honor of Austin's receiving first prize in the University of Connecticut Music Department's composition reading competition.

10. GEDOK has affiliations in many cities throughout Germany and in Vienna; Austin was selected to represent the region of Mannheim-Ludwigshafen for the GEDOK exhibition in Lübeck.

11. Austin recalls with gratitude the efforts of Pro-Rektor Gerald Kegelmann, Pro-Rektor Hermann Jung (who provided introductions to each concert), and the current Pro-Rektor Rudolf Meister and Pro-Rektor Michael Flaksman. She also credits Mannheim's Stadtbibliothek, Musikabteilung, which is known for its catalog and holdings of music by women composers. Austin's music was performed in many of this library's concert series, "through the good graces of its music library director, Frau Brigitte Höft," emeritus.

12. *Hommage for Hildegard* is based on the antiphon *Caritas abundat* by Hildegard von Bingen. With this work, Austin won the IAWM's Miriam Gideon first prize in 1998.

13. Gerhard Austin was professor of German literature at the University of Connecticut.

14. Further, if one adds a minor third *within* the minor sixth, such as might be spelled E-G-C, and then stacks a minor third from C to E-flat, a major triad, first inversion, plus a minor triad, second inversion, results.

15. Paraphrased from Michael Slayton, "In der Hand der Frau: Elizabeth Austin's *Frauenliebe und -leben* in Comparison to Schumann's Setting" (lecture paper, November 2005).

16. English translation by Elizabeth R. Austin.

17. Goethe was responsible for Jena's botanical garden at that time. Serendipitously, Austin's daughter Susan and her family now live in Jena, and so the composer is even further compelled to visit her beloved ginkgo tree.

18. This oboe, violoncello, and piano trio was formed in Weimar, Germany, in 1992 by pianist Reinhard Wolschina of the Weimar conservatory "Franz Liszt."

19. From the composer's notes about *Ginkgo Novo*.

20. From the composer's notes about *Ginkgo Novo*.

21. From the composer's notes about *Rose Sonata*.

22. Specifically, the Fibonacci sequence consists of a string of numbers where, after two starting values, each integer is the sum of the two preceding integers. The first Fibonacci numbers are therefore 0, 1, 1, 2, 3, 5, 8, 13, 21, 34, 55, 89, etc. The Fibonacci numbers are named after Leonardo of Pisa, known as Fibonacci.

23. See, for instance, Ernö Lendvai, *Béla Bartók: An Analysis of His Music* (London: Kahn and Averill, 1971).

24. The remarkable mathematic property of the Fibonacci numbers lies within their quotients. As each integer is divided by the one previous, the resulting quotient steadily approaches *PHI*, the number of the so-called golden mean, or "divine proportion": 1.618. Music theorists have debated for decades over Bartók's (and other composers') apparent usage of Fibonacci intervals and golden mean proportions in his music.

25. The golden mean can also be expressed as $(1 + \sqrt{5}) / 2$. And we must concede that mathematically, 1.618 (*PHI*) and 0.618 (*phi*) are really expressing the same thing. The difference is only which number is divided by which (i.e., 5 divided by 3 yields 1.6, and 3 divided by 5 yields 0.6). To effectively express this, mathematicians have referred to 1.618 as *PHI* and 0.618 as *phi*. But they are both golden mean numbers.

26. For instance, attempts have been made to posthumously attribute golden mean principles to the Beethoven piano sonatas. But we must consider that if the "climactic" moment in sonata form is the recapitulation (i.e., the return of the primary thematic material and, more importantly, the return of the tonic key), then *every* sonata form is constructed around the general golden mean principle. So while there is some evidence of golden mean influences in the Beethoven sonatas, perhaps the better question is not, did Beethoven employ golden mean proportions in the sonatas? but rather, why did the sonata form *naturally* develop into an approximate 2/3–1/3 proportional makeup? This speaks to the innate humanness of its formal design.

27. The composer's words, concerning *Wie eine Blume*.

28. The included texts are: Rainer Maria Rilke, *Gedichte* 1922–1926 (two poems from this collection); Rilke, *Die Sonnette an Orpheus, Erster Teil, XII*; Rilke, *op. cit., V, XXII, XXV, XV* (quoted in two separate places), *XIV*; Rilke, *op. cit., Zweiter Teil, VI*; Ewald Von Kleist, *Der Frühling*; Friederich Holderlin, *An eine Rose, Erstes Gelingen* (1790–1797).

29. There are many others, including the *Cantata Beatitudines* (1982), which culminates with a quote from Messiaen's *Outburst of Joy*; *Klavier Double* (1983), in which the predominant thematic element is derived from the Schumann *Phantasie in C Major*; *Gathering Threads* (1990) for solo clarinet, which contains the theme from Strauss's *Macbeth*; *To Begin* (1990) for brass quintet, which quotes a theme from *Fidelio*; the *Sonata for Soprano Recorder* (1991), which quotes the German song, *Ich hat' einen Kameraden*; and *Sans Souci Souvenir* (1996), a piece for viola d'amore and harpsichord, which quotes both Frederick the Great's composer-sister, Wilhelmine von Bayreuth, and Stamitz.

30. From the composer's notes about *Puzzle Preludes*.

31. From the composer's notes about *Puzzle Preludes*.

32. Personal interview with the author, in Austin's Connecticut home, 2005.

33. Austin is referring to Ruth Dahlstrom (now Ruth Galkin), harpist and friend who accompanied her to France, also to study at the Conservatoire Americain.

34. Used with kind permission of Rowohlt Verlag (translation by the composer). This prefatory poem is included in the score as an optional reading, movement I, p. 18.

35. See LighthouseFriends.com, www.lighthousefriends.com/light.asp?ID=688.

36. See www.mvv-life.de/de/pub/wasser/wasserturmmannheim.cfm.

37. The recording of the Mannheim bells is provided with the score; the recording was made by the composer.

38. *L'isle joyeuse* is believed to have been inspired by *L'embarquement pour Cythère*, a painting by Antoine Watteau (1684–1721).

39. These are the composer's words. Austin refers to the on and off of the light as its rotational time, when it is either facing toward or away from the observer.

40. The photograph here is of Austin at the Goethe ginkgo in Jena; it was made by the author in 2003.

APPENDIX A: LIST OF WORKS

[Unless otherwise noted, all scores are published through ACA Publishing or are available from the composer]

Orchestral

Chamber Symphony (1960)—string orchestra
Symphony no. 1, "Wilderness" (1987)—symphony orchestra, two reciters
Symphony no. 2, "Lighthouse" (1993)—symphony orchestra

Choral

Christ Being Raised (1955)—SATB, organ (optional) [published by Arsis Press]
Christmas, the Reason (1981)—SSAA, piano
Song of Simeon (Nunc Dimittis) (1981, rev. 2008)—SATB, organ
Mass of Thanksgiving (1987)—SATB, organ
An Die Nachgeborenen (To Those Born Later) (1991)—SATB, piano
The Master's Hands (1994)—SATB, organ/piano
Kyrie (from *"Transatlantic Mass"*) (2001)—SATB, organ
Like the Grass of These Fields (2001)—SATB, B-flat trumpet, organ
When the Song of the Angels Is Stilled (2005)—SATB, a cappella
Psalm 22 (2009)—SATB, a cappella

Choral with Ensemble

Cantata Beatitudines (1982)—SATB with soloists, wind ensemble, organ

Songs, Sets/Cycles

Three Sandburg Songs (1954)—soprano, piano
Drei Rilke-Lieder (1958)—mezzo-soprano, piano; soprano version available [published by Tonger Musikverlag]
The Heart's Journey (1978)—soprano, piano
Set Me as a Seal (1978)—mezzo-soprano, piano
Measure Me, Sky! (1979)—soprano, piano
Songs from Advent Poems (1979)—soprano, horn, piano
A Prayer for Christian Burial (1981)—middle voice, organ
Sonnets from the Portuguese (1988)—soprano, piano
A Birthday Bouquet (1990)—high voice, piano
Litauische Lieder (Lithuanian Songs) (1995)—baritone, piano
Hommage for Hildegard (1997)—mezzo-soprano, baritone, flute, clarinet, percussion, piano
Frauenliebe und -leben (1999)—mezzo-soprano, piano; soprano version available
Showings (2000)—soprano, trombone, organ/piano
Ausländer Arien (2004)—soprano, flute, violoncello, piano

Instrumental

KEYBOARD

Capers of a Clock (1953)—piano five hands
Zodiac Suite (full version) (1980)—piano
Elegy (1984)—piano duet
Lighthouse I (1989)—harpsichord [published by Tonger Musikverlag]
Puzzle Preludes (1994)—piano

A Child's Garden of Music (2000)—piano
An American Triptych (2001)—piano
Rose Sonata (2002)—piano
Waitin' and Wailin' Blues (2005)—piano [published by Peer Music]
Wachet auf . . . der Morgenstern (2006)—organ
I Felt a Funeral in My Brain (2007)—carillon [published by the Guild of Carillon-neurs in North America (GCNA)]

STRINGS

Inscapes (1981)—string quartet
Circling-Kreisen (1982)—violoncello, piano [published by Tonger Musikverlag]
Sans Souci Souvenir (1996)—viola d'amore, harpsichord
Water Music I: Beside Still Waters (1996)—violoncello octet
B-A-C-Homage (2007)—viola, piano
Brainstorm (2008)—concert double bass, piano

WINDS

Gathering Threads (1990)—clarinet in B-flat [published by Tonger Musikverlag]
Sonata for Soprano Recorder (1991)—soprano recorder
Sans Souci Suite (1996)—Baroque flute, percussion
Capricornus Caribbicus (1998)—flute, oboe, piano
Weep No More (2009)—clarinet (B-flat) quartet

BRASS

Bantam! (1978)—trumpet, piano
To Begin (1990)—brass quintet
Prague Sonata (1999)—French horn, piano
A Triadic Tribute (2000)—brass quintet, organ

Mixed Chamber Ensemble

Wie eine Blume . . . Orchid Ideas and Roses (2001)—wind sextet, percussion
Ginkgo Novo (2002)—English horn, cello, piano
A Falcon Fantasy (2004)—guitar, piano

Soloist with Ensemble

Celebration Concerto (2007)—piano soloist, child soprano, wind ensemble

Electroacoustic

Ghosts (1982)—bassoon and tape
Klavier Double (1983)—piano and tape

APPENDIX B: DISCOGRAPHY

An American Triptych. Ulrich Urban, piano. Capstone CPS 8710. "Spectra: A Concert of Music for Piano by Connecticut Composers Inc."

An Die Nachgeborenen (To Those Born Later). Veronika Winter, Kirsten Grunepult, Alex Bassermann, voice; Sibylle Dotzauer, piano; Staatliche Hochschule für Musik Heidelberg-Mannheim Chamber Choir; Gerald Kegelmann, conductor. Capstone CPS 8625. "Reflected Light."

A Birthday Bouquet. Susan Gonzalez, soprano; Marcia Eckert, piano. Leonarda LE 352. "Songs by Women."

A Birthday Bouquet. Gregory Wiest, tenor; Oresta Cybriwsky, piano. Capstone CPS 8646. "Time Marches On . . . More Modern American Songs."

Circling. Mary Lou Rylands, cello; Jeananne Albee, piano. Capstone CPS 8625. "Reflected Light."

Falkenfantasie (Falcon Phantasy). Chris Bilobram, guitar; Reinhard Wolschina, piano. Querstand VKJK 0422. "Composition Feminine: Musik von Komponistinnen für klassiche Gitarre."

Five Sonnets from the Portuguese. Melinda Liebermann, soprano; Cornelius Witthoeft, piano. Capstone CPS 8618. "Songfest," Society of Composers Inc.

Frauenliebe und -leben. Eun-Jung Auh, soprano; Teresa Crane, piano. Arizona University Recordings AUR CD 3148. "Spectra: A Concert of Vocal Music by Connecticut Composers Inc."

Gathering Threads. Markus Lucke, clarinet. Capstone CPS 8625. "Reflected Light."

Ich kann's nicht fassen from *Frauenliebe und -leben.* Suzanne Summerville, mezzo-soprano; Raminta Lampsatis, piano. ArtsVenture, Hamburg, Germany, and Fairbanks, Alaska. "Auf Der Wanderschaft."

Klavier Double. Jerome Reed, piano. Capstone CPS 8625. "Reflected Light."

Lighthouse I. Ursula Trede-Bottcher, harpsichord. Capstone CPS 8625. "Reflected Light."

The Master's Hands. The Kent Singers; Marguerite Mullée, director. Capstone CPS 8710. "Spectra: A Concert of Music for Voices by Connecticut Composers Inc."

Puzzle Preludes. Ulrich Urban, piano. Capstone CPS 8710. "Spectra: A Concert of Music For Piano by Connecticut Composers Inc."

Sonate für Blockflöte (Sonata for Soprano Recorder). "Bläserkammermusik von der Staatliche Hochschule für Musik Heidelberg-Mannheim." Available from the Hochschule or the composer (under the name Elizabeth Scheidel-Austin).

Sonnets from the Portuguese (poems by Elizabeth Barrett Browning). Linda McNeil, soprano; Carolyn True, piano. Leonarda LE 357. "Songs and Cycles: Contemporary Women Composers."

Symphony no. 1, "Wilderness." Krakau Radio/TV Orchestra; Szymon Kawalla, conductor. Capstone CPS 8634. ". . . and the eagle flies . . . new American orchestral music."

Symphony no. 2, "Lighthouse." The Moravian Philharmonic Orchestra; Joel Eric Suben, conductor. Capstone CPS 8779. "Spectra: A Concert of Music for Orchestra by Connecticut Composers Inc."

To Begin. Constitution Brass. Capstone CPS 8625. "Reflected Light."

Zodiac Suite. Jerome Reed, piano. Capstone CPS 8625. "Reflected Light."

SOURCES

Crane, Teresa. "Selected Music of Elizabeth R. Austin." University of Illinois at Urbana-Champaign, 2007.

Leonard, Kendra Preston. *The Conservatoire Américain: A History.* Lanham, MD: Scarecrow Press, 2007.

Olivier/Braun. "Scheidel Austin, Elizabeth." In *Komponistin Aus 800 Jahren,* 357. Germany: Sequentia-Verlag, 1996.

Republik der Kuenste. "Scheidel-Austin." In *70 Jahre,* 118–123. Germany: GEDOK, Bundesausstellung, 1996.

Slayton, Michael K. "Elizabeth R. Austin: An Interview with the Composer." *Journal of the International Alliance for Women in Music* 7 (2001): 17–23.

———. "*In der Hand der Frau*: Elizabeth R. Austin's *Frauenliebe und -leben* in Comparison to Schumann's Setting." Paper presented as part of the Society of Composers National Conference, Greensboro, NC, October 12–15, 2005.

Carson Cooman

SUSAN BOTTI (1962–)

For me, composing first came out of theater and acting work that I was doing. Eventually I started gravitating more toward music because I saw a potential freedom in the craft that wasn't possible for me in the particular theater projects I was doing. To this day, the way that I plan and shape pieces comes out of this background, which is a crucial part of my life as both performer and composer.[1]

The notion of being a composer was not something Susan Botti considered in her youth. Trained as an actor and singer, she is a born performer, and during her years of work in these fields, she gradually came to see music composition as a vehicle for the sort of dramatic self-expression she wished to pursue. Botti began composing seriously in college, and since that time, her career has skyrocketed through a series of prestigious awards, major commissions, and significant teaching posts. Despite the relative smallness of her catalog, her output has been deeply appreciated by instrumental and vocal performers and includes works commissioned by the Orpheus Chamber Orchestra, the New York Philharmonic, and the Cleveland Orchestra.

Susan Botti was born on Friday, April 13, 1962,[2] in Wichita Falls, TX. Growing up in Cleveland, Ohio, she began studies in voice, piano, acting, and art at an early age. Her precollege music studies were conducted at the Cleveland Institute of Music. Botti graduated from the Berklee College of Music (Boston, MA) in 1984 with a bachelor of music degree; her principal teachers were Robert Freedman, Allan Chase, and Matt Glaser. Graduate studies in composition followed at the Manhattan School of Music (New York, NY), where she studied with Ludmila Ulehla and Giampaolo Bracali, earning a master of music degree in 1990.

In the years that followed, Botti built an active life in New York City; she primarily undertook work as a composer, vocalist, and actor. In these latter two capacities, she acted in theater, film, and television productions and sang in national television commercials and film scores. During that time, she collaborated frequently with composer Tan Dun, and two of Tan's major works included parts specifically written for Botti. *Orchestral Theatre III: Red Forecast* (1996) is a forty-minute work for soprano and large orchestra; Botti gave the world premiere of this work with the BBC Scottish Symphony, and the American premiere with the American Composers Orchestra in Carnegie Hall. Tan also composed the role of "Water" for her in his major opera *Marco Polo* (1995). Botti appeared in this role in the world premiere production at the Münchener Biennale, in subsequent productions throughout Europe and Asia, in the American premiere at New York City Opera, and on the Sony Classical recording. Later, she also appeared as a soloist in the soundtrack for Tan's film score *The Banquet (Ye yan)* (2006).

Botti's life as a freelance performer in New York City changed when she accepted her first major faculty position as associate professor of music composition at the University of Michigan, Ann Arbor. Botti held this post from 2000 to 2007, achieving tenure and serving on the faculty with William Bolcom, Michael Daugherty, Bright Sheng, and others. During Botti's years in Michigan, she began collaboration with a fellow faculty member, the poet Linda Gregerson, and they have collaborated on several large works, including *Dido Refuses to Speak* from the *Gates of Silence* trilogy. Other poets whose works Botti has set to music include Denise Levertov, Phillippe Jaccottet, Rabindranath Tagore, e. e. cummings, Gaspara Stampa, and Lewis Carroll.

During Botti's Michigan years, she received several major awards, notably the Goddard Lieberson fellowship from the American Academy of Arts and Letters (2004) and a Guggenheim fellowship (2005). For the years 2003 to 2005, Botti was appointed as the Daniel R. Lewis young composer fellow with the Cleveland Orchestra.

In the 2005–2006 season, Botti was awarded the prestigious Rome Prize from the American Academy in Rome. The award allows the artist to spend a year living at the academy, and Botti used her time there to develop new works and collaborate with local Roman musicians from different musical areas: classical (pianist Brunella De Socio and harpist Lucia Bova); jazz (pianist Riccardo Fassi); and world music (Iranian percussion master, Mohssen Kasirossafar). In 2007, Botti moved back to the New York City area, settling in the Hudson Valley, and began a new teaching appointment as a member of the composition faculty at the Manhattan School of Music.

Even Botti's purely instrumental works are infused with a sense of drama and stagecraft. If there is a single unifying thread that runs throughout Botti's output, it is a sense of creative drama expressed through a colorfully lyrical language. She has often emphasized how important her background and experience as an actor are to the way she conceives and plans music.

Botti's style of vocal writing is significant, because it has been formed out of both her own performance style and her compositional language. Even when composing for instruments, aspects of her vocal style are present. Perhaps the most notable feature of Botti's vocal writing is the seemingly free mix of strictly notated and improvisational material, always in the service of the dramatic impulse. Her texts are set in a manner that includes singing, speaking, extended vocal techniques, and performance gestures.

Her early setting of an e. e. cummings text, *listen, it's snowing* (1990), is a good example of such integration. Notably, the text comes not from one of cummings's many poems, but rather from one of his plays: *HIM* (1927). Botti's setting begins by unfolding the opening words of the poem in the manner in which they might be spoken to another person.

Example 2.1. *listen it's snowing*, mm. 1–4

Later in the piece, the singer eschews traditional pitch for some non-pitched exclamations and the dramatic gesture of reaching inside and striking the bass strings of the piano with palm.

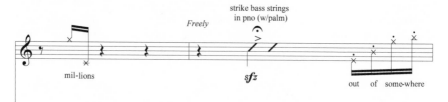

Example 2.2.   *listen it's snowing,* mm. 11–12

The final measures of the work involve a lack of synchronization between the soprano and piano, and several of the notes in the soprano's final phrases are inflected up or down by a quarter-tone. The musical language is employed with absolute freedom in the service of the dramatic projection of the text.

Botti's harmonic-melodic idiom is largely gestural and multitonal. Greatly favored are chords and root sonorities built to include combinations of major or minor seconds and perfect fourths or fifths. These harmonies are useful building blocks for the composer because they allow her to move between atonal and modal contexts rather easily, as such sonorities have identities connecting them to both types of harmony. Uses of idiosyncratic modality (particularly textural usage of open fourths and fifths) permeates her output (especially the early songs), but in general, Botti's language is key reflective, nondependent on direct triadic resolutions. Her pitch materials are often chosen with sensitivity for their sound and relative enharmonic or overtone-driven structures. Botti conceives the shape and pacing of the pieces first in careful detail; then, once she is completely satisfied with the line and shape, and has lived with it in real time, she composes the musical specifics that fill in the work. One method of approaching Botti's work is from a perspective of line, shape, texture, and stagecraft.[3]

One of Botti's most well-known works is *Jabberwocky* (1990) for soprano and percussion. She wrote this setting of Lewis Carroll's fantastical poem as a showpiece for herself and solo percussionist, and indeed it became one of her early signature works as a performer. Taking the dramatic aspects of presentation to an extreme, the score of the work is entirely graphical (and in color). A representative page is shown below.

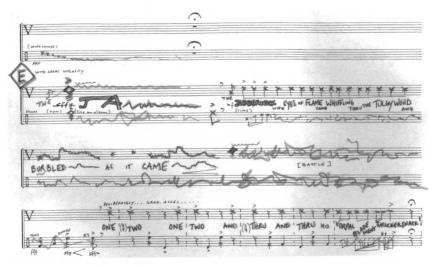

Example 2.3. *Jabberwocky*, p. 3

The poem is conveyed through gestural, graphical notation in which the hand-drawn elements are intended to visually inspire the singer-actor into shaping his or her presentation. In a sense, it is a notation of the way an actor might prepare a soliloquy, developed from the improvisational ways Botti herself performed the poem.[4]

Botti's music incorporates free and aleatoric notation. She credits her study of the music of Polish composer Witold Lutosławski with first introducing her to this sort of structured aleatory. Indeed, Lutosławski's notational style (largely developed by his wife Danuta, who had trained as an architect before becoming her husband's copyist) has been influential on a great many composers. In Botti's hands, this style of notation has become a vehicle to provide the organized freedom she wishes to give performers to allow for individual dramatic expression.

The composer also credits singing works of Russian composer Sofia Gubaidulina and Hungarian composer György Kurtág with providing models for freely expressive vocal notation that allows performers to shape elements of the line based on personal expressive choices. Botti's music is full of such notation; in fact, some of her works are written entirely in this manner. Examples 2.4a and 2.4b are from the fourth movement of *Telaio: Desdemona* (1995). The first is a texted vocal line; the second is a musical response by the solo second violin. The notation employs a free mix of structured and unstructured elements; pitch content and basic rhythmic guidelines are provided, but the specific rhythmic identity and pacing are left to the performer.

Example 2.4a. **"Aria: Mesta e pentita . . ." from *Telaio: Desdemona*, m. 1**

Example 2.4b. **"Aria: Mesta e pentita . . ." from *Telaio: Desdemona*, m. 4**

In 1994 and 1995, Botti created two significant explicitly operatic works. First came *Wonderglass*, a chamber opera based upon the writings of Lewis Carroll and scored for six singers and small chamber ensemble. Other than the young girl who exclusively plays the role of Alice, the other five singers take on many roles, creating a variety of Carroll's characters in the work's ten scenes, two bridges, prologue, and epilogue. Carroll's fantastical images are portrayed through dramatic scenes that involve the entire ensemble (including the instrumentalists) in the drama.

> *Wonderglass is a journey following some of the adventures of Lewis Carroll's Alice. The sequence of events unfolds as it might in a dream. In order to recapture the essence of the mythical worlds of* Wonderland *and* Through the Looking Glass, Wonderglass *holds up a mirror to the audience itself, allowing a reflection of each person's own imagination. Because these characters and their scenes are already so familiar, it is possible to use them as a point of departure. The words mean what we want them to mean. There are no answers in Lewis Carroll's world, only questions and formulas and puzzles. Answers become questions in and of themselves. As a result, we realize the events and participate in our own unique way—each encounter belongs not just in Alice's or Lewis Carroll's dreamworld, but in our own.*[5]

Botti's *Jabberwocky* was interpolated as scene 10 of *Wonderglass*. In the context of the larger opera, *Jabberwocky* becomes a story recited by a hooded, blindfolded figure, dressed in black, surrounded by darkness. This setting of Lewis Caroll's poem "is intended to present the story as it might have been told in an oral tradition."[6] The crucial importance Botti places on dramatic communication is evident in her usage of *Jabberwocky*; the poem is transformed into dramatic soliloquy.

> *By isolating the performer's expression to mouth and hands, a concentrated intimate visual space is established, which communicates the story while inspiring the*

imagination of the spectator. Carroll's abstract and fantastical language is explored through the use of extended vocal techniques, further communicating the atmosphere. The function of the storyteller and his/her accompanist [percussionist] is to excite the imagination of the spectator. However they choose to interpret the poem, they must communicate the story, its events, and characters.[7]

The second of these major theatrical works, actually subtitled *Dramatic Soliloquy*, is the before-mentioned *Telaio: Desdemona*. The piece was commissioned by Joann Freeman, artistic director of the American Artists Series of Detroit (comprised of Detroit Symphony players) and premiered in the 1994–1995 season with Botti as soloist. The work was first staged in a 1997 production at the Society for Ethical Culture in New York City. *Telaio: Desdemona* is a character study of Desdemona from William Shakespeare's *Othello*. The soloist is tasked with portraying both Desdemona and a narrator. The narrator's text consists of a collagelike collection of Shakespeare's descriptions of his tragic heroine. When Desdemona herself sings arias, Botti uses texts from two non-Shakespearian sources: the Italian Renaissance poet Gaspara Stampa (1523–1554) and traditional Italian folk songs.

The Italian word telaio *literally means frame—as in the frame of a loom used for weaving.* Telaio: Desdemona *explores this image in several ways. First, the entire piece serves as a frame within which threads of the character of Desdemona are woven, and out of which her portrait emerges. Secondly, I have used the traditional forms of recitative and aria to serve as a series of smaller frames within the overall structure. Lastly, the word* telaio *is a pun—in Shakespeare's* Othello, *Desdemona is in essence "framed" by Iago.[8]*

The work is approximately forty-five minutes in duration. A separate instrumental piece, Botti's *Prelude for 7 Instruments* (1996; 10 mins.), was designed as a purely instrumental overture to *Telaio* and is often played beforehand.[9]

During her before-mentioned residency with the Cleveland Orchestra from 2003 to 2005, Botti composed two works for large orchestra, each about ten minutes in duration. The first, *Impetuosity* (2003), is a vibrant concert overture, as its title might suggest.

Impetuosity is an exploration of momentum. The piece begins with a buildup of energy from a static state, gradually increasing in tension until it is unleashed. The orchestra is the energy force careening in many directions, focusing strongly as a rhythmic unit, finding precarious balances, held at a still point momentarily by the concert master until the free-flying pendulum again starts to swing. Impetus: "the force or energy associated with a moving body" [Webster's Dictionary]. This piece is inspired by the freedom of great jazz artists I admire such as Thelonius Monk, John Coltrane, and Gonzalo Rubalcaba.[10]

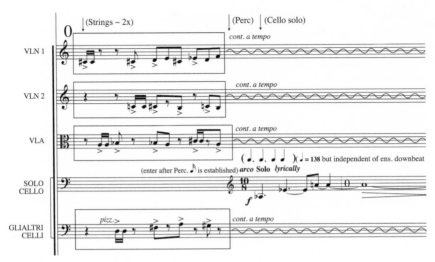

Example 2.5. *Impetuosity*, m. 164

The second work for the Cleveland Orchestra, *Translucence* (2005), is a much different sort of piece. Botti states that one of the best things about the Cleveland residency was the opportunity (unlike most commissions) to write two pieces; thus, she did not feel any pressure to "do everything" in one piece. Thus *Impetuosity* and *Translucence* are virtually opposite. Whereas *Impetuosity* is about harnessing the orchestra's energy toward bold, dramatic ends, *Translucence* is more lyrical and oriented toward more traditional utilization of the orchestra. The lyrical, unfolding nature of the piece stems from the fact that Botti based the work upon one of her songs, *The Exchange* (2003) for tenor and harp, a setting of a poem by American poet May Swenson (1913–1989).

> *Translucence is in one continuous movement, but there are two parts. The first part is an abstract exploration of central images from the poem—a journey through which to pass before arriving at the second part, which is based on the song itself. Some images are prominent . . . a murmur that builds into a complex mix of voices ("Populous and mixed is mind"), multiple string parts with superimposed wind and brass layers, released into a kind of plea ("Earth, take thought"). This leads to a rhythmic section—"I will be time"—which is an earthly dance. Although the song is greatly expanded—exploded is perhaps a better term—and reinterpreted, I wanted to retain its essence, its lyricism, and my direct reaction to the powerful poem.*[11]

The two-part structure of *Translucence* is readily audible; the piece begins with a shimmering bang and remains quietly energetic, building in layered intensity. As in the music of Lutosławski, Botti adeptly uses seamless integration between metric and aleatoric material to shape the drama of the piece (Lutosławski used the terms *a battuta* and *ad libitum* for these two sorts of music). As the first section reaches its powerful climax, the woodwinds sustain and *decrescendo* while brass, percussion, and harp begin aleatoric patterning. This evocative, nonmetrical section serves as the turning point between the two sections of *Translucence*. In the final section of the work—the free elaboration and expansion of the source song—Botti employs integration and interplay between the metrical material (including the song's lyrical textures) and coloristic bits of aleatory.

Though the two Cleveland residency works are not explicitly intended to be connected, they would make an exquisite diptych if programmed together. In these pieces, Botti demonstrates the versatility and flexibility of her musical style to create works that are nonvocal and non-*concertante*. In pieces for voice or instrumental soloist, the genre itself provides the composer an inherent dramatic structure to play against. It is notable, however, that in these purely orchestral works (which do not meaningfully feature the orchestra members as soloists), Botti creates compelling and memorable dramatic structures, which keep a listener engaged throughout.

Having a hands-on experience with such a tremendous orchestra is unlike anything else. Impetuosity is really about gesture, and the orchestra as an entity invoking those gestures. It has this sense of what an impulse does within this "energy source." Translucence came from a whole different place. It was from a more traditional sense of the orchestra and connected much more to lyricism and development.

One of Susan Botti's most original and distinctive creations is *Cosmosis* (2004), the only known work for the combination of soprano soloist, women's chorus, and symphonic wind ensemble. The work was created for a consortium of bands, led by Michael Haithcock and the University of Michigan Symphony Band. The other ensembles in the consortium came from Baylor University, Florida State University, Michigan State University, and the University of Texas at Austin. *Cosmosis* is based upon two poems by May Swenson. The primary focus is the poem "The Cross Spider," which Swenson wrote after hearing the news of a Skylab experiment in which a student proposed to see how well a spider could spin a web in outer space.[12] Botti describes Swenson's portrayal of the spider as "mythical," and the resulting musical work is indeed large scale and universal in its conception. The opening prologue sets Swenson's short shape poem "Overboard" in a jagged interplay of rhythmic speaking from the wind ensemble, chorus, and soprano. The poem is in an arch form, beginning with "What throws you out is what drags you in," folding down to a single word and then back out again. Botti sets this with machinelike interplay between the punchy spoken text and colorful pitched gestures of the wind ensemble.

Example 2.6. *Cosmosis*, mm. 22–23

Following the prologue, the principal poem is set in colorful discourse in three movements. Botti employs an abundance of aleatoric writing and nonpitched colors (e.g., laughing, chanting, quasi-*Sprechstimme*, etc.) in the chorus and soprano parts. The final section of the work is inspired by the idea of the myriad radio waves that are bouncing around in outer space. At its conclusion is a structured improvisation for the entire ensemble. Instructions are given entirely in words, shown partially in example 2.7 (see the next page).

Cosmosis is significant because there is nothing else like it in the wind ensemble repertoire. Legendary conductor and scholar Frank Battisti calls *Cosmosis* one of the most unusual, creative, and compelling works he had ever heard for the genre of wind ensemble.[13]

As with any composer, Susan Botti's personal background has shaped not only the kind of music she has written, but also her approach to writing it. There are few other composers (Mauricio Kagel is another example) for whom the essence of stagecraft and theatrical drama is at the heart of every piece composed. Perhaps it is easier to be dramatic or attuned to

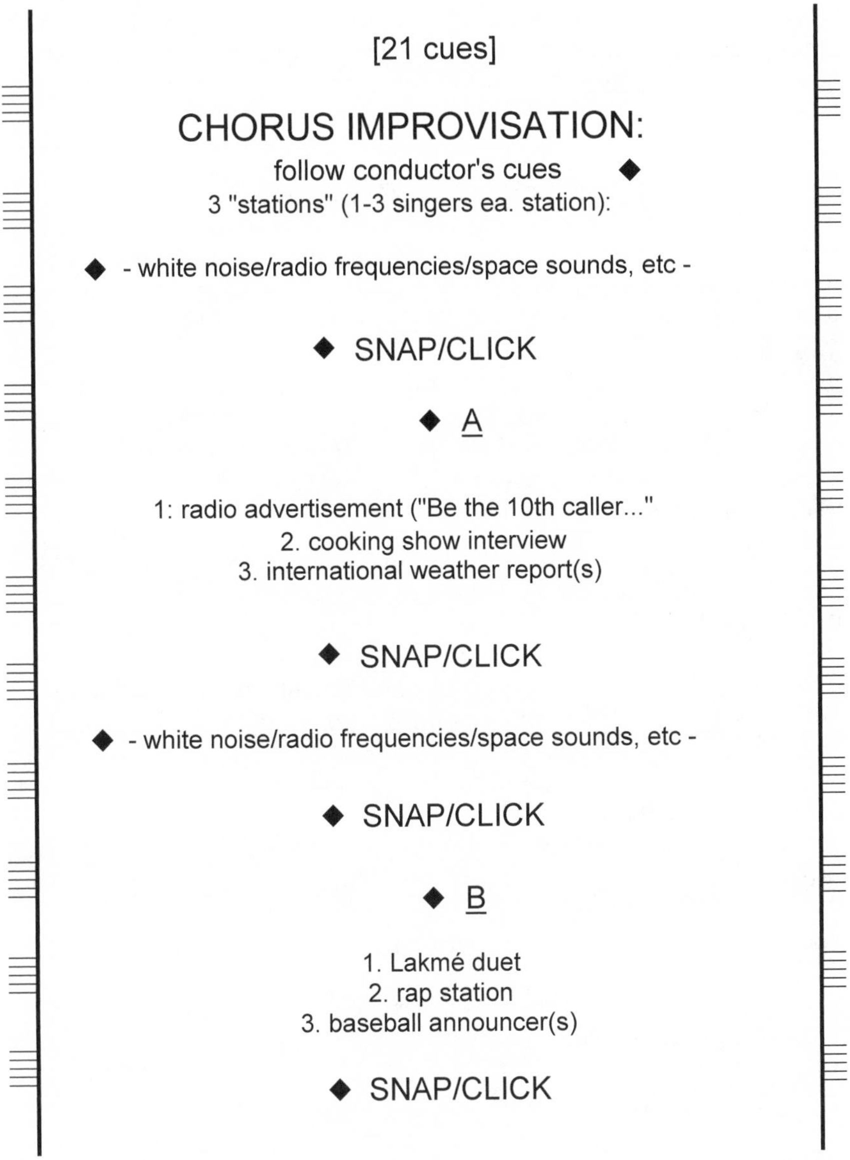

[21 cues]

CHORUS IMPROVISATION:

follow conductor's cues ◆

3 "stations" (1-3 singers ea. station):

◆ - white noise/radio frequencies/space sounds, etc -

◆ SNAP/CLICK

◆ A

1: radio advertisement ("Be the 10th caller..."
2. cooking show interview
3. international weather report(s)

◆ SNAP/CLICK

◆ - white noise/radio frequencies/space sounds, etc -

◆ SNAP/CLICK

◆ B

1. Lakmé duet
2. rap station
3. baseball announcer(s)

◆ SNAP/CLICK

Example 2.7. *Cosmosis,* m. 68 (partial)

the pacing of the theater when one is writing a theatrical work, such as an opera, but to integrate this sense of timing and gesture into one's entire output requires personal commitment, serious training, and determination. Susan Botti certainly possesses all of these qualities.

A CONVERSATION WITH SUSAN BOTTI

Though Susan and I had communicated through e-mail correspondence for a number of years, we had never met in person. Finally, when I had to be in the Hudson Valley for other business in December 2007, we got together at a bakery in downtown Rhinebeck, near her current home of Red Hook, New York. Amidst the bustle of the surroundings, we had a lovely discussion about all sorts of things in both our lives and, of course, about her music. As somebody who has been as active as a stage performer as she has a composer, Botti has an infectious and warm personality, and it was a real delight to speak with her in person about her work and career.–Carson Cooman

COOMAN: The first questions you are most often asked probably deal with your dual life as a composer and a performer. How do you see those two parts of your life interacting, and has that interaction changed over time?

BOTTI: I see the duality as an incredible benefit, and I think that I have grown tremendously as a composer because of my performing and vice versa. Since I was not an instrumentalist, I didn't have the advantage of sitting in the orchestra, but I did have the advantage of being able to perform with orchestras as a vocalist. I think that you can study a work over and over again, but by performing it, you get inside it in a way that you just can't otherwise. You breathe (in my case literally breathing!) with the piece and absorb it on a deeper level. My reactions to performing the music of others have a visceral impact on what I want (or don't want) for my own writing. I can really sense how things feel, and I decide whether or not that's something I want as a part of my own music.

COOMAN: Why do you think so few composers have the voice as their instrument?

BOTTI: I think it's just that the typical training of a singer involves even less new music than it does for other kinds of instruments. Thus, most singers are not exposed to that much new music; it's outside their experience and training.

COOMAN: Were you always composing, then?

BOTTI: No, I didn't start composing until later in my musical life. I was creating things, although I might not call it composing because it didn't use the same sort of craft that we've come to associate with composition.

One of the earliest experiences I had connecting music to theater came from the plays of Samuel Beckett. I was acting in *Endgame,* and I had a very strong feeling that the script was a musical score. So I decide to approach it from that standpoint. I countered the director, who was trying to find other motivations, and I really went on my own path with developing my character. It wasn't until much later that I saw a video of Beckett working with an actor, and I saw that he was basically "conducting" her—the impulses were so musical. At that point, I really started to focus on composing and went back to Berklee to finish my degree. That's when I began seriously writing.

COOMAN: What has it felt like to see pieces you originally created for yourself performed by others?

BOTTI: I absolutely love it. You know this little *Jabberwocky* piece of mine—I was invited to do a workshop with singers in Canada, and one of them chose *Jabberwocky* to perform. I was very curious how she was going to interpret it. The score is graphical, and she didn't listen to my recording first. She just used the score to develop her own interpretation. I was really quite relieved that the score conveyed what I wanted, and it had a lot of things in common with my performance.

COOMAN: Are you doing less performing now than you did before?

BOTTI: Actually, I'm doing more. That was one of the main reasons that I left the University of Michigan; I really wanted to get back to performing more and spending less time on the academic teaching. I enjoyed my time at Michigan, and it was a school very much about performance, but my role as a composition professor didn't always allow me the room for growth as a performer that I sought.

COOMAN: Had you taught before Michigan?

BOTTI: No.

COOMAN: How did it feel being in that rather traditional academic composition scene after coming into it from the world of theater originally?

BOTTI: It was challenging at first. I had enough of the academic training myself to appreciate it, and I still do enjoy it. It was nice to work with the students privately, but things really took off for me when we got to the level of putting it together with the players. That's where I felt completely connected and felt that I had a lot to offer. I shared an office with Bill Bolcom for six years, and he was a terrific person to be around. I learned a lot in my time there, but the environment wasn't right for me, long term.

COOMAN: In what ways do you think your residency with the Cleveland Orchestra was important to you?

BOTTI: It was important on many levels. On one level, they did not want a vocal work from me. I'm thrilled when people want me to involve myself as a performer, but it was really wonderful for them to say, "We just want orchestra pieces without soloists and without you." That made a big statement in terms of my writing. On another level, I grew up in the Cleveland area, and it was a homecoming to be working with this amazing orchestra. It was also a really heavenly opportunity to have the chance to write two pieces. I didn't feel the pressure that one might feel with one piece to make it "do everything." I was able to do one thing and then try something different in the other.

Cooman: Have you often felt a sense of being pigeonholed into writing vocal music?

Botti: The Cleveland Orchestra residency and the Orpheus Chamber Orchestra commission [*Within Darkness*] were big steps away from that. But when you're a vocalist, there is a sense that some people always think of you in that world. I remember when my chamber opera *Wonderglass* was produced in New York in the mid-1990s; my husband was in the audience and was privy to someone's saying, "Wow, did she actually orchestrate it too?" But I've felt that I've been able to move past that in large part as I've received more commissions for instrumental and orchestral music. On the other hand, writing good vocal music isn't easy and is a very noble pursuit. So I don't feel like I'll be giving up that aspect of my life.

Cooman: How did the New York Philharmonic commission for *EchoTempo* come about?

Botti: One thing that I'm very proud of is that most of the major commissions and connections I've had have come from the initiative of players themselves. Christopher Lamb (the principal percussionist) had a few new works commissioned for him by the Philharmonic (concerti by Joseph Schwantner and Tan Dun), and he was the instigator for that commission.

Cooman: Has the piece been performed since the New York premiere?

Botti: Yes, I've done it four times. I've done it with three different percussionists and also with chamber orchestra.

Cooman: Do you want to write more theater music in the future?

Botti: I'd love to do opera again. I feel it's very natural to me to incorporate theatrical elements. The piece that I'm currently working on [*Gates of Silence*] has dramatic elements, in fact. It's a work for the resident Blakemore Trio at Vanderbilt University.[14] I'm creating three independent pieces—violin and piano, piano trio, and piano trio plus soprano (myself)—but they are very much linked. We're going to perform them in the 2009–2010 season, first at Vanderbilt and then in New York City.

Cooman: What do you look for in texts?

BOTTI: Space for music! Some texts are entirely complete on their own, and music would just interfere. If that's the case, I leave it alone, no matter how much I like it. I like texts that are evocative, not didactic in language.

COOMAN: Have you done much with texts that have been chosen by other people, or do you normally make those choices yourself?

BOTTI: I make them myself. I've never had somebody choose a text, and I'm not sure how I'd react to that. I suppose it would depend on the text. The text is so important. When I'm performing a piece (by anybody), if I can't connect to the text, then I know I can't really perform it as well as I'd like.

COOMAN: Do you think your interest in text came mainly through drama, or were you interested in literature in a nondramatic way?

BOTTI: I certainly was interested in literature in all forms, but my experience with text did come through theater. That's where I'm most well versed in the world of literature.

COOMAN: How does it feel to be teaching at the Manhattan School where you studied?

BOTTI: It's wonderful. They've been so incredibly welcoming and supportive; my colleagues have been terrific. It's so familiar too.

COOMAN: Do you work on your music daily?

BOTTI: When possible. Even if I don't get to that dedicated space, I find a way to work. I've been in transition or on tour so often in my life that I've learned to adjust and work in nearly any context. I value the quiet time. These days the train trip into New York gives me two hours of just "sitting there," which is remarkable! It was after the birth of my second child that I really learned to find quiet time whenever I could. You have to create whenever you can and develop a discipline that's specific to what is happening in your life.

COOMAN: When you're writing, do you find yourself singing at some point in the compositional process?

BOTTI: I probably wouldn't use the word *singing*, but I do have a process in which, at a certain point, the crucial step becomes the conception of what I call a "line through the piece." The form and timing are so important to me. What's most crucial is spending time with the piece in its real time, experiencing the pacing as it happens. I need to sit there and live with the piece as if I'm experiencing it. This definitely comes from theater. When the timing and overall shape feel right, then I know that the piece will be fine, and I can fill in the specific musical details.

COOMAN: Have your feelings about notation and score preparation been influenced by the scores you've performed by other composers?

BOTTI: Absolutely. Lutosławski was a great icebreaker for me in terms of the sense of using structured aleatory. The freedom of vocal phrasing in Kurtág and Gubaidulina has been very important. I love the natural notation of the vocal lines, and I've adopted some of that. I always compose without bar lines, and then I put them in later where I feel they will help the most for performance. I really enjoy the freedom and naturalness that one gets by writing without them. Even if something is in an obvious metrical structure, I don't put in the bar lines while writing, because I want to leave room for something to stretch or move later in the process. I never want to lock myself in. I've found this idea is sometimes very scary for my students. They often start by writing directly into the computer; the bar lines are all there, and they just map things onto the grid. So when I ask them to write something without the computer or bar lines, it is a healthy challenge.

COOMAN: How did *Cosmosis* come about?

BOTTI: While I was at Michigan, Michael Haithcock [director of bands] asked for a band work, and so I went to their concert. I heard piece after piece (from the traditional band repertoire), and I kept thinking, "What could I possibly do with this medium?" But then I heard a wind ensemble piece by Leslie Bassett, and I then started to have ideas for how I could make this work. Michael asked me to write the piece for me to perform with the band, but I didn't want to write just another work for vocalist and ensemble. Thus I added the women's chorus to be a foil or shadow for the voice. The band world has really welcomed the piece.

COOMAN: What does the term *woman composer* mean to you? Does it make you upset to be categorized in that way?

BOTTI: I guess my first response to this whenever it comes up (and it does often come up) is that if you really think of the world and think of women in the world, how can I in good conscience claim that it's difficult to be a woman composer? I mean, there are women being killed in certain parts of the world just for being women, and so many women who are treated as less than human. I realize that generations of women before me did have difficulty getting their works performed. I certainly owe them a debt for having persevered through that. Now we are at a point where it is much less of an issue than it ever was. Also, one's personal background has a good deal to do with how one views the issue. When I was very young, I never imagined myself as a composer, perhaps partly because I wasn't ever playing any music by women composers during my piano lessons, so how would I relate to that occupation? Of course, that's now changed quite a bit, even since I was growing up. Encouragement from one's family also plays a major role. I'm the sixth of seven children; I have three sisters, two of whom are physicians, the other a teacher. Education was key, and in my family you could imagine yourself as doing whatever you wanted to do if you applied yourself toward that goal.

COOMAN: Do you think concerts that focus just on women composers are good things?

BOTTI: I have tended not to seek out those sequestered opportunities, although when they've happened, I've never objected to being a part of them. This sense of being a woman composer didn't really hit me until I went to Michigan, where I was the first woman to join the composition faculty. I saw it as well with young women entering the composition program, many of whom really wanted to seek a female mentor.

COOMAN: What would you say about the general direction of contemporary concert music?

BOTTI: I think there is an enormous amount of potential and diversity. I love the fact that new music is being performed in galleries and alternative spaces. There seem to be a lot of different perspectives about the orchestra world and contemporary music's place in it. I feel strongly that education and accessibility are important keys to music and culture thriving. The Bronx Zoo is a fabulous place, but one of the best times to go is on the day that it is free to the community—vibrant and alive and full of the diversity that makes New York amazing. Wouldn't it be thrilling if we could generate that kind of diversity and excitement at a concert hall? Museums have free evenings, why not the symphony? The Cleveland Orchestra is having a free concert this season with an exclusively contemporary music program (each of the Lewis Fellows will have a work in the concert). A recent performance at Blair School of Music [Vanderbilt] was held in beautiful Ingram Hall—and was free. This is wonderful.

COOMAN: And how do you see your own work evolving?

BOTTI: I'm evolving (or devolving) back to my theater roots. I'd love to create new works for alternative spaces (or transform existing spaces). I'd love to get more involved in education, in addition to my conservatory teaching. The work of someone like composer-bassist Jon Deak, for instance [Very Young Composers], is deeply inspiring and important.

ANALYSIS: *ECHO TEMPO* (2001)

Unsurprisingly, given her active performance life as a vocalist, music for the voice forms a large part of Susan Botti's output as a composer. Though the majority of her vocal music was originally written for her own performance use, this percentage will probably change in the coming years as she spends more of her time fulfilling commissions that arise from other performers. Though there have been various songs and monodramas that feature her voice, perhaps her most ambitious vocal work (and also her most prestigious commission to date) is *EchoTempo* (2001), a double concerto for soprano, percussion, and orchestra.

This work was commissioned by the New York Philharmonic and was premiered on its subscriptions concerts on November 1, 2, and 6, 2001. The orchestra was conducted by music director Kurt Masur, and the two soloists were Botti and the orchestra's principal percussionist, Christopher Lamb. This commission immediately preceded the two works written as part of her residency with the Cleveland Orchestra, *Impetuosity* (2003) and *Translucence* (2005), and is the first acknowledged work in her catalog scored for full symphony orchestra (the only preceding orchestra work of any sort was *Within Darkness*, written for the Orpheus Chamber Orchestra with violin soloist Martha Caplin).

EchoTempo is thus a quite significant work, as it is the piece that draws together the elements of vocal writing and monodrama Botti had previously explored, but this time with the resources and colors of the full symphony orchestra. Unlike most composers, Botti had the remarkable opportunity to write her first major orchestral piece for one of America's finest orchestras. It is a testament to the brilliant expressive potential shown in Botti's previous music that she was awarded this prestigious commission at such a point in her career.

EchoTempo is scored for standard symphony orchestra: three flutes (second doubling alto flute; third doubling piccolo), two oboes, English horn, two clarinets, bass clarinet, two bassoons, contrabassoon, four horns, three trumpets, two tenor trombones, bass trombone, tuba, three orchestral percussionists, harp, and strings. Botti has also made a slight rescoring of the piece for use with chamber orchestra (mostly reducing the number of brass). It is notable that the work includes not only the solo percussionist, but also three orchestral percussionists. Whereas many percussion concerti eschew orchestral percussion to focus on the soloist, Botti involves them fully in the discourse.[15]

It is worth quoting Botti's program notes about the work in their entirety, since they provide a good bit of insight into the work.

> *EchoTempo* is a setting of Native American translations for soprano, percussion, and orchestra. . . . The first aspect of this unusual combination of solo instruments that intrigued me was the idea that the voice and drums were the "original" instruments. I felt that the texts that I chose needed to reflect a timelessness. The simple elegance and power of these texts not only fulfilled that quality, but also offered me a wonderful doorway into the spirit of these inspiring cultures. The Native American connection to and reverence for nature and the human experience resonate through the translations. My settings of these texts do not incorporate the original songs or dances with which they were conceived. Rather, I looked for my inspiration to the rhythms and sounds from the natural world around us—animal movements and sounds, elemental and emotion-based sounds as interpreted through my musical vocabulary.

The four texts are set in a continuous cycle (performed without pause).

Song 1 ("Spring Is Opening"/Pawnee) is a celebration of the vibrant renewal of spring.

Song 2 ("Neither Spirit nor Bird"/Shoshone) is a love song.

Song 3 ("War God's Horse Song II"/Navajo) comes out of the fantastic and beautiful Navajo mythology. "War God"—also known as "Enemy Slayer"—is one of twin sons born to Changing Woman and the Sun. Changing Woman is the principal Navajo deity, whose name comes from the cycle of changes in her age: young in the spring, mature in the late summer, old in the winter, and young again the following spring. The warrior twins were sent by the deities to rid the world of monsters born of the quarreling people of the earth who were ravaging the land. The twins were sent to restore harmony to the world.

Song 4 ("In the Great Night"/Papago) is also known as "Owl Woman's Death Song."

Each song represents a season, joined in an endless cycle, renewed again each spring. When I was compiling the texts I would set, I hoped to find expressions of human experience common across time, across cultures. The delight in the senses of spring, the passion of love, and the transcendence of death were evident choices. Sadly, so was the choice of a text that portrays the senseless repetition of human conflict. As disturbing an issue as this was when I began *EchoTempo*, it became even more so in the wake of the horrifying events in New York City and Washington, D.C., on September 11.[16]

EchoTempo falls within the considerable body of concert music inspired by Native American sources. In his book *Imagining Native America in Music*, musicologist Michael Pisani traces the ongoing musical interest that "outsiders" have had in Native American culture: from the earliest engagement of Western European composers to present day composers of Native American background who choose to compose for modern Western ensembles. For some composers (such as Kyle Gann or James DeMars), the interest has been in the Native American musical materials (primarily rhythms and microtonality). In Botti's case, as her notes make clear, she became interested in Native American source material after thinking about the fact that this work was to feature voice and percussion (the bedrocks of Native American music-making) as its soloists. Though she did not use Native American source material, there is a clear connection made between the personal drama of Botti's style and the full body/gestural attributes that are an essential part of the performance of Native American traditional music. The four movements of *EchoTempo* are about 8 minutes, 8 minutes, 11.5 minutes, and 5 minutes, respectively, for a total duration of approximately 33 minutes. Each will be discussed in turn.

"Spring Is Opening" sets a brief, two-line traditional text (translated by Frances Densmore) from the Pawnee tribe. The poem is a celebration of the coming of spring and the sensuous enjoyment of the "white weeds used in the dance." The work begins with both soloists quietly improvising on percussion instruments:

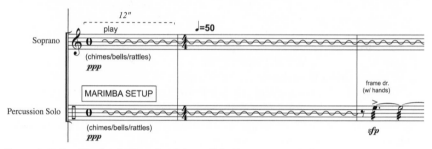

Example 2.8. "Spring Is Opening," from *EchoTempo*, mm. 1–3

After a dramatic entry from the orchestra (minus the brass), the two soloists engage in the first of many cadenza-like, imitative passages, which are found scattered throughout the work. This is a significant hallmark of Botti's writing in *EchoTempo*. Very often, the soprano is called upon to imitate the textures and sounds produced by the percussion soloist. Sometimes this is done through explicitly notated ideas; in other cases (such as the first passage shown below), it is simply marked "imitate percussion." In the second example below, the percussionist plays a pitched arpeggio on the marimba, which is immediately answered by the voice imitating the arpeggio. Because vocal arpeggios are extremely difficult, Botti does not specify the pitches, since it is not significant to the effect.

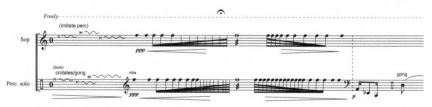

Example 2.9a. "Spring Is Opening," from *EchoTempo*, mm. 7–8

Example 2.9b. "Spring Is Opening," from *EchoTempo,* mm. 10–15

Calling to mind the numerous references she has made to Lutosławski may aid in our understanding of Botti's remarkable sense of pacing and contrast, specifically employed in the integration of these free, cadenza-like improvisatory sections with the more straightforward rhythmic textures (whether lyrically songlike or drivingly rhythmic). From a listener's perspective, the work's pacing has a remarkable sense of "giving you what you want when you want it." It is this seamless discourse between these free and metrical ideas that give the work a shape both accessible and fresh.

Because the movement's text is so short, it is not until nearly four minutes into the piece that the soprano even begins to unfold the initial words. The text is first presented over a rhythmic "groove" established with the percussion and double bass (see example 2.10 on the next page).

A faster rhythmic section, including a featured section for the percussion soloist, responds to the soprano's intonation of "Spring is opening." After the singer finishes the last line of text, the percussion leads directly into the second movement, "Neither Spirit nor Bird." This movement begins with a flurry of evocative color from strings playing high aleatoric patterns, accompanied by quiet percussion strokes on the wind chimes and rattles. The text for the movement (translated by Mary Austen) comes from the Shoshone tribe. The text states "Neither spirit nor bird; / That was my flute you heard / Last night by the River."[17] Each stanza compares the sounds made by the speaker's "flute," "blood," and "heart" to sounds of the natural world. Again, the movement moves in and out of free and metrical passages. The metrical passages have a particularly songlike character, accompanied by an arpeggiated, almost *Lieder*-esque texture (see example 2.11).

The songlike lyricism of the metrical parts often quickly dissolves into the free, imitative cadenza-like writing via seamless transitions. Botti usually accomplishes this transitional effect by beginning the rhythmic freedom within the end of the metrical section, so that the switch into meterless music is effectively masked (see example 2.12).

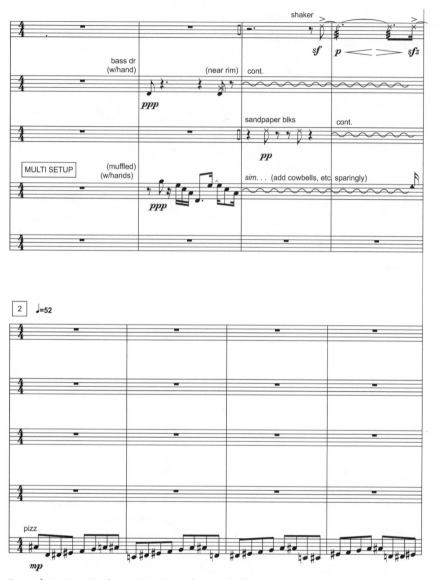

Example 2.10. "Spring Is Opening," from *EchoTempo*, mm. 36–39

The final section sets the stanza beginning, "That was no beast that stirred / that was my heart you heard," with a jagged dramatic texture. In the final lines of the movement, Botti employs chantlike vocal notation akin to that of *Telaio: Desdemona* (see example 2.13).

The solo percussion leads directly into the third movement with a brief transitional passage, while the soprano prepares to play the Navajo rattles used in the opening of the third movement.

Example 2.11. "Neither Spirit nor Bird," from *EchoTempo*, mm. 16–20

The third movement, "War God's Horse Song II," is the most extended section of the work and is based on a Navajo poem by Frank Mitchell, translated by David P. McAllester. It is a long poem in a call-and-response style. In the original text, every line is followed by a refrain line stating, "With their voices they are calling me." With very colorful imagery, the poem describes the environmental raiment of the war god. Botti does not repeat the refrain line after each line as in the original. Rather, she saves it for emphasis at specific moments.

Other than the introduction—an evocation for rattles, rain sticks, and soprano (on the text's repeated refrain)—and a brief cadenza-like elaboration of the final lines of the text by soprano and percussion, the entire movement is set within a tense, constantly pushing rhythmic structure. The introduction provides an optional improvisation for the soloists. In Botti and Lamb's performance, this improvisation lasted

Example 2.12.   "Neither Spirit nor Bird," from *EchoTempo*, mm. 35–36 (partial)

several minutes and incorporated many patterns and musical ideas, which are not notated.

The rhythmic body of the movement reaches its climax in a passage with a repeated half-step motive (G♯–A) in the soprano and high orchestra voices. It is accompanied by sweeping gestures in the middle and lower orchestral voices. Botti brings this evocative passage back twice, and it sticks in the ear as one of the most memorable sections of this movement (see example 2.15).

At the end of the text, the soprano speaks the final line ("With their voices they are calling me") with an authentically primal method of

Example 2.13.   "Neither Spirit nor Bird," from *EchoTempo*, m. 106

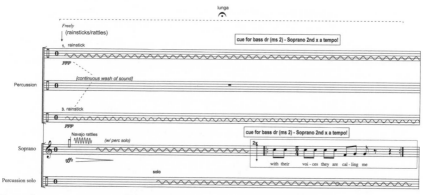

Example 2.14. "War God's Horse Song II," from *EchoTempo*, m. 1

Example 2.15. "War God's Horse Song II," from *EchoTempo*, mm. 119–122

declamation. There is nothing in the score's notation to denote these vocal inflections, but Botti incorporates them in her performances. Her voice dies away with each repetition and is immediately answered by a percussion ostinato, followed by a musical section featuring the percussion soloist.

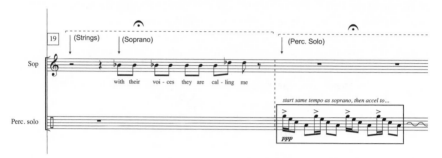

Example 2.16.   "War God's Horse Song II," from *EchoTempo,* **mm. 151–152**

After this free declamation of the poem's final lines, the orchestra presents a driving coda that leads directly into a languorous string passage, evoking the mood of the next movement.

The brief final movement, "In the Great Night," is very simply scored—using only soprano, percussion, and strings. The text (translated by Frances Densmore) is by Juana Manwell, "Owl Woman" of the Papago tribe. As with the first movement, the text is only a few lines long. It celebrates the coming of "the great night" (death), in which the "darkness comes rattling" and "my heart will go out." The seemingly free interplay between soprano and percussion returns.

Example 2.17.   "In the Great Night," from *EchoTempo,* **m. 1**

A marimba passage of quietly moving energy in the solo percussion begins to move upward leading to a final, unified declamation of the concluding words, "go out," in a pattern of two upward surges. The music dies away with a quiet coda of bowed crotales, rain stick, and soprano *vocalise.*

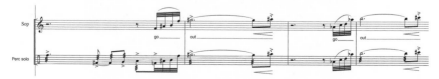

Example 2.18.   "In the Great Night," from *EchoTempo,* **mm. 17–20**

The overall emotional affect created by *EchoTempo* is that of an atmospheric ceremony. Botti does not explicitly employ Native American rhythms or melodies, but she nevertheless evokes a primal sense of communal music making within the dramatic structures she creates. The mix of free and rhythmic notation provides a vehicle for the theatrical articulation of the inherent drama in the texts. Unlike some other composers, for whom aleatory is simply a device for articulating points in purely musical structure, Botti uses these elements to provide a communicative space for the performers' expression of programmatic ideas. It allows her to achieve effects that would simply not be possible with traditional notation.

CODA

Living again in the New York City area and serving on the faculty of the Manhattan School of Music, Susan Botti continues her busy schedule of composing, teaching, and performing.[18] She is currently writing a wind ensemble work for the National Wind Ensemble Consortium Group, as well as other ongoing projects. As the artist in residence for the National Symphony Orchestra in Taipei, Taiwan (2009–2010 season), she will have the

opportunity to perform her work (*Telaio: Desdemona*) in Asia. The orchestra will also perform her *Within Darkness*, with Maestro Gunther Herbig.

Though not a prolific composer, Botti has produced a catalog in which each work is a carefully crafted, substantial artistic statement. The prestigious prizes she has received serve as recognition from the outside world of the considerable creative personality that surges within her. A performer from a very young age, Botti consistently imbues her music with a notable and genuine drama. Her theatrical pacing allows her music to unfold its story (whether programmatic or nonprogrammatic) with gripping intensity, and her compositional training allows her to present these ideas in richly expressive language. Susan Botti still has a large portion of her career ahead of her, and there is no question that she will remain a vital and personal voice in the landscape of contemporary music.

NOTES

1. Author interview with the composer, December 3, 2007. Unless otherwise cited, all quotations and personal information are from direct correspondences with the author, and permission for their usage has been granted by the composer. Photograph used by permission, Waring Abbott.

2. Botti is proud to share both her birthday (April 13) and her initials with Samuel Beckett, one of her great influences.

3. Though his music is immensely different from Susan Botti's, it is worth pointing out another composer, Harrison Birtwistle (1934–), whose output possesses these same properties, i.e., a focus on the theatrical drama of musical shapes more than any other element.

4. Despite its notational demands, the work has been taken on by other performers. Botti has not, to date, composed another work whose notation is quite so graphical.

5. Susan Botti, *Wonderglass*, SUBO Music, 1994.

6. Botti, *Wonderglass*.

7. Botti, *Wonderglass*.

8. Susan Botti, *Telaio: Desdemona*, SUBO Music, 1995.

9. This is the first purely instrumental piece in Botti's catalog.

10. Susan Botti, "Program Note for *Impetuosity*" (program booklet of the Cleveland Orchestra, 2004).

11. Susan Botti, "Program Note for *Translucence*" (program booklet of the Cleveland Orchestra, 2005).

12. May Swenson, *In Other Words* (New York: Knopf, 1987).

13. Author conversation with Frank Battisti, April 12, 2005.

14. The Blakemore Trio consists of violinist Carolyn Huebl, cellist Felix Wang, and pianist Amy Dorfman.

15. A model in this regard is Joeseph Schwantner's *Concerto for Percussion and Orchestra* (1994), also written for Christopher Lamb. Schwantner's concerto has become a repertoire standard.

16. Susan Botti, "Program Note for *EchoTempo*" (program booklet of the New York Philharmonic, 2001).

17. George W. Cronyn, ed., *Native American Poetry* (New York: Ballantine, 1962).

18. Photograph of Susan Botti as Desdemona, used by permission of Waring Abbott.

APPENDIX A: LIST OF WORKS

[All works are published by SUBO Music (ASCAP), with the exception of *Silent Movie* (included in Boosey & Hawkes's and the New York Festival of Song's *Songbook for a New Century*)]

Opera/Stage

Wonderglass (1994)—chamber opera (soprano, mezzo-soprano, 2 tenors, bass-baritone, flute, clarinet, saxophone, trombone, harp, piano, percussion, contrabass); Lewis Carroll, text

Telaio: Desdemona (1995)—operatic soliloquy (soprano, harp, piano, percussion, string quartet); William Shakespeare and Gaspara Stampa, text

Orchestral/Large Ensemble

Within Darkness (1999)—violin, chamber orchestra

EchoTempo (2001)—soprano, solo percussion, full orchestra; Native American traditional texts in translation

Impetuosity (2003)—full orchestra

Cosmosis (2004)—soprano, women's chorus, wind ensemble; May Swenson, text

Translucence (2005)—full orchestra

Choral

Stelle (2006)—6 voices, harp, piano; Rabindranath Tagore, text

Tagore Madrigals (2006)—6 voices; Rabindranath Tagore, text

Make-Falcon (2006–present; work in progress)—chorus and ensemble; Linda Gregerson, text

Vocal

listen, it's snowing (1990)—soprano, piano; e. e. cummings, text

Jabberwocky (1990)—soprano, percussion; Lewis Carroll, text [incorporated into *Wonderglass*; see Opera/Stage]

Her Vision (1996)—high voice, harp; Denise Levertov, text [adapted/excerpted from *Pig Dreams*]

Pig Dreams (1996)—soprano, flute, harp; Denise Levertov, text
. *Trois poèmes de Jaccottet* (1997)—soprano, piano; Philippe Jaccottet, text
Silent Movie (2001)—tenor, piano; David Kirby, text
The Exchange (2003)—tenor, harp; May Swenson, text
Two Gregerson Songs (2006)—soprano, piano; Linda Gregerson, text
un bacio (2007)—soprano, baritone, 2 flutes, bass clarinet, cello, steel drums; [phonemes of the title], text
Dido Refuses to Speak (2008–2009)—soprano, piano trio; Linda Gregerson, text [part of *Gates of Silence* trilogy]

Instrumental

Prelude for 7 Instruments (1996)—harp, piano, percussion, string quartet
The Journey without Her (2008–2009)—piano trio [part of *Gates of Silence* trilogy]
Lament: The Fallen City (2008–2009)—violin, piano [part of *Gates of Silence* trilogy]

APPENDIX B: DISCOGRAPHY

Cosmosis. Susan Botti, soprano; University of Michigan Women's Chorus and Symphony Band; Michael Haithcock, conductor. Equilibrium, CD 75. "Brooklyn Bridge."

Jabberwocky. Susan Botti, soprano; Paul Guerguerian, percussion. CRI/New World Records, NWCR 802. "listen, it's snowing."

listen, it's snowing. Susan Botti, soprano; Daniel Kirk-Foster, piano. CRI/New World Records, NWCR 802. "listen, it's snowing."

Telaio: Desdemona. Susan Botti, soprano; Susan Jolles, harp; Paul Guerguerian, percussion; Martha Caplin, violin; Renée Jolles, violin; Liuh-Wen Ting, viola; Dorothy Lawson, cello. CRI/New World Records, NWCR 802. "listen, it's snowing"

Trois poèmes de Jaccottet. Susan Botti, soprano; Daniel Kirk-Foster, piano. CRI/New World Records, NWCR 802. "listen, it's snowing."

SOURCES

Ellison, Cori. "Downtown Divas Expand Their Horizons." *New York Times*, October 28, 2001, 31, 36.

Guinn, John. "*Wonderglass* Explores Lewis Carroll's Mind." *Detroit Free Press*, February 19, D4, D6.

Hauptman, Fred. "The Sound of New Music." *Seattle Weekly*, April 25, 1990, 12.

Leonard, James. "Burning Down the House." *Ann Arbor Observer* 27, no. 8 (April 2003): C4.

Oteri, Frank J. "Native Song." *Stagebill*, October 2001, 30–31.

Pisani, Michael. *Imagining Native America in Music*. New Haven: Yale University Press, 2005.

Mays, Desiree. "Telaio: Desdemona." *20th Century Unlimited Program Book*, March 1999, 1–6.
Nisbett, Susan Isaacs. "Botti Works Magic with Words." *Ann Arbor News*, April 5, 2003, C3.
———. "Theatrical Music." *Ann Arbor News*, March 30, 2003, C2.
Smith, Craig. "Musical Drama Plumbs Depth of Desdemona." *Pasatiempo*, March 26, 1999, 4.

Deborah Hayes

GABRIELA LENA FRANK
(1972–)

The musicians I've been exposed to have been hardcore conservatory brats. They're the ones that I write for. I really understand the conservatory mentality. I trained in it. And I also understand, while they respect Beethoven and all that, they also long for something contemporary, something "cool." These are youngsters. So this made a really big impression on me, this kind of identity crisis that we had. The CDs that we put on when we went back to our dorm rooms were pop music. But the music we lived with, and loved, and put in a certain place in our lives, was this old stuff. The response that I would get, to music that I enjoyed writing more, was tremendous. But I also knew that I benefited from—and I liked the challenge of—staying with a certain repertoire.[1]

Gabriela Lena Frank is an extraordinary young American composer whose work is adding distinction and enthusiasm to the new music scene. As her words suggest, her music has the emotional depth and technical complexity of the masterworks of the Western concert tradition, along with the excitement and immediate appeal of popular music. With a Jewish American father and a Peruvian mother of Spanish, Chinese, and Quechua Indian descent, she identifies herself as an American *mestiza*, a woman of mixed European and Native American ancestry. As a composer, she explores the concept of *mestizaje* ("mestizo-ism") in music. Thus, she says, "I'm intensely interested in recasting traditional folk music of South America using the resources of Western classical instruments and forms."[2] In a more general sense, *mestizaje*, in which cultures exist in harmony, "is something that everybody needs to think about," she notes, "because we're all living in a *mestizo* society now."

At the turn of the twenty-first century, Frank's professional career blossomed in ways she had never imagined as a student. She earned a doctor of musical arts (D.M.A.) degree in composition from the University of Michigan in 2001, and in early 2003, much to her surprise, the prestigious New York City publishing firm of G. Schirmer Inc., offered her a contract—which she accepted. Today, numerous commissions, residencies, performances, and awards support her work. From her home in Berkeley, California, Frank travels extensively in the United States, South America, and throughout the world. A virtuoso pianist, she often performs her own works. Her music is sought by leading performers and attracts a wide range of audiences, whether in concert halls or in community centers, schools, prisons, or even less traditional venues. She connects further with performers and listeners through her informative and extensive writing and speaking. She is committed to arts-oriented outreach projects to engage new audiences, often consisting of people of diverse racial backgrounds.

Much of the music in Gabriela Frank's professional catalog reflects her ongoing private study of Peruvian music, geography, and ethnology, especially indigenous, preconquest traditions—Inca and pre-Inca. She finds inspiration in Latino and Latin American mythology, art, and poetry. She draws upon her own experience as a *mestiza* and an American-born Latina. She evokes her favorite music from her earliest years. She calls up her memories and brings her dreams to consciousness. For Gabriela Frank, her life story is the foundation of her compositional identity.

Frank was born on September 26, 1972, in Berkeley, California. Her father, Michael Barry Frank, who was born in New York of Lithuanian Jewish descent, is a Mark Twain scholar and editor at the University of California's Bancroft Library. Her mother, Sabina Cam Villanueva de Frank, whom he met when he was a Peace Corps volunteer in Peru in the 1960s, is a stained glass artist. Gabriela grew up, in her words, "comfortably middle class," in Berkeley's "post-hippie heyday," in a cosmopolitan, multicultural university milieu.

She was drawn to the piano at a very early age and started piano lessons before she turned five. She attributes the "music gene" to the Frank side of the family. "My paternal grandmother [Lucille Frank] and her brother were gifted pianists, picking up songs played on the radio by ear." Gabriela's family acquired a spinet piano when she was about two years old, when her brother, Marcos Gabriel Frank, almost five years older than she, asked for lessons. She loved improvising and imitating music she had heard.

As a baby, I was attracted to the instrument, and we have numerous pictures of me picking out notes at the keyboard, or playing little songs I was making up to picture books propped up on the stand, or even asleep at the keyboard. From such small beginnings, my grandmother immediately identified the music talent in me, and there are pictures of us sitting at the piano together, improvising songs and having a grand old time.

When she did not speak properly and seemed unresponsive to people calling her name, young Gabriela's parents began to worry. Both Spanish and English were spoken at home, so perhaps she was confused. But young children easily learn languages, so confusion was unlikely. She seemed normal in other ways, and she was learning to read. Every night, her parents read to her, holding her close to their chests so she would feel the words come through, much the same way as she experienced music coming through the piano.[3] When she entered kindergarten, she had the good fortune to have a teacher who recognized the patterns exhibited in hearing-impaired children. Tests revealed that Gabriela had been born with a high moderate to profound neurosensory hearing loss. She was fitted with hearing aids.

I remember how the world came to new life. The piano sounded amazing, and I remember turning out song after song after song with all of that verve and imagination that only little kids have. In my kindergarten class, we had an upright, so I had access to a piano both at school and home.

Still, Frank remembers not liking the way the piano was speaking to her with hearing aids, and to this day she takes them off when she practices. She had years of speech therapy and learned to lip-read for complete understanding.

While still very young, she began studying with a neighborhood piano teacher, Babette Salamon, from South Africa, who had trained in London at the Royal College of Music. Gabriela's first lessons were without hearing aids; she would imitate what she saw her teacher play. "I didn't really hear the piano; I felt the vibrations through the instrument. It's possible I got my perfect pitch that way, at that formative time for brain development."[4] With Salamon, who remained her piano teacher throughout high school, she learned standard piano repertoire.

I had the normal diet of Clementi, Haydn, Scarlatti, Beethoven, and Mozart. About once a month, I would go over to her house and spend the evening with her and her husband, listening to selections from their vast LP collection. We never listened to contemporary music. I didn't know composers could be living, or that they could be women. I never thought about being a composer professionally, even though my teacher did encourage me to play my compositions at her annual piano recitals. She also helped me write down my first piece on paper when I was in high school.

At the same time, she found herself particularly drawn to folkloric music of the Andes, which she heard, through the seventies and eighties, when musicians came up from Peru, Ecuador, and Bolivia to the Bay Area to give concerts. The sounds—and sights—had a significant, lasting influence on her own music.

While I could listen to the Peruvian LPs my parents had at home, the concerts gave me an important visual where I could attach sounds to their instruments, see the traditional dress of the musicians, watch their ensemble work, and watch how they danced.

The concerts became an important family ritual. "I had special little costumes I wore, especially colorful." After the concerts, she was "jazzed up" and wanted to go to the piano to try to replicate what she had heard. Her parents allowed her to stay up an extra hour. "They understood that creative buzz." Cassette tapes they had bought at the concerts wore out from continued playing. "My piano teacher would gently scold me, with good humor, when I tried to 'Latin-ize' my Clementi or Bach by adding little touches reminiscent of the folkloric concerts I heard." Apart from the music, she was only aware of "a certain ambiance of Peruvian-ness" at home.

Although I identified such things as my particular brand of humor and my love of certain foods as distinctly Latina, my nostalgia for the old country was kept in check for many years by tales of hyper-inflation, drug wars, machismo, and the ongoing genocide of Latin America's indigenous peoples.[5]

Between the ages of nine and twelve, she learned violin through public school instruction, but even with perfect pitch, she could not learn to play in tune. Still, those few years with the violin have made her very comfortable in writing for string instruments. Another childhood experience of lasting value was her training in aikido, a nonviolent martial art. Her father enrolled both children, and soon they were instructors in weekly Saturday morning classes. Public speaking and teaching seemed very natural to her.

Frank became a self-described "conservatory brat" in her mid-teens, in 1988, just before her last year of high school.

On a whim, I took a summer music program for composition at the San Francisco Conservatory of Music and, overnight, had a change of everything. I remember walking into the building and being amazed to see a grand piano in every room, staff lines painted onto the chalkboard, and a huge library filled with nothing but books on music, and records. And I started to learn the canon of twentieth-century music, much of which seemed such a strange beast to me. Discovering that composers could indeed be living, and furthermore that I did have a special talent, pivoted me irrevo-

cably in a new direction. On a giant leap of faith, I decided that I was going to be a composer, and really never looked back. I was sixteen.

She continued at the preparatory department that year, receiving her first "hardcore training in theory and ear training." Accustomed to depending upon her quick ear, she struggled to learn how to read music well so that she could write down her ideas more quickly. "My initial pieces were very tonal, very short, and tempered by whatever piece I happened to hear last—a Bach cello suite, a Boccherini guitar quintet, or the clarinet solo from Messiaen's *Quartet for the End of Time*." As her gifts became apparent, her parents were always very supportive. "They never told me to abandon a music career just because I couldn't hear," recalls Frank, "so I grew up with the idea that I could do whatever I set my mind to."[6]

After graduating from high school, Frank attended Rice University's Shepherd School of Music, in Houston, Texas, majoring in composition and studying piano as well. She graduated with a bachelor's degree in 1994 and two years later earned a master's degree in composition. Her composition teachers were Paul Cooper (1926–1996), Ellsworth Milburn (1938–2007), and Samuel Jones (1935–). With her piano teacher, Jeanne Kierman Fischer, she learned the music of Alberto Ginastera (1916–1983), Béla Bartók (1881–1945), and other composers who incorporated folk and traditional musics in various ways. Their work was a revelation. "I hadn't even realized it was possible to do a multicultural kind of music."

At Rice University, Frank was active as a pianist, accompanist, and chamber music player, and she wrote a great deal of music.[7] With its first-class performance faculty and students, the school was a young composer's paradise, where even pieces by inexperienced students like herself received world-class level performances. To learn more about writing for instruments other than the piano, she started working with her players as she composed. The experience taught her "how rich and important the performers' imagination and talents are for a composer," and she began making audiotapes of the workshop sessions for further reference. She won a composition prize with *String Quartet no. 3* (1992) and tasted "anonymous recognition," an aspect of competitions that she still considers strange. She rarely entered competitions.

Two of the five pieces on Frank's master's composition recital program are still in circulation. The jazzy *Manhattan Serenades* (1995), for cello and piano, is the earliest work in her professional catalog; in 2007, she estimated that a dozen teams were performing it in different parts of the world. Her master's thesis, *Movement for String Quartet* (1995),[8] influenced by the work of Witold Lutoslawski (1913–1994), is now the fourth movement of the string quartet *Inkarrí* (2005).

Frank also pursued new interests. During an undergraduate music history class taught by Marcia Citron, Frank became interested in Beethoven's deafness and its effects on his piano writing as his increasing hearing loss altered his perceptions of musical sound, texture, and voicing. Encouraged by Citron, she wrote a five-page paper on this intriguing topic. As a composition major, however, she was not satisfied with the traditional conservatory curriculum of Western classical music. "I respect it," she says, "the way I respected my *sensei* [teacher] in aikido. But it just wasn't really for me." Then she came across the writings of the Peruvian novelist, poet, and ethnologist José María Arguedas (1911–1969), whose concept of *mestizaje* envisioned Quechuas and their Spanish conquerors living in harmony. Recognizing a core idea that she had been seeking for so long, she nearly wept. To her, *mestizaje* suggested a wider, transforming vision of a world that encompasses many cultures without oppression.

Paganini's caprices had always conjured up a hidden memory of the frenetic energy of Peruvian kashwa dances. Bach's contrapuntal lines jogged my mind for Andean duo-panpipe tunes. Beethoven's stormy sonatas smacked of vibrating Bolivian wuankara *drums. Debussy's flute writing paralleled the melancholy* harawis *of the Andes. The list goes on. It didn't take long to realize that embers burned deep in my consciousness, unattended. The question was, what was I going to do about it?*[9]

Frank made an extraordinary commitment to figure out for herself over the span of her life what Arguedas' concept of cultural *mestizaje* might mean to her as an individual and an artist. More time passed before anything distinctly Peruvian or Latina emerged in her own music, at least anything that she could single out. She was aware that some of the Rice faculty members did not believe in her, perhaps because of her interests outside the conservatory curriculum, perhaps because she was a female in an all-male department, or perhaps for some other reason entirely. Their doubt was subtle. She took it as a challenge.

After Rice, she entered the Ph.D. program in composition at the School of Music of the University of Michigan in Ann Arbor where she studied composition with William Albright (1944–1998), William Bolcom (1938–), Leslie Bassett (1923–), and Michael Daugherty (1954–), and piano with Logan Skelton. Encouraged by her music history professor, Steven Whiting, to pursue her study of the effects of Beethoven's deafness upon his piano writing, she wrote a thirty-page paper and planned to expand the research into a Ph.D. dissertation. Then the school instituted a D.M.A. degree program in composition with less emphasis on research and music theory, and she switched to that. She continued to develop her compositional skills through performance and even wrote her own piano concerto to play in the annual student concerto competition for all instrumentalists. She won the competition (the orchestral part, in piano reduction, was played by Gordon Beeferman); then she performed the work with orchestra, conducted by Kenneth Kiesler.[10]

She studied with Leslie Bassett for one semester and later recorded a CD of his piano and chamber music as a tribute to him.

> *When word circulated that Leslie would be stepping out of retirement for a single semester to teach a few lucky students, I scrambled furiously for the front of the line, and so began a fortuitous mentorship. Our lessons consisted of admonishments ("Young lady, good orchestration can hide a multitude of sins"); humorous warnings ("Trombone players are boobs, and I'm speaking, of course, as a former trombonist myself!"); and enthusiastic advice ("Put oboes snarling down around a cluster on middle C. What a marvelous effect!")*[11]

She studied over a longer period with Bolcom, who is known for his encyclopedic knowledge of American popular song; a virtuoso pianist, he tours widely with his wife, the singer Joan Morris. "I was especially intrigued by Bolcom's choice when to incorporate and not incorporate American vernacular into his music," Frank recalls. "Not everything I write has overtly Latin overtones, and I think it's important to know when to draw organically on such idioms. Seeing how Bolcom handled this had a big effect on me."

Bolcom encouraged her to travel to South America; she received university grants for her research, which began in 1998 with visits to Venezuela and Argentina. Although she did not take any classes in Latin American music, her piano teacher, Logan Skelton, had introduced her to Bartók's essays and ethnomusicological research, and she tried to replicate his methods. Frank decided to learn Spanish, but because of the hearing loss, she could not pick it up in normal conversation. "I watched Spanish soap operas on TV," she recalls. "They were great because everyone was so dramatic. Then I graduated to news broadcasts, which were fast paced but still very clearly spoken. Finally I moved on to regular programming, with the less precise speech, slang, and so on."[12] Somewhat as at Rice, her multicultural interests created some distance between her and other students at Michigan. To some, the "Latin thing" was just a current fad that Frank was latching on to. She protested at first but soon gave up.

> *There was a lot of pressure in Michigan to get on the latest bandwagon of trends, technical trends. It could be improv, it could be avant-garde extended techniques, it could be trying to make the music sound like rock and roll or pop, or using discotheque beats, and the goals were to be super cool, super bad. It was done so tritely and badly, it just didn't appeal to me. It seemed to be macho, also. You didn't see a lot of women going out for that. They were all twenty-something-year-old guys; of course they're thinking about getting their kicks. It was fun to be with a lot of these guys, but I didn't see a lot of longevity or a lot of future in what they were doing.*

Although during her time at Michigan she was "very focused on working, not on making a *career*," by graduation she had produced what she now realizes was a "very interesting—small but interesting—body of work" that "ended up helping the career." In the five pieces she completed from 1998 to 2001, she devised ways of expressing her concept of *mestizaje* through stories, poetry, and sounds.

The first of the pieces, *Las Sombras de los Apus* (*The Shadows of the Apus*) (1998–1999), a ten-minute work for cello quartet commissioned by Gregory Beaver, cellist of the Chiara Quartet, depicts the avalanche-summoning spirits (*apus*) of the Andes, according to Quechua mythology. Though the scenario is Latin American, she describes the music as not Latin but, like the fourth quartet, Lutoslawskian. "This was a certain direction that I was taking for a while; I call it my Lutoslawski-aleatoric direction, with a bit of [Sofia] Gubaidulina [1931–] thrown in. I was really taken with the sound of their work; I still am. It's just a totally different handling of sound, but still for a dramatic effect that can be grasped by the audience."

Using Lutoslawski's technique of limited aleatory from the 1960s, Frank writes chance passages in which only the number of repetitions of pitches within the aleatoric wheel is left to chance or the player's discretion; pitches and relative note values are specified. Three cellos depict the *neblina* (mist) that (according to the program note) warns travelers that the *apu* is about to unleash a *huayco*, or avalanche.[13] Cello parts I, III, and IV are written in three different *scordatura* tunings to enable a variety of open-string pitches (score examples are in sounding score, not *scordatura*).

Example 3.1.   *Las Sombras de los Apus* (1999), opening section[14]

Frank makes imaginative use of vibrato-less sustained notes, *fp* attacks, quiet *pizzicatos*, and a central F pitch blurred with its neighboring semitones E and F-sharp to create a misty texture that is both static and forward moving.

In the next section, cello I introduces the theme of *El Apu*, to be played *molto espressivo e legato*, free and unhurried; left-hand *pizzicatos* are all open strings (C♯–G♯ *scordatura*, D–A standard). As accompaniment, the other three cellos repeat pitches notated in their aleatoric wheels; the resulting dense *pianissimo* cluster D♯-E-F-F♯ suggests the misty mountain atmosphere.

Example 3.2. *Las Sombras de los Apus,* 2nd section

In subsequent sections, cellos II and III continue the *apu*'s theme in turn, and then the *neblina* returns briefly. In the section labeled *"El Apu y Su Sombra"* the "shadow" (cello II) of the *apu* (cello I) begins each phrase slightly behind; a score notation directs that the two parts "should not line up," thus suggesting the echoing quality of sounds at high altitude. Intensity builds in semitone glissandos and fast arpeggiated intervals, *más agitato,* leading to the climactic section labeled *"¡El Huayco!"* Then the earth emits *gruñidos* (groans) and *machacas* (grindings), the *apu* is but a memory (*"Como Memoria"*), and all is silence.

Frank uses Latin musical elements for the first time, but only sparingly, in the second of these five works, *Ríos Profundos: Música para Violoncello y Piano* (*Deep Rivers: Music for Violoncello and Piano*) (1999). In seven short, connected scenes or movements, the music depicts experiences of young Ernesto, the central character in Arguedas's 1958 novel *Los Rios Profundos,* as he tries to find his place in a Peruvian society that pits dark-skinned Indians and fairer Hispanics against each other. The cello's opening melody, based on motifs representing Ernesto, returns in the seventh movement, Ernesto's final summation of himself.

In the third work, *Cuatro Canciones Andinas* (*Four Andean Songs*) (1999), for voice and piano, Frank sets texts in Spanish for the first time—Indian poetry that Arguedas collected and translated from Quechua into Spanish. In the liner notes to the 2005 CD recording of the songs, Frank notes that Arguedas's efforts to "validate the native culture of the Andes" by collecting "the tunes, poetry, and folklore of the Quechua Indians, the descendants of the ancient Incas," remind one of Bartók's efforts in Europe.[15] The piano accompaniment incorporates sounds of guitars and flute; the dramatic voice part includes spoken passages, whispering, *Sprechstimme* (half-singing, half-speaking), and fast trills. "I hadn't traveled to Peru yet by this point," Frank recalled in 2007. "It was a big stretch for me just to grapple with the words, and my goal was just to convey them beautifully, in a way that wasn't obviously Western."[16]

In 2000, Frank made her first visit to her mother's family in the Peruvian Andes, and the fourth and fifth works are informed by that trip. She dedicates the stunningly virtuosic *Sonata Andina* (*Andean Sonata*) to her Peruvian *abuelita* (grandmother), Griselda Villanueva de Cam. The *Elegía Andina* [*Andean Elegy*], a vivid twelve-minute tone poem for chamber orchestra, is Frank's doctoral thesis and the earliest orchestral work in her catalog. The Albany (New York) Symphony Orchestra commissioned the piece and premiered it in December 2000. Frank strengthened the orchestration for performance in February 2008 by the Fort Worth (Texas) Symphony Orchestra, which has issued the work on CD.

Of these five works, *Sonata Andina* proved to be the most immediately significant to her further career. The eighteen-minute sonata won the 2000 Search for New Music award from the International Alliance for Women in Music, and Frank has come to regard her performance of the work at the IAWM concert in June 2000 at the National Museum of Women in the Arts in Washington, D.C., as a "turning point," her first venture into the wider professional world outside academe. In her first significant review, the *Washington Post* found the sonata to be "crafted with unself-conscious mastery."[17] Two years later, her impromptu performance of the *bravura* last movement at an ASCAP reception in New York City contributed to G. Schirmer's decision to sign her on.

The first movement's title, "Allegro Aymara," refers to the Aymara people who lived slightly south of the Quechua in the Inca Empire, in what is now western Bolivia, southern Peru, and northern Chile. Frank labels the opening measures as imitating the sounds of a large Bolivian *tambor* drum and a heavy wooden end-blown *tarka* flute. To suggest the tarka's hoarse overblown tone, she writes fifths, seconds, and three-note chords instead of single notes. Dotted bar lines suggest that the performer may exercise some metric freedom.

Example 3.3.   *Sonata Andina* (2000), I, "Allegro Aymara," mm. 1–11[18]

At the beginning of the B section (the movement's form is A-B-A coda) a *pinkillo* flute made of thick jungle reed plays a catchy tune accompanied by a small *tinya* drum.

Example 3.4. *Sonata Andina*, I, "Allegro Aymara," mm. 105–110

At the end of the coda, motives from earlier tunes are extended and transformed into grand pianistic gestures.

Example 3.5. *Sonata Andina*, I, "Allegro Aymara," mm. 281–294

The second movement, "Himno Inca," mimics a performance style of the Andes in which a number of *zampoña* (panpipe) players stand in a semicircle, each playing a constricted range of notes, preceded, accompanied, and followed by brief percussion. The movement opens with percussion in the form of the pianist's strictly measured hand clapping and tongue clicks. The effect is quite striking: a photo of the composer performing this section in 2003, at Merkin Concert Hall in New York City, appeared in the *New York Times* with Allan Kozinn's review of the concert.[19] To create the perception of ascending pitches, Frank's "performance hints" suggest changing from clapping to using the fingertips to strike different parts of the palm or even the wrist.

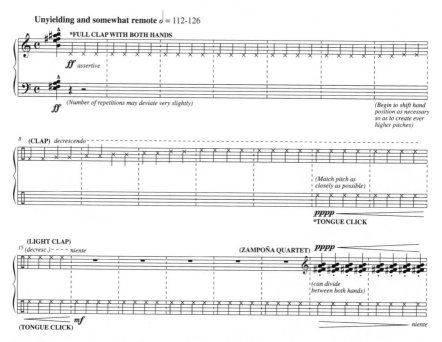

Example 3.6. *Sonata Andina*, II, "Himno Inca," mm. 1–22

In the final two measures of the example, the *zampoña* ensemble enters; its pulsating chords continue for the next sixty measures, with first one and then another of the four pitches becoming prominent; example 3.7 shows how Frank notates this effect (Kozinn described it as "a pounding chordal shimmer à la early Steve Reich").

Example 3.7. *Sonata Andina*, II, "Himno Inca," mm. 58–66

In the third movement, "Adagio Illariy" (*Illariy* is the Quechua word for a specific kind of light seen at dawn), a *quena* flute meditates on a new day. Score notations ask the pianist to produce phrases that are variously "in supplication," "like a catch in one's breath," "drifting," like "bleeding watercolors," and "feather light." Example 3.8 is the opening of the movement.

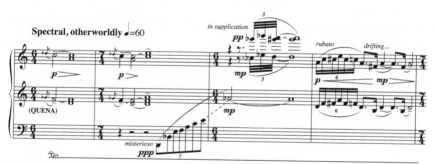

Example 3.8. *Sonata Andina*, III, "Adagio Illariy," mm. 1–4

The "Finale Saqsampillo," which Frank inscribes to the memory of Ginastera, refers in its title to the "warrior devils" of the Amazonian jungle. The movement is also published separately, with slight adjustments, as *Danza de los Saqsampillos* (2006), for two pianos, alternatively two marimbas. The introductory section of this A-B-A form opens with the beat of *tambores* and the strumming of Spanish guitars, to which is later added the *charango*, a higher-pitched ten-string instrument made out of an armadillo shell.

Example 3.9. *Sonata Andina*, IV, "Finale Saqsampillo," mm. 1–12

Chords of superimposed fourths suggest guitar tunings; the dissonance of the charango's G against G-sharp, which blurs the E triads and thickens the resonance, also suggests the casual out-of-tune qualities of the charango. A *zampoña* panpipe begins the B section with a quick dance tune in a characteristic Iberian American *sesquiáltera* rhythmic pattern that juxtaposes compound duple meter (6/8) with simple triple (3/4).

Example 3.10. *Sonata Andina*, IV, "Finale Saqsampillo," mm. 56–64

The marimba enters in measure 127 as the *sesquiáltera* rhythm continues.

Example 3.11. *Sonata Andina*, IV, "Finale Saqsampillo," mm. 127–133

Material from the A section returns and expands into a gusty, violent rainstorm, or *vendaval*, and expands further still, for one-hundred-plus measures.

Example 3.12. *Sonata Andina*, IV, "Finale Saqsampillo," mm. 213–219

The coda ends calmly with a fading remnant of the A theme *"quasi lontano."*

Example 3.13. *Sonata Andina*, IV, "Finale Saqsampillo," mm. 360–368

Most of the stylistic features of these five pieces, completed by the time Frank left Michigan, remain characteristic of her music. In *Leyendas* [*Legends*]: *An Andean Walkabout* (2001), for string quartet, written for the Chiara Quartet, she highlights Andean mythology and music as in *Sonata Andina*. In the first three movements, the string writing re-creates the sounds of *toyos* (large panpipes), small tarka, and *zampoñas*, respectively; the fourth movement depicts an Inca *chasqui* runner, the fifth movement a funeral that combines Gregorian chant and the wailing of local mourners, and the sixth movement some *romanceros* (gallant men) singing with guitars. (An analysis of *Leyendas* appears later in this chapter.) In her next instrumental work, *Sueños de Chambi* [*Dreams of Chambi*]: *Snapshots for an Andean Album* (2002), for violin and piano, she turns to visual sources and interprets seven photographs by Martin Chambi (1892–1973), the acclaimed Amerindian photographer of Peruvian life, architecture, and landscape. Two of the movements are in the style of the *harawi*, one of Frank's favorite forms, which she describes as a melancholy song with pre-Columbian Inca origins, usually comprised of repeated musical phrases with melismatic passages and *glissandos*. At the opening, the violin part is sparsely accompanied; in the middle section of the movement, for solo violin, a brief passage is marked "a Bartók (*Sonata no. 2 for Violin and Piano*)."

Example 3.14. *Sueños de Chambi* (2002), VI, "Harawi de Chambi," violin part, mm. 1–14[20]

Sueños de Chambi was premiered in Oregon in June 2002 by Sergiu Luca, violin, and Brian Connelly, piano. In July, in Brazil, Frank and flutist Lucas Robatto premiered her arrangement of the work for alto flute/flute in

C and piano. Five of the pieces are arranged for viola and piano in *Cinco Danzas de Chambi* (2006).

Frank entered *Leyendas* in the ASCAP Foundation Morton Gould Young Composer Awards, for composers under the age of thirty (she was twenty-nine), and was among the winners; in May 2002, she was awarded $500. Frances Richard of ASCAP, whom she had met as an undergraduate when Richard was visiting schools to explain performing rights and royalties to composition students, persuaded her to come to New York for the awards ceremony and reception and even found money for her plane ticket. Only much later did Frank realize that Richard wanted to introduce her to Susan Feder, who as vice president of G. Schirmer had already developed many leading composers' careers. At the reception, in spite of Frank's protests ("No, Fran!"), Richard led her to the piano, tapped on her glass for silence, and announced, "Gabi's going to play." Frank played the rousing finale of *Sonata Andina*, and Feder asked her to send some scores. A few months later, although convinced that, as so often happens with score requests, she would have no response, Frank sent *Las Sombras de los Apus, Sonata Andina, Leyendas,* and *Sueños de Chambi*. "Four chamber works. No vocal works. No orchestral works. And on the strength of that, they signed me up."

> *I thought it was a shot out of the dark. I mean, they hadn't seen my name on student competitions. I wasn't studying in New York City, so it wasn't as though a local teacher had recommended me for them to look at. This was a time when they were considering signing on younger composers whom they could mentor, nurture their careers. But the composer had to have the potential to connect with an audience. Susan saw me at my best.*

As Frank was gaining recognition, she was also coping with illness. About the time she was completing her work at the University of Michigan, she had the misfortune to develop Graves' disease, an autoimmune condition characterized by severe hyperthyroidism. The first indication came when she was accompanying Joan Morris in concert and her hands were shaking. She underwent treatment to stop the overactive thyroid, but the disease progressed.

By the end of 2002, the Graves' disease was affecting her eye muscles; inflammation was pressing on her optic nerve. "My first sign of this was that my eyes weren't blinking together. Then I noticed that everything was darker."[21]

> *One day I awoke and opened my eyes and still saw complete blackness. I had not yet developed the habit of placing my hearing aids in the same place when I took them off, and I spent two hours looking for them before I could make a phone call! . . . [D]ealing with my hearing loss was simple, while dealing with my vision loss has been so hard. I think the main difference is being born with one and acquiring the other, and the resulting attitude differences.[22]*

In December, Frank met with Schirmer executives in New York, and in February 2003 she signed a contract for exclusive representation. At the celebratory lunch after the signing, "I could *not* understand what the others were saying. It was because my eyes were failing and I couldn't lip-read." Others at the lunch—Susan Feder, Peggy Monastra, and David Fetherolf—remember this too.[23] The condition only worsened. Soon afterward, in Peru, there was blood in her tears. Toward the end of 2003, she had her first surgery, bilateral orbital decompression, to enlarge the eye socket. Since then, she has undergone more surgery and other therapies.

When Frank started traveling to Peru in 2000, she began to cultivate relationships with her family there. "My mom comes from a family of fourteen children, so there are a lot of people that I'm connected to." But it was a gradual process.

The first time I went I thought it was going to be this magical homecoming, and instead I was such a gringa! I got sick from the water. I got sick from the food. I sunburned. I got ear infections. I got lost. I lost money. I was in culture shock. I didn't know how things worked in the country, and I felt rejected by the land. Yet there were enough moments where I felt so connected and I was so happy that I kept going back. And as I kept going back, I realized more through familiarity, but it also felt like remembering.[24]

With her relatives as guides, she continued her research, recording instrumental music and singing at festivals in the mountain areas. "While I was rather innocently conducting this one-woman show," she remembers, "I discovered a whole network of Latin American ethnomusicologists who had already 'been there, done that.' . . . I count many of those wonderful scholars among my friends now."

She also turned her attention to her father's musical roots, after he gave her a stack of Jewish music CDs with the note, "Because I have to compete." She laughed long and hard, she remembers, but the inspiration was born. In 2002, she received a generous commission[25] to write *An American in Peru*, for violin and instrumental ensemble, a musical depiction in six movements of her father's Peace Corps experiences that blends Jewish traditions with the music he heard in Peru. The piece has been withdrawn, but two of the movements remain in her catalog as separate pieces. Growing up in New York, her father had been particularly moved by the skilled singing of the many renowned Jewish cantors (*khazn*) of the time. "To him, they sounded like grown men crying, and crying without embarrassment or inhibition in front of the congregation," the composer writes. *Khazn's Recitative: Elu D'vorim* is a four-minute Shabbat recitation for unaccompanied violin in the style of one of her father's favorite cantors, Moshe Koussevitzky (1899–1966). The other remaining piece, *Havana Gila* (*Girl from Havana*), is based on the popular Peruvian slang-Spanish reinterpretation of the well-known Jewish tune *Hava Nagila* (*Come Let Us Be Glad*).

In 2003, the year she began her association with G. Schirmer, Frank returned to orchestral writing with *Three Latin American Dances*, which was premiered in 2004 by the Salt Lake City Symphony, conducted by Keith Lockhart, and issued on CD two years later. Referring to Peru's three geographical regions, the three movements correspond to *selva* (jungle), *sierra* (mountains), and *costa* (coast), respectively. The first movement, "Introduction: Jungle Jaunt," moves through material derived (according to her program note) "from the harmonies and rhythms of various pan-American dance forms"; here, as in the *Sonata Andina* finale, her model is Ginastera's driving, energetic style. The extensive middle movement, "Highland Harawi," is in three big sections, slow-fast-slow; half of the string players play the slow harawi melody slightly behind the others to convey "the wet, reverberating effect of Andean echoes," as in *Las Sombras de los Apus*. The movement's fast, rollicking middle section depicts the *zumballyu*, spinning top, of Illapa, the Peruvian-Inca weather deity of thunder, lightning, and rain, with which he unleashes a terrible storm. The lighthearted final movement, "The Mestizo Waltz"—the title is a pun on Franz Liszt's *Mephisto Waltzes* (1859–1885)—is an arrangement of the sixth movement of the string quartet *Leyendas*.

In her works since 2004, Frank has found further ways to fan the embers of *mestizaje* deep within. In pieces with titles such as *Illapa*, *Inkarrí*, and *La Llorona*, she reflects further upon Quechua-Inca mythology. In *Cuatro Bosquejos Pre-Incaicos* (*Four Pre-Inca Sketches*) (2006), for flute and cello, she creates imaginative musical profiles of four of her favorite museum figures from the Moche, Lambayeque, and other ancient coastal cultures. In *Ritmos Anchinos*, she honors her mother's Quechua-Chinese ancestry. Even more personal in origin are pieces she describes as responding to her own dream life and memory, such as *Manchay Tiempo* and *Hypnagogia*. Moving to other traditions, she sets Nicaraguan poetry in *Songs of Cifar and the Sweet Sea*, and Chicano poetry in *Jalapeño Blues*. She focuses on Spain in *Quijotadas*, her native California in *Two American Portraits*, and immigrant populations in *Peregrinos*.

Frank begins to explore mythology in greater musical depth in *Illapa: Tone Poem for Flute and Orchestra* (2004), her expansion of the dramatic "Highland Harawi" movement of *Three Latin American Dances* into a two-movement, fifteen-minute flute concerto. In the harawi sections, Frank explains in her descriptive program note, the weather god is calmly playing his quena flute before and after the storm. In 2005, she traveled to Brazil, where *Illapa* was performed by the Orquestra Sinfonica da Bahia, with Lucas Robatto, the orchestra's principal flutist, as soloist. She reported to friends that "I have become a one-name entity here, like Madonna and Cher. 'Gabriela!' has been advertised on billboards and in newspapers for the concert of my concerto. It makes me both laugh and try to duck out of sight." The Chicago Symphony Orchestra performed the work in April 2009.

In the string quartet *Inkarrí* (2005), written for the Kronos Quartet, Frank considers an important Inca myth that foretells a return to the naturally evolving cycles of *pachacuti*—accession and renewal—that were interrupted by the cataclysm of the Spanish conquest. Inkarrí (the word is a hybrid of the Quechua *inka* and Spanish *rey*, both meaning king or ruler) foretells a time when the last Inca king, Atahuallpa, dethroned by Pizarro and his men and beheaded in 1532, will be reinstated as supreme ruler, thereby returning justice to the world. Atahuallpa's *aullido* (howl, shriek) at his demise "continues to ring in Andean folklore," Frank writes. "El Aullido de Atahuallpa," the quartet's fourth movement, is her fourth string quartet (1995), the Lutoslawskian master's degree thesis, which, at six minutes, was difficult to program. "I'd been looking for a multi-movement piece to put it in." She surrounds it with four new movements that illustrate the Inkarri myth; the overall style is rather simple and un-adorned, almost austere, as befits the subject (see example 3.15).

The first movement of *Inkarrí*, "Harawi de Viracocha," one of Frank's loveliest harawis, is named for the supreme Inca deity, creator of the universe (see example 3.15).

The second movement, "Himno de la Runakuna: Palos y Piedras," paints a picture of the first humans (*runakuna*) before Viracocha's tutoring in fire or language, who communicate—and even produce music—with *palos* (sticks) and *piedras* (stones), interspersed with whistling (*silbando*). Dry sounds of sticks and stones, notated in aleatoric wheels, are repeated against whistling string harmonics, also in aleatoric wheels. The vigorous third movement, "Escaramuza de Tawantinsuyu," depicts the *escaramuza* (struggle or skirmish) in the *Tawantinsuyu* (land of the four tribes = Inca Empire) after evolving cycles of *pachacuti*.

The fourth movement, "Atahuallpa's Howl," forms a dynamic curve that reaches its dramatic high point at the king's demise and the cataclysmic destruction of the *pachacuti* of the Inca universe, marked *Cataclismático* (see example 3.16).

The two lower instruments are soon joined by violin II and finally violin I. The intensity decreases and the movement ends with the sparse pitches with which it began. The peaceful fifth movement, "Inkarrí," develops from a return of the "Harawi de Viracocha," suggesting the hoped-for return of the Inkarrí, which will harken a return of Viracocha.

Example 3.15. *Inkarrí* (2005), I, "Harawi de Viracocha," mm. 1–14[26]

Another religious observance is Frank's subject in *Requiem for a Magical America: El Día de los Muertos* (2006), which depicts the annual celebration of the Day of the Dead, a mixture of Catholic and preconquest religious beliefs. The piece, which accompanied a University of Kansas dance presentation, includes many ingenious instrumental effects and wonderfully rhythmic tunes; it is scored for large wind ensemble, including saxophones, plus brass and six percussion players commanding a large *batterie* of traditional and nontraditional instruments. In *La Llorona: Tone Poem for Viola and Orchestra* (2007), Frank turns to a popular legend. The solo viola depicts the ghostly spirit of the mythological "crying woman" (*llorona*) which haunts riverbanks. There are no explicit indications of *guitarras* or quenas; the music is predominantly in the European tradition. Frank returned to Houston, home of her alma mater, for the premiere by the Houston Symphony; the piece's enthusiastic reception was particularly gratifying.

Ritmos Anchinos (2006), for string quartet, sheng in D, and *pipa*, is Frank's first piece for Yo-Yo Ma's Silk Road Ensemble; she coined the word *anchino* from *chino* (Chinese) and *andino* (Andean). She dedicates

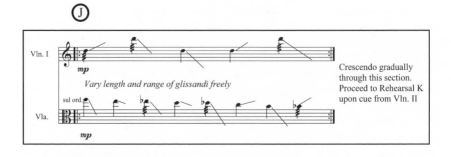

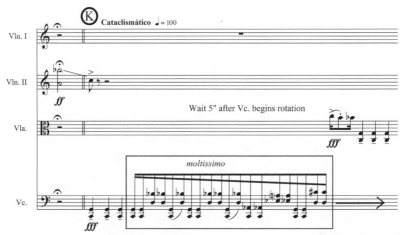

Example 3.16.   *Inkarrí,* IV, "El Aullido de Atahuallpa," rehearsal J to first brace of rehearsal K

the work to her mother's half-Chinese father, Máximo Cam Velazques (1911–1968). (*His* father, her mother's grandfather, left China in the late 1800s to open a country store in the Andes.) *Ritmos Anchinos* has been performed widely and released on a CD recording. Frank became a member of the Silk Road Ensemble and continues to write for it.

Her highly original choral settings reflect similarly expanding interests. *Ccollanan María* (*Holy Mary*) (2004), for chamber choir, is a traditional religious song to the Virgin Mary from Cuzco, Peru; as with *Cuatro Canciones Andinas*, the text is in Spanish and Quechua. In subsequent choral works, Frank draws on other traditions. *Why Am I So Brown* (2005), for children's choir, uses poetry from the 1991 collection by the same name by the Chicano poet Trinidad Sánchez Jr. (1943–2006). *Pollerita Roja* (2006), for women's chorus SSAA, is also contemporary, using poetry of Lily Flores Palomino. In *Jalapeño Blues* (2007), for mixed chorus SSAATTBB, written for the acclaimed male chorus Chanticleer, she sets four poems from Sánchez's 2006 collection of the same name (which seems to be a pun on a popular brand of corn chip)—"Jalapeño Blues," "Chicanofóbia," "Why Do Men Wear Earrings on One Ear?" and "A Poem about Brandon Dever." Texts are in English and Spanish—the "Spanglish" of bilingual Americans.

In *Songs of Cifar and the Sweet Sea*, for voice and piano, she sets poems of the Nicaraguan poet Pablo Antonio Cuadra (1919–2002) and evokes sounds and styles from Nicaragua. She began the cycle in 2004 at a Carnegie Hall workshop for singers and composers led by the composer John Harbison and the soprano Dawn Upshaw.[27] In the fifth song, "Me diste ¡oh Dios! una hija," for baritone and piano, Cifar, a mariner on the Sea of Nicaragua, asks that God spare his daughter the hardships that have been thrown his way. After the piano introduction of *tambores y guitarras* from the opening to the *Sonata Andina* finale (see example 3.9), Frank sets the poem as a *Barcarola Nicaragüense* (*Nicaraguan Barcarolle*), transforming the introduction's E-A-D chords into an E minor accompanying figure in gentle barcarolle rhythm (see example 3.17).

At the end of the refrain, "*Me diste ¡oh Dios! una hija con el cielo de mi patria en sus ojos. . . . ¡No permitas, Señor! que el viento la arroje como a mi a lo insaciable*" (You gave me, oh God! a daughter with the sky of my country in her eyes. . . . Don't permit, Lord! the wind to hurl her as it hurled me to the ravenous), the word *insaciable* is repeated in falsetto voice a seemingly insatiable number of times, over the unmistakably dominant chord of B major; cadential resolution to E minor is delayed until the next phrase begins, avoiding a break in the action. Frank has said she is not sure herself why Cifar goes into falsetto, whether it is true emotion or self-jest. Frank develops ideas from this song in the *Barcarola Latinoamericana* (2007), a grand fantasy for solo piano.

The composer's waking memories of dreams are the inspiration for *Manchay Tiempo*, for piano, harp, strings, and percussion, which was premiered in Seattle in November 2005; the title, a hybrid of Quechua and Spanish, means "Time of Fear." As children, she and her brother would relate their dreams to each other; her brother, now a neuroscientist, has made several discoveries regarding sleep and dreaming.[29] *Manchay Tiempo* (actually "mancha dempo") was her childhood label

Example 3.17. *Songs of Cifar and the Sweet Sea* (2004), "Me diste ¡oh Dios! una hija," (a) mm. 63–67 and (b) mm. 87–93[28]

for her feelings of "terror and tenderness" because of a recurring dream that her mother was "but a hair's breadth away from some unspeakable danger." Later, as a college student, Frank saw a TV documentary about Sendero Luminoso, the Shining Path group, wreaking murderous havoc in Peru during the late 1970s and 1980s; she realized she had seen the documentary as a child and interpreted it with a child's imagination.

Hypnagogia (2008), for string sextet, written for the Concertante ensemble, takes its title from the term for the altered state of consciousness when one is falling asleep and waking up, when a variety of visions, apparitions, inspiration, and other sensory perceptions are experienced, along with a fluid association of ideas. Frank describes this state as "the roadmap into our psyche." Her program note begins, "My dream life is an active one, almost unbearably so." She describes the "ghosts" that accompany the descent into sleep and dreaming—"a bizarre and highly condensed slideshow of family members' faces, mythical llamas from Peruvian fairy tales, a crucified yet laughing Christ, an abandoned playground swing, a dewinged butterfly." The disconnected, fleeting ghosts are "capable of leaving me quietly stunned, emotional." In *Hypnagogia*, she incorporates fragments of Peruvian folkloric music; *scordatura* tunings "help lend an otherworldly sound" that suggests "hypnagogic reverie."

The string quartet *Quijotadas* (2007) is about dreams that supersede reality. *Quijotadas* is the Spanish word for extravagant delusions in the spirit of Don Quixote, the hero of Cervantes' tale from the early 1600s. In writing the piece for the Brentano Quartet, Frank discovered that the material was taking her in a new direction, toward "a very muscular, dissonant, craggy, very detailed and compressed, and less accessible piece," and when she heard the Brentano play it, she was surprised—actually scared—by how it sounded.[30] In the second movement, "Seguidilla para La Mancha," she evokes traditional music of Spain for the first time, in a free interpretation of the seguidilla, a spirited dance of Quixote's homeland of La Mancha. The opening rhythmic pattern, *pizzicato*, in alternating 2/4 and 3/8 meters, imitates the sounds of guitar and bandurria, a mandolin-like Spanish folk instrument.

*BANDURRIA Y GUITTARA

Example 3.18. *Quijotadas* (2007), II, "Seguidilla para La Mancha," mm. 1–6[31]

The second violin introduces the melody in short phrases, with answering motives in the other three instruments. Uneven meters suggest a stylized version of the dance (see example 3.19).

In 2008, Frank held a residency with the Modesto (California) Symphony and completed *Two American Portraits*, for orchestra. The first movement, "Frank's Alborada," pays homage to Frank Mancini, the late founder of the Modesto orchestra, who was a clarinetist; the *alborada* is a traditional welcome song from Spain. The second movement, "Old

Example 3.19. *Quijotadas,* II, "Seguidilla para La Mancha," mm. 46–51

Modesto," is intended to convey the spirit of the valley's miners, farmers, and horsemen; Frank drew inspiration from visits to local museums and a steer ranch. A reporter who covered Frank's preparations for the local newspaper described her as "friendly, curious and bursting with energy" and commented that "her easygoing manner comes as a bit of a surprise considering her impressive credentials."[32]

A two-year residency with the Indianapolis Symphony Orchestra from 2007 to 2009 resulted in *Peregrinos* (*Pilgrims*) (2009), for orchestra, inspired by the composer's work with the city's Latino immigrant populations, mostly young people. The orchestra posted a video online about Frank and her plans for the piece. Her work from the beginning of the residency through the premiere performance is the subject of a documentary video, "Peregrinos/Pilgrims: *A Musical Journey*," produced by WFYI-TV Indianapolis and broadcast in central Indiana.[33] At the October 2009 performance by the Berkeley Symphony, conducted by Joana Carneiro, special guests included members of the Indianapolis-based Latino Youth Collective who inspired the composition.

This story of Gabriela Frank and her music through 2009 has been the story of her emergence as an articulate composer, writer, and musical ambassador. The work of the many distinguished performers and conductors—Frank prefers to call them collaborators—who are indispensible to her efforts has scarcely been mentioned. A full listing of Frank's awards, commissions, composer-in-residence assignments, and public appearances of all kinds would fill many more pages. Being able to support herself as a freelance composer is, for Frank, a dream come true. But collaborators, funding, and professional contacts would not be enough without the essential factor, the inspired and inspiring musician herself.

A CONVERSATION WITH GABRIELA LENA FRANK

I first met Gabriela Frank in Washington, D.C., in June 2000, after hearing her famously breathtaking performance of the Sonata Andina. *In 2007, preparing to write this chapter, I introduced myself and my assignment to her via e-mail. Gabriela responded with her usual friendliness and enthusiasm for new projects. I sent her some introductory interview questions which she answered candidly and at length. We arranged to meet in September, in Berkeley. Over a long lunch in her sunny apartment, she talked about her work and showed me scores, recordings, and notes. The next evening, I took some of my Bay Area friends and family members with me to hear Chanticleer premiere* Jalapeño Blues *in the San Francisco Conservatory's elegant new concert hall. After the extraordinary concert, when the audience was invited onstage for champagne with the celebrated composer and chorus members, we saw how Gabriela's warmth and love of her art encompass everyone around her. A few weeks later, she and I completed the interview via e-mail.—Deborah Hayes*

HAYES: Gabriela, in only a few years you have built an impressive list of works and performances. Have you been surprised by the kinds of response your music has received?

FRANK: This is still a trip for me, that someone's writing about me. I'm looking at these pieces that I wrote with no awareness, ever, of anybody coming in and putting them into the big picture—no awareness that others would be interested in my work that way. I thought the interest would extend as far as the performer's interest in learning it and presenting it to an audience. I am more aware now of how my music is much more than just about the music. It's about how it represents somebody tackling larger issues. You realize you own yourself even less, if that makes any sense. You know that you are the starting point for a lot of people's thoughts, a lot of people trying to come to grips with stuff.

HAYES: With your solid academic training, do you find yourself taking an academic approach to your own creative work? Building your own theoretical systems? Analyzing your own style in its historical context?

FRANK: It's really funny. Although I have a doctorate, I don't see it as an academic degree. My time in school didn't feel academic, per se, but felt like an apprenticeship. I was gathering so much real-world experience by playing so much, writing for real musicians and workshopping the music with them, transcribing music, traveling in Latin America, memorizing scores, and then spending a *lot* of time trying to put things in context. I was constantly trying to figure out the connection between Latin music and its nonmusical context, but in a living way, not an academic one. I wasn't really developing methodologies or theories, although I certainly did a lot of journal writing through all of this, trying to puzzle out why I wanted to write my *mestiza* music, and whom I was writing it for. I have definitely developed perspectives, but I wouldn't call them theories. Music's been my ticket to see the world, and I know that I want my composing to reflect real-life experiences, real questions I'm asking about what it means to me to be Gabriela. I don't want someone to hear my music and hear an academic approach. I want them to feel like they've heard a story because that's what I feel and draw on when I compose.

HAYES: What is your method of creating a new work?

FRANK: I've definitely been inspired by Bartók's approach to creative work—a deft handling of harmony, form, and folkloric style as dictated by the needs of the music. I might start with a blueprint among these salient elements, and then I'm quick to deviate when the music breathes itself into a different direction. Staying open to diverting the path like this means keeping your intuitive eye observant even while your intellectual self "disciplines" the pitches and rhythms. I'm also very, very aware of what it must feel like to perform this music. If the chords thicken up, that makes me want to bear down to control them at the keyboard. Is this coinciding naturally with the mood intensifying too? And is this logical with the folkloric style I'm alluding to? Or an indigenous instrument I want to evoke?

HAYES: In what ways do you work differently?

FRANK: One thing that I'm noticing that is different from Bartók is that I really am much more of a programmatic composer than him. I could listen to someone tell stories the livelong day, and so there's often a story line behind my music, or at least a scenario or character. And although one can find spots where Bartók seems to be imitating that Bulgarian wobbly vibrato singing, or a gypsy fiddle, I think I've been more transparent in how I've tried to evoke the sounds of indigenous instruments and performance practices. For example, in *Leyendas: An Andean Walkabout*, I try to make the string quartet sometimes sound like a string quartet, and sometimes like breathy panpipes, singing quena flutes, strummed guitars, crying Indian women, and the like.

HAYES: Yes, you are more transparent; you label these indigenous sounds in your scores.

FRANK: I like to create these sounds without asking for very avant-garde techniques; I find you can do rather a lot sticking to the traditional vocabulary of the instrument. In the first movement, I needed to make the quartet sound like a toyo, which is an extremely large panpipe. The notes are connected with these little scooping *glissandi*. It's very breathy, and you can hear a spit attack sound at the initial onset of each note [see example 3.20]. So I have part of the ensemble *pizz* their strings in dissonance with one another while the viola bows its note in the normal fashion, but a bit farther up the fingerboard, producing a more breathy sound. I ask for a wide vibrato instead of the traditional tight one that string players normally use, and the effect is extraordinarily close to what a toyo sounds like.

HAYES: So you have the four string players sound like a wind instrument.

FRANK: I'm wondering if it seems as though I've worked out how to achieve that toyos sound in a very intellectual way. But it doesn't *feel* intellectual when I'm doing this. Rather, it feels like a game. Sometimes, I just look at the two halves: "viola, meet panpipe; panpipe, meet viola." And then I wait for them to morph into one another, find that common ground where the ideas just come roaring to life. I feel as though my job is to widen that common ground. So my approach to my creative work involves a lot of just playing around and discovering. But before any of this can happen it is absolutely important to sit on a heap of knowledge.

HAYES: Could you talk more about your methods of acquiring that knowledge?

FRANK: I've definitely listened and studied a lot of folkloric music—in my own haphazard way that would probably give a well-trained ethnomusicologist the shudders. Yet it works for me. Once I have this bank of styles in my understanding, the ideas flow. Without the knowledge, the ideas don't come. So half of my composing time does involve my writing notes down on a page. The other half involves my acquiring the knowledge—out-and-out study, in other words. And the study is not just music. I've amassed a huge library of books on history, myths and fairy tales, archeology, poetry, literature, and so on. My job is to be a storyteller, and I can do that better if I know the story behind the music.

HAYES: What kinds of field recordings do you use?

FRANK: Raúl Romero, a Peruvian ethnomusicologist at the Archives of Traditional Andean Music in Lima, handles a lot of the recordings for Smithsonian Folkways—CDs and a whole series of videotapes. I'm cataloging the CDs I have. I listen to them, make notes on all the tracks, and transcribe the music. A lot of these CDs are done by ethnomusicologists who are colleagues of mine. I know their work; I trust their methodology when they're in the field. What's great about the Lima archive, too, is that if I want to hear more of a certain example, I can go to this person who compiled the CD next time I'm in Lima, and I know he'll have hours—*hours*—more. I've gone there and studied a lot of stuff.

HAYES: So far you seem to be concentrating on the Andean mountain culture more than the jungle or coastal areas of Peru—although you have written in the style of "coastal *romanceros*."

FRANK: Yes, and also, a lot of the music that's played these days in the Andes has coastal influences. The music has traveled so much that it's very rare that you hear something you think is exclusively *serrano*, mountain, in influence, there's been so much cross-fertilization.

HAYES: Do you know Quechua too? Is it quite different from Spanish?

FRANK: Yes, very different. That was the native language, well, the main native language of the Incas. They forced Quechua on all their tribes that *they* were subjugating. There were pockets, and hints, of other native languages around Peru that are very, very old, which we think come from those tribes. But it's very hard to know for sure. One of the tribes is a people called the Qeros people. And there are others. I don't know much about the music of the *selva* culture, jungle culture, of Peru, I have to say. I've read a few articles now, have a few CDs. It has always been really hard to penetrate. The Spaniards did not really go in there much. And to this day the government makes laws and policy, and people in the jungle live pretty much the same way as they always have. They suffered a lot in the various terrorist waves that have hit Peru. A lot of the fighting would happen in very rural parts of the mountains and in the jungle areas. The last time I was in the jungle area, in 2003—we were only on the perimeter, in an area called Tingo Maria—from terrorist movements about fifteen years earlier you could still see bridges that had been blown up that they hadn't repaired yet, massive areas of trees and bushes that have been cut down by fighting, and something that looked like old artillery from the government as well.

HAYES: Could you talk more about how you learned to compose for orchestral instruments?

FRANK: That was really a thorn in my side when I was starting out in school. I was writing piano music for violin, and piano music for anybody else. And I said, "How am I going to get around it? I can never learn the violin as well as I play the piano. How am I going to do this? And I have a whole orchestra to learn. I'll do the best I can, which is: play with them." I learned a lot when I played with a string quartet and they'd forgotten me—I was the pianist in the back. They're working on intonation or saying, "Are you going up-bow or down-bow here?" I'm *learning* this. I'm learning the repertoire. I started playing for studios; I was learning what the teachers were fixing. It was a slow process, gradually adding in my knowledge like that, and then going with specific questions. It was kind of like this interview, where you have a set body of questions and then more questions come out of the conversation, and ideas occur to you—spinoffs. And you go back and codify the new body of questions. You just keep building on it. It's starter for the next level of understanding of the subject. So I'm always adding to what I know about strings. Other than piano, strings are what I'm most comfortable with. When I did the big band piece, *Requiem for a Magical America*, whew! Finally I did something just all out like that for winds and brasses. I learned a lot, and I have a lot of ideas for future pieces now. I also know the questions to ask. I have a lot of questions, things I'm unsure about. But now I have those questions.

HAYES: You also mentioned collecting information from fellow performers about instrumental technique—Western classical performers, I mean.

FRANK: I love workshopping pieces as I compose, for real collaboration with performers. Since my earliest student days as an undergrad, I will grab friends and just ask them a lot of questions about their instrument. I will often have little snippets of music I've composed, little combinations of things I've tried, and I want to see if they work and if my friends have suggestions for how to make them more comfortable. They will usually drop little gems of wisdom—things their teachers have said, pieces I should look into for a really good example of such-and-such technique, or some nerdy insider joke I would never otherwise be privy to. I have dozens and dozens of recordings that I've made of all these sessions. The earliest one is "Nick Walker, Double Bass, March 1993," and they continue into this year with "Monica Scott, Cello, May 2007." I keep my notes from all of these workshop sessions in binders. And I will not just meet with solo performers, but entire groups of people. Some of my best workshopping has been done with formed quartets. I feed the players a really good South American meal afterward as my thank-you.

HAYES: How do you organize the material you are collecting so that you can use it in your music?

FRANK: This way of composing generates a *lot* of material. I've always been prodigious, and I go a little nuts with all of these ideas that keep coming at me. In recent years, I've begun to organize all of this extra material into binders. The ideas serve as wonderful "starters" (like for a good sourdough!) for future pieces. It's even better that I can get a little distance from the ideas before going back to them and working them into a piece. The starters could be an actual melody, or a combination of instruments that produce a cool sound, or a great opening gesture for a concerto soloist, or a mythological figure I've read about that I hear music for. The possibilities are really endless. As a result, I never start with a blank piece of paper anymore. I've got binders and binders of stuff now, and I'm constantly organizing new categories for the binders as my ideas take me into new places.

HAYES: What kinds of precompositional planning do you do?

FRANK: One thing that I do that I've not seen a lot of composers do is to make frequent use of my scissors. Here's an analogy. When I was in college, I wrote my best papers if I simply wrote down all of my thoughts and reactions as I read. These were haphazard and personal, and they touched on themes that we didn't even talk about in class. It didn't matter; I wrote them all down. By the end of the book, I had a wealth of interesting insights I'd produced—raw material, in other words. Then I would take my scissors and start cutting up my notes, organizing the thoughts into the categories that seemed to naturally emerge. I would always turn in very solid papers as a result of so much directly connected evidence. I compose in a similar way. I'll just sit down and write, perhaps starting off with an idea, and perhaps not. By the end of the day, I'll look at what I have and throw out the stuff that's not exemplary and cut everything else up. Some of the ideas I'll put up on my bulletin boards as ideas to develop for the project on my desk that day. Others go directly into my binders.

HAYES: When you are writing a piece, do you sketch in manuscript, or write in manuscript at any stage? Do you do your own computer engraving?

FRANK: The actual composing itself is a mix of writing with pen on paper, occasionally composing into the computer, occasionally using a sequencing program to hear some music being played back to me with MIDI sounds. I'll compose both at the piano and away, and I'll sometimes compose full score, sometimes short score. I'm not a slave to any one method, in other words. Different pieces, different passages, have different needs. I have a shorthand that I've developed, too, that only I can read. It's simple. To save time, I'll omit writing out accidentals in the traditional way. Instead, if the slash for the note head is backward, that's a flattened note. If it's straight up and down, that's a natural note. If it's slanted forward, that's a sharpened note. It's rare now that I do my own engraving, and in this way, I'm pretty lucky. That's the advantage of having a wonderful publisher like G. Schirmer. For me, it's important to have someone else do the engraving because of the Graves' disease. I've lost most of the eyesight in one of my eyes and still deal with some pain issues. So, being able to have the amazing engravers at G. Schirmer look after my work is a true blessing. I was just laughing about this with the Schirmer people when I was in New York. I said, "I was so green! The only thing I heard when you guys wanted to sign me up was, you'd copy out my music." (This was only, you know, three or four years ago.) I did not understand promotion. I did not understand that I could say, "I want to do a piano concerto. Can you hunt around and see if there's any orchestra that would be interested in my doing a piano concerto?" I didn't understand that kind of thing. And I don't do that. Even now, they ask, "What do you want to do?" And I don't know. I don't abuse it. For me it seems like the opportunities have been so plentiful, there's not much for me to ask for.

HAYES: You are certainly represented by a superb publishing house.

FRANK: The relationship with Schirmer has been a dream. When my eye condition was diagnosed, a few months after I signed with them, I had to tell them, "I can't do these commissions"—a few were due right away. The Schirmer people could have lost faith in me, you know. But they stayed by my side, they continued promoting the stuff that I did have;

they got performances, they told people. It takes time for them to get your name out consistently. I benefited from their decades of relationships with orchestras and chamber music societies, all of that. And they know that I deliver. I deliver in terms of the music. I also deliver in person. I go and meet people. I'm cordial. I'm not a diva. I'm just very straight up and friendly. I'm willing to do outreach—more than willing. It's a big part of my life, what I can do with that. The whole gesture of composing has been a gift for others.

HAYES: Once the piece is in the hands of performers and conductors, do you work with them?

FRANK: It really depends on the piece and the musicians. Orchestra music has very limited rehearsal time, so as much as possible I will workshop the piece months ahead of time with performer friends. They may just look at their own part, and I use my imagination to blow up the part to an entire orchestra section. When I worked on my viola concerto, *La Llorona*, I checked a lot of difficult double stops and *tremolos* with the premiering soloist, and we traded PDFs for several weeks by e-mail. I also made a visit to where he lives in Houston and stayed with him for a couple of days so that we could work on stuff.

HAYES: Are there artists other than composers and musicians who have influenced you?

FRANK: Mark Twain's approach to creativity is one that I like. Here's where you can detect the influence of my father, a Mark Twain scholar. Mark Twain was so much an observer, and a cultural anthropologist, but in his own way, and he expressed his knowledge in his creative writing. So his observations about what it means to be an American went through this mill in his head and came out in *Tom Sawyer* and *Huck Finn*, or *A Connecticut Yankee in King Arthur's Court*. And of course he had a lot to say, coming out of the Civil War (of all things), about his place in history. I think that's a really admirable goal to have. I guess I'm aiming for the same thing with the music. He was the first great American writer to use the everyday speech of ordinary people in his stories, and this doesn't come at the expense of tremendous craft, profundity, and heart. His stories are so modern and immediate, and decidedly not "academic," although there is a lot there that is ripe for academic study. I think he concentrated on telling a good yarn that was rich with commentary on the human condition, and to tell this story with skill. I'm trying to do something similar.

HAYES: You seem to have little trouble explaining your work to interviewers—to me. To what do you attribute this fluency?

FRANK: A lot of your questions I've thought about before. Also, I journalize a lot. Every night I spend about twenty, thirty minutes. I summarize what I've done. I summarize my thoughts about my work and about how it's tying to my personal life. I gave rather personal answers to a lot of your questions about my music, too. I don't see work as all that separate from how I think about myself. It's still tied up with my identity and tied up with my thinking about my relationship with my family in Peru, or what I want to accomplish in my life. I chose music as my main vocation. I'm tying all my desires onto music. So it's very personal.

HAYES: Have you experienced what seems to be special treatment, either positive or negative, as a woman in the traditionally mostly male profession of "serious" composer?

FRANK: On the negative side, only in very subtle ways. There was nothing that held me back seriously. I remember a prominent, quite old composer telling me in a single guest lesson when I was a sophomore that women didn't write aggressive music. This was in response to a phrase I had that featured *fff* dynamic. I wasn't offended, to be honest. I saw this guy as from another era, and the remark was simply old-fashioned. There were perhaps little vibes of doubt from other male teachers that I picked up on, but they were simply challenges for me to prove them wrong—if their doubt was indeed not a figment of my imagination. No one ever put a real obstacle in my path. This I can honestly say. On the positive side, G. Schirmer is a women-dominated office. The women are *fantastic*. They are people I would want to be friends with, you know, outside of "the biz." I just got very, very lucky. They've been consistently hiring really good people. I have had not a single complaint in the four years with them. And I've been very happy for the other composers on the roster. I've noticed that I'm not covetous or anything. I have so much going on that I can't imagine what they could do that's more.

HAYES: How much are you able to choose what kinds of pieces to write, from among all the requests and opportunities?

FRANK: It's very important to me to make sure that the successful career doesn't always dictate the same kinds of works being done over and over again. Because we have so many string quartet ensembles that are well known, with a nice body of backers, money, or presenters to help them stay in demand, a lot of commissions for chamber music come for string quartet. So I've been approached by a number of string quartets. Now, I *love* writing string quartets, but at the same time, I know I benefit by writing chamber music for other instruments. And musicians who play other instruments are so hungry for good repertoire that I've really identified that as something to watch out for. I'm very happy I have a thriving career and all these opportunities, people knocking on my door. But I have to make sure that I don't just let the dictates of demand determine what I write. There are some pieces I have anxiety about because I haven't been able to work on them. I might have players in mind, but the pieces are not commissioned; they are just things that I want to do.

HAYES: In what stylistic directions do you see music composition heading in the next decade or so of the twenty-first century?

FRANK: Such a tough question! I do see our music becoming more multicultural as more people of mixed heritages, nonwhite heritages, wield more social, political, economic, and artistic power. Latinos are the fastest growing minority in the States; here in California, we recently reached a new benchmark where more babies born are of Latino heritage than any other. This is going to affect our cultural expression in literature sold in shops, music written and programmed, screenplays turned into movies, and so on.

HAYES: What do you see in your future?

FRANK: My goal is to work on fewer projects, but bigger ones. I *really* want to finish a big book of piano pieces, the *Book of Quipus*. [Quipus—colored knotted bunches of strings containing encoded information—are what the Incas used in lieu of a written language.] I would love to do something in the magic number of twenty-four, or twelve, or a series of concerti. Something I really want to do is do a series of tone poems. I've been wanting to finish a very large evening-length song cycle, *Songs of Cifar and the Sweet Sea*, and I know who my singers would be for it. Quite a bit of it has been commissioned along the way.

HAYES: Do you have projects in mind other than writing music?

FRANK: I would love to take some time off from composing and just study and do some other things. It's still startling to me that I spend so much time composing, because even when I was in school, composing was only one part of my life. I did other things just as much as I did composing. I think it's healthy to do other things. I have things to say.

ANALYSIS: *LEYENDAS: AN ANDEAN WALKABOUT,* FOR STRING QUARTET (2001)

Gabriela Frank's music embodies her concept of multicultural *mestizaje* in a number of ways. In her program notes and other public statements, she tends to emphasize the Latin/Latino and other personal sources of her inspiration. In interviews and correspondence, she also relates her compositional techniques to the Western traditions—mainly Romantic, post-Romantic, and modernist—of her academic training and performing repertoire.

Titles and song texts are typically in Spanish, whether or not the music *sounds* particularly Latin. In the Romantic and post-Romantic tradition of the tone poem, she favors music that tells a story, evokes an image, or highlights a character; her punning use of Liszt's title *Mephisto Waltz* is but one of her references to the nineteenth-century European origins of the genre. Her programmatic explanations, whether historical or personal, are often visual, recalling her early attraction to concerts with costumes and movement. She likes to use a solo instrument to represent the story's major character—cello for Ernesto, flute for Illapa, viola for *la llorona*. She favors formal structures that are sectional or episodic, like dramatic scenes or events in a story. In the twentieth-century modernist tradition, she builds formal structures upon contrasting timbres. She devises new sounds on Western instruments to suggest Andean instrumental ensembles, high-altitude acoustics, and the like. Her writing for orchestral percussion and her innovative, colorful instrumental combinations are extraordinarily striking. Melodies in parallel intervals, *glissandi*, *vibrato*, *tremolos*, varieties of attack, guitarlike strumming, heterophonic doubling, echoing, and indistinct atmospheric passages are among the effects in her repertoire of imaginative tone colors with programmatic associations.

Still, she realizes that a piece can arouse different associations in a listener and must be able to stand on purely musical values alone.

In a certain respect, I think everybody needs to be the owner of their own listening experience. Do they like to read a program note? Sometimes they do, they're in the mood for it; sometimes they're not. I don't want people to be more accepting of the music just because it's a "marginalized voice." I don't want them to be overloaded with information.[34]

Among musical influences on her work, she cites several composers and effects, including Lutoslawski's aleatoric atmospheres, Ginastera's energetic dance rhythms, Bartók's simulation of vocal and instrumental sounds, and even Debussy's parallelism. She knows much twentieth-century avant-garde music, both as a pianist and from her academic training in music theory, but she does not write for the musical elite alone. She does not write electronic music. She writes for performers, usually quite virtuosic, conservatory-trained players and conductors. Her primary considerations are how a piece works in performance and whether listeners will be moved by hearing it.

She writes melodies, often tonal melodies, rather than atonal rows. She explores a tune by repeating it in a variety of contexts. Developing a theme from germ motives is not her typical approach. She seldom devises thematic transformation as found in tone poems of Liszt and other Romantics. Frank's textures are typically melody-and-accompaniment or melody-and-atmosphere, sometimes melody and atmosphere in alternating sections. Heterophonic, simultaneous versions of a melodic line are frequent, as are contrapuntal juxtapositions of individual lines. Her harmonic language is quite classically conceived—dissonances resolving to consonances—but seldom classical in sound: tonic-function chords are not always unadorned triads, and dominant-function combinations can contain all kinds of dissonant combinations. Contrasts in voicing and range help convey degrees of tension and resolution. Intriguingly complex rhythms typically occur within a steady beat, as in popular music. In short, while she works within the Romantic and modernist traditions, Frank maintains a highly selective twenty-first-century sensibility in adopting ideas and techniques from either one.

What is difficult to represent on paper is Frank's extraordinary sense of rhythm, including the timing of events, whether from bar to bar, phrase to phrase, or over the course of an entire movement or multimovement piece. Listeners are drawn to the directness and intensity of Frank's sound and to the energy that seems to propel the music forward, taking the audience along with it. Repetitions and returns of material—a melody, rhythm, harmonic progression, or texture—are frequent enough to ensure the listener's comprehension; returning material is almost always varied in some way so that the listener has a sense of progression.

Frank's approach to musical rhythm as energy and physical movement may have been enhanced by her early training in aikido; it has certainly been strengthened by her wide-ranging experience as a performer. "Her music always turns the corner at the right time," says the pianist Wu Han.[35] Holding listeners' attention by presenting relatively short sections of contrasting character is perhaps a trait borrowed from popular music. The term *totalism* is sometimes used for music that, like Frank's, "combines visceral audience appeal with a complexity that can hold the interest of the sophisticated expert." Totalism, writes the musicologist Richard Crocker, is classical music freed of its snobbishness, combined with popular music without voracious commercialism.[36]

The six movements of the string quartet *Leyendas: An Andean Walkabout* provide a sampling of Frank's characteristic compositional techniques and kinds of expression. Perhaps because she loves writing them, her string quartets seem to represent significant steps in her discovery of her compositional voice. With *String Quartet no. 3* (1992), she wins an undergraduate competition, an early validation of her skill. Three years later, in the *Movement for String Quartet* (Quartet no. 4), her master's thesis, she demonstrates her facility with modernist techniques. *Leyendas* (2001), the earliest quartet in her professional catalog, is among her first works to evoke specific Peruvian musical sounds. *Inkarrí* (2005) appears four years later, when much of Frank's music reflects her deeper explorations of Inca history and mythology. Where *Leyendas* is pictorial and celebratory, *Inkarrí* is a reflection on colonial oppression and the Inca hope of renewal. Two years after that, in *Quijotadas* (2007), Frank confronts the fragility of heroic dreams and noble ideals; the music takes on an abstract quality that even she does not yet fully understand. With references that are less local and specific than those in *Leyendas*, the music speaks to universal human concerns.

Leyendas remains one of Frank's most frequently performed works. Its initial title, *Mestiza: Letters from the Motherland for String Quartet*, underlines its conception as a celebration of the composer's maternal heritage and her deepening emotional attachment to the Peruvian sierra; she inscribes *Leyendas* to her mother, "from whom I received the gift of Peru." The subtitle, *An Andean Walkabout*, suggests meandering and enjoying the sights and sounds; the word *walkabout* further suggests a spiritual journey, a rite of passage like the walkabout of young Australian Aborigines who walk the land to learn the paths or "song lines" of their ancestors.

In creating *Leyendas*, Frank workshopped the piece with a quartet that included violinist Wendy Olson and cellist Katri Ervamaa. She gave the members of the Chiara Quartet—violinists Rebecca Fischer and Julie Yoon, violist Jonah Sirota, and cellist Gregory Beaver—a CD of field recordings of Andean instruments and voices, collected by herself and by professional ethnomusicologists, so that they could hear her original sources of inspiration. In the score, besides the sounds of tarka, guitarras, charangos, quenas, and zampoñas heard earlier in the *Sonata Andina*, Frank evokes the large panpipe called a toyo, and the singing of women and men. She describes the brief first movement, "Toyos," in the conversation section above, and her scoring merits a closer look here. To re-create the instrument's particular timbre, the four quartet members play a melody together, heterophonically, each producing components of the toyo sound. Violin II and cello pluck the melody notes close to the bridge (*pizzicato, sul ponticello*) to produce short, brittle sounds, and in parallel minor seconds to make the pitch less precise; the total effect simulates the toyo's spit attacks. Viola plays the melody in parallel fourths as a toyos ensemble would, and in short pulsations to imitate the sound of a large wind instrument blown with great force; the violist is directed to bow the strings lightly over the fingerboard and use a wide vibrato (*flautando, sul tasto, molto vibrato*) to produce the toyo's breathy tone. After the first phrase, violin I enters with more spit attacks on the second half of each melody note, *pizzicatto, sul ponticello*. The movement is quiet and calm, its structure simple and effective. Two six-measure phrases are followed by an eleven-measure phrase that extends initial motives, and then a six-measure ending, *pianississimo*. Quiet *pizzicato* B minor chords in violin II and cello mark the ends of phrases, providing a Western classical framework (see example 3.20).

The second movement, the fast-paced "Tarqueada," is named for a dance from the Aymara area of Bolivia, which is accompanied by tarka flute. At the opening, violin I, playing in high-pitched fourths, is labeled

Example 3.20. *Leyendas: An Andean Walkabout* (2001), I, "Toyos," mm. 1–6[37]

"tarka"—a smaller tarka than the low-pitched one in *Sonata Andina*, I (see example 3.3, above)—while the other three instruments, playing fast *tremolo* chords, are labeled "*guitarras y charangos.*"

After this arresting introduction, the main idea, the fast dance music, begins; short phrases are separated by waves of sixteenth notes. Metric ambiguity propels the music forward: in 8/8 bars, the three lower parts are 3+3+2, while violin I's accents fall differently. Melodic motives are repeated and varied; the melody gradually fades out, leaving the accompanying sixteenth-note patterns, which finally fade out as well. The overall effect is of a burst of energy that gradually dissipates.

Example 3.21. *Leyendas*, II, "Tarqueada," mm. 21–24

In the third movement, "Himno de Zampoñas," the quartet depicts the sound of a *zampoña* (panpipe) ensemble playing in two alternating styles, each varied in pitch and timbre upon its reappearance, ABA'B'A"B". In the A sections, while one instrument plays all the melody notes, five per measure, *pizzicato*, the other three instruments practice the characteristic *zampoña* hocketing technique, taking turns sounding melody notes while the others rest. They play each note with its upper twelfth as a harmonic, in imitation of *zampoña* overtones. The B section consists of pulsating chords with first one and then another of the four instruments becoming prominent, as in *Sonata Andina*, II (see example 3.7). The notes undergo several changes in pitch, range, and timbre—single notes or thirds, *pizzicato* or *arco*, normal bowing or bouncing the tip of the bow against the string (*battuto a punta*), and so on.

Movement IV, "Chasqui" (Courier), presents an array of small units in quick succession that finally achieve resolution. The title of movement IV refers to the highly trained runners or couriers in the Inca Empire who carried messages and goods for thousands of miles using a relay system over a vast web of trails in the Andes range. The chasqui carried a *pututu*, or conch-shell "trumpet," to announce his arrival. Messages consisted of knotted-cord records known as *quipus*, along with a spoken message. In her program notes, Frank explains that she has exercised "artistic license" to imagine the chasqui's choice of instruments to be the charango and quena.

Events in this three-minute movement happen at great speed, suggesting a chasqui running to the next relay station, then another chasqui taking his message and running on. Three times a chasqui evidently arrives at a village and announces himself by playing a slower, almost shrill, exceptionally arresting tune on his quena; the sound echoes from peak to peak. Overall, as shown in figure 3.1, the music conveys a sense of progression through passages of restless instability (xx) associated with running (R) that alternate with the tonal quena melody (Q).

motives:	R1	-	R2	-	R1	-	Q1	-	R1	-	Q2	-	R1	-	Q3	-	Ending (R1)	‖
tonalities:	xx		clusters	xx			Emi		xx		DMa?		xx		Cmi___Cmi___			‖
mm.	1	-	29	-	55	-	69	-	95	-	104	-	144	-	158	-	177 - 198	‖

Figure 3.1.

At the beginning, the effect of dashing from place to place is created by a succession of bursts of sixteenth notes, permutations of the five-note pattern C-D-F-G-A (T-mi3-T-T) in uneven and unpredictable lengths which seem to spring from the anchoring quarter-note *pizzicatos* (see example 3.22).

Parallel major ninths along with the very fast tempo create a blur of sound. Conveying the idea of running in segments, several times a second motive interrupts; its pitches are in the same relationship as the sixteenth-note motive but in a different rhythm (see example 3.23).

Dissonant seconds on weak beats continue the blurring effect. Alternating, the two motives constitute the first "running" motive (R1). The

Fleet ♩ = 156-160

Example 3.22. *Leyendas,* IV, "Chasqui," mm. 1–4

second "running" motive (R2) consists of strummed open strings, then slightly dissonant, repeated eighth-note chords.

After an eight-measure vamp, violin I begins the quena melody; the second phrase is echoed by violin II. The violin parts are labeled "quena," and players are even asked to imitate flutter tonguing. The melody is in E minor the first time (Q1), accompanied by a strummed chord progression with guitar associations, E minor, D major, C major, D major, E minor (see example 3.24).

The second time (Q2), the melody is in the lower two instruments in a chromatically inflected D major; harmonies are D major, A minor, D minor, D major. The third time (Q3), the melody is solidly in C minor, with the key enforced by chord progressions of tonic-subdominant-dominant-tonic. The R1 passage before Q3 repeats the R1 before Q1, but a major third lower, just as Q3 is a major third lower than Q1, the repetitions reinforcing the sense of resolution and symmetry. The movement ends with a perfect cadence in C minor.

While it is unlikely that listeners, even if "overloaded with information," would assess this movement only on how accurately it portrays the Inca chasqui runner, the title and program note do provide listeners—including performers—with a way into the music itself. Besides its pictorial associations, the movement can be enjoyed as a scherzo-and-trio, or as the portrait of a flutist trying to overcome distractions, or with any number of other scenarios, programmatic and musical.

Movement V, "Canto de Velorio" (*velorio,* wake for the dead), portrays the singing of two *lloronas*—not the ghosts of the tone poem *La Llorona,* but living, professional crying women hired to make funeral rituals even sadder. Movement V, which at seven minutes is the longest of the

Example 3.23. *Leyendas*, IV, "Chasqui," mm. 11–14

quartet's six movements, is a study in intensity rather than action. Its various elements form a dynamic curve somewhat like the "El Aullido de Atahuallpa" movement of *Inkarrí*. Sustained tone clusters introduce the funereal scene (see example 3.25).

Then, to signify the combination of Christian and indigenous religion (as in *Requiem for a Magical America*), Frank uses soft, high-pitched fragments of the *Dies Irae* chant, notated in aleatoric wheels, to accompany the wailing of the two *lloronas*. A *coro de mujeres* (chorus of women) echoes the *lloronas'* mourning (see example 3.26a–b).

Intensity increases in the second entrance of the *lloronas* with the addition of another echo in violin II, and new ornamentation in the cello, as *llorona primera* (see example 3.27).

Example 3.24. *Leyendas,* IV, "Chasqui," mm. 76–88

Example 3.25. *Leyendas,* V, "Canto de Velorio," mm. 1–3

Example 3.26a. *Leyendas,* V, "Canto de Velorio," mm. 11–21

Example 3.26b. *Leyendas*, V, "Canto de Velorio," mm. 22–25

Example 3.27. *Leyendas*, V, "Canto de Velorio," mm. 30–35

The texture continues to build in intensity with extensions of the introductory clusters plus fragments of the *llorona* melody and the responses of the *coro de mujeres*. After the *fff* climax, the intensity promptly dissipates, and the movement ends with a slow, quiet return of the *Dies Irae* and the *lloronas*.

In the final movement, "Coqueteos," a flirtatious love song is sung by a group of gallant men called *romanceros*.[38] In its orchestral version, as the third of the *Three Latin American Dances*, Frank describes it as a "light-hearted tribute to the *mestizo* or mixed-race music of the South American Pacific coast" that mixes influences from "indigenous Indian cultures,

African slave cultures and Western brass bands." The movement is in E minor throughout. The *romanceros* introduce their song in thirds over "guitars"—cello *pizzicato* chords plus the "strumming" of violin II and cello *tremolos* of octave-wide *glissandos*; this bold introduction, continuing for a full twenty-eight measures, the last eight over a constant dominant-seventh harmony, creates a keen sense of anticipation.

Example 3.28.   *Leyendas*, VI, "Coqueteos," mm. 1–7

The main melody is in violin I alone with highly accented guitarlike accompaniment.

Example 3.29.   *Leyendas*, VI, "Coqueteos," mm. 31–37

The melody is harmonized by E minor tonic triads (as in mm. 31–33 and 35), set off by contrasting aggregations—the second half of m. 34 includes G, D, A, C, F, B. In the cello line, the lowest pitches of each three eighth notes repeat the pattern E-F-G, but the makeup of the chords and the cello's other pitches are wonderfully unpredictable. This main melody is followed by a bridge passage, a return of the *romanceros* in cello, then in violin I, and a final statement of the main melody accompanied by a "*vendaval de guitarras*" (storm of guitars) as in m. 2 (octave *glissandos*).

In the orchestra version, titled "The Mestizo Waltz," the effect is even more festive; Frank marks the movement "*¡Felíz!*" (Happy!). In the final appearance of the main melody, first violins are doubled by flute, oboe, clarinet, trumpets, and piano (in octaves); accompaniment includes, besides strings, an English horn, three bassoons, four horns, three trombones, harp, timpani, and four percussion players on bass drum, conga, *chekere*, wood block, and bongo.

Example 3.30. *Three Latin American Dances*, orchestra, III, "The Mestizo Waltz," mm. 91–96, percussion and piano[39]

The Chiara Quartet premiered *Leyendas* in July 2001, issued the work on CD in 2006, and continues to perform it frequently. They have organized programs around *Leyendas*, playing the first two movements at the beginning, the second two just before intermission, and the last two at the end.[40] They have held audiences' attention with the piece at Rose Live Music concerts in a Brooklyn nightclub.[41] In 2004, the quartet was presented by the Los Angeles Philharmonic New Music Group on their Green Umbrella series. In 2003, Frank arranged *Leyendas* for string orchestra for performance by the Kalistos Chamber Orchestra in Massachusetts. In 2008, it was programmed by the Fort Worth Symphony Orchestra, which issued it on CD as part of the orchestra's *Caminos del Inka* series.

Leyendas remains significant to its composer both in itself and for the ideas or "starters" that it generated for subsequent works. Techniques she devised in *Leyendas* for producing Andean music on Western stringed instruments, as well as ways of celebrating Andean life in music, have become major components of her compositional vocabulary. Encouraged by the enthusiastic reception of *Leyendas* among players, audiences, and critics, the composer continues on her remarkable quest.

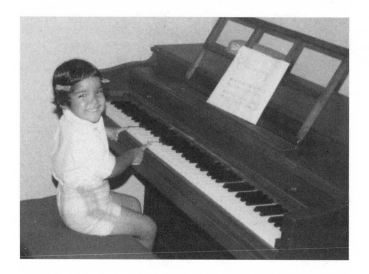

CODA

This account ends at the close of 2009, another eventful year in an eventful decade for Gabriela Frank. Early in the year, she received a prestigious John Simon Guggenheim Memorial Foundation Fellowship. Toward the end of the year, her *Inca Dances*, recorded by guitarist Manuel Barrueco and the Cuarteto Latinoamericano, won a Latin Grammy for best contemporary classical composition from the Latin Academy of Recording Arts and Sciences. She completed a new vocal work, *Tres Mitos de mi Tierra* (*Three Myths from My Land*), for the British six-man vocal ensemble the King's Singers; in this piece, for the first time, she wrote the text herself, a new direction for her. She also began collaboration with the Pulitzer Prize-winning Cuban American playwright Nilo Cruz (1960–) on several projects, beginning with songs for Dawn Upshaw and the St. Paul Chamber Orchestra. At least one future project will feature Frank as co-writer. She was named Creative Advisor to the Berkeley Symphony Orchestra, working with the orchestra's conductor, Joana Carneiro (another former University of Michigan student), to raise the orchestra's national profile and promote new music, particularly the work of young composers. New CDs are in preparation, including a much anticipated all-Frank CD from

Naxos, in collaboration with the Nashville-based ALIAS ensemble; Frank is pianist for the disc's three works with piano. An extraordinarily gifted and generous artist, Gabriela Frank is still searching her conscience and finding more ways of sharing her inspiring vision of *mestizaje*—in her music, her writing and speaking, her participation in community projects, and her collaborations with other artists. In turn, her understanding expands as her work evokes affirming responses. In our increasingly mixed society, her vision of harmonious coexistence is a compelling one. The future holds great promise.

NOTES

1. Gabriela Frank, interviewed by the author in Berkeley, CA, September 14, 2007. Unless otherwise indicated, quotations in this chapter are from that interview and from the composer's e-mail messages to the author on July 22, 2007, and October 30, 2007; permission for their usage has been granted by the composer.

2. Frank, quoted in "Gabriela Lena Frank" (G. Schirmer composer brochure, 2009), www.schirmer.com/Default.aspx?TabId=2419&State_2872=2&composerId_2872=2388.

3. "President's Luncheon: Speaker, Gabriela Frank," in *ALDAcon 2005: Selected Proceedings*, Association of Late Deafened Adults Convention, Salt Lake City, September 7–11, 2005, edited by Douglas Watson and Carolyn Piper, www.uark.edu/depts/rehabres/ALDAcon2005/ALDA2005.htm, "President's Luncheon."

4. "Gabriela Lena Frank: Composite Identity," interview by Frank J. Oteri, February 5, 2008, *NewMusicBox*, April 1, 2008, http://newmusicbox.com/article.nmbx?id=5517.

5. Frank, "*Kachkaniraqmi*—I still exist," artistic statement, ca. 2005. The Quechua word *Kachkaniraqmi* is used by Arguedas.

6. Frank, "ALDAcon Keynote Presentation," *HOH-LD (Hard Of Hearing–Late Deafened) News* 25, no. 12 (December 17, 2005), www.hearinglossweb.com/res/hlorg/alda/cn/2005/gab.htm.

7. Various university music libraries hold scores of some of Frank's unpublished student works: *Four Sketches for Double Bass Duet* (1993); *Ying* (soprano, 2 marimbas), *Synapse* (solo piano), *Mischief* (violoncello, marimba) (all 1995); *Good Karma* (violin, piano), *Dreams of Dali* (vibes, piano), and *Jabberwocky* (3 sopranos, baritone, violin, marimba) (all 1996).

8. It was published as String Quartet no. 4 (1995) (Bryn Mawr, PA: Hildegard Publishing, 2000). The "Movement for String Quartet" score is in the Rice University library and is available online as a digital file.

9. Frank, "*Kachkaniraqmi*—I still exist," artistic statement, ca. 2005.

10. A score of the competition concerto, *Runaway* (1997–1998), is held in the Stanford University library; Dr. Allen Ho of Southern Illinois University at Edwardsville includes a score and tape of the work in his archive of music for piano and orchestra.

11. Frank, liner notes to *Leslie Bassett: Music for Piano and Piano-Violin Duo*, ℗ 2002.

12. Frank, "ALDAcon Keynote Presentation" (2005).

13. Unless otherwise indicated, quotations from here to the beginning of the next section ("A Conversation with Gabriela Lena Frank") are from Frank's program notes in the scores and on G. Schirmer's Web pages.

14. Excerpts from *Las Sombras de los Apus*, music by Gabriela Frank © 1999 by G. Schirmer Inc. (ASCAP). International copyright secured. All rights reserved. Used by permission.

15. Frank, quoted by Rae Linda Brown, liner notes for *Cuatro Canciones Andinas*, ℗ 2005.

16. Frank, interviewed by the author, September 14, 2007.

17. Joan Reinthaler, "Music by Women: Notes from All Over," *Washington Post*, June 13, 2000.

18. Excerpts from *Sonata Andina*, music by Gabriela Frank © 2000 by G. Schirmer Inc. (ASCAP). International copyright secured. All rights reserved. Used by permission.

19. Allan Kozinn, "Drawn to What's Next, Not What Has Been," *New York Times*, December 8, 2003, E7.

20. Excerpts from *Sueños de Chambi*, music by Gabriela Frank © 2002 by G. Schirmer Inc. (ASCAP). International copyright secured. All rights reserved. Used by permission.

21. Frank, "ALDAcon Keynote Presentation" (2005).

22. Frank, "ALDAcon Keynote Presentation" (2005).

23. Frank, interviewed by the author, September 14, 2007.

24. Frank, "Composite Identity."

25. Allison Thompson, "First Winner of Sackler Composition Prize Named," *Advance* (University of Connecticut newsletter), November 11, 2002, http://advance.uconn.edu/2002/021118/02111801.htm.

26. Excerpts from *Inkarrí*, music by Gabriela Frank © 2005 by G. Schirmer Inc. (ASCAP). International copyright secured. All rights reserved. Used by permission.

27. Anthony Tommasini, "Composers Build to Suit," *New York Times*, October 17, 2004, AR26.

28. Excerpt from *Songs of Cifar and the Sweet Sea*, music by Gabriela Frank © 2004 by G. Schirmer Inc. (ASCAP). International copyright secured. All rights reserved. Used by permission.

29. Greg Beaver, "Reviews and Reviewers: Gabriela Frank and April 10," Greg Beaver's blog, April 13, 2005, http://greg.chiaraquartet.net/archives/41-Reviews-and-reviewers-Gabriela-Frank-and-April-10.html.

30. Frank, "Composite Identity."

31. Excerpts from *Quijotadas*, music by Gabriela Frank © 2007 by G. Schirmer Inc. (ASCAP). International copyright secured. All rights reserved. Used by permission.

32. Lisa Millegan, "Sketching a Musical Portrait," *Modesto Bee*, January 27, 2008; the article is illustrated with a photograph of the composer at a local steer ranch.

33. "Peregrinos/Pilgrims: A Musical Journey," video and illustrated script, www.wfyi.org/peregrinos.asp. WFYI is a PBS (Public Broadcasting System) affiliate.

34. Frank, "Composite Identity."

35. Wu Han, quoted in "Composer Gabriela Lena Frank Is Featured Composer at Great Lakes Festival," *Detroit Free Press*, June 5, 2006, http://peacecorpsonline. org/messages/messages/2629/2047831.html.

36. Richard Crocker, *America's Musical Life: A History* (New York: Norton, 2001), 822, cites Kyle Gann, *American Music in the Twentieth Century* (New York: Schirmer Books, 1997).

37. Excerpts from *Leyendas*, music by Gabriela Frank © 2003 by G. Schirmer Inc. (ASCAP). International copyright secured. All rights reserved. Used by permission.

38. A video of this movement performed by the Cuarteto Latinoamericano is posted at www.youtube.com/watch?v=SCL8vA3y_jU&feature=related.

39. Excerpt from *Three Latin American Dances*, music by Gabriela Frank © 2004 by G. Schirmer Inc. (ASCAP). International copyright secured. All rights reserved. Used by permission.

40. Allan Kozinn, "Bringing Disparate Ethnic and Cultural Worlds Together," *New York Times*, January 13, 2007.

41. Daniel Felsenfeld, "Chiara String Quartet," *Strings* 21, no. 9 (April 1, 2007): 95, reviews a January 2007 concert at Rose; Bernard Holland, "Bar Chatter, Weekend Cheer, Intimate Tables and, Yes, Chamber Music," *New York Times*, July 2, 2007, reviews a summer concert.

APPENDIX A: LIST OF WORKS

[current list at www.schirmer.com]

Orchestra

Elegía Andina for Orchestra (2000)
Leyendas: An Andean Walkabout, arr. (2003)—string orchestra
Three Latin American Dances for Orchestra (2004)
Manchay Tiempo (2005)
Two American Portraits (2008)

I. Frank's Alborado
II. Old Modesto

Peregrinos (2009)

Soloist(s) with Orchestra

Havana Jila (2003)—violin and orchestra
Illapa (2004)—flute and orchestra
Compadrazgo (2007)—piano, cello, with orchestra
La Llorona (2007)—viola and orchestra

Works for Band/Wind/Brass Ensemble

Requiem for a Magic America: El Día de los Muertos (2006)—orchestra winds and percussion

Works for 2–6 Players

Manhattan Serenades (1995)—cello and piano
Las Sombras de los Apus (1998–1999)—violoncello quartet
Rios Profundos (1999)—violoncello and piano
Leyendas: An Andean Walkabout (2001)—string quartet
Sueños de Chambi: Snapshots for an Andean Album (original) (2002)—violin and piano
Sueños de Chambi: Snapshots for an Andean Album, arr. (2002)—flute/alto flute and piano
Ghosts in the Dream Machine (2005)—piano quintet: piano, 2 violins, viola, cello
Canto de Harawi "Amadeoso" (2005)—flute, clarinet, piano
Cinco Danzas de Chambi (2006)—viola, piano
Cuatro Bosquejos Pre-Incaicos (2006)—flute, cello
Danza de los Saqsampillos (2006)—2 pianos, alt. 2 marimbas
Inkarrí (Inca Rey) (2006)—string quartet
Ritmos Anchinos (2006)—string quartet, sheng, pipa
Adagio para Amantani (2007)—cello, piano
Quijotadas (2007)—string quartet
Tres Homenajes: Compadrazgo (2007)—2 violins, viola, cello, piano
Hypnagogia (2008)—2 violins, 2 violas, 2 cellos
Inca Dances (2008)—guitar, 2 violins, viola, cello

Solo Works (Excluding Keyboards)

Khazn's Recitative: Elu D'vorim (2003)—violin
Soliloquio Serrano (2007)—pipa

Solo Keyboard

Sonata Andina (2000)—piano
Barcarola Latinoamericana (2007)—piano

Chorus a Cappella/Chorus Plus 1 Instrument

Hombre Errante (2002)—SATB a cappella
Ccollanan María (2004)—a cappella chorus
Why Am I So Brown? (2005)—SATB children's choir
Pollerita Roja (2006)—SSAA a cappella
Jalapeño Blues (2007)—SSAATTBB a cappella
Two Mountain Songs: Envuelto por el Viento; Picaflor Esmeralda (2008)—SSAA youth choir; SSAA women's choir
Tres Mitos de Mi Tierra (2009)—CtCtTBarBarB men's ensemble

Solo Voice(s) and Up To 6 Players

Cuatro Canciones Andinas (1999)—mezzo-soprano and piano
Songs of Cifar and the Sweet Sea: 1, 5, 6 (1–3), 9 (2004)—soprano, baritone and piano
New Andean Songs (2007)—soprano, mezzo-soprano, 2 percussion, 2 pianos

Opera / Musical Theatre

A Night at the Alhambra Café: Act I, Finale (2006)—Latina soprano, tenor, baritone, onstage violin, with guitar, percussion, piano

APPENDIX B: DISCOGRAPHY

I. Gabriela Lena Frank as composer

Barcarola Latinoamericana. Nicola Melville, piano. Innova 691 (compact disc). "Melville's Dozen." 2008.

Ccollanan María. Volti San Francisco; Robert Geary, director. Innova 759 (compact disc). "Turn the Page: New Directions in American Choral Music."

Cuatro Bosquejos Pre-Incaicos. Jessica Warren-Acosta, flute; Cheng-Hon Lee, cello. Filarmonika CD. "Acentos," *Caminos del Inka* recording series.

Cuatro Canciones Andinas. Bonnie Pomfret, soprano; Laura Gordy, piano. ACA Digital Recording CD CM20090. "De Toda La Eternidad: Songs of American Women Composers." 2005.

Cuatro Canciones Andinas. Susanna Eyton-Jones, soprano; Craig Ketter, piano. MSR Classics MS1344. "Voice of the People." 2009.

Elegia Andina. Fort Worth Symphony Orchestra; Miguel Harth-Bedoya, conductor. Filarmonika CD. "The Composer's Voice." (With: *Leyendas,* arr. string orchestra.)

Elegía Andina. Fort Worth Symphony Orchestra; Miguel Harth-Bedoya, conductor. Filarmonika CD. "Inti," *Caminos del Inka* recording series.

Inca Dances: Lamento del Panaca; Danza de Maliqui Rey. Manuel Barrueco, guitar; Cuarteto Latinoamericano. Tonar CD. "Sounds of the Americas." 2008. Also available as MP3 file.

Jalapeño Blues. Chanticleer. Video at http://slhwnotes.blogspot.com/2007/07/chanticleerperforms-jalapeno-blues.html (accessed August 5, 2009). Recorded 2007.

Leyendas: An Andean Walkabout. Chiara String Quartet: Rebecca Fischer and Julie Yoon, violins; Jonah Sirota, viola; Gregory Beaver, cello. New Voice Singles CD CNVS 002. 2006.

Leyendas: An Andean Walkabout: "Chasqui" (movt. IV). Del Sol String Quartet: Kate Stenberg and Rick Shinozaki, violins; Charlton Lee, viola; Hannah Addario-Berry, cello. Other Minds CD. "Ring of Fire: Music of the Pacific Rim." 2007.

Leyendas: An Andean Walkabout, arr. string orchestra. Fort Worth Symphony Orchestra; Miguel Harth-Bedoya, conductor. Filarmonika CD. "The Composer's Voice." (With: *Elegia Andina.*)

Leyendas, An Andean Walkabout, arr. string orchestra. The Knights; Eric Jacobsen, conductor. Sony CD 759978. "New Worlds." 2010.

Manhattan Serenades. Lin/Castro-Balbi Duo: Gloria Lin, piano; Jesús Castro-Balbi, cello. Filarmonika CD. 2007. "Rapsodia Latina," *Caminos del Inka* recording series.

Peregrinos/Pilgrims: A Musical Journey. FYI Productions DVD. 2009.

Rios Profundos. Mallarmé Chamber Players. Capstone CD 8684. "It Won't Be the Same River." 2001.

Ritmos Anchinos. Silk Road Ensemble: Jonathan Gandelsman and Shaw Pong Liu, violins; Andrea Hemmenway, viola; Nicholas Finch, cello; Wu Man, pipa; Wu Tong, sheng. World Village and In A Circle Records. "Off the Map." 2009.
Sueños de Chambi: Snapshots for an Andean Album. Shem Guibbory, violin; Sonia Rubinsky, piano. Innovative Music Programs CD MS1344. "Voice of the People." 2009.
Songs of Cifar and the Sweet Sea: "¡Me Diste, oh Dios! una hija"; "El Rebelde"; "Tomasito, el Cuque"; "Eufemia"; "En La Vela del Angelito." Robert Gardner, baritone; Anna Polonsky, piano. "The Unfolding of Music II: Disc 5." Atherton, CA: Music@Menlo. 2008.
Three Latin American Dances. Utah Symphony; Keith Lockhart, conductor. Reference Recordings CD RR-105. "Symphonic Dances." 2006.
Three Latin American Dances: no. 3, "The Mestizo Waltz." Utah Symphony; Keith Lockhart, conductor. Reference Recordings. "Utah Symphony 30th Anniversary Sampler." 2006.
Two Mountain Songs: Envuelto por el Viento; Picaflor Esmeralda. San Francisco Girls Chorus; Susan McMane, director. San Francisco Girls Chorus CD. "Heaven and Earth: Joining the Chorus."

II. Gabriela Frank as Pianist

Leslie Bassett: Music for Piano and Piano-Violin Duo. Gabriela Lena Frank, piano; Wendolyn Olson, violin. Dexter, MI: Equilibrium CD EQ 51. 2002.

SOURCES

Beaver, Gregory. "Gabriela Frank and Apr 10." *Greg Beaver's Blog*, Lot 49, April 13, 2005. http://greg.chiaraquartet.net/archives/41-Reviews-and-reviewers-Gabriela-Frank-and-April-10.html.
Carneiro, Joana, and Gabriela Lena Frank. "Joint Interview with Berkeley Symphony's New Director and Its Creative Advisor." By Michael Zwiebach. *San Francisco Classical Voice*, August 18, 2009. www.sfcv.org/article/joint-interview-with-berkeley-symphonysbrnew-director-and-its-creative-advisor.
Frank, Gabriela Lena. "ALDAcon Keynote Presentation." *HOH-LD [Hard Of Hearing-Late Deafened] News* 25, no. 12 (December 17, 2005). www.hearinglossweb.com/res/hlorg/alda/cn/2005/gab.htm.
———. "The Beautiful Next Step: An In-Depth Interview with Gabriela Frank." By Yolanda O'Bannon. July 2009. www.yowangdu.com/the-world/north-america.html.
———. "Composer Inspired by Central Valley." Video interview by Lisa Millegan. http://videos.modbee.com/vmix_hosted_apps/p/media?id=1867665.
———. "Composite Identity." Interview by Frank J. Oteri, February 5, 2008. *NewMusicBox*, April 1, 2008. http://newmusicbox.com/article.nmbx?id=5514 through 5518.
———. "Gabriela Lena Frank and the Indianapolis Symphony Orchestra." Video interview. February 13, 2007. www.youtube.com/watch?v=A17SRoXZlM.

————. *"Kachkaniraqmi*—I still exist." Artistic statement, ca. 2005.

————. "Keynote Address." In *ALDAcon 2005: Selected Proceedings of the Association of Late Deafened Adults Convention*, Salt Lake City, September 7–11, 2005, edited by Douglas Watson and Carolyn Piper. www.uark.edu/depts/rehabres/ALDAcon2005/ALDA2005.htm (link "4: President's Luncheon").

————. Liner notes to *Leslie Bassett: Music for Piano and Piano-Violin Duo*. Gabriela Lena Frank, piano; Wendolyn Olson, violin. ℗ 2002. Equilibrium CD EQ 51.

Felsenfeld, Daniel. "Chiara String Quartet." *Strings* 21, no. 9 (April 1, 2007): 95.

"Gabriela Lena Frank." New York: G. Schirmer, 2003. www.schirmer.com/Default.aspx?TabId=2419&State_ 2872=2&composerId_2872=2388.

Holland, Bernard. "Bar Chatter, Weekend Cheer, Intimate Tables and, Yes, Chamber Music." *New York Times*, July 2, 2007. www.nytimes.com/2007/07/02/arts/music/02chia.html?scp=1&sq=Holland,%20%22Bar%20Chatter,%20weekend%20cheer&st=cse.

Kozinn, Allan. "Drawn to What's Next, Not What Has Been." *New York Times*, December 8, 2003, E7.

————. "Bringing Disparate Ethnic and Cultural Worlds Together." *New York Times*, January 13, 2007.

Millegan, Lisa. "Musical Impressions." *Modesto Bee*, May 2, 2008. www.modbee.com/scene/v-print/story/286700.html.

————. "Sketching a Musical Portrait." *Modesto Bee*, January 27, 2008.

Thompson, Allison. "First Winner of Sackler Composition Prize Named." *Advance* (University of Connecticut newsletter), November 11, 2002. http://advance.uconn.edu/2002/021118/02111801.htm.

Tommasini, Anthony. "Composers Build to Suit." *New York Times*, October 17, 2004, AR26.

Donald McKinney

JENNIFER HIGDON (1962–)

I've been fortunate in that my parents never told me I could not do something. A lot of people along the way have said "You're never going to be able to do this—you started flute too late—there's no way you're going to be able to have a career as a composer; you didn't major in composition as an undergraduate— you're never going to be able to make it as a freelance composer." But every step along the way, I was pretty defiant and said, "Watch me!"[1]

Determination and willpower—these hallmarks of Jennifer Higdon's professional persona help explain her success in the competitive world of classical concert music. Higdon's enthusiasm—her passion for life— infuses her works, yielding a lasting affection for her music on the part of performers and audiences. Higdon's music maintains a potent communicative quality, inviting listeners into its embrace and establishing a simple human connection.

Currently living in Philadelphia, Higdon maintains a rigorous schedule at the Curtis Institute of Music, where she teaches composition and courses in counterpoint and twentieth-century music. She and her partner, Cheryl Lawson, run Lawdon Press—the name is a combination of their last names—which publishes and distributes Higdon's works exclusively. Over the first decade of the new millennium, Higdon has emerged as one of the most frequently performed composers in America. She has received numerous awards from prestigious sources such as the Guggenheim Foundation, the American Academy of Arts and Letters, the Pew Fellowship in the Arts, Meet the Composer, the National Endowment for the Arts, and the American Society of Composers, Authors and Publishers (ASCAP). Her compositional output is diverse, including chamber, choral, solo, and large-scale instrumental works. She has scored seven string quartets, numerous woodwind quintets, and a collage of music for various mixed ensembles. Higdon's attraction to chamber music and the intimacy of the small stage is central to her approach. A feeling of intimate communication also carries over into her many highly acclaimed works for large orchestra.

> *My job is to communicate. I feel that you should be able to come to my music without having any kind of knowledge about classical music. I want to be able to speak to you on a kind of visceral level. "Accessibility" doesn't seem like a negative word to me.*[2]

Born in Brooklyn, Higdon grew up in Atlanta and in rural Tennessee and still considers herself a southerner. When she was six months old, her family moved from New York to Atlanta, Georgia. Her father, Charles "Kenny" Higdon, a professional painter and filmmaker, taught at the Atlanta College of Art; he took Jennifer and her brother, Andrew Blue, with him to festivals and exhibitions of new, experimental art. Higdon's early experiences of visual art have been of undeniable importance in shaping her compositional thought processes. The two movements of the *Piano Trio* (2003), a work inspired by the piano trios of Copland and Shostakovich, bear visual titles, "Pale Yellow" and "Fiery Red."

> *During the 1960s we saw things, and both my brother and I would look at these things and say, "This is art? I don't know." It helped me formulate early on what my idea of what art was. By the time I was seven or eight, I began to find the need to experiment out of my system; because I had been around so much experimental art, I realized, even at that age, that I needed a little more form.*

After approximately ten years in Atlanta, the family moved to a forty-acre farm in Seymour, Tennessee, in the Appalachian Mountains. Higdon was not raised on the music of Bach, Beethoven, and Brahms; she grew up in a household without classical music. As a teenager, she was surrounded instead with bluegrass, rock, and folk music. Her composers were John Lennon, Paul McCartney, Bob Marley, and Peter, Paul and Mary. The accessibility of popular music has remained one of Higdon's goals for her writing. Her extraordinary ability to recognize melodies from the popular music of the 1960s and 1970s has strongly influenced her own melodic structures, and she endeavors to write melodies that a wide variety of listeners find memorable. The vibrant rhythmic pulse that dominates much of the popular music of the 1960s is likewise a trademark of Higdon's concert music.

I think I have a need for clear rhythm or pulse. I think that is a very prominent thing because I listened to so much of the Beatles growing up. I listened to an extraordinary amount of the Beatles!

In her large-scale works, she relies on the percussion section of the orchestra not only for this pulse but also for melodic and timbral contributions. Higdon utilizes the nonpitched and pitched percussion instruments in a continual web of rhythmic activity that animates the musical structure. Her orchestral work, *Fanfare Ritmico*, written in 1999 for the Women's Philharmonic Orchestra, opens with a frenzy of activity, immediately demonstrating the composer's propensity for rhythm and pulse.

Example 4.1. *Fanfare Ritmico* (2000), mm. 1–7

People often tell me they can't believe that I grew up in the south because my music has such an active energy to it. Part of it is my excitement about music!

Higdon's musical pursuits began in the high school marching band. She recalls how performing and touring with the band resonated with her as a teenager. At fifteen, she taught herself to play the flute using a band method book she found in her house. Before long, she auditioned for the flute section of the school's concert band and was placed first chair. Higdon's flute playing advanced throughout high school, and for a short period she studied with Jan Vinci in the nearby town of Maryville, Tennessee. With Vinci's help, in 1980 Higdon was able to attend a summer flute camp at Bowling Green State University in Ohio, where she studied with Judith Bentley. Higdon was drawn to Bentley's teaching style, and so she enrolled as a flute performance major at the university, with a limited knowledge of classical repertoire but a tremendous thirst for music. Higdon met Cheryl Lawson during these high school years; the two have remained life partners.

It was Judith Bentley who kindled Higdon's interest in composition. In the tradition of legendary flutists William Kincaid and Marcel Tabuteau, Bentley emphasized the importance of the musical line—how to dissect a musical entity and effectively discuss its construction and development. In her own music, Higdon still strives to incorporate a clear musical line into every piece. In the third movement of her string quartet *Autumn's Cricket*, to cite one example, she unfolds the musical material in a solely linear fashion. And the melodic line, which is persistently maintained by the first violin and cello, is constructed with careful detail, enhanced by *accelerando* and *ritardando*.

Example 4.2.   *Autumn's Cricket* (1987), III, mm. 2–15

Though Higdon describes *Autumn's Cricket* (and many of her other works) as formless, it may be concretely stated that her music is not devoid of structure. Higdon's pieces tend to find structural identity through the composer's judicious utilization of small motives, and *Autumn's Cricket* is a prime example. At the beginning of the first movement, Higdon introduces a unison motivic line in the first and second violins and viola; after a fermata, the motive is then developed contrapuntally.

Example 4.3. *Autumn's Cricket* (1987), I, mm. 1–10

After the secondary theme, Higdon uses the motivic material from the opening measures in retransitional fashion. This technique, evident in her early chamber music, has continued to govern her compositional style.

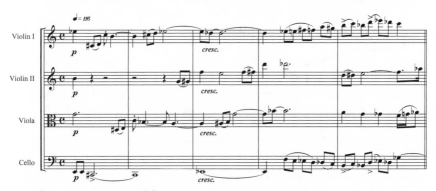

Example 4.4. *Autumn's Cricket* (1987), I, mm. 126–130

I can remember when I was in school sitting in an orchestra playing with a swirl of sound around me. We did Daphnis et Chloe *in my undergraduate, and I was amazed by the incredible sound rising (I was playing one of the flute parts). It was*

*such a visceral experience, and I often think when I'm writing I'm trying to recreate
that experience for other people, to get them excited about the music.*

During her time at Bowling Green, Higdon gained much practical experience as an ensemble performer, which helped to shape her perspective on constructing music from the performer's perspective. Her years
as an orchestral player enable her to adroitly address specific technical
demands performers face when tackling new and unusual works. Careful attention to detail instills Higdon's music with malleability, allowing
her to shift her style according to exactly for whom she is writing. She
consistently addresses the needs of the specific persons involved while
maintaining her original voice.

*My style changes from piece to piece depending on the commissioner. For instance,
last year I wrote something for a junior high band. That's really different from what
I might write for a professional symphony orchestra. And occasionally I'll change the
language of a piece to reflect what kind of piece it is.*[3]

Nearing graduation from Bowling Green, Higdon began to consider
what would come next; she turned to conductor Robert Spano (director of
the university orchestra and Higdon's conducting teacher) for guidance.
Spano, a Curtis Institute of Music graduate, strongly encouraged Higdon
to enroll at the Curtis Institute. She took his advice, beginning a professional connection with Spano that would ultimately prove a central force
in the propulsion of her career.

Upon arriving at Curtis in September 1986, Higdon again felt herself
at a disadvantage, with little practical training in harmony and counterpoint. But she dedicated herself to composition studies with David
Loeb and Ned Rorem. Rorem's style of thinking related well to Higdon,
paralleling her studies with Judith Bentley, and Rorem has continued to
be a strong supporter of Jennifer Higdon's career. In a recent article, he
praised Higdon, stating, "If I were asked to name fifteen American composers of quality writing today, Jennifer Higdon would be on the list. Her
music is honest, she has something to say, and she knows how to say it."[4]

Higdon's compositional style began to develop and evolve during her
years at Curtis; her in-depth study of counterpoint and vocal writing continue to play a role in her current compositions. She received her artist's
diploma from Curtis in 1988 and then decided to take a year away from
school before enrolling in further degree programs.

Higdon remained in Philadelphia until the fall of 1989, when she entered the University of Pennsylvania (Penn). She completed her master's
and doctoral degrees at Penn; the first movement of her string quartet,
Voices (1993), helped fulfill her degree requirements. Composition students were afforded the opportunity to study with a variety of compos-

ers in a rotating system. Her most influential teacher during this time period was George Crumb. Higdon found a like-minded contemporary in Crumb, who is a West Virginia native, and the two shared a common bond in their similar upbringings near the Appalachian Mountains. Crumb's biggest contribution to Higdon's style was his insistence that she continually focus on color and texture in music. His own remarkable ear for timbre opened a new aesthetic in twentieth-century music, and his influence on Higdon is certainly evidenced in her music. The enriched palette of interesting color combinations Higdon gleaned from her time with Crumb has continued to season her compositional style, specifically in her writing for percussion instruments. A notable example is the second movement of Higdon's *City Scape* (2002).

Example 4.5. *City Scape* (2002), II, mm. 1–3

The movement calls for a variety of intriguing sounds, including water gong (a gong submerged in and out of water while a performer plays a roll on the gong). She also calls for the timpani player to strike a crotale, strategically placed on the head of the timpani, while moving the timpani pedal to create a sirenlike sound.

City Scape *is a metropolitan sound picture written in orchestral tones. Every city has a distinctive downtown skyline—that steely profile jutting into the sky—with shapes and monumental buildings that represent that city's particular signature.*

Higdon's choral setting of *O Magnum Mysterium* (2002) provides another example of her interest in creating intriguing sonic landscapes. The piece requires a small instrumentation of two flutes, water crystals, and chimes, which contributes a unique timbre to interlace with the human voice.

Example 4.6.   *O Magnum Mysterium* (2002), mm. 46–48

I tend to teach like I was taught flute, not like I was taught composition. When you're in a performance lesson, it's much more one-on-one, talking about every detail and discussing the possibilities. I have worked with composers who always wanted me to write like them, or only know how to teach the way they write, but my flute teacher was a little more flexible. She seemed to be able to change her style of teaching with each individual student, which I think valuable, because everybody is different.[5]

In 1996, Higdon received widespread recognition when *USA Today* named her orchestral work *Shine* (1995) as the best new piece in classical music for the year. Her compositional style was compared to that of Béla Bartók. The six-minute work was written to fulfill a commission from ASCAP to commemorate the one-hundredth anniversary of the Oregon Symphony, as well as ASCAP's past president, composer Morton Gould. *Shine*, which clearly demonstrates the energetic rhythmic pace pervasive to much of Higdon's oeuvre, brought immediate national recognition to her music and served as a harbinger for the outpouring of orchestral works to come.

Example 4.7. *Shine* (1995), mm. 269–277

I was thinking how we all cross paths with various people, and we're touched by them. It's a memorial to the paths we cross, and all the people who cross ours, and how we learn and grow from them. It's a nice way to put a positive tone poem out in the world.

Higdon's prowess as a composer of orchestral works steadily rose, primarily through commissions from major symphony orchestras, but the signal moment came in 1999, when the Curtis Institute of Music asked her to compose a work in commemoration of its seventy-fifth anniversary. For this special endeavor, Higdon chose to honor her late brother Andrew Blue Higdon, who had recently passed away after a long battle with cancer. This work, entitled *blue cathedral*, would prove to spark the most providential events of Higdon's escalating career.

In tribute to my brother, I feature solos for the clarinet (the instrument he played) and the flute (the instrument I play). Because I am the older sibling, it is the flute that appears first in this dialogue. At the end of the work, the two instruments continue their dialogue, but it is the flute that drops out and the clarinet that continues on in the upward progressing journey.

Robert Spano conducted the first performance of *blue cathedral* with the Curtis Institute Orchestra in May 2000. The premiere was hailed as an enormous success with both audiences and critics. Higdon's ability to inculcate lyrical and contemplative writing with her characteristic rhythmic aggression is markedly demonstrated in the work, as, true to her artistic upbringing, she utilizes stark visual imagery to conjure a mental picture. The image of an enormous floating cathedral of glass not only provides the listener with a focus for the sound but also aids the composer in identifying the particular sonorities that will most precisely complement the given scenario. To establish an aural impression of the cathedral, Higdon employs metallic percussion instruments, creating an ethereal, otherworldly environment. She enhances the distinct metallic qualities of the crotales, triangles, vibraphone, glockenspiel, and chimes by asking that they be struck with triangle beaters.

Example 4.8.   *blue cathedral* (1999), mm. 1–4

As the percussion instruments actualize the soundscape of the cathedral's walls, Higdon introduces the strings in signature polychordal style, an undercurrent of sound through which the solo flute and clarinet are gently woven.

Example 4.9.   *blue cathedral* (1999), mm. 7–15

> *Cathedrals represent a place of beginnings, endings, solitude, fellowship, contemplation, knowledge, and growth. As I was writing this piece, I found myself imagining a journey through a glass cathedral in the sky. Because the walls would be transparent, I saw the image of clouds and blueness permeating from the outside of this church. In my mind's eye, the listener would enter from the back of the sanctuary, floating along the corridor amongst giant crystal pillars, moving in a contemplative stance.*

After its highly successful premiere, *blue cathedral* lay dormant for several years until 2003, when Spano recorded the piece with the Atlanta Symphony Orchestra, thus spawning the work's rebirth. By 2004, *blue cathedral* had received over one hundred performances, making it the most frequently performed work by a living composer. It is programmed regularly by high-quality orchestras all over the world. And Robert Spano, who had once impelled a young flute student from Tennessee to pursue composition at the Curtis Institute, had effectively aided in the construction of Higdon's mighty cathedral.

Spano's remarkable role in Higdon's career did not end there. Shortly after the premiere of Higdon's *Concerto for Orchestra* in 2002, the conductor heard a recording of the Philadelphia performance and immediately expressed his interest. Upon discovering the composer was Jennifer Higdon, he committed himself to performing and recording the concerto in his inaugural season with the Atlanta Symphony Orchestra. In order to complete the recording project for Telarc Records, Spano and the Atlanta Symphony also commissioned Higdon's next large-scale work, a three-movement orchestral suite entitled *City Scape*. In *City Scape*, Higdon pays musical tribute to her childhood home (although she believes it applicable to any city). Knowing the piece would be recorded on the same disc as the concerto, Higdon sought to balance the frenetic energy of the former with something comparably calm and subdued. "I knew I would need to write something that had bigger building blocks," remembers the composer, "as if I were creating a sculpture of giant stones." Those giant stones were eventually molded into the second movement of *City Scape*, "river sings a song to trees," the longest of the three movements and an exhibition of Higdon's superior ability to shape extended lyrical thought.

In recent years, Higdon has begun to work out a series of solo-with-orchestra pieces, beginning with a commission from the Brooklyn Philharmonic in 2004. The resultant work, *Dooryard Bloom*, is a piece for baritone solo and orchestra based on texts selected from Walt Whitman's poems. In 2005, she composed three works for solo instruments, including an *Oboe Concerto*, a *Trombone Concerto*, and a *Percussion Concerto*, which was written for percussionist Colin Currie. A recording by the London Philharmonic and Currie earned Higdon a 2010 Grammy Award for best classical contemporary composition. Her most recent contributions are *Concerto 4-3* for string trio and orchestra that was written for Time for Three; *The Singing Rooms* for solo violin, chorus, and orchestra; a *Violin Concerto* for Hilary Hahn; and a *Piano Concerto*, which was commissioned by the National Symphony Orchestra and premiered in December 2009. Higdon continues to receive widespread recognition through numerous commissions, residencies, and performances. Her decidedly nonconformist upbringing, coupled with the very best musical training, has instilled in Jennifer Higdon a distinct compositional voice within the world of twenty-first-century concert music. With an innate ability to shift from delicate chamber music to energetic, virtuosic orchestral writing, she continues to compose works that resonate with performers and audiences worldwide.

A CONVERSATION WITH JENNIFER HIGDON

Jennifer Higdon has been described by many as having pure and positive energy. She portrays these qualities not just with her music but with her everyday interactions with people. I met Higdon during her residency with the Pittsburgh Symphony Orchestra in 2006, after which she made time to meet with our students at Duquesne University. All were captivated by her enthusiasm and passion for what she was doing. When we met for this interview in May 2007, Higdon was completing a busy concert season by attending a performance of CityScape by the National Symphony Orchestra. And as we sat in the lobby of Washington, D.C.'s, Melrose Hotel, discussing music, yes, but also just life in general, I realized how I have always been struck by her simple genuineness. Couple that with southern charm, a vivacious spirit, and an infectious smile, and it is easy to see why Jennifer Higdon continues to reach so many people.–Donald McKinney

McKinney: Tell me about your family upbringing and background; what types of music did you listen to as a child?

Higdon: I grew up in the south, although I was born in Brooklyn. This is often a confusing part of my biography because I don't sound like I'm from Brooklyn. I grew up in Tennessee and Georgia, and my dad was an artist who worked at home. We had a lot of music there. He always had music playing when he was drawing or doing illustrations. It was usually rock, 70s folk music, or sometimes a little bluegrass, but not really any classical in the household. When I was a kid, he used to take me to rock concerts in Chastain Park in Atlanta. Totally backward of what you would think for a classical composer, I had no classical background through the age of eighteen. It's hard to believe!

McKinney: Maybe that's what makes you so interesting.

Higdon: Well, it is such a different kind of story. I played percussion in the high school marching band, and I taught myself to play the flute. That was pretty much my entrance into music: going through those band method books and playing flute in the concert band. We did a lot of Marvin Hamlisch (if I remember correctly!). When I went off to college in Bowling Green, I went to study flute performance with this phenomenal teacher, Judith Bentley. She really got me started in classical music. When I think back now, it's really unusual; I went to college not knowing any classical music. I didn't even know the Beethoven symphonies, which just seems weird for an eighteen-year-old who wants to major in music, especially knowing what I know now. I guess I didn't know enough to be intimidated!

McKinney: So you really threw yourself into it.

Higdon: That's it! I also think I was really hungry. I was so fascinated by the whole field of classical music that I just started absorbing as much as I possibly could. When I started college, I was playing catch-up with my colleagues. They had all had music lessons, and they knew quite a bit of repertoire. And it was that way all the way through my schooling; I always felt like I was trying to catch up. I'm not sure if it was actually a disadvantage, but it felt like it at the time.

McKinney: What were some of your musical influences prior to undergraduate training?

HIGDON: It was definitely the Beatles—that would have been the first thing. My dad had bought the *Sergeant Pepper*'s album when it first came out. Dad, being an artist, wanted to look at that cover; it was quite radical, with all of these wax figures. My brother and I got a hold of it, and we just listened to that music over and over and over again. I loved the Beatles. I remember thinking, "Wow, what incredible rhythms." Just the feel of their music really made an impression. After that, I was influenced by virtually anything I happen to run across. My dad would take me to animation festivals or film festivals, or experimental art happenings in Atlanta. The other music I picked up was usually that sort of stuff, the seemingly random things you grab out of the air if you're attending events at a museum. I remember one time in Atlanta, we did go to an orchestra concert because my parents wanted me to experience the orchestra. But we only went to that one concert (they also took us to one ballet). I can't even remember what was on the program, but I do remember it was the Atlanta Symphony, and it was at the Woodruff Arts Center. I have done enough stuff with Atlanta now that it's pretty amazing for me to think back on that. I can actually remember where we sat in the Woodruff Center.

McKINNEY: So it was just after you were born that your family moved to Atlanta?

HIGDON: Yes. I think we moved six months after I was born. We lived in the Lenox Square area for most of the time. I think my parents decided that they wanted us to have the experience of living in the country, which is why they decided to move to a rural part of Tennessee. They bought a forty-acre farm there.

McKINNEY: What age were you then?

HIGDON: I probably was ten or eleven. So half of my childhood was in Atlanta proper, and the other half was way out in the middle of nowhere.

McKINNEY: Was it an actual working farm?

HIGDON: Well, we didn't work it; our neighbors worked it. There was a dairyman who lived on the next farm over, and we let his cattle graze on the grounds. My dad was what I guess you would call a "gentleman farmer." He basically only had a garden—tomatoes, potatoes, those sorts of things—but he had an art studio at the back of the house. He was self-employed. We had one of the earliest fax machines; it used to be called literally the "facsimile machine," and one image coming over that thing would take about an hour. It was so slow. But that's how he kept connected with art agencies in Atlanta. They would send him images and orders, and he would draw them up and send them back, via Delta airlines (Delta Dash). This is before FedEx and UPS really got going. It was a nice contrast, having lived in the city and then going to the country. I sometimes draw on that country, the sounds that occur in a place like that, where you are at the base of a mountain and it's really quiet. Having studied with George Crumb, who grew up in West Virginia, I gained a real appreciation for it, talking with him about those eerie sounds one hears coming through the woods on a summer evening. It was pretty amazing, nice and quiet there. It was such a different world.

McKINNEY: Tell me about your compositional history. When did you start?

HIGDON: I started in college. I can't remember what it was, exactly, but I must have expressed some sort of interest in writing, because I came into my flute lesson one day and Judith Bentley said, "I want you to write a piece of music." It was something that simple. And I said, "Well, how do you write a piece of music?"

McKINNEY: You had no interest up to that point in writing?

HIGDON: I don't think I did. I am thinking I must have said something to trigger her, because she didn't do this to all of her students. I can't figure out for the life of me what made her do it. But that woman could teach music like no one I have ever seen. I developed a sense of the importance of line from her. Mrs. Bentley would take a piece apart, and then we would talk about how things were actually put together and where you are going with this or that particular line. She had a profound influence on the way I thought about music.

McKINNEY: What year was this? Were you a sophomore?

HIGDON: It might have been the end of my freshman year. It was on the early side of my time at Bowling Green. She told me Harvey Sollberger was coming; he's a flutist and a composer. He was going to do a master class. Instead of my doing the regular flute repertoire, she wanted me to write a little work. So I asked her how to go about composing a piece of music, and she showed me how to do a six-tone row! I wrote this funny little piece called *Night Creatures* for piano and flute. There wasn't much to it, actually. I played that for the Sollberger master class. There was something about the idea of organizing tones that I just thought was totally cool. It was such a unique form of self-expression. Something about it really clicked for me. I kept playing flute, but I started writing things on the side by myself. At some point—I think it might have been during my junior year at Bowling Green—I did take some lessons with Marilyn Shrude and Wallace DePue. Because I was a flute performance major, I couldn't really do the regular composition track. I couldn't handle both degrees. In order to go to the composition track, I would have had to dump a lot of my classes.

McKINNEY: How would you say your earlier music differs from your current music?

HIGDON: Well, it seems like I was all over the map tonally in the early stuff, because I was trying to find my own voice. It's interesting; people hear my earlier stuff and they say they can hear me in it. I think I'm too close to it to know. I'm not actually sure. There are things that connect— the rhythmic energy does show up in the early works. Some of those early pieces actually still get played.

McKINNEY: Most of your earlier pieces seem to be chamber and solo works. Your orchestral material seems to have come later.

HIGDON: That's absolutely accurate. It feels like I have only been doing orchestra for the past decade. I think I must have done twenty, thirty, forty, or fifty chamber works before I ever got into the orchestral world. I was writing for friends, or for myself to play on flute. Usually, if you are an inexperienced composer, orchestras don't really ask you to write something.

McKINNEY: How did you come to composition as a profession? What path has led to your current success?

HIGDON: Halfway through my undergraduate days at Bowling Green, I realized that I really wanted to compose. I loved playing the flute, and I had a good time doing it, but there was an extra dimension to the composing part. The interest was so all-consuming I decided I needed to apply to graduate school in composition. I needed to make a switch. I wanted to finish out my performance degree, but then after that, I wanted to be in composition. I never thought twice about it. My parents never said, "Are you sure you want to do this?" or, "Are you crazy?" They were completely supportive. That might have been because my dad was a commercial artist, working at home, and I'm sure his parents probably said that to him.

McKINNEY: And this is when Robert Spano appeared in your life?

HIGDON: Right. My last year at Bowling Green was the first year that Robert Spano came into that school to run the orchestra. He was very young, but his conducting style was already there. I remember sitting in on his audition and thinking, "Wow! This guy is really something." So in my last year I took a conducting seminar with him. It was a graduate class, but he let me come in—I was like a little peon in the room! When I got accepted into a couple of different schools, I went to him and asked where he thought I should go, and he said, "Curtis—no doubt about it." That became the switching point for me. I kept playing flute, but I wasn't practicing six hours a day like I had been. I started focusing on fundamentals like counterpoint and harmony. Working with such good musicians just made my imagination blossom. It's kind of startling, the difference between the pieces I wrote before I started Curtis and those that came while I was there. You can hear a complete shift. It was like someone had opened a Technicolor door.

McKINNEY: Who were your teachers at Curtis?

HIGDON: David Loeb was my primary teacher, and I also studied with Ned Rorem. We had this thing at Curtis where only five students would attend. Ned would come down and basically do seminars on songwriting. He would give one text to all of the students, and we would all set it in our own way. We would talk a lot about that. Ned provided a perspective different from David Loeb. Loeb is a very intelligent man, and he gave me a lot of the historical background on just about everything related to music. Ned made me think about the voice a lot. And also I think he was a good example of a professional musician, which is always nice for young students.

McKINNEY: So you were at Curtis for how many years?

HIGDON: Two. Then I took one year off before going to the University of Pennsylvania. I started there on a master's degree and then a doctorate. I was there five years, I think.

McKINNEY: And this is where you studied with Crumb.

HIGDON: Right. They also had a rotating system where you moved between different teachers, not that different from the way Curtis has done their thing. I think George was probably the person I was with the most. It was great—George's southern accent and my southern accent! He really made me think about color, though. That was the important lesson for me, just listening to him talk about color. I think that actually fed into my preexisting experiences with my dad's paintings and all the art I had seen; I had grown up in such a visual environment that the word *color* had many meanings to me. That really affected the way I wrote or thought, or hoped to write music. But even watching the way Crumb speaks about music, or when he sits down to play the piano—it taught me something about timing. George's music has this magical timing to it. It's a hard thing to describe, but watching him play anything—even if it was Bach— or talking about some piece he loves was pretty amazing.

McKINNEY: Your music has a remarkable ability to move from lyricism to aggressive rhythmic energy; how would you say you balance these qualities? What characteristics best describe your musical language?

HIGDON: I have no idea! I actually do it by instinct. I don't think about how long something has been there or how long I've been doing something in the music. I just try to follow my instinct. I'm sure my instinct has probably been developed from all the stuff I listened to when I was young, and I think a lot of times textural changes occur pretty fast in my music. I'm certain it's just the amount and type of art I had as a kid. There was an interesting point in one of my lessons with Crumb that may have triggered something. We were having a conversation about the final test of a piece, and he said, "Well, the final test is how it sounds." That's it— not how it analyzes but just how it sounds. Is it interesting? And I remember thinking, "Wow! If that's the final test, then maybe I should just start from that point and see if I can write things that just sound interesting." If that's the final test, let's just work backward from there.

McKINNEY: It's interesting trying to find form in your music; it doesn't fall into any box of standardized forms. What is your approach to form?

HIGDON: I'm pretty formless! Again, my test is always, "Is it interesting?" That's the number-one question. I try to shape the music. I guess I'm chiseling away, trying to find the sculpture within the stone. It never has a distinct form. Now someone could probably analyze it and find something there that I didn't realize, but I'm doing it instinctively. I think you can step outside the bounds all the time, so long as you make it a logical world for the listener. Does the choice sound logical? Instinct and ear are my guides. I have only one piece where I purposefully used a standard form: the last movement of *City Scape* is a rondo, but that is only because the Atlanta Symphony asked for it. They wanted something in rondo form because the schoolkids were going to be studying it the following year. It's the only time I have ever approached form that way, very unusual.

McKINNEY: What other sorts of elements do you find must be taken into consideration when completing a commissioned work?

HIGDON: I always think about the ensemble involved. What I write for a junior high band (which I did not that long ago) will be very different from what I write for the Chicago Symphony—very different demands! For the junior high band, the goal was to do something that would stretch the kids a little—not frustrate them, but help teach them about rhythm. I geared the whole piece around that; it's called *Rhythm Stand*. I had these kids not only playing their instruments but also playing rhythms with pencils on music stands to give them a feel for how different rhythms operate. It mixed up the sound enough so the kids began to realize they could make music out of a lot of different things—it didn't have to be the instrument in their hands! The very next piece I wrote was for Chicago, one of their train commissions. They did a whole series of these pieces for Ravinia, where the train runs through the yard. I wrote a piece called *Loco* about a crazy train! There weren't the same limitations as you would have for a junior high band, but both pieces are valid in what they do for their respective players and audiences.

McKINNEY: How do you make your pitch language decisions, either tonal or atonal?

HIGDON: Usually I just look at the nature of the piece—how edgy a sound I want and the performers involved. I only have one or two pieces that are pretty atonal; one is a solo piece, called *rapid.fire*, for flute. It needed to be more nontonal because I was trying to create a sensation of fear and violence in the city—not an easy thing to pull off with a solo flute, but I thought that would be an interesting challenge. I also look at whom I am writing for. I've been fortunate enough to always write on commission, and so I look at the ensemble and their history. Then I try to figure what sound world is appearing in my head, in my subconscious. What does it dig up when I think about what I'm supposed to be writing? More often I think the stuff tends to be tonal. That seems to fit the groups that I'm writing for. It's funny—my pieces do change; their harmonic language changes from piece to piece. But I think it needs to be that way because it keeps it interesting for me. I set up some sort of challenge in there, something to explore for myself.

McKINNEY: I noticed a lot of your scale structures are octatonic. Is that purposeful, or do you think it is a naturally occurring by-product of that "sound world" you alluded to?

HIGDON: I use it purposefully. But I think what happens is stuff just kind of comes in because I'm examining it with my students. Especially in the case of *Concerto for Orchestra*, I remember we were doing Stravinsky and Bartók in my classes during that time. I had a lot of kids in those classes, so we were looking theoretically. I think that's actually what happened: "These are cool scales! Let's see how this sounds!"

McKINNEY: How has composing chamber works affected your approach to large-scale orchestral music?

HIGDON: I have a tendency to use chamber textures in my orchestral music. I think it makes a great contrast in the orchestral palette. I also realize—and this probably comes from writing so much chamber music—that even in orchestras, the players are so good now you could easily draw out any group of people and they would be able to play really good chamber music. The level of musicianship in the world has gotten to such a point that musicians can do things like they've never been able to do in history. So I have a tendency to write pretty virtuosic orchestra works. Maybe it's because I went through the chamber experience. I do this a lot in the *Concerto for Orchestra*; I make little chamber sections.

McKINNEY: There are quite a few quartets, for instance.

HIGDON: Exactly. Quartets, quintets, sextets, and I even go to the extent of writing a solo violin part for the principal second (which sometimes freaks them out a little bit). It's just that they are really good players, and they all deserve a chance to shine. So it makes me think a lot about the fact that this itself is an interesting color: chamber versus orchestral. Why can't you have a chamber piece within the orchestra setting?

McKINNEY: What is your approach to orchestration?

HIGDON: I'm very careful. I always wonder if I know what I'm doing every time I start a new piece to orchestrate. I look at the blank page and think, "Oh boy."

McKINNEY: Do you start with a short score, or do you go straight into orchestrating?

HIGDON: I always go into short score. What happens is, at some point in the writing, my head will start composing too fast for me to orchestrate it out on the full page. I try to balance out the shifting between the sections, the color changes. The best way for me to do that is with a short score; I'll make little notations here and there. Sometimes I know exactly how something is going to be orchestrated later, so my short scores get pretty messy in the notations! Then I'll go back and orchestrate maybe fifteen or twenty pages and then lay those out and ask myself, "What would make a contrasting color shift? As I move into the next section, what do I need to do that will make this sound different?"

McKINNEY: In the third movement of the *Concerto for Orchestra*, did you plan out the instrumental combinations?

HIGDON: That movement came out of requests from some of the players in the Philadelphia Orchestra about solos they wanted. And why not? It's a concerto for orchestra, and individuals make up an orchestra. So I actually drew out a little map for myself. Because the second movement was going to be just strings, I knew I couldn't start the third movement with string solos—the color contrast wouldn't be enough. So I decided right off the bat to start with the winds. I knew the brass would be the best to push the emotion up in a piece. So I thought I should do the winds first, then the string solos, and then I'll put the brass after. Just simply thinking about color made me design the piece the way that I did. I wasn't sure it was going to work, because that's a lot of different music compacted into small segments. But they seem to flow into each other, to my great surprise!

McKINNEY: Could you discuss the relationship between the composer and performer?

HIGDON: It's a symbiotic relationship. People often ask me if I work with the performers, and the answer is yes, definitely. I often work with the performers before I ever put pencil to paper. I find out what they like to play, what repertoire they've been playing. I look at the characteristics of the music that they choose for themselves. And then I figure out how I can make a sound world just for them—kind of like tailoring clothes that fit the individual. If I can't locate the ensemble or the soloist, which sometimes happens, I will ask the kids at Curtis to look at something. I might go into one of my classes and just ask them, "Does this work?" A perfect example is the second movement of the *Concerto for Orchestra*, the string movement. I have a series of *pizzicatos* moving quickly between the string sections. I took in a fragment of that to the students and said, "This is the tempo. How long can you do this *pizzicato* before you start feeling strain on your hands? Where is this going to be a problem for the players?" They actually showed me what for them was the straining point, and that's how I decided to divide up the *pizzicato*. I don't want it to be so uncomfortable it becomes problematic. So, talking with them actually helped design the architecture of the piece.

McKINNEY: Have you ever encountered sexism toward female composers in our musical culture?

HIGDON: You know, I don't think I have. I actually think that there are a lot of composers who have gone ahead of me, like Joan Tower and Libby Larsen, who helped kick the doors down. I think those women probably went through a lot more than I have, but I get enough performances, and hardly anyone ever says anything about the fact that I'm a woman. I don't think I have run into any barriers, but I think the women who have gone before definitely did. They have stories; those ladies did pave the way for us.

McKINNEY: In what direction do you see composition heading in the twenty-first century?

HIGDON: I suspect more new music is going to get done, because I notice younger people tend to respond to the newer stuff. The energy level of it, the rhythm, is closer to their pace of life than some of the older music. I think they'll eventually come to the older music by going through the new stuff. I think the new stuff is a doorway. In terms of where does the music go? I'm not really sure. I think it's better not to know; it will be a nice surprise to see how things develop. I like that there are so many different styles right now, because I love having variety in my concerts. For me, it's great having a mixture of styles and time periods in concerts, or even a mixture of instrumentation. I don't mind having concerts that mix up large ensembles, small ensembles, and solo works. I find that type of concert experience intriguing; it kind of feeds everyone's need. I often tell my composition students to pay attention to the audience. Find the point where they are getting restless in a piece, where you lose them, because that will teach you more about timing than anything. I notice our audiences and demographics—their expectation of the concert experience is shifting.

McKINNEY: Have you seen a shift in how audiences are responding to "new music"?

HIGDON: I've seen a major shift, and it surprises me how often people come up to me and say, "Thank goodness there's something new on the program!" This didn't used to be the case. It used to be people coming up and complaining about the new stuff. I just finished a residency with an orchestra where I had a bunch of public speaking engagements at bookstores and colleges. Quite a few people have said to me, "You know, I think I'm going to come back to the orchestra." They told me they had stopped going because the orchestras were doing the same pieces over and over. But now, because orchestras are doing some new stuff, these people were going to come back. I think in the past couple of weeks I've had three or four people say that to me. We have really turned some sort of corner.

McKINNEY: What do you think has made your music in particular more accessible?

HIGDON: I think it's the melody and the clear rhythm. Then the listener is able to follow the ideas. If you go into a room as a composer and say, "I believe in melody," usually the audience erupts into applause. I'm always amazed at the intensity of the reaction, even if you are just talking about the music and that you love a good tune. I think there's a certain clarity that has occurred, not that the other stuff wasn't clear, but it's just that we've had a change in the harmonic language, and people feel more comfortable now. I think there is a willingness to explore the more tonal aspects—both the performers and the audience members.

McKINNEY: How do you approach young composers who come to study with you?

HIGDON: I look at everyone individually. I look at my own background and how radically bizarre it was! I realize that every student needs something different. I don't have a set method for teaching. I literally spend time getting to know the students and their work processes—what they go through, what their problems are, what languages they write in—then I try to stretch them. I try to move them in directions they're not used to going so they can build a big toolbox of ways they can conquer problems. I have to teach them to problem solve. If it's a composer who is very prolific, I try to slow her down and have her write something over a longer period, where she really has to take time to think about each step. If it's a composer who has problems writing, and he can only write one piece a year, we'll do exercises where he only has two weeks to write a work. I'll push students to their extremes so they can figure out the method that works best for them. I've discovered some individuals who are more creative at night; some work better in the day. Some students need a huge amount of time; some need little chunks of time, with things in between. The kids often don't know what they need, so I try to find all the different things I can give them so they can problem solve on their own.

McKINNEY: And in what ways do you see yourself specifically trying to mentor this next generation of composers?

HIGDON: Just exploring. Questioning and exploring. Writing as much music as possible and making sure young composers get their music played, so they can hear it. I try to stay up on what's going on—not only in classical music, but also in rap, rock, all areas. I'm finding that a lot of the kids have so much background in other areas—it's good, for instance, to be able to address what's happening in the rap world in terms of rhythm! Sometimes I feel I learn just as much from my students as they do from me. It amazes me how much I learn from them.

ANALYSIS: *CONCERTO FOR ORCHESTRA* (2002)

Of the many turning points in Jennifer Higdon's career, the most significant came in the form of a 1998 commission from the Philadelphia Orchestra. The orchestra asked Higdon to write a commemorative piece as part of their centennial celebration, and the resultant work would become the composer's greatest orchestral contribution to date: the *Concerto for Orchestra.*[6]

Because of her affiliations with the Curtis Institute and the University of Pennsylvania, Jennifer Higdon was a perfect match for the Philadelphia Orchestra's centennial celebration commissioning series. Simon Woods, then artistic administrator for the orchestra, knew they were taking a chance on a relative unknown, but he clearly recalls that "there was just something about Higdon's music that we really liked, especially her distinctive harmonic vocabulary."[7] It was Woods who, early in the process, suggested to Higdon that her piece should be an orchestral concerto. Higdon had worked closely with members of the orchestra in chamber ensembles, and Woods felt this personal knowledge of the performers would enable the composer to tailor the work toward their individual talents.

The June 2002 premiere coincided with an annual meeting of the American Symphony Orchestra League, as well as the opening gala festivities for Philadelphia's new Verizon Hall at the Kimmel Center for the Performing Arts. At the time of the premiere, Higdon considered herself an unknown and believed everyone to have rather low expectations, but by the following morning, she found herself with sudden newfound notoriety, including a front-page picture in the *Philadelphia Inquirer. Inquirer* music critic and columnist David Patrick Stearns covered the premiere:

> No longer will Jennifer Higdon be just another promising Philadelphia composer. Last night, her first major orchestral work was premiered by the Philadelphia Orchestra—talk about starting at the top—with the kind of success many classical composers don't experience until after they're dead. . . . Higdon represents a conservative turn in composing styles—at least on the surface. Her "Concerto for Orchestra" has shamelessly ecstatic climaxes, scintillating interplay among instruments, and an orchestration that delivers wave after heart-stopping wave of intoxicating color.[8]

Higdon considers the time of the *Concerto for Orchestra* to have been pivotal, when musicians and audiences began to take notice of her music. Since the premiere, the work has received numerous performances by major orchestras, including the Dallas Symphony, the Pittsburgh Symphony, the Atlanta Symphony, the Milwaukee Symphony, the National Symphony, the Eugene Symphony, the Malmo Symphony (Sweden), and the New World Symphony. Additionally, it has been performed at music festivals around the world, including the 2003 Tanglewood Contemporary Music Festival and the 2004 Cabrillo Music Festival. The Telarc recording of the concerto, with Robert Spano and the Atlanta Symphony Orchestra, won the 2004 Grammy Award for best engineered album (classical), and the work was also nominated for best classical contemporary composition and best orchestral performance.

The moment I walked out onto the stage, and the audience rose to its feet, I don't think there was anyone more shocked than I was. My life literally changed within that week.

If there is a governing ideology over the whole of the piece, it is one of fluctuating color and texture. Undoubtedly linked to her study with George Crumb, Higdon's sentient, almost hyperacute awareness of tone color is perhaps the primary component of her compositional style, a gift regularly demonstrated through her orchestrations. But even for Higdon, the task of writing her first large-scale orchestral work was a daunting one. Before that time, she had composed several lengthy pieces for chamber ensembles but had never written an extended piece for orchestra, and she realized early in the process that she would need to rely heavily upon her instincts.

In addition to the formidable pressures of writing for the Philadelphia Orchestra, Higdon found herself fatefully contending with the events of September 11, 2001. Before the events of that day, she had been writing a largely bright and vivacious work, but afterward, her emotional status was understandably altered. To dilute the emotional impact, she was forced to set aside work on the *Concerto for Orchestra* until she was able to cleanse her spirit and finish it with the same energetic pace with which it began.

It was an interesting examination of how the emotion affects composing. It was as if someone had dumped black paint into my oranges, yellows, and reds. I knew if I tried to write immediately on top of that event, I would alter what the piece was about. I had to step back.

Higdon's *Concerto for Orchestra* follows the role models established by twentieth-century composers Béla Bartók and Witold Lutoslawski. Bartók's *Concerto for Orchestra* of 1943 and Lutoslawski's of 1954 are monumental pieces that heroically reflect the stalwart European tradition of the mid-twentieth century. These two landmark works have challenged orchestras for half a century, but Higdon believes her contribution to the genre to be the "most virtuosic in existence." She is quick to describe the difficulty of following those great masters:

The first thing I did was put away my Bartók score and recording. I love that piece! That and the Lutoslawski. I love them both so much, I knew if I didn't stop looking and listening to those pieces I wouldn't be able to write my own concerto. They are such strong works with such an incredible harmonic language—even the way the instruments relate to each other. For four years I didn't look at or listen to either one of them; it was a moratorium for those two.

As part of the planning process for the *Concerto for Orchestra*, Higdon laid out for herself a map of the individual movements, in order to establish what would eventually be the high and low points of the work. She hoped such careful planning would aid her in creating smooth transitions and a logical flow between (and within) each movement. Her working relationships with individual players in the orchestra also helped in this endeavor, as she began to consider shaping the numerous solo passages within.

The *Concerto* is scored for a large orchestra, including an extensive battery of percussion. Higdon constructed the piece in five movements, with no pause between the fourth and fifth. The overall shape takes on an arch form, where the outer movements are designed to feature the full orchestra, while the inner movements focus on individual sections: the string section (movement II), the wind section (movement III), and the percussion section (movement IV). In an effort to understand the composer's compositional processes and the various elements that have helped make her *Concerto for Orchestra* such an enormous success, we will examine the first movement in some detail. But because Higdon actually composed the first movement last of the five, let us first consider synopses of the other movements so that we may appropriately place the opening in the context of the work entire.

Movement II

The laconic second movement is the shortest in duration and functions as a scherzo, in which Higdon was seeking to centerpiece the much celebrated Philadelphia Orchestra string section. The movement begins with *pizzicato*; various string techniques, including *sul tasto* and *à la guitara*, heighten the drama; and Higdon closes the movement with a final "snap" *pizzicato* (à la Bartók). To speak to the concerto format, she features a quintet of *arco* strings accompanied by *pizzicato*.

Example 4.10. *Concerto for Orchestra*, II, mm. 22–25

Higdon provides solo passages for each of the principal players as she creates contrast and shape with various idiomatic string techniques, clever orchestration, and divergence between rhythmic and lyrical styles. We find also in the second movement an example of the composer utilizing polyrhythm to create textural density. In the following example, note how the violins and violas move in parallel octaves, while the cello and bass maintain a polyrhythmic ostinato. The scalar material is diatonic, but the added F-sharp makes a move toward Lydian mode. Contrary motion toward the end of this flowing passage creates a strong sense of arrival at the end of the phrase.

Example 4.11.   *Concerto for Orchestra,* II, mm. 103–106

The second movement was written around bodies of water. First, I was in Pensacola, Florida, at a music festival; then in Los Angeles where Cheryl had a convention; and then in Chicago, where I kept looking out the window at Lake Michigan. I think it did influence the music (which reminds me of wind blowing on water), and I can still see those hotel rooms very vividly in my mind.[9]

Movement III

The third movement is the longest in duration and functions as the apex of the overall arch form. This movement, composed first of the five, features mystical, ethereal sounds created by *portamento* effects and miscellaneous harmonics in the string section. Higdon utilizes extensive solo writing in a primarily tonal harmonic language, relying heavily upon major chord structures. She uses such structures, however, in a manner as to rather disguise their traditional tonal contexts. In several sections of the third movement, we find a series of major chords in an accompanimental role to the primary melodic material.

Example 4.12. *Concerto for Orchestra*, III, mm. 42–55

In the above passage, the trombones are moving through a series of major chords while the cello and contrabass emphasize particular pitches within those triadic structures. It is the oboe, then, that weaves the melodic line, introducing Higdon's cardinal intervallic motive of the minor sixth.

> *I worried about the oboe solo accompanied by three trombones, so at the first rehearsal, I tried having those trombones muted. But it wasn't a lush sound. So we removed the mutes, and I said, "That's it, right there!"*[10]

A similar moment occurs later in the movement, when the woodwind section is introduced. The first phrase utilizes three clarinets moving in the key of D-flat major, while the second violin oscillates between G-flat and A-flat (this oscillation between two pitches in a dramatic rhythmic pattern is another favored Higdon technique). The composer's penchant for counterpoint is evidenced by the clarinet parts.

Example 4.13. *Concerto for Orchestra*, III, mm. 78–84

During the second phrase, Higdon eliminates the second clarinet and bass clarinet to bring forth a lyrical solo passage. While the previous rhythmic phrase was established in D-flat, the clarinet solo moves directly into the key of B-flat major. For the accompaniment, Higdon returns to major chord structures, this time presented by muted trumpets. The chordal structures, having little to do with B-flat, functionally speaking, create an opaque harmonic foundation for the tonal melody.

Example 4.14. *Concerto for Orchestra*, III, mm. 85–94

This movement of the concerto features the bulk of the solo writing, much of which was tailor-made for specific players in the Philadelphia Orchestra (Higdon was often approached by individual players who would make specific requests for their exclusive moments). There are solo opportunities for every principal string, woodwind, and brass player in the orchestra, a difficult (and rarely attempted) feat for any composer. The myriad solo passages, which employ the minor sixth as the primary intervallic motive, unfold in the following manner:

m. 13: Flute 1, 2, and 3, accompanied by harp, piano, and major chords in viola and cello.

m. 42: Oboe 1, 2, and 3, accompanied by major chords in the trombones and lower strings.

m. 78: Clarinet 1, 2, and bass, accompanied by major chords in the trumpets (muted).

m. 95: Bassoon 1, 2, and contra, accompanied by punctuated major chords in the flutes and violins.

m. 113: A *tutti* orchestra moment built on various major chords.

m. 131: Contrabass solo, accompanied by oscillating figures in the flute and clarinet.

m. 140: Second violin solo, accompanied by oscillating figures in the oboe and bassoon.

m. 146: Cello solo, accompanied by oscillating figures in the flute and vibraphone.

m. 152: Viola solo.

m. 159: First violin solo.

m. 172: A return to the opening "mystical" sounds: *portamento* and harmonics.

m. 177: Brass chorale with prominent usage of minor sixth interval. Solos are provided for every player in the brass section. The brass is used to propel the energy into the following *tutti*.

m. 210: *Tutti* moment relying on major chord structures.

m. 239: A woodwind quartet (flute, oboe, clarinet, and bassoon).

m. 246: A contrapuntal first violin solo in the key of C major. The movement finishes with a return to metallic percussion and string harmonics to create a smooth transition into the fourth movement.

Movement IV

The fourth movement was born of a conversation between Higdon and Philadelphia Orchestra timpanist Don Liuzzi. Liuzzi requested that Higdon write a timpani part which would also require him to play traditional percussion, an opportunity rarely afforded an orchestral player. That discussion evolved into an entire movement designed to showcase the percussion section. But Higdon was after something more than just giving the percussionists "more to do." Higdon's percussion writing is melodious, even lyrical; she purposely tries to break traditional expectations of the percussion section by beginning the movement with delicate and subdued sounds. At the opening, Higdon calls for four bowed vibraphones and crotales (see example 4.15).

I realized that percussion is the section of the orchestra that has grown and advanced the most during the twentieth century. So, this being a new work at the beginning of the twenty-first century, it seemed logical to highlight that section. Coupled with this was the fact that I love percussion, and I've had the good fortune of working with the various members of the Philadelphia Orchestra percussion section. I wanted to write something for them specifically.[11]

Example 4.15.   *Concerto for Orchestra*, IV, mm. 1–5

I used bowing to start that movement because I wanted the percussion movement to contain the quietest part of the entire piece, which is not what most people would expect.[12]

An additional challenge for the performers in this movement is its progressive temporal evolution. The movement begins at quarter note equal to forty-two and steadily accelerates through sixty, eighty, and ninety. The final arrival tempo establishes a direct transition into the fifth movement. During this gradual *accelerando*, the percussionists are also shifting from the pitched percussion instruments toward the nonpitched instruments. Higdon describes this entire process as "a Victrola being wound up." An additional level of energy is accomplished through *portamento* in the timpani and the strident chromaticism of the piano.

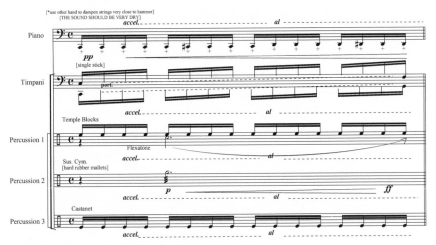

Example 4.16.   *Concerto for Orchestra,* IV, m. 50

Movement V

In 1999, Higdon completed a six-minute orchestral work entitled *Fanfare Ritmico*. Realizing she was about to begin the commission for the *Concerto for Orchestra*, Higdon used *Fanfare Ritmico* to experiment with textures and sonorities she thought she might employ in the upcoming concerto. It is interesting to note correlations between the two works; for instance, in both *Fanfare Ritmico* and the fifth movement of the *Concerto for Orchestra*, Higdon favors a pointillistic orchestrational style. In examples 4.17a and 4.17b, the piano figure is accenting the different voices of the brass section.

Example 4.17a.   *Fanfare Ritmico,* mm. 202–205

Example 4.17b. *Concerto for Orchestra,* V, mm. 160–163

The polychords in example 4.17b, divorced by a major second, are another part of the natural "sound world" of Higdon's harmonic language,
an instinctual sonoral choice. The composer has stated that she often
"chases sounds" and will experiment and improvise until she finds a suitable match for her aural imagery.

Analysis of Movement I

With a basic understanding of the other four movements in hindsight, we
may more readily understand the problem Higdon was confronting as
she approached conception of the opening movement. She remembers it
being by far the most difficult to write because she had already composed
such a vast amount of material, and finding a way to go back and begin
the piece proved a real challenge. "It took writing the other four movements to create a clear picture of what was needed to start this virtuosic
tour-de-force," Higdon recalls.[13]

The first movement utilizes the full orchestra in a frenzy of rhythmic
and harmonic activity. On the surface, the movement may seem to have
little melodic content; however, Higdon's compositional style allows
the harmonic structure and orchestral texture to function as melody.
Additionally, she relies heavily on intricate rhythmic counterpoint to
achieve the overall melodic content. Her ability to manipulate orchestral sound is a vital contributing factor to the success of this work and
many others.

To speak to the formal design of the first movement, we must remember that Higdon typically achieves form not through application of any

standardized structure but through scrupulous manipulation of melodic and intervallic motives. She unites small armies of motivic cells, rallying them together as a unifying force. For the listener, this approach laces her music with the aural perception of form, along with a palpable sense of perpetual development. We find ourselves repeatedly struck by the same thought: "Hey, there's that *thing* again, but it's changed—it's evolving." The design of the first movement of the *Concerto for Orchestra* is no exception; herein lies a complicated amalgamation of ideas, meticulously woven together:

mm. 1–28:	Introduction of the primary intervallic motive by timpani and chimes.
mm. 29–50:	*Tutti* arrival, extensive use of polychordal structures.
mm. 51–57:	Transition utilizing octatonic scales by bass clarinet and piccolo.
mm. 58–81:	Intervallic motive outlined in various instruments.
mm. 82–122:	Series of quartets (strings, woodwinds, and brasses).
mm. 123–152:	Retransition to the opening texture using primary intervallic motives.
mm. 153–166:	*Tutti* arrival, similar to measure 29.
mm. 167–186:	Transition utilizing perfect fifth intervals and whole-tone scales.
mm. 187–196:	Transition, similar to measure 51, utilizing octatonic scales.
mm. 197–204:	Woodwind quartet.
mm. 205–213:	Transition utilizing metallic percussion and solo harp.
mm. 214–235:	Brass quartet, similar to measure 104.
mm. 236–end:	Coda, D-flat/A-flat pedal point, major chords and the opening motive.

I just let the music unfold. That causes funny responses. At universities, people will ask about the form of one of my pieces, and I say it's through-composed. And then they always look at me very puzzled.[14]

The *Concerto for Orchestra* begins with the timpani and chimes stating the primary motivic material in octave doublings. This motive, featuring a perfect fourth quickly expanding to a tritone, returns periodically throughout the movement in various guises and serves to unify the movement. To complement the primary motive, Higdon layers scalar patterns in the strings with sparse rhythmic interruptions in the horns. Many of the scale patterns rely on the octatonic scale or some derivative of it.

Example 4.18.   *Concerto for Orchestra*, I, mm. 1–7

As the piece gains momentum, Higdon begins to layer the woodwinds and strings in similar scalar patterns while transplanting the rhythmic interruptions to the trombones. The opening timpani-chime motive returns in measure 17, but at a new pitch level. By layering these many diverse lines, Higdon begins to fill her canvas with a dense texture of orchestral color. This type of contrapuntal aggregation is central to her style, a technique described by the composer as "clocks moving at different speeds." In example 4.19, we see the composer outlining four strands of counterpoint, and the instrumental doublings create an aural sense of even further contrapuntal activity. As the musical lines suddenly shift upward by a major second, the listener is swept along with them—Higdon has captured the ear through utilization of recognizable gestures, and now she is able to lead the listener willingly forward.

Example 4.19. *Concerto for Orchestra, I, mm. 23–26*

Higdon's partiality for polychordal structures, evidenced throughout the *Concerto*, is exhibited again in this opening movement. She typically employs these structures at climactic moments, or occasionally as a transitional tool, and the usual arrangement is that of two major triads stacked a major second apart. We find this precise arrangement within the string section (and doubled by upper woodwinds) beginning measure 29 (see example 4.20).

The rapid scalar passages in the piano are largely diatonic and function within the harmonic structure of the polychords, and the trumpets supply a descending pattern of major triads. But because Higdon marks them to be played *mezzo piano*, she achieves a unique texture in which the trumpets find themselves in a subsidiary role to the polychordal strings. Robert Spano remarked that Higdon "can make a common triad sound fresh, inventive and new."[15]

Example 4.20.   *Concerto for Orchestra*, I, mm. 29–34

After the first large-scale point of arrival in measure 29, Higdon returns to the opening motive, again placed in the orchestral bells, but this time found in sequences of a perfect fourth followed by a tritone.

Example 4.21.   *Concerto for Orchestra*, I, mm. 46–49

She has manipulated a change, christening what was a rather simple motive into a powerful unifying entity of the entire movement. But there is such subtlety to her process; the listener doesn't feel coerced, but simply led forward by a calculated hand. This is another Higdon thumbprint—her exceptional ability to appeal to both sides of the audience's brain. She offers logic and grace simultaneously, so all hearers feel welcomed.

During a brief transition, beginning measure 51, Higdon features a fanciful duet between bass clarinet and piccolo. The bass clarinet employs the octatonic scale based on A-natural, but the piccolo scale is constructed around C-natural. These polyharmonic scale patterns are accompanied by an E-natural pedal point in the flutes and vibraphone (common tone to both scales), affording a satisfying "centeredness" to the sound. The unlikely pair makes their dance together, twisting and spinning to Higdon's music.

Example 4.22. *Concerto for Orchestra*, I, mm. 51–57

Higdon's overall objective in the first movement is to provide precisely these sorts of solo opportunities for various players in the orchestra. And during the next section she begins the process in earnest, exposing the strings, woodwinds, and brass instruments in a series of quartets. The string and woodwind quartets maintain the energetic pulse fundamental to the rest of the movement, but the brass quartet offers a rather significant lyrical contrast (see example 4.23).

This quartet features an accompanimental ostinato in the marimba that settles into a D-flat/A-flat pedal point, while the brass centers in the key of G-flat major. Higdon injects further variety into the tonality by fluctuating between B-flat and B-natural (this is particularly evident in the trumpet part, which takes on the primary melodic material). We should also note the before-mentioned pitch oscillation technique, seen here in the harp part. At the end of the brass quartet, Higdon lands squarely on an E-natural/B-natural open fifth, followed by a return of the string quartet, performing a series of descending major triads (see example 4.24).

This series of chords begins a short retransition section constructed with fragments of the opening motive. Higdon places whole-tone scale patterns in the woodwinds while the strings and muted trumpet add to the texture through a series of trills. This is a typical Higdonesque moment, as a series of overlapping lines work together to create a sonorous background. As the retransition draws to a close, the second trumpet signals the return of the opening motive at the original pitch level (see example 4.25).

Example 4.23. *Concerto for Orchestra,* I, mm. 105–114

The following *tutti* section yields a texture reminiscent of the opening. There is, again, extensive use of polychords in the strings and upper woodwinds, while the brass instruments sound a series of major chords. In these *tutti* passages, the rhythmically active polychordal structures

Example 4.24. *Concerto for Orchestra,* I, mm. 116–117

Example 4.25. *Concerto for Orchestra*, I, mm. 133–136

actually form the melodic material, as Higdon draws forth melodic lines from the existing harmonic substructure. Similar to the passage at measure 29, the horns play a significant role by supplying a countermelody, enhancing the overall direction of the musical phrase. The trumpets accompany this countermelody with parallel major chords.

Example 4.26. *Concerto for Orchestra*, I, mm. 153–157

But unlike the opening *tutti* passage, where the counterpoint remained independent, this section climaxes with a grand-scale statement from the winds and strings, powerfully outlining a series of major triads before crashing to an end with a barrage of scalar passages in measure 164. A combination of whole-tone, chromatic, and octatonic scales is interwoven, creating a clouded atmosphere of variegated sound. The intermixture of these scale structures in contrary motion toward the end of measure 166 propels the music toward the apex of the movement (see example 4.27).

As the scale patterns complete the musical phrases leading into the next section, we find Higdon exploring perfect fifth intervals, both vertically and horizontally. These perfect fifths serve as underpinning for another statement of the opening motive (this time in the lower strings, tuba, and contrabassoon), while the woodwinds furnish accompanying whole-tone scales. The layering of these elements again reveals the complexities within Higdon's writing (see example 4.28).

The brass instruments continue the flowing undercurrent of perfect fifths until the texture finally dissipates into music reminiscent of the passage beginning in measure 51 (see example 4.24). But unlike that earlier passage, which paired bass clarinet with piccolo, Higdon writes this later passage for bassoon and oboe, in similar roles. The octatonic scale construction remains the same, as does the E-natural pedal point, but to bring further variety to the passage, Higdon transposes the scale patterns down a minor second to be centered on A-flat in the bassoon and C-sharp in the oboe (see example 4.29).

Example 4.27. *Concerto for Orchestra*, I, mm. 164–166

Remembering the composer's proclivity for metallic percussion sounds, we might have anticipated her choosing to accompany a delicate duet between harp and celesta (beginning measure 205) with a variety of ringing percussion instruments, including triangle, glockenspiel, crotales, and vibraphone. The pitch array she employs during this section signifies B-flat major, but Higdon alternates freely between D-natural and D-flat.

Example 4.28. *Concerto for Orchestra*, I, mm. 172–174

Example 4.29. *Concerto for Orchestra*, I, mm. 190–194

Because she is a composer who writes by instinct, her relationship to a tonal center is fleeting, far less important than the individual line.

Example 4.30. *Concerto for Orchestra*, I, mm. 205–213

As the metallic sounds retreat into the background, Higdon continues to recapitulate her primary materials, ending with a return of the brass quartet (from measure 104). She uses a similar marimba pedal point and melodic material but expands this section with an additional ten measures, leading directly to the coda.

Throughout this first movement, Higdon has, with minimal diversion, maintained an intense rhythmic energy; the calm nature of the coda may therefore come as something of a surprise to the listener. She chose to end in this manner in order to establish an appropriate atmosphere for the dawn of the second movement (which we remember begins with *pizzicato* strings). For the coda, Higdon maintains the D-flat/A-flat pedal point established by the marimba, and she continues to accompany with major chord structures, but there are many other layers cleverly hidden within the texture of the orchestra, including a statement of the opening motive in the vibraphone. The combination of these myriad elements brings unity to the first movement, which ends quietly with D-flat major against E-flat major, a final souvenir of the polyharmonicism that dominates the work.

Example 4.31. *Concerto for Orchestra*, I, mm. 236–243

With Jennifer Higdon's *Concerto for Orchestra* comes a notable representation of the composer's stylistic approaches. Throughout each of the concerto's five movements, Higdon exhibits a musical voice proven to be accessible to a widespread audience. She has likewise confirmed that, as a composer of contemporary music, it is conceivable to rise from beneath the shadows of the great masters, to create something new and provocative which will invigorate, educate, and yes, even entertain the listener. A triumph on many fronts, this monumental work is already shaping and forming a new vision of what it means to write concert music in the twenty-first century.

CODA

That's what I love about music—it speaks to everyone, and I love that possibility![16]

In April of 2010, Jennifer Higdon was awarded the Pulitzer Prize in music for her dazzling *Violin Concerto*. The work was premiered on February 6, 2009, with Hilary Hahn and the Indianapolis Symphony, conducted by Mario Venzago. Higdon's concerto is the first orchestral score by a self-published composer to receive this accolade. The premiere recording, on the *Deutsche Grammophon* label, is slated for release in September 2010, with Hahn and the Royal Liverpool Philharmonic Orchestra, conducted by Vasily Petrenko. The Higdon piece will be paired with the Tchaikovsky violin concerto for the recording.[17]

Higdon continues to be active as one of the most-performed compos-ers of the early twenty-first century. She describes her process as almost purely instinctual. Her keen ear, coupled with a lack of adherence to any traditional stylized system, has allowed her to develop a remarkably individual voice. Her harmonic and melodic inventiveness has certainly struck a chord with today's audiences.

Many commissions will keep Higdon busy through the 2010–2011 concert season and beyond. Current works include *On a Wire*, commis-sioned by the chamber ensemble eighth blackbird, which will premiere it in June of 2010 with the Atlanta Symphony Orchestra. Additionally, the San Francisco Opera has commissioned Higdon's first opera, which is set to premiere in the fall of 2013.

As a Renaissance woman, with expertise in composition, publishing, performance, and conducting, not to mention her insatiable enthusiasm for life, Higdon continues to provide significant contributions to the classical music world and inspire the next generation of musicians and patrons. There can be little doubt that the precedent she has set will remain strong through generations. With such an impassioned torch-bearer, how could one but follow?

NOTES

1. Unless otherwise cited, all quotes and personal information stem from personal correspondence between the author and the composer; permission for their usage has been granted by the composer. The photograph here is used by permission of J. D. Scott.

2. Andrew Quint, "Speaking with Composer Jennifer Higdon: The Communication Thing," *Fanfare* 27, no. 5 (May/June 2005): 44.

3. Jason Victor Serinus, "The Award-Winning Jennifer Higdon," *Secrets of Home Theater and High Fidelity*, June 2005, www.hometheaterhifi.com (accessed March 6, 2007).

4. Diana Burgwyn, "Positive Energy: With Characteristic Enterprise and Exuberance, Composer Jennifer Higdon Has Built a Multi-Layered Life in Music," *Symphony Magazine* 53 (July/August 2002): 56.

5. Molly Sheridan, "Jennifer Higdon Promoted at Curtis," *NewMusicBox*, November 1, 2001, www.newmusicbox.org (accessed March 12, 2007).

6. As part of the celebration, the orchestra commissioned eight works from leading composers: James MacMillan, Aaron Jay Kernis, Richard Danielpour, Einojuhani Rautavaara, Hannibal Peterson, Michael Daugherty, and Roberto Sierra. The commissioned works were performed over a four-year period.

7. Burgwyn, "Positive Energy," 53.

8. David Patrick Stearns, "Jennifer Higdon: 'Concerto for Orchestra,'" *International Alliance for Women in Music Journal* 8, no. 3 (2002): 46.

9. David Patrick Stearns, "Jennifer Higdon," *Andante Magazine*, June 2002, www.andante.com (accessed March 4, 2007).

10. Stearns, "Jennifer Higdon."

11. John Tafoya, "Jennifer Higdon's 'Concerto for Orchestra,'" *Percussive Notes* 42 (April 2004): 49.

12. Tafoya, "Jennifer Higdon's 'Concerto for Orchestra,'" 49.

13. Robert Spano, liner notes, *City Scape: Concerto for Orchestra*, compact disc, Telarc CD-80620.

14. Stearns, "Jennifer Higdon."

15. Richard Dyer, "Composer Has Emotional Reach, Direct Appeal: Jennifer Higdon Touches Many with Her Work," *Boston Globe*, July 13, 2003, N4.

16. Photo here used by permission of Candace DiCarlo.

17. "Jennifer Higdon Awarded Pulitzer Prize in Music." *NewMusicBox*, April 12, 2010, www.newmusicbox.org/article.nmbx?id=6335&utm_source=twitterfeed &utm_medium=twitter.

APPENDIX A: LIST OF WORKS

[All works, unless noted, are published by Lawdon Press and are available through www.jenniferhigdon.com]

Orchestral

Shine (1995)—symphony orchestra
blue cathedral (1999)—symphony orchestra
Fanfare Ritmico (1999)—symphony orchestra
Wind Shear (2000)—orchestral winds and horns
City Scape (2002)—symphony orchestra

Movements:

- *SkyLine*
- *river sings a song to trees*
- *Peachtree Street*

Concerto for Orchestra (2002)—symphony orchestra
Machine (2002)—symphony orchestra
Dooryard Bloom (2004)—baritone solo, orchestra; Walt Whitman, text
Loco (2004)—symphony orchestra
Oboe Concerto (2005)—oboe solo, orchestra
Percussion Concerto (2005)—percussion solo, orchestra
Trombone Concerto (2005)—trombone solo, orchestra
Light (2006)—symphony orchestra
Piano Concerto (2006)—piano solo, orchestra
Spirit (2006)—orchestral brass, percussion

String Orchestra

"String" from *Concerto for Orchestra* (2002)
Celebration Fanfare (2003)
To The Point (2004)

Wind Ensemble and Band

Fanfare Ritmico (2002-wind ensemble version/1999-orchestral version)
Rhythm Stand (2004)—young concert band
    *Note: This piece is not published by Lawdon Press.
Kelly's Field (2006)—concert band

Choral

Deep in the Night (1997)—SATB choir
Southern Grace (1998)—SATB choir
Imagine (1999)—TTBB choir (also arranged for SATB choir); Donna Red Wing, text
A Quiet Moment (1999)—TTBB choir/SSAA choir (also arranged for SATB choir)
Sing, Sing (1999)—SATB choir
Sanctus (2001)—SSAATTBB choir (text in English and Latin)
O magnum mysterium (2002)—SATB choir, 2 flutes, 2 crystal glasses, chimes
This Singing Art (2004)—SATB choir, chimes, and organ
Voice of the Bard (2005)—TTBB choir; William Blake, text
somewhere i have never travelled, gladly beyond (2006)—SATB choir, vibraphone,
    piano; e. e. cummings, text

Songs, Sets, Cycles

In Our Quiet (1992)—soprano or mezzo-soprano, piano
Notes on Love (1992)—soprano, flute, piano
Lake Blue Sky (1994)—mezzo-soprano, flute, clarinet, violin, cello, piano, percussion
Wedding Hymn (1995)—soprano, flute, piano (version A); 2 flutes, piano (version B); Sidney Lanier, text
Morning Opens (1997)—soprano, piano
To Home (1998)—soprano, piano
breaking (1999)—soprano, piano
Hop & Toe Dance (2001)—soprano, piano
Bentley Roses (2002)—mezzo-soprano, flute, piano; James Whitcomb Riley, text
Falling (2003)—voice, piano; text by the composer, part of a collection of Valentine songs written over the years
Songs (2003)—soprano, piano
Threaded (2003)—mezzo-soprano, piano
Dooryard Bloom (2004)—baritone, orchestra
Red (2004)—bass-baritone and piano; Eric Owens, text

Instrumental

KEYBOARD

Secret & Glass Gardens (2000)—solo piano

WINDS

When Souls Meet (1982)—flute, piano
The Jeffrey Mode (1984)—flute, piano
Mountain Songs (1985)—flute choir
Solitudes (1987)—3 C flutes, alto flute
Steeley Pause (1988)—4 C flutes
rapid.fire (1992)—solo flute
Autumn Reflection (1994)—flute, piano
Autumn Music (1995)—woodwind quintet
Song (1995)—solo flute
running the edgE (1996)—2 flutes, piano
Short Stories (1996)—saxophone quartet
Legacy (1999)—flute, piano
Amazing Grace (2002)—flute choir
Bop (2004)—saxophone quartet

BRASS

Ceremonies (2001)—organ, brass
Movements: 7 (3 for solo organ)
Trumpet Songs (2004)—trumpet, piano

STRINGS

Autumn's Cricket (1987)—string quartet
String Trio (1988)—violin, viola, cello
Sonata for Viola and Piano (1990)—viola, piano
Voices (1993)—string quartet
Sky Quartet (1997, rev. 2001)—string quartet
Legacy (2003)—violin, piano
Amazing Grace (2003)—string quartet
Impressions (2003)—string quartet
Southern Harmony (2003)—string quartet
An Exaltation of Larks (2005)—string quartet
Quiet Art (2006)—string octet (4 violins, 2 violas, 2 cellos)
String Poetic (2006)—violin, piano

PERCUSSION

ZONES (1991/ version B completed 2003)—percussion quartet, CD (version A); percussion quintet, CD (version B)
Splendid Wood (2006)—marimba ensemble (3 marimbas; 6 players)

MIXED CHAMBER ENSEMBLE

Soliloquy (1989)—3 scorings

- English horn, string orchestra
- Cello, string orchestra
- Clarinet, string quartet (2004)

Lullaby (1991)—8 scorings

- mezzo-soprano, flute, piano (version A)
- 2 flutes, piano (version B)
- flute quartet (version C)
- soprano saxophone, flute, piano (version D)
- 2 alto saxophones, piano (version E)
- soprano saxophone, alto saxophone, piano (version F)
- soprano, alto saxophone, piano (version G)
- flute, clarinet, piano (version H)

Notes on Love (1992)—soprano, flute, piano (8 songs, which may be performed individually and/or in any combination)
Lake Blue Sky (1994)—mezzo-soprano, flute, clarinet, violin, cello, piano, percussion
Wild Man Dances (1995)—3 flutes, clarinet, 2 saxophones, trumpet, trombone, 3 percussion

Wedding Hymn (1995)—3 scorings; Sidney Lanier, text

- soprano, flute, piano (version A)
- 2 flutes, piano (version B)
- flute, clarinet, piano (version C)

wissahickon poeTrees (1998)—flute, clarinet, violin, viola, cello, piano, percussion
Scenes from the Poet's Dreams (1999)—piano quintet (piano left hand, string quartet)
Celestial Hymns (2000)—clarinet, violin, viola, cello, piano
Dark Wood (2001)—bassoon, violin, cello, piano

DASH (2001)—(2 scorings)

- clarinet, violin, piano (version A)
- flute, clarinet, piano (version B)

Light Refracted (2002)—clarinet, violin, viola, cello, piano
Piano Trio (2003)—violin, cello, piano
Trio Song (2003)—2 flutes, cello
Zaka (2003)—flute, clarinet, violin, cello, piano, percussion
Zango Bandango (2003)—flute, clarinet, violin, cello, marimba, piano
Summer Shimmers (2004)—piano, woodwind quintet
Smash (2005)—flute, clarinet, violin, viola, cello, and piano

APPENDIX B: DISCOGRAPHY

Autumn Music. Moran Woodwind Quintet. Crystal Records. "Postcards from the Center."
Autumn Reflection. Jeffrey Khaner, flute; Hugh Sung, piano. Avie AV 0004. "American Flute Music."
Autumn Reflection. The Jeffrey Mode. Lullaby. rapid.fire. Steeley Pause. Sonata for Viola and Piano. Voices. Jennifer Higdon, flute; Hugh Sung, piano; Michael Isaac Strauss, viola; Pat Spencer, Jayn Rosenfeld, Jennifer Higdon, Stephanie Starin, flutes; Nicholas Kitchen, violin; Melissa Kleinbart, violin; Hsin-Yun Huang, viola; Wilhelmina Smith, cello. I Virtuosi IVR 501. "rapid.fire."
blue cathedral. Atlanta Symphony Orchestra—Robert Spano, conductor. Telarc 80596. "Rainbow Body."
blue cathedral. Bowling Green Philharmonia; Emily Freeman Brown, conductor. Albany Records TROY 633. "New Music From Bowling Green, Vol. 3."
City Scape. Atlanta Symphony Orchestra; Robert Spano, conductor. Telarc 80620. "Higdon: City Scape/Concerto for Orchestra."
Concerto for Orchestra. Atlanta Symphony Orchestra; Robert Spano, conductor. Telarc 80620. "Higdon: City Scape/Concerto for Orchestra."
DASH. Verdehr Trio. Crystal Records 946. "Making of a Medium, Vol. 16: International Connections."
Deep in the Night. New York Concert Singers; Judith Clurman, conductor. New World Records 80592-2. "A Season's Promise."
Impressions. Piano Trio. Voices. Cypress String Quartet, Anne Akiko Meyers, Alisa Weilerstein, Adam Neiman, Nick Kitchen, Melissa Kleinbart, Hsin-Yun Huang, and Mina Smith. Naxos 8.559298. "Jennifer Higdon: Piano Trio/Voices / Impressions."
O magnum mysterium. Handel and Haydn Society Chorus and Orchestra; Grant Llewellyn, conductor. Avie AVI 2078. "All Is Bright."

rapid.fire. Patti Monson, flute. Composers Recordings CRI 867. "Conspirare: Chamber Music for Solo Flute."

running the edge. Claudia Anderson, Jill Felber, flute; John Piirainen, piano. Composers Recordings (CRI) CD 780. "Lesbian American Composers."

running the edge. Jill Felber, Claudia Anderson, flutes; Betty Oberacker, Jeremy Haladyna, piano. Neuma 450-101. "Zawa! Landmark Duos for Flutes."

Soliloquy. Kate Dilligham, cello; Moscow Symphony Orchestra; Alexei Kornienko, conductor. Kate Dillingham. "Kate Dillingham, cello with the Moscow Symphony Orchestra."

Song. Laurel Zucker, flute. Cantilena Records. "Inflorescence II—Music for Solo Flute."

Southern Harmony. Ying Quartet. Quartz QTZ 2055. "United States: Life Music 2."

Steeley Pause. Claudia Anderson, Jill Felber, Julianna Moore, Karen Yonovitz, flute. Centaur CRC 2203. "American Flute."

wissahickon poeTrees. Network for New Music Ensemble; Jan Krzywicki, conductor. Albany Records TROY 488. "Dream Journal."

Zaka. eighth blackbird. Cedille 9000-094. "Strange Imaginary Animals."

SOURCES

Aquilina, Florence. "An Interview with Jennifer Higdon." *Journal of the International Alliance for Women in Music* 6, nos. 1/2 (2000): 1–4.

Burgwyn, Diana. "Positive Energy: With Characteristic Enterprise and Exuberance, Composer Jennifer Higdon Has Built a Multi-Layered Life in Music." *Symphony Magazine* 53 (July/August 2002): 52–57.

Dyer, Richard. "Composer Has Emotional Reach: Direct Appeal Jennifer Higdon Touches Many with Her Work." *The Boston Globe*, July 13, 2003, N4.

Phillips, Brenda Rossow. "Jennifer Higdon: A Stylistic Analysis of Selected Flute and Orchestral Works." D.M.A. diss., Arizona State University, 2005.

Quint, Andrew. "Speaking with Composer Jennifer Higdon: The Communication Thing." *Fanfare* 27, no. 5 (May/June 2005): 42–46.

Serinius, Jason Victor. "The Award-Winning Jennifer Higdon." *Secrets of Home Theater and High Fidelity*, June 2005. www.hometheaterhifi.com (accessed March 6, 2007).

Sheridan, Molly. "Jennifer Higdon Promoted at Curtis." *NewMusicBox*, November 1, 2001. www.newmusicbox.org (accessed March 12, 2007).

Spano, Robert. Liner notes, *City Scape, Concerto for Orchestra*. Compact Disc. Telarc CD-80620.

Stearns, David Patrick. "Jennifer Higdon." *Andante Magazine*, June 2002. www.andante.com (accessed March 4, 2007).

———. "Jennifer Higdon: 'Concerto for Orchestra.'" *Journal of the International Alliance for Women in Music* 8, no. 3 (2002): 46.

Tafoya, John. "Jennifer Higdon's 'Concerto for Orchestra.'" *Percussive Notes* 42 (April 2004): 48–55.

Valdes, Lesley. "Renaissance Woman." *Penn Sounds* 11 (Spring 2000): 4.

Tina Milhorn Stallard

LIBBY LARSEN (1950–)

*Maybe it's exuberance that people don't really know about me. I actually am
exuberant, which makes for a very active mind. There's a lot of exuberance in
my music. That's not a value that has been talked about much at all in relationship to music. Mozart was an exuberant. Bach probably was, too. How could
they do all of that? People always ask me how I do all of this. I think to myself,
"I can't not do this"*[1]

Libby Larsen's scores exhibit a pronounced *joie de vivre*, along with a
seemingly keen understanding of the spiritual soul. A midwestern upbringing instilled within this composer a broad global view and the value
of the life of the mind, manifested in the cultural awareness central to her
compositions and her staunch dedication to arts advocacy.

Elizabeth "Libby" Larsen was born in Wilmington, Delaware, on December 24, 1950. At the age of three, her family moved to Minneapolis,
Minnesota, where she continues to reside. Larsen's first musical memories are as observer—her older sister received piano lessons in the home,
and a three-year-old Larsen would carefully watch and listen. Following
the lesson, she would make her way to the piano and imitate the sounds
she had heard. Larsen often credits her midwestern roots as a particularly important influence, in that there was so much group music making
in the home. She sometimes mentions Garrison Keillor's popular radio

program "Prairie Home Companion" when she wants to explain Minnesota's thriving amateur music culture to non-Minnesotans.

Larsen's earliest formal musical training began at Christ the King School in Minneapolis, where she learned to read and sing Gregorian chant. The rhythmic flexibility and prosody of text found in chant offered to her the idea that there was *freedom* in music, an idea which would permeate her future compositions. Larsen's was an eclectic musical upbringing; her father was an amateur clarinetist in a Dixieland band, her mother played boogie-woogie on the record player, and young Libby received classical instruction at school.

Surrounded by musical influences, Larsen didn't realize that "not everybody in the world could read and write music"[2] until she entered a public high school, where students in the choir were taught by rote. In direct opposition to the budding prodigy within, the experience was what the composer calls her "first truly hideous musical experience."[3] Years later, as she watched her daughter's organic interest in music wane upon joining her school band, Larsen gained an even greater perspective into the flawed nature of public school music curricula. These experiences, alongside her acute awareness of the already tenuous state of classical music in the current American culture, account for Larsen's commitment to the propagation of school music programs. She has consistently evidenced a penetrating insight into the communicative and restorative powers of music, as well as the dangers facing funding and programming. As a result, she was named the 2003 Harissios Papamarkou Chair in Education and Technology for the John W. Kluge Center of the Library of Congress and further served on national boards of the American Symphony Orchestra League, Meet the Composer, and the College Music Society.

While an undergraduate at the University of Minnesota in the 1970s, Larsen soon realized there did not exist a proper outlet for young composers to discuss the implementation of academic compositional techniques into their own unique style; in addition, she found it difficult for composers to find venues in which to perform new compositions, as directors of major ensembles were becoming increasingly reluctant to program contemporary music. And so, together with fellow student Stephen Paulus, Larsen set about the task of establishing the Minnesota Composers' Forum (currently the American Composers' Forum), an organization which serves to champion the work of American composers and provide a connection between composers, musicians, and communities. From humble beginnings, this organization has grown into an entity that now consists of over 1,700 members and offers programming in all fifty states.

Larsen's recent endeavors include residencies at universities and national conferences on music education, including the National Association of Schools of Music conference and the Music Educators National

Conference. Her speeches emphasize the need for educational models and professional performance practice to adapt to current musical and technological advances. Through these ventures, Larsen is given frequent opportunity to travel, and consequently, she spends much of her time with university students across the United States.

> *American English is more rhythmic than melodic. It's truncated and full of body language punctuation. I'm not sure that we have a sense of what is lyrical in this culture we're forming other than moments of nostalgia. My* String Symphony *asks the question: What is the lyricism of American life and American English, and what, if anything, does this have to do with a European-evolved string section?*[4]

Larsen's focus on incorporating American vernacular into her compositions naturally applies to rhythm and melody; yet many of her instrumental works are idea based, incorporating her knack for storytelling and communicating broader concepts, such as the way different audiences embrace the synthesis of traditional performance and contemporary media. Her *String Symphony*, for example, is Larsen's musical essay on the role of stringed instruments in contemporary culture. This commission from the Minnesota Orchestra represents a recurrent theme found in Larsen's work: the ability of music to comment on culture, past and present, and to evoke emotional as well as intellectual responses from the listener. She views the work as "both a celebration of orchestral strings and a search for their melody as it comes through our language. Most of all, it is a way to express beauty."[5]

> *We live in a percussive world. Can you imagine American music, all kinds of American music, without the drum set? The tough thing about writing for strings is there's no percussion. So the challenge is, what do those strings mean? What do they mean to the flow of life? Why do strings exist?*[6]

But the crowning illustration of Larsen's synthesis of traditional and contemporary is her opera *Frankenstein: The Modern Prometheus* (1990). She approached the story as one of cultural significance rather than a mere iconographic Hollywood tale. "It transcends the limits of its time," says the composer, "because it deals with the notion of scientific progress at human expense."[7] To heighten the impact for modern audiences, Larsen considered the most stylish sources of contemporary visual entertainment: film and television. She carefully studied the craft of scene construction, from the specific relationship between music and dialogue to the relative length of each scene. The vantage point of the audience— what Larsen terms the "new proscenium"—came to the forefront, "for if we are going to attract a permanent place in the heart of the younger audience, we need to think about their point of view—not in terms of what's going on dramatically, but in terms of how people view the stage."[8] In an attempt to make such new vision a reality, Larsen incorporated large video screens placed above the stage to project images of various operatic scenes. Central to the story is the flashback tableau, "What the Monster Saw," during which the screens depict images as seen through the eyes of Dr. Frankenstein's malformed creation.

Larsen also calls for rather atypical orchestration in this piece, including a small ensemble of strings, brass, winds, and percussion, combined with multiple keyboards, a computer, and an acoustic piano. Rather than forcing the amalgamation of acoustic and electronic sounds, Larsen indicates that all sounds are to be mixed electronically. The composer's vision for *Frankenstein* thereby yields a compelling dramatic work that effectively employs traditional and contemporary instruments within a medium deeply rooted in historical convention. Acclaimed by audiences and critics alike, the work has been hailed by *USA Today* as "one of the eight best classical music events of 1990."[9]

Beyond *Frankenstein*, many of Larsen's other works likewise possess underlying themes of social awareness; an example from her choral compositions is *May Sky* (2002), which musically sets the haikus of Japanese inmates incarcerated in American internment camps during World War II. When approached about composing this piece, Larsen was immediately drawn to the idea, acknowledging that "our cultures need to talk, not through Beethoven but through our own words!" Larsen includes text in both English and Japanese, a direct connection to the imprisonment of the poets on foreign soil. She states, "The texts express the ability of confinement to foster timelessness and spiritual freedom. The poetry is not about escape. The image of barbed wire feels like the filament of a spider's web, in its fragility, because of the strength of the spirit."[10]

Even Larsen's instrumental compositions aim to elicit an experiential response from the listener, such as *Dancing Solo* (1994) for clarinet. The clarinet has long been integral to the composer's musical makeup; since childhood, she has found herself enamored with the wide timbral palette of the instrument, likening it to the human voice. Larsen hails the instrument as "a cultural vehicle in American music," recognizing the integral role of the clarinet in the development of big band and jazz music—purely American art forms.[11]

Dancing alone—improvising with the shadows, the air, on an inner beat, upon a fleeting feeling—has always enthralled me. In Dancing Solo, *I am making a dance for the clarinet, a dance composed of color, rhythm, beat implied and explicit, and breath: the music is the dance and the dance is the music.*[12]

An improvisatory quality pervades each movement of this work, befitting both the freedom of movement in dance and the typical role of the clarinet in jazz repertoire. Caroline Hartig, the clarinetist for whom Larsen composed the piece, suggests that the piece "is inspired by instrumental virtuosity, which parallels the kinesthetic motions of the human body."[13] In the first movement, entitled "with shadows," the primary motive is a free-spirited sextuplet figure; Hartig suggests the shadows are depicted by the eighth-note neighbor tone figure (on A^3 and B^3), which anchors the piece and interrupts the texture like another voice. The title of the third movement, "in ten slow circles," is derived from its form, which consists of ten musical phrases in a slow tempo, resulting in an intimate, unrestrained dance.

If *Dancing Solo* captures the visualization of the human form, *Aspects of Glory* (1997), for organ, concentrates on the intangible spirit. While contemplating writing the piece, the stylized role of the organist piqued her curiosity: "Unlike any other member of the liturgical staff, the organist has the responsibility and vision to create a context for praise."[14] Eventually, Larsen's focus turned to actual words of exaltation, and she settled upon three facets of "glory": the ancient metaphysical roots of the word, the view of heaven as depicted in African American spirituals, and the use of instruments in various worship settings. Each movement is prefaced by a poetic text that provides additional commentary on the given aspect of glory. The texts are excerpts from the seventh-century Caedmon's Hymn (*Wuldor*), a spiritual (*My Home in Glory*), and a Langston Hughes poem (*Tambourines*).

Though many of Larsen's works contain extramusical concepts, the hallmarks of her compositions are rooted in basic craft—rhythmic vitality, motivic structure, and harmonic language. Her affinity toward the inherent traits of the American vernacular, along with her eclectic musical background and interests, serve to inform the rhythmic nature of her compositions.

From the beginning, I had a natural interest in rhythm. When I heard rhythms and words that caught my attention, I started writing them down and manipulating them on paper. My path to composition came through an interest in words and rhythm and the ability to notate those.[15]

Larsen's early training in Gregorian chant is evidenced by her rhythmic vocabulary. Many of her pieces, such as *Aubade* (1982) for solo flute, employ no bar lines; the composer simply includes phrase markings for grouping metrically free musical ideas. Such sections are often interwoven into her more structured works as well; this is the case in the first movement of *Dancing Solo*. In her vocal compositions, where prosody of text is paramount, Larsen regularly utilizes unaccompanied recitative phrases, as in this opening passage from *Songs from Letters: Calamity Jane to Her Daughter Janey, 1880–1902* (1989), for soprano and piano.

Example 5.1. "So Like Your Father's," from *Songs from Letters*, mm. 1–3[16]

Typically, the influence of chant is less overt, as she strives for a more sparkling rhythmic dynamic. The insertion of bar lines, in fact, is a later phase of composition for Larsen; often she freely composes and subsequently adds bar lines and meters to follow her instinctual phrasing.[17] As a result, many of her compositions contain frequent, often abrupt, changes of meter.

The third movement of *String Symphony* (1999), entitled "Ferocious Rhythm," demonstrates Larsen's intuitive process. Infused with energy, the movement utilizes many unorthodox string articulations, including snap *pizzicato* and strumming (a reference to the popularity of the guitar in American music), yet it is Larsen's rhythmic articulation that creates variety and intensity. Organically grown from the seeds of a few fragmented statements in the opening measures, the instruments expound upon these fragments, heightening the rhythmic tension. Sudden shifts toward lyricism, contrasting meters, or an unexpected *tutti pizzicato* create the diversity that results in a "ferocious" rhythm. Similar combinations permeate the movement, showcasing the versatility of the string section while infusing the piece with vibrancy (see example 5.2).

Outside rhythmic parameters, the degree to which Larsen's music is characterized by its composite tonal palette must be acknowledged. Rather than following the fundamentals of functional harmony, it is Larsen's intention to create areas of tonality in which color and suggestion are paramount. She composes freely inside of inferred tonal areas, supported by intervallic saturation and usage of pedal points. While the resultant sound may contain observable vertical harmonies, it is primarily conceived linearly.

I like to create "D-ness" or "A-ness" by placing allusions to functional harmony in and around it, so that you can reference your own allusion to tonality. It is meant to have so much air around it that you really aren't feeling as though one thing is leading to another.

Example 5.2. *String Symphony*, III, "Ferocious Rhythm," mm. 183–187[18]

One example of Larsen's intervallic tonicization occurs in "Deep Blue," the first piece from *Blue Third Pieces* (2000), for flute and guitar. In tribute to the blues, Larsen uses the interval of the third as the structural groundwork of the piece. The guitar opens with vertical sonorities containing thirds, while the opening phrase of the flute is comprised almost entirely of major and minor thirds, establishing the architectural importance of the interval. As the piece evolves, passing tones and appoggiaturas decorate movement by thirds, but the interval remains integral to the melodic structure.

Example 5.3. "Deep Blue," from *Blue Third Pieces*, mm. 4–6, flute[19]

Another common intervallic color in Larsen's music is the tritone, often used in conjunction with more consonant intervals to produce sonorities that seem neither consonant nor dissonant. In *Four on the Floor* (1983), a boogie-woogie-inspired chamber piece for violin, cello, bass, and piano, the tritone saturates the piano, evoking the chromatic character of boogie-woogie. A motivic device featuring the interval begins in the right hand, measure 4; here, the resolution of the tritone to the minor third provides linear motion that belies its inherently dissonant nature.

Example 5.4. *Four on the floor*, mm. 4–7, piano[20]

But while intervallic tonicization is a common feature of her music, arguably Larsen's primary means of creating and maintaining a tonal center is the utilization of pedal points in one or more voices; around these pedal points, the residual notes defy functionality and serve to produce tonal, but nonfunctional sonorities. A prime example of this may be found in "Gale," the fourth movement from *Water Music* (1984), a poetic symphony based on water studies. In the following passage, a strong framework is established with a D pedal point in the violins, violas, timpani, and harp; but while the pedal tone strives to denote D as a tonic of sorts, several devices are employed to evade functional references.

The ascending chromatic motive in the cello, which expands by adding one semitone per repetition, cuts through the pedal point and weakens its stronghold; this motive appears in several instruments, and the D is decorated throughout the section with neighbor tones C and E-flat. The result is a surge of activity vaguely centered around, but not in, the key of D.

Example 5.5. "Gale," from *Water Music*, mm. 35–41, harp, timpani, strings[21]

The goal of the music is not to portray the storm, but to dwell in its force, expressing the feelings aroused by such violence rather than fury, assaulted from all sides by strong, tonal images.[22]

Strong hints of lyricism are undoubtedly present in Larsen's music, but melodic contour is conventionally not at the forefront of her architecture. She seems far more interested in creating colorful musical gestures—motives rich in harmonic potential—than in generating memorable tunes. The aforementioned rhythmic and tonal qualities of her writing combine to create motivic structures that are at the core of her processes. Larsen's motives, which are often operating as ostinati, have marked potential for both melodic and rhythmic developmental procedures. Her works for voice, choir, or chamber ensemble often contain only a few motives, well designed and malleable; and though her large-scale works may promote a greater number of motives, they are often found to be less subject to steep varietal usage and rather are employed as tools for momentum or rhythmic propulsion.

The motive has to have potential for many solutions. Especially when working with texts, I try to understand that oneness—how the motive and the word cannot be separated. I work very hard on the motives, which may look simple on the page, but then you find it's here and it's there, and it means seventeen other things in relationship to the overall structure.

The *Prelude on "Veni Creator Spiritus"* (2002), for organ, is a premier example of Larsen's motivic economy. In this piece, she treats the four vocal phrases of a borrowed chant tune as individual units; they appear in their original order but are not always presented successively. Melodic contour and modal influences are generally preserved, yet the original rhythms are altered slightly, and the metric placement does not always follow the prosody of the original text. The piece begins with an additional motivic element, the contour of which is loosely derived from the final five pitches of the chant.

Example 5.6a. *Veni Creator Spiritus,* chant melody

Example 5.6b. Larsen, *Prelude on "Veni Creator Spiritus,"* mm. 1–2[23]

In vocal works, Larsen's motives often have a direct connection with the text. For instance, *May Sky* begins with the following three-measure figure:

Example 5.7. *May Sky*, mm. 1–3, tenor[24]

This motive, onomatopoeic of the cicada that buzzes outside a prisoner's window, is used throughout the piece as a sort of ostinato-like drone, typically concurrent with the Japanese lyrics. The melodic structure is derived from the pentatonic scale, prevalent in the music of Asian cultures and reminiscent of the poets' homeland, and the gentle compound meter belies their captivity and suggests a newfound serenity. While there is little traditional development of this motive, its rhythmic and harmonic properties permeate the whole of the piece.

For a final example, Larsen's adroit usage of motive and ostinato in *Songs from Letters* serves to illustrate a meeting between Calamity Jane and Wild Bill Hickok during a shootout near Abilene, Texas. Larsen captures the essence of the wild American frontier with two thoughtfully constructed motives, introduced successively.

Example 5.8. "He Never Misses," from *Songs from Letters*, mm. 1–5[25]

The first motive is the aural depiction of riding a horse, the oscillation between E and D in the left hand tracing the motion of the rider while the *staccato* figure in the right hand mimics the sound of hooves. The second motive is characterized by a short–long rhythm and a melodic construction of minor thirds; it is marked to be played "as if shooting a Colt 45." The text dictates Hickok carried two guns; therefore Larsen presents the figure in dual groupings, culminating in a shootout later in the movement.

If the two motives from "He Never Misses" conjure a stark visual image, the primary figure in "A Man Can Love Two Women" rather summons an emotional one. The opening line of text reads, "Don't let jealousy get you, Janey"; Larsen characterizes this jealously with a fierce left-hand gesture.

Example 5.9. "A Man Can Love Two Women," from *Songs from Letters*, mm. 1–7[26]

The left hand plummets to the low register of the piano, a dark presage of the deeply rooted germ of envy that destroys love and leaves a lover hollow; this theme returns in several forms, fragmented and inverted. The apogee of Jane's suffering is depicted in measures 15 through 18, as the motive simultaneously occurs in both hands (inverted in the left hand), converging on a cluster of semitones.

Example 5.10. "A Man Can Love Two Women," mm. 15–18

Libby Larsen's works possess an air of accessibility, inviting the listener—from novice to scholar—to embark upon a journey, often revolving around an historical or humanistic subject. Likewise, with her keen wit and exuberant soul, Larsen possesses a magnetic personality; she is the person with whom one would like to share a cup of coffee and discuss the vicissitudes of life.

A CONVERSATION WITH LIBBY LARSEN

I had heard tell of Libby Larsen's girl-next-door charm, quick wit, and boundless energy. As I stood in a hotel lobby in Greensboro, North Carolina, I wondered if I would recognize Larsen when she entered. I shouldn't have worried; the moment I saw her bounding down the staircase to the lobby below, her presence was unmistakable. The University of North Carolina at Greensboro has commissioned an opera from Larsen, and she was observing voice auditions to gauge the talent level of incoming graduate students under consideration for supporting roles. Amidst her very busy schedule, Larsen made time for dinner and this interview. Over the course of the next few hours, we were often interrupted by tangential stories of our lives as individuals, musicians, and mothers (I was eight months pregnant with my first child). At the conclusion of our time together, I had not only gained a greater understanding of the composer; I had found new zeal for my own singing and teaching, so infectious is Larsen's dynamic spirit.—Tina Milhorn Stallard

STALLARD: We are all, to some extent, products of our culture. How do you feel your midwestern upbringing has shaped you as an individual? And how does that factor into your writing?

LARSEN: I grew up in a family that values the life of the mind and can articulate that value. I can't remember a time when I didn't feel uniquely positioned—in the middle of the United States—to know, to read, and to take advantage of what was around me. At the same time, I've always

felt I was very lucky. Coastal influences were so strong in all of the stereotypes when I was growing up—via television from one coast or the
other—and I simply didn't see it where I was. I've always felt able to be
at the fulcrum and see three-hundred-and-sixty degrees around. I know
that sounds odd, but I value it. Maybe it has a broader view. I never had
the feeling I needed to be in any other place than where I was. I don't
know if that's midwestern, but I do know it is from my family. Wherever
I am, I am.

STALLARD: Do you find you are creative in nonmusical ways as well?
Self-evolving? Learning?

LARSEN: Oh, yeah! I am a systems planner. If there is a problem at hand,
and there is some traditional way of going about solving it, I tend to look
at the problem and think to myself, "you could go about it this way or
this way" and develop full-blown systems of how to get to the heart of
the issue. That's part of composition—systems planning through oral representation. I take great delight in this. That's one of the reasons I accept
positions on boards of directors or advisory panels; I can see many quality
ways to get at an issue. That's just the way my mind is. There are myriad
possibilities that are practically useful.

STALLARD: Clearly you are very good at communicating through the
medium of music, but you are also quite verbally articulate. What makes
you such a good communicator?

LARSEN: I was born with that. When I was very little, it was Saturday
afternoon sport in our neighborhood that fathers would get together to
hang out, and I would be there with my dad. I clearly remember sitting in
one of those fold-out chairs, and how the men would talk to me because
they wanted to hear me speak. I apparently came out in full sentences
with all the verb tenses in place. But then for years of my childhood I
was punished severely for talking in school, or at inappropriate family
moments. I think that's why I started composing—I started composing in
my head. I had to have an outlet for something that must be genetic. For
me, composition was a haven because it was a language I could speak.

STALLARD: How did your early training at Christ the King School prepare you for a life in music?

LARSEN: If there is grace, that was it for me, because we were taught in
the four medieval logics of the educated brain. We were taught sequentially about symbols. The letter *A* is a letter, but it is also a cipher in math,
and it also represents a musical tone. We were taught to think in many
layers about abstractions. Being taught sequentially how to represent
those abstractions with numbers, letters, notes, and color has completely
influenced the way I think about music. A composer makes an order of
sound through time and space. Any sound (this is not because I am a
daughter of Cage—although I am) is potentially musical, depending on

the culture and the interpretation of the sound in a context. I talk about this a lot, especially in music education circles.

STALLARD: Your musical background is quite eclectic. Who were your major musical influences when you were a young person?

LARSEN: One of them was Rimsky-Korsakov—my mother took me to see *Scheherazade*. It was the orchestration that struck me, the totality of the music and the orchestration—not the orchestra—all the gestures in the music that cannot be separated. You really can't separate the music from the color; it is one. I just remember thinking, "What is that? I need to breathe that." Yeats said, "How can you tell the dancer from the dance?" That's the kind of music I try to write, so that when the performer is performing the music, it feels like they are one. Music will let you do whatever you want to it, but it does not speak to the abstract human essential of us. It tries to fit into a niche or appeal to the mind. The hardest thing to do is reach the place you can't articulate. Painting can do that, sculpture can do that, and music can do that; it is the *non*articulate part of us that is mystical. I keep trying to get there. The musical moments that grabbed me as a child are the ones that went there. Again, I don't care about style or genre; it's about language.

STALLARD: What did you gain from your composition teachers at the University of Minnesota?

LARSEN: Paul Fetler is one of the best teachers I've ever come across for the very young composer. He was able to teach the principles of unity and variety, of tension and release, the quality of range and its relationship to these areas, the value of a single note. I don't know many teachers that are even thinking about the value of a single note. Fetler was able to draw out in all of us abstract thinking as the first wave of composition. Eric Stokes used to say to us, "You know, you should listen to everything; it won't hurt you." He would listen to a rock; he created a piece called *Rock and Roll*, which is all about rocks rolling. On the other hand, he would create a piece for flute quartet, equally effective. He gave a joy to listening. Dominic Argento's teaching style suited me best, because he didn't teach aurally. In lessons, you would bring him your music and sit next to him in a wicker chair with a broken seat. He would light a cigarette and flip through your score without saying anything. So you questioned every single thing you were doing. You became lightning fast at self-analyzing everything that goes onto the page. Then he would say something like, "too many triads," or if it was an opera, "you really need to think about what the first ten minutes is about." He would offer something pithy and expect you to figure it out for yourself. I was really ready for him. It suited me well—but I had been writing music since I was five! Argento and Stokes both had completely brilliant, creative ears. Color was a playground for them; any instrument was game for any color.

STALLARD: Did you ever consider studying at another institution or abroad?

LARSEN: Once I thought I would study with William Woods at Albuquerque. I loved the way his mind worked. I thought really hard about going to study with him, but there wasn't a very rich performance tradition in Albuquerque. Minneapolis and St. Paul have seven orchestras, and there are choirs everywhere. For a composer, it is wonderful—a playground. I had friends in Minneapolis who were professional performers and wanted to do my music. Why would I leave? That's a defining thing in my life. I don't put much stock in going for prizes; I've never wanted to look to other composers for validation. It's just not in me. I look to great performers for validation, because for me, that's where the oneness comes from.

STALLARD: What is your relationship with the performer when composing?

LARSEN: It is an abstract point of respect—a respect for the performer's talent and commitment to their talent. I have a strange habit I'm trying to get over. My respect for performers is so deep I can't talk to them. I write a piece, and it is successful; and they like the piece, and everything's fine; but I still can't talk to them. That point of respect is where great collaboration happens. If you really have found the crossroads where everybody in the collaboration respects the other person's talent and commitment to their talent, then even if you don't like the way it's being realized, the collaboration still works.

STALLARD: As a composer, how much artistic license do you feel a performer has?

LARSEN: I'd like to say a lot, but I don't mean it. I worked very hard to put down those notes. I can tell you where I am often flexible: tempo. I often mark my tempos just a hair off from what the music really wants. That's the place where I will easily say, "What tempo do you think works?" Over the years, different tempos have worked because the culture is changing. So, tempo, I am finding, is a result of cultural consensus. Where I really get upset is when people start messing with the form or applying pedagogical rules. I'm finding this with choral music. A conductor will call up and say, "You have this phrase repeated, but it isn't repeated the same way." Pedagogy says we have to repeat it the same way. I have to say to them, "You can't do that. I'm sorry. There's a reason for it, and I'm really glad you called. Let me tell you the reason." It infuriates me when the pedagogy gives the teacher the idea that there is something wrong with the music because the pedagogy says so. Also, I get really angry when people change the order of a set. That happens a lot in choral music—never in instrumental music, but in choral music a lot. And sometimes it occurs in song cycles. With singers, though, I am willing to consider other notes. Occasionally, a singer will contact me and say, "I just don't have that A-flat. Is there another note?" So there are a couple of recordings out there that don't match my score; the score is what I wanted, but the recording, which is often a great recording by a very fine singer, was simply better for them. If a singer calls and says, "What do you prefer?" I say, "Well, I prefer the score, however. . . ."

STALLARD: Do you prefer that the song cycle be performed in its entirety?

LARSEN: Some of them yes, some of them no. *Love After 1950* can be performed individually, though they are nice as a group. With *Sonnets from the Portuguese*, a lot of people want to perform only three of the six. It's okay with me, but we worked very hard at the progression of the soul within the cycle. I guess it depends. There is something at work when people change the order of sets. A lot of times it's because they want a happy, up-tempo last piece. That's a cultural thing; it's very Hollywood, very American. It goes over with the audience if the last piece of a set is [she hums a merry tune], and that's just conditioning. I'm very careful about the way I construct a set.

STALLARD: And what about alterations to dynamics?

LARSEN: Well, dynamics have changed so much in thirty years, it is almost impossible for anybody to gauge. They are hall specific and acoustic specific. I think of dynamics as guidelines. I wouldn't want a *piano* to be *forte*, or something to be *sforzando* that isn't marked *sforzando*. But dynamics are another thing that must sometimes be elastic.

STALLARD: Before you put pencil to paper, what are some of the steps you take to conceptualize the piece?

LARSEN: I spend a fair amount of time feeling the piece. I think what that means is feeling the architecture of the piece and the energy that will support that architecture. Then there is a moment when I've got it. Usually by that time, I know a little about how the music sounds. After that, I generally think through the piece in my mind in another abstract layer. I hear *tessituras*, ranges and rhythms, but it isn't ready for paper. When that last layer feels right, I go to the piano and improvise briefly, and I know whether I have it or not. Then I write the piece, and that goes really fast. For me, a whole piece will come out. All I need is the mechanical time to write it out.

STALLARD: Are you sometimes surprised at how quickly it happens?

LARSEN: No, I just do it. Other people may say, "How did you come up with a seven-hundred-measure piece in a day?" The answer is, I didn't; I had been working on it for a year. I'm sure that's the way Mozart and Bach wrote. That's the abstract part of the brain working in time that we in our culture refuse to comprehend. We have a stubborn resistance to the fact that time operates in several very deep ways. We want to put a quantitative name on it that has nothing to do with abstract thinking. That's a very American thing.

STALLARD: You compose pencil to paper, right?

LARSEN: Yes. It is so much faster. There's a question of time and space that the computer is not allowing notators access to. The computer does not offer time and space dimensions to people who are putting notes in line.

STALLARD: There is an art form to writing a score. Does using the computer feel less organic?

LARSEN: Yes. There is much detail that goes from in here [the brain], down your arm, into the pencil, and onto the page. Lightning-fast decisions are made. By computer, it takes forever. There's a lot of music now that is lacking dimension coming out of composers; it lacks space and time. It is inevitable that the instrument will affect the music. I can see it, and I can hear it in young composers.

STALLARD: Harmonically speaking, your music is tonal, but it typically doesn't follow functional harmony or rational extensions of functional harmony. How do you make decisions regarding pitch selection?

LARSEN: I compose in areas of tonalities, but the operative word is *tonality*. For some people, that means functional tonality—one note leads to another. The problem is one note doesn't necessarily lead to another.

STALLARD: It seems that color is the most important element for you.

LARSEN: It is color and suggestion. The song "Lift Me to Heaven" [from *Cowboy Songs*] has a D-flat blues scale. You can analyze it that way, but it's really the color of space that is much more important than the tonality. It is meant to have so much air around it that you aren't really feeling as though one thing is leading to another.

STALLARD: The music is melodic, but melody is not the driving focus?

LARSEN: The overall architecture is so important—and that's where I do most of my work—because you never hear music in the present. The only thing you can hear is a pitch in a moment in time. The overall shape for the listener is what makes you hear what came before and anticipate what might come after. This is the big game for the composer. Shape is more important than melody.

STALLARD: So you would say your music is more linearly based.

LARSEN: That's a direct result of chant.

STALLARD: Your music might look simple on the page; however, when one looks at the various levels, one sees the complexity of it. The vocal music, for instance, may not be appropriate for a young singer, who is musically, or cognitively, incapable of putting all the pieces of a set together. That requires a higher level of thinking.

LARSEN: This has been really interesting for me to watch. At first glance, my music, both vocal and instrumental, looks easy on the page, but invariably performers will say, "I should have given this more time," or, "this is not what I thought I saw on the page."

STALLARD: I think it is because the music is so rhythmically derived—if you are not in the moment constantly, it doesn't work.

LARSEN: Even in the easiest instrumental pieces, you have to be there the whole time. Otherwise the textures don't work; the pitches don't work.

STALLARD: How do you go about constructing your motives?

LARSEN: I work very hard on that. I keep saying to young composers, "The motives aren't good enough." I used to construct much more intricate motives, especially in my clarinet music. I would construct a gesture that had the potential for a hundred variations in the space of three beats. That's really fun to do. Lately, I've gotten more interested in finding just the right note. I'm finding that the cleaner the notes, the more depth of experience for the listener.

STALLARD: You've often spoken of your interest in evoking potential for listening.

LARSEN: The potential of just three notes is almost infinite. What's so scary is that you have to face yourself. You have to ask yourself the question, "Do I own this?" And the answer is, of course not. It is a complete antithesis to the way composers are trained. We are training composers to believe they own the music. Nobody owns it. You may be the only one working on it, but all you're doing is guessing what goes where. It's a terribly vulnerable situation; you come face to face with your naked self. You are trying to control on the page something that is solely generous. The question of getting down to three notes—or one note—is what makes me work so hard on motives. I don't think students know the value of a note anymore. We're not teaching it in grade school or high school—we aren't even teaching it in college. Everywhere else, even in rap, people are feeling the value of notes. I'm not even sure we're teaching music anymore.

STALLARD: Your scores are characterized by their economy of means—you don't fill them with too much information, but rather you utilize a handful of motives to be developed. Do you think that's part of what makes your music accessible to audiences?

LARSEN: I am always concerned with how people listen to the music. I want to engage the curiosity of the listener, but that's where it stops. It feels pretentious to tell the listener how to listen to music. I simply want to engage an audience in a journey of pitches and rhythms, exploring a fundamental human theme. I try to put the essential piece on paper, hoping to invite the curiosity of the mind. But it depends on who is listening or looking at the score. My very best musical friends are the ones that open a score and say, "Oh, I can read it at this level or this level. . . ." The conductors I work best with are the ones who can hear, by looking at what's on the page, what is really in my head. It is a choice, an opinion, a value judgment about who can hear what I write. I ask this of a lot of composers: "Do you think about who can hear what you write?"

STALLARD: Your vocal works are vivid in their musical portraits, and obviously the text adds another layer of interpretation. And many of your instrumental compositions have extramusical concepts as well. Do those tangible images make it easier to bring the music to life on the page?

LARSEN: I don't think it's visual, but it is a way of organizing thought. I would call it "idea based." Again, it's aimed at who can hear the music and how we listen to music. It is not for pitch and rhythm. To me, saying we should teach people to listen for pitch and rhythm is quite narrow-minded. That's quite academic. Even pieces that aren't about an idea—that's an idea.

STALLARD: After having so much success, do you have more confidence in your abilities? Do things come easier for you now?

LARSEN: Did you think I didn't have confidence?

STALLARD: No, but you once mentioned having a balance between ego and self-doubt.

LARSEN: I think I meant self-criticism. I never doubted, not even once. But self-criticism, that's another thing. It doesn't mean beating up on oneself; a really good critique system says, "I can do that better." You have to have a good sense of humor and a sense of servitude. So many people succumb to the idea of mastery or celebrity as the endgame in music. Once you succumb to that, you can't grow. Like it or not, you've entered a field of mastery which can never produce a master.

STALLARD: When working with composition students, what is your primary objective?

LARSEN: I'm trying to foster their growth in the area of critique so they can master the critique of their own writing. Then they can find their own voice. They are hungry for their own voice. I try to use all the techniques available to help them understand what they need to put in service of their instinct, and what critiquing mastery they need to develop in order to work with that instinct.

STALLARD: You have stated that, growing up in a family of girls, gender bias wasn't a part of your family story. I read that it wasn't until you were a graduate student, when a male colleague made a comment that women are unable to write in large forms, that you experienced gender bias. Do you feel any of that now? Do you begrudge the terminology "female composer"?

LARSEN: The only people who do it are academicians, when they are trying to create categories or bins or arguments. I don't think it will get better; I think the academy will make it worse. It's just not an issue anywhere else, but it is an issue in the academy. I'm watching it become a serious problem in jazz studies and electroacoustic music programs.

STALLARD: Limiting access to females in the field?

LARSEN: Yes, defining roles. It's infuriating, but it's only in the academy. I'm really not sure why it's happening. It verges on academic bigotry; it is putting the wrong thing under the spotlight. I'm not angry about it; it's just so curious.

STALLARD: Do you think it is easier for a composer who is married to devote her time solely to composition?

LARSEN: [emphatically] No! And I'm married and have a child. Two women who come to my mind are Clara Schumann and Mrs. H. H. A. Beach, neither of whom is here to talk about her life. But it feels like the model of the "protected study" is being applied there—the idea that in order to think great thoughts you have to be in a protected place, forty days in the desert. This is an unrealistic model for the contemporary world because no one gets the protected study anymore. I've been tossing around a different model because it's the life that I lead. The brain has several capacities, and one of them is to hold on to a large, complex thought while doing a million busy-making things. In other words, there is a study, but it's in the brain—it's not a building, and there aren't housekeepers. Sometimes people may infer that the reason I'm able to do what I do is because I'm married and have a husband with an income. I quickly disabuse them of that idea; I talk about the value of oneself and one's work. In the culture the way it is now, even if you have a mind that does great thinking, you must take care of all the day-to-day stuff, too. That's the twenty-first century.

STALLARD: Has motherhood affected you professionally?

LARSEN: I can tell you how it's affected my process. Before I had a child, I didn't understand how accessible my whole brain was at any time I wanted it. After my daughter arrived, my brain started having insomnia. I began working toward figuring out why. It turns out that the part of my brain devoted to the detail work in composition was completely kidnapped trying to understand all of the language my daughter was speaking. It was the communication of the various googles and coos and cries of a human who does not yet have formal language. Here is this one person speaking five foreign languages to you at once, and she is completely dependent upon you. It made me a much better composer, actually, because I had to recognize and organize my thoughts much more quickly and make decisions about infinity—the infinity of decisions that are available when working on a piece of music. I couldn't graze around in them. I couldn't luxuriate in the "what ifs," but I didn't want to sacrifice standard or quality. So I became much more efficient.

STALLARD: What do you see for the future? In what direction do you see classical musical composition heading in the twenty-first century?

LARSEN: I see two trends that are currently developing. Many colleges and universities I visit are moving toward electronic and electroacoustic music as the definition of composition. I see it happening and grow concerned about the value of the performer in the process—also, the question of who can listen to what you write and why. This trend, for whatever reason, seems to be limiting the number of women who are coming in as graduate students; I see a decline in the number of women, particularly Caucasian women, in graduate schools. The other thing I see happening is a trend toward world music as compositional inspiration. It may be that we are still in search of a definition of "self" in how we teach composers to write. We are still looking for our own definition but are unwilling to find it in the music we have produced as a culture; we are still in the European appropriation—appropriate, consider, assimilate. I'm not sure what the value is of these trends. I thought for a while I was seeing academies with great performing traditions integrating composer and performer much more, but it is beginning to disappear again.

STALLARD: Where do you see traditional instruments fitting into the electronic age, strings in particular? Will there be a neoclassicism that emerges, in which traditional instruments are used in a technological way?

LARSEN: I don't know where I see it going. I think it's possible that the culture at large may somehow come to prefer the sound of synthesized and mixed strings over live strings. I'm finding that students in general are learning all of their sound through mediated mixing; I'm coming across composers now who don't really know they can't hear acoustic sound. They'll bring me a score, and in the foreground is a harp, and in the background is a full horn section playing in their meat-and-potatoes range. I will say to them, "You will not hear the harp; you have to trust me on this." But they will swear they do hear it! And who's right? I think it's possible that this whole next generation, the one that feels so radically different, actually *is* radically different—I mean in the way they perceive what they hear in the musical mix. So I believe the real issue of the twenty-first century is going to be mediated sound, which tends to even out and compress the overtones and give everything a level quality. For those of us who can hear acoustically, how do we teach that experience and the value of it? I think it's going to be a challenge; it means we're going to have to really shake ourselves up. I'm afraid the system is just going to "ostrich"; it looks that way at the moment. The system is full of people my age, who are not yet ready to retire, and people your age are coming in who can change it.

STALLARD: So it's up to us.

LARSEN: Yes, and I'll help. I've been trying for about ten years. Maybe it will be when music departments don't exist anymore. That seems to be the way things change.

STALLARD: Is there anything you would like people to know about you that hasn't been published?

LARSEN: [After much pondering] There is something. I very much wanted to take voice lessons with Ella Fitzgerald. I couldn't figure out any way to get to her. She was singing in Minneapolis, believe it or not, at a department store. In the middle of the clothing department at Dayton's department store, there she was. I went up to her, but I couldn't ask her. I left not having done it. I realized I wanted to be Ella Fitzgerald, to feel the mastery of all of what she had—the best scat, the best *coloratura*, the best understanding of phrase, the best flow of music. I realized what I really wanted was to be that music, that oneness.

ANALYSIS: *TRY ME, GOOD KING:*
LAST WORDS OF THE WIVES OF HENRY VIII (2000)

Vocal works comprise a substantial portion of Libby Larsen's compositional output. A number of those, including operas, a mass, a choral cantata, and various songs and song cycles, contain female characters and historical figures.[27] Not only are many of Larsen's subjects female, but the majority of her solo vocal repertoire is composed for the female voice, and she primarily selects texts written by female writers, including Elizabeth Barrett Browning, Emily Dickinson, and Brenda Ueland. Larsen maintains she is drawn solely to the expressive nature of language and that she selects only those texts possessing the indigenous musical qualities with which she is able to find an intimate connection. The composer readily confesses her attraction to the inherent vulnerability of personal narrative.

> *I am drawn to first-person texts, and a certain expression of spiritual struggle. When I study texts for men to sing, it's very difficult to find the raw struggle towards honesty that interests me in first-person female texts. There's a distancing that I often find in male texts. Almost all of the emotions are held at arm's length to be extracted and examined objectively through technique and a particular kind of language. In many texts written by women, the language is subjective and very personal. The author risks exposing herself directly to the reader.*[28]

The musical setting of language is paramount to Larsen's compositional style because, for her, a text's certain musical and emotional qualities generate rhythm, melody, form, and texture. Notwithstanding the composer's dedication to syllabic naturalness, her vocal music often maintains a passionate, lyrical quality. As a student during the height of serialism and indeterminacy in America—styles which were, at times, quite the antithesis of lyricism—Larsen credits her studies with Dominick Argento for ingraining within her the "knowledge that lyricism is a concept and not an act."[29] Larsen's background as a vocalist greatly influences her work, although many expansive lyrical gestures are found in her instrumental pieces as well. By her own admission, Larsen is more concerned with rhythm—its inbuilt ability to convey psychological and physical colors— than with melody.[30] But in the vocal medium, even along rhythmic lines, her commitment to word and language is the prevailing factor.

> *When I compose for the voice, I work from two premises; first, the vocal lines must proceed idiomatically; second, the word setting must flow naturally. . . . The rhythm of American English is like the rhythm of no other language. The phrases are uneven. There is a choppy flow from one sentence to the next. Emphatic statements are made by pitch variation. Generally, however, the pitch of American English falls within the interval of a fifth. Within its hodgepodge of Americanized foreign words, it has a difficult time rhyming elegantly. I love American English. In my music, I generally let the rhythm of the words, the varying length of phrases, and the word emphasis dictate specific rhythms, phrase structures, and melodic materials. When my music is performed, the words and phrases should flow quite naturally, almost conversationally.*[31]

Try Me, Good King: Last Words of the Wives of Henry VIII, a song cycle for solo soprano and piano, presents final moments in the lives of five women irrevocably linked by their successive marriages to King Henry VIII.[32] The chosen texts, extracted primarily from letters written by the misfortunate queens (as well as applicable execution statements), shed light on the lives of each of these women, born over a span of thirty-eight years and hailing from three different countries. Each musical setting embodies the spirit of its representative queen and her individual experiences in Tudor England.

Through the utilization of specific unifying elements, Larsen seeks to elucidate a sense of commonality among the women, exploring means of linking them together musically. The first of these elements is the bell "toll," which occurs in every song, with the exception of "Anne of Cleves." Though each bell toll is structurally dissimilar, each represents a potent omen for the reigning queen: the clang of impending death for three, the antithetical joy of childbirth for another.

The other important unifying tool in this cycle is the interpolation of lute song into each movement. The lute is perhaps the most representative instrument of the sixteenth century, and the song was the chief vehicle for passionate expression by English composers.[33] *Try Me, Good King* contains melodies by the two leading composers of the genre, John Dowland and Thomas Campion, as well as one by Michael Praetorius. Though these borrowed tunes were not composed during the reign of Henry VIII, Larsen suggests they nonetheless "create a tapestry of unsung words, which comment on the real situation of each doomed queen." Larsen captures the unique qualities of each woman in a single moment in time, while simultaneously demonstrating the bond shared by all; the result is what she calls "a monodrama of anguish and power."[34]

This cycle provides a case study for us to examine Larsen's primary principles of composition: careful text setting, creation and subsequent employment of rhythmic motives and ostinati, and compositional economy. Through analysis of this work, Larsen's propensity for creating vivid imagery through various texts will be illumined; for although the rhythmic and tonal hallmarks of her compositional style must be addressed, our principal focus should be upon the painstaking care with which Larsen approaches the "oneness" between language and sound.

Katherine of Aragon

Katherine of Aragon was the daughter of Ferdinand and Isabella of Spain, a powerful political partnership. Katherine learned much from Isabella's reign and later proved herself a valuable leader in her own right. Regardless of political successes, it was Katherine's failure to produce a male heir that led to her demise. Though she actually conceived five times, two of the pregnancies resulted in stillbirths, and two sons died in infancy. The only surviving child of Katherine and Henry was Mary, born February 18, 1516.[35] Desperate to produce a male heir, and unable to receive the proper dispensation from the pope to annul his marriage to Katherine, Henry made a radical move to sever ties with Rome and create the Church of England, thereby forever altering the course of British history. Free from papal authority, Henry was now at liberty to divorce his wife of twenty-four years and marry his mistress, Anne Boleyn. Katherine spent her remaining years as a virtual prisoner; she was allowed no visitors (including her daughter) and felt she had been stripped of the rights ordained to her by God. Katherine repeatedly refused to officially recognize the annulment of the marriage, and she referred to herself as queen until the end of her life.[36] She signed her final letter to Henry, written on the eve of her death, "Katherine, Queen of England"; it is from this letter Larsen draws her text for the opening movement.

Katherine's words to Henry exhibit the wisdom of one aware that her time has come. In spite of the manner in which she has been treated, Katherine's strong inner constitution compels her to remain respectful of Henry and his position as king. She addresses him as "my most dear lord, king, and husband." Her unswerving dedication to him is manifested in words of concern, as she expresses fear for his well-being and the political danger he faces. Larsen's musical setting of the letter is lavish with rich text painting; the most overt technique is the relentless sixteenth-note pedal point (see example 5.11).

In one aspect, this persistent figure symbolizes Katherine's strength; it is the pulse of her love for Henry and devotion to her faith. But the motive also indicates the queen's isolation, as the pitch F is texturally secluded (with one exception, all other pitches are located above the F).

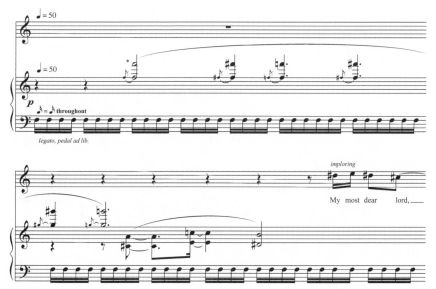

Example 5.11. "Katherine of Aragon," p. 1[37]

This figure, however, is but one thread of Larsen's fabric. Working outside the restrictions of bar line and meter creates a flexible vocal line that remains independent of the pedal point. Indeed, the rhythmic setting is primarily syllabic, simply following the prosody of the text. There are a few brief instances of *melisma*, which serve to highlight certain words, as in the following phrase, "you have cast me into many calamities and yourself into many troubles."

We may also see in this example the before-mentioned bell toll motive, represented here by descending octaves on the pitch A, with added C-sharp. The bell toll represents Katherine's mortality (or at least her acknowledgement of it), as she announces, "The hour of my death [is] now drawing on" in the opening measures. Later, when Katherine warns Henry about the "welfare of [his] soul," the bell toll signifies spiritual death for the wayward king. As a motivic fragment, Larsen uses the toll to punctuate exposed vocal lines (see example 5.12), and the final passage of this song features five successive statements of it. This incessant repetition, coupled with the only *ritenuto* marking in the entire piece, signifies Katherine's physical death, which took place the day after she wrote the letter.

Throughout this movement, fragments of Dowland's lute song, *In Darkness Let Me Dwell*, appear in the piano. There are three statements in total. The first and third lie bare in parallel octaves, highlighted by grace notes (see example 5.13b; lute song marked by *), but the second entrance is perhaps the most recognizable, as it follows the melodic contour of the original, but with altered rhythm (see examples 5.13a and 5.13b).

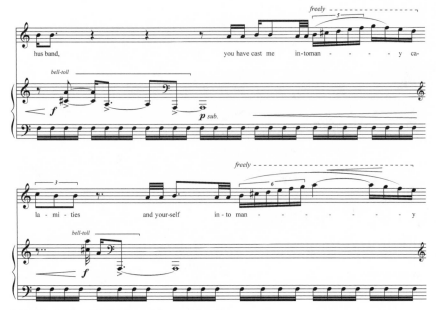

Example 5.12. "Katherine of Aragon," p. 5

Example 5.13a. John Dowland, *In Darkness Let Me Dwell*, mm. 8–18

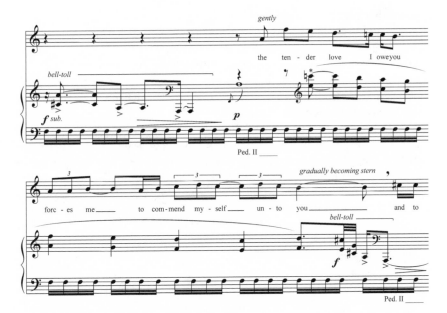

Example 5.13b. "Katherine of Aragon," p. 4

Larsen develops an interesting symbiosis between her vocal melodies and these lute song fragments. When the two are occurring simultaneously, she clearly derives the vocal line from the lute tune, as with the phrase, "the tender love I owe you," seen above (see example 5.13b); however, although the vocal melody initially follows the contour of the lute song (and utilizes the same pitch content), we must note the way in which it retains its autonomy, quickly veering toward its own path. We may say then that Larsen imbeds only the *essence* of the lute song into her melody, an important distinction when considering the various compositional possibilities for adaptation of extant source material.

Anne Boleyn

Perhaps the most remembered of Henry's wives, Anne Boleyn suffered a rather more theatrical fate than did her predecessor. In the beginning of their time together, the newlyweds were quite happy (and fertile), and Anne gave birth to Princess Elizabeth on August 26, 1533; the problem was that the future queen would be the couple's *only* child.[38] Frustrated by "his wife's failure" to produce a male heir, Henry's interests again turned away from his wife and toward another woman—this time, Jane Seymour. In an effort to repudiate the current marriage, Henry's advisor, Thomas Cromwell, fabricated a scheme, accusing Anne of having multiple lovers; she was promptly convicted of adultery, an act considered treasonous against the king and punishable by death. Some reports state that Anne was mentally unstable during her imprisonment in the Tower of London, as she was not only being wrongfully accused and facing death, but had also recently suffered a miscarriage.[39] The text for this movement is drawn from three sources: a letter from Anne to Henry (written two weeks prior to her being beheaded); an undated love letter from Henry to Anne; and Anne's execution speech.

In her letter to Henry, Anne's words are desperate; she begs him to grant her a fair trial and asserts that she has been loyal in both duty and affection. Similar to Katherine's letter, Anne is respectful, addressing Henry as "good king." When Anne asks Henry to remember the amorous words they had once spoken, Larsen cleverly interjects portions of Henry's love letter into the score. The composer, in fact, generates the musical form from this arrangement. The two portions of Anne's letter, separated by Henry's, result in a convincing ternary design. And the queen's words on the day of her execution, primarily those from her speech upon the scaffold, constitute a coda.

Larsen again draws much of her dramatic tension from inventive utilization of a rhythmic motive as driving force. In this movement, repeated triplets aid in creating the atmosphere, in much the same way as the sixteenth-note motive in the previous piece; however, whereas in "Katherine of Aragon" the repetitive figure symbolized the queen's inner strength, the triplet motive in "Anne Boleyn" rather means to expose mounting instability.

Example 5.14. "Anne Boleyn," mm. 14–17[40]

Unaccompanied vocal lines, typically associated with the text "Try me, good king," further explicate Anne's isolation and frustration. The climactic moment of the movement depicts her final act of desperation, as the voice soars to a high C (see example 5.15).

Larsen quotes Dowland again in this movement, this time with the suitably appropriate lute song *If My Complaints.* This melody first appears in the beginning of the B section, as Anne's anger and exasperation begin to be replaced by more plaintive reasoning (see examples 5.16a and 5.16b).

Example 5.15. "Anne Boleyn," mm. 69–71

The tempo and harmonic rhythm are much slower in the B section, and the longer note values and rolled chords are idiomatic to the lute. Larsen's eerie harmonization of the Dowland melody further envelops the listener into what is rapidly becoming a gloomy circumstance. Larsen returns to the lute melody in the coda, during Anne's execution speech; here the solo right hand, joined by a descending chromatic line, denotes her inevitable fate. Unlike prior sections, the voice is mostly independent in the coda—a simple recitative, sparsely decorated by the piano—a symbol of Anne's isolation upon the block (see example 5.17).

Larsen evolves the descending chromatic line of Dowland's melody into the bell toll motive for this movement, which occurs six times in the coda.

Example 5.16a. John Dowland, *If My Complaints*, mm. 1–4

Example 5.16b. "Anne Boleyn," mm. 25–28

Example 5.17. "Anne Boleyn," mm. 75–84

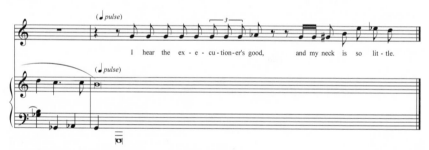

Example 5.18. "Anne Boleyn," mm. 86–87

The rhythm of the first five is a sixteenth note followed by a whole or half note (see example 5.17, m. 75) lending an element of aural suspense; the final toll contains two quarter notes followed by a downward octave leap, rendering dark and bitter resignation to the verdict (see example 5.18).

Jane Seymour

Jane Seymour's relationship to Henry VIII tenders the most enigmatic tale from Larsen's set. The couple married on May 30, 1536, and in October of the following year, Jane bore the long-awaited male heir, Prince Edward. The beautiful, healthy child was celebrated throughout England, but Jane could not recover from the difficult labor and died just twelve days after the birth.[41] For the first time, the king truly mourned the loss of a spouse.

Throughout the remainder of his life, Henry visited Jane's family home, and he later referred to her his "true and loving wife." At his request, Henry was interred beside Jane.

The first half of the text for "Jane Seymour" is taken from the official announcement Jane wrote to the council on the day of Edward's birth, while the latter portion comes from an anonymous poem, entitled "Tudor Rose."[42] Neither the text nor the music suggests Jane's fate; rather, Larsen focuses our attention on the joyous birth of the prince. She achieves this new sense of hope and promise primarily through infusion of Michael Praetorius's fifteenth-century carol arrangement *Lo, How a Rose E're Blooming*. Fragments of the carol appear periodically in the right hand of the piano (and Larsen employs its descending third as her primary motivic device); a first glimpse occurs in the opening measures.

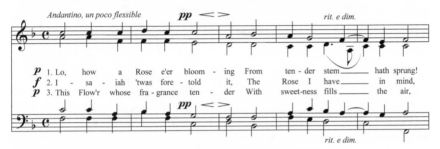

Example 5.19a.   Praetorius, *Lo, How a Rose E're Blooming*, mm. 1–5

Example 5.19b.   "Jane Seymour," mm. 1–3[43]

The symbolic relationship between the Praetorius melody, the text of the anonymous poem, and the dramatic scenery surrounding this movement must be noted. The Tudor rose was the heraldic emblem for that particular line of monarchs, and Edward's birth ("blooming") was in essence the "flowering of a new rose"; furthermore, the poetry celebrates the significance of the male heir by comparing Jane and Edward to the Virgin Mary and Christ as child. Larsen deftly cauterizes these ideas, capturing both the austere delectation of the monarchy as it hails the future king, and the comparative simple contentment of a mother's delight.

That there is no sense of sadness or impending doom to the bell toll is unique to this movement; here its peal is one of joy, announcing the arrival of the long-anticipated prince. Larsen actually uses two different sonoral landscapes for the toll. The first features remnants of the Praetorius tune in upper-register octaves, over an inner texture reminiscent of large church bells, as the whole of England rejoices as one.

Example 5.20. "Jane Seymour," mm. 10–12

The second toll is comprised of five pitches sounded individually yet sustained, depicting the natural acoustic envelope of bells; this more intimate ringing illuminates Jane's reverent, maternal bliss. In the last measures of this movement, the two bell toll motives are integrated. The listener is invited to witness the gentle mother rocking her newborn babe, but joy and sorrow are intertwined, for we know she is fading.

Example 5.21. "Jane Seymour," mm. 28–30

Anne of Cleves

While Henry mourned the loss of Jane Seymour, Thomas Cromwell began an international search for the next queen. Given the king's marital history, finding a suitable and willing bride was no easy task. Eventually, a political partnership was formed with Cleves, an important group of territories on the lower Rhine, ruled by a Protestant family. Upon meeting his betrothed, Henry quickly realized the vast cultural divide that lay between them; in addition, he found Anne to be quite unattractive. On his wedding day (January 6, 1540), he remarked to Cromwell, "If it were not to satisfy the world and my realm, I would not do that I must do this day for none earthly thing."[44] The marriage was annulled six months later, and Henry offered himself to Anne as "her loving brother." Anne never remarried, but she formed close relationships with Henry's daughters and remained in friendly contact with the king for the remainder of his life. And upon Anne's death, Queen Mary ensured that she was buried in Westminster Abbey—the only of Henry's wives so honored.[45]

This song's text is lifted from a letter from Anne to Henry just after the marriage was dissolved. She is quite gracious in her writing, not only expressing approval of the decision, but accepting Henry's offer to become her brother. Cleverly, Anne signs the letter "Anne, daughter of Cleves," which indicated to the king that she was not only accepting the circumstances but joyfully reclaiming her maiden name. Larsen's setting means to capture the irony of this peculiar situation.

Due to language barriers and myriad cultural differences between the couple (not to mention Henry's distaste for her physical appearance), Anne of Cleves is often unfairly portrayed as being unintelligent and gauche. Larsen's piano accompaniment seizes upon this misconception; the primary motivic figure for this movement is clearly derived from the rustic flavor of Thomas Campion's *I Care Not for These Ladies*, the composer's whimsical lute song selection for this movement. Though Larsen retains the rhythmic structure of the original song, she harmonizes Campion's melody with parallel tritones, allowing Henry and Anne's mutual dissatisfaction with their brief marriage to resound in the dissonance.

Example 5.22a. Thomas Campion (Campian), *I Care Not for These Ladies*, mm. 1–8

Example 5.22b. "Anne of Cleves," mm. 1–6[46]

Larsen seeks to restore Anne's dignity and grace through the vocal line, which is primarily lyrical and melodious against the existing discord. The opening phrases are unaccompanied; the first two consist primarily of semitones, while the third is diatonic, outlining F major. The composer seeks to paint a sonoral picture of the anomalous relationship; Henry's markedly offbeat proposition, for instance, to metamorphose Anne into his sibling rather than his spouse, is met with somewhat mocking enthusiasm.

Example 5.23. "Anne of Cleves," mm. 53–63

The final phrases are sung a cappella, decorated with slight punctuations in the piano, as Anne willingly accepts the end of her blighted marriage, the jocular sound of the queen's words ringing with irony as she signs away her royal name.

Example 5.24. "Anne of Cleves," mm. 65–72

Katherine Howard

Given Henry's visceral disapproval of Anne of Cleves, it is no surprise that he rather immediately sought the company of a younger, more attractive woman. True to form, he looked no further than the queen's ladies-in-waiting, where he discovered Katherine Howard, the teenage cousin of Anne Boleyn. The king was immediately attracted to Katherine and began to pursue her, lavishing her with gifts and property, but his affections were unrequited (young Katherine's true feelings toward Henry were never clear). By this time, he was in poor shape and quite overweight; armor made for him had a chest measurement of fifty-seven inches and a waist measurement of fifty-four inches. He had also aged considerably.[47] His physical appearance, coupled with his frequent illness, could not have been appealing to a vibrant young woman. Katherine and Henry married within three weeks of the annulment of the king's fourth marriage, but at some point in the spring of 1541, Katherine was revealed to be involved in an affair with Thomas Culpeper, whom she had met two years before her involvement with the king.[48] Henry, furious that he had been cuckolded, had Culpeper summarily executed for treason on December 10, and Katherine met a similar fate the following February, executed on the same block as was her cousin six years earlier.

Larsen chose as the text for this movement the speech Katherine delivered at her execution. This is the most dramatic piece in the set; Katherine pleads with God and her people to show mercy, claiming she has not "wronged the king." Though much evidence to the contrary has been offered, Katherine insists that the affair with her young lover ended prior to her involvement with Henry. But the unmistakable truth in her final words unmasks her: her deepest feelings revealed, her fate certain, Katherine stands with strength upon the executioner's block and declares, "I die a queen, but I would rather die the wife of Culpeper."

The movement begins with an eerie ostinato in the right hand, which is based upon semitones in displaced octaves. This figure is pervasive to the piece, but at times it is slightly altered, fragmented, or placed in the lower register. Permeating the vocal line and the piano score, the imbalance of the semitone reflects Katherine's fragile emotional state.

Within these opening measures, the virtual whole of Larsen's compositional template is revealed. The lute song, *In Darkness Let Me Dwell,*

Example 5.25. "Katherine Howard," mm. 1–7[49]

makes a reappearance, thereby bookending the set; this time, however, only Dowland's initial vocal phrase is incorporated. The tune is generally presented in conjunction with the ostinato, and it becomes readily apparent that Larsen is in fact deriving the ostinato from the half-step neighbor tones in Dowland's melody (see example 5.25, mm. 5–6).

The bell toll motive, first stated in measure two, is comprised of descending parallel minor sixths with a short-long rhythm, similar to tolls in other movements (see example 5.25, m. 2, m. 7). In "Katherine Howard," the bell toll is typically employed either to introduce a new thought or to punctuate a phrase of heightened emotion from the terrified queen. A striking example occurs late in the movement, where the bell toll, texturally isolated and marked *subito piano*, provides sudden contrast to a preceding outburst.

Example 5.26. "Katherine Howard," mm. 36–39

The above passage is representative of an intriguing trait unique to this final movement: Larsen's rather affecting utilization of fluctuating *tempi*. The initial pulse, at sixty beats per minute, surely represents Katherine's palpitating heartbeat; the tempo then varies with her agitation and distress but invariably returns to the *tempo primo*, as though the young woman is forcibly willing herself to calm only to become frantic again.

As the text progresses, Katherine's words are divided between public and private statements; she addresses God, the people, and the council, in addition to uttering phrases seemingly to herself only. Following the young queen's last words, Larsen presents a series of bell tolls, moving from agitated to resigned, marking the actual execution moment. As all ebbs toward solemn quietness, the lute tune concludes the work—"in darkness let me dwell."

Example 5.27. "Katherine Howard," mm. 42–45

This work, depicting patriarchal tyranny and human tragedy, demonstrates those elements which have helped usher Libby Larsen to the forefront of American music. Her intrinsic setting of English-language text breathes life into the letters and speeches, allowing the musical notes to shape the way we hear the queens as they speak, and meaning to evince that, though each of the queens was quite a different woman, each was similarly star-crossed, shaped by common circumstance. Larsen's music seeks to make the case, in a profound way, that there was simply no escaping the malignancy that was marriage to King Henry.

CODA

At home in Minneapolis, Libby Larsen continues her life of composition and arts advocacy.[50] She recently completed a commission by the Buglisi Dance Theatre (based in New York), and is currently composing the opera

Picnic, commissioned by the University of North Carolina at Greensboro. The libretto by David Holley, an adaptation of the Pulitzer Prize-winning play by William Inge, contains several of Larsen's favorite compositional muses: human nature, jazz, and the American vernacular.

> *Opera is about a central human theme, usually told through a taboo of the culture at the time. The love affair at the center of the play turns on the fact of a dance, and the dance is based in jazz. Cultural taboo is jazz in this, and although it is not mentioned, it really is the question of wantonness that is deeply American.*

Larsen is also working on a number of other commissions, including pieces for the St. Paul Chamber Orchestra, the American Organist Guild, the International Double Reed Society, the Brigham Young University Philharmonic Orchestra, and the Winona Symphony, as well as a theater piece revolving around Mesmer, Mozart, and Marie Paradis. Upcoming professional appearances include the following: Gettysburg College, a symposium on music education at Tanglewood, guest lecturer at the University of South Carolina Conductor's Institute, and guest composer

at the Women in Music Festival in New York, as well as residencies in Fort Collins, Colorado; the University of North Carolina at Greensboro; and Florida Atlantic University. In addition, Larsen is overseeing new recordings of two compositions: *Gavel Patter*, for four-hand piano, will be recorded at St. Paul's Sundin Music Hall, while *Bronze Veils*, for trombone and percussion, will be recorded at the University of Wisconsin at Eau Claire.

Even in light of the considerable number of current projects, Larsen's beacon of exuberance doesn't appear to be waning; rather, the composer's energy and creativity seem to be renewed with each opportunity. In Larsen, we find one whose work imitates her midwestern upbringing; subjects or ideas central to her compositions reflect a broad global view and great respect for humanity, while her unswerving commitment to education reveals passion and determination in securing musical literacy for future generations. Likewise, her compositional style embodies the environment in which Larsen was raised. Clear textures and motivic economy mirror the fresh Minnesotan air, while the many lakes and rivers in the Minneapolis area are embodied in the rhythmic vitality coursing throughout her opus.

When asked about her artistic legacy, Larsen suggests it is primarily "the value of breath in music; just breathing, dwelling in breath," but adds that "musics are evolved by cultures in order to study themselves through the logic and language of music." She feels herself to be merely a voice for contemporary culture. How fitting for a woman who does not seek validation from others by means of composition prizes or academic positions; Libby Larsen is content simply to give her music room to breathe.

NOTES

1. Author interview with the composer, February 10, 2007. Unless otherwise cited, all quotations and personal information are from direct communication between the author and the composer; permission for their usage has been granted by the composer. Photograph used by permission, Ann Marsden.

2. Linda R. Moorhouse, "Libby Larsen," in *A Composer's Insight: Thoughts, Analysis, and Commentary on Contemporary Masterpieces for Wind Band*, ed. Timothy Salzman (Galesville, MD: Meredith Music Publications, 2003), 54.

3. Libby Larsen, "MENC Vision 2020 Conference Address: Music Instruction for 2020," www.libbylarsen.com/MainFrame.html?page=Resources.html (accessed December 14, 2006).

4. Richard Kessler, "Interview with Libby Larsen," *NewMusicBox*, February 1999, www.newmusicbox.org/archive/firstperson/larsen/interview2.html (accessed December 19, 2006).

5. Libby Larsen, composer's preface, *String Symphony* (London: Oxford University Press, 1999).

6. Susan M. Barbieri, "The Language of Strings: Composer Libby Larsen's Music Speaks in American Vernacular," *Strings* (November/December 1999): 71.

7. Nancy Malitz, "Song of the Monster: Libby Larsen Breaks New Ground in *Frankenstein: The Modern Prometheus*, Due for Its Premier in Minnesota This Month," Opera News, May 1990, 45.

8. Malitz, "Song of the Monster," 44.

9. *USA Today*, December 24, 1990, 02.D.

10. Kathy Romey, "Interview with Libby Larsen," held June 10, 2002, for the Sixth World Symposium on Choral Music, Minneapolis, MN, August 3–10, 2002, www.libbylarsen.com/resources_icb_2.jpg (accessed December 16, 2006).

11. Stefan Harg, "An Interview with Libby Larsen," *The Clarinet*, June 2003, 58.

12. Libby Larsen, composer's preface, Dancing Solo (London: Oxford University Press, 1994).

13. Caroline Hartig, "Dancing Solo for Solo Clarinet (1994), Libby Larsen," *The Clarinet*, December 2002, 6.

14. Libby Larsen, composer's preface, Aspects of Glory (Boston: E. C. Schirmer, 1990).

15. Moorehouse, "Libby Larsen," 55.

16. "So Like Your Father's" by Libby Larsen, from *Songs from Letters* © Oxford University Press Inc. 1989. Assigned to Oxford University Press 2010. Extract reproduced by permission. All rights reserved.

17. Moorehouse, "Libby Larsen," 56.

18. "Ferocious Rhythm" by Libby Larsen, from *String Symphony* © Oxford University Press Inc. 2001. Assigned to Oxford University Press 2010. Extract reproduced by permission. All rights reserved.

19. "Deep Blue" by Libby Larsen, from Blue Third Pieces © Oxford University Press Inc. 2000. Assigned to Oxford University Press 2010. Extract reproduced by permission. All rights reserved.

20. *Four on the Floor* by Libby Larsen © Oxford University Press Inc. 1998. Assigned to Oxford University Press 2010. Extract reproduced by permission. All rights reserved.

21. © 1987 by E. C. Schirmer Music Company, a division of ECS Publishing, Boston, MA. Used by permission.

22. Program notes on the composer's website: www.libbylarsen.com.

23. *Prelude on "Veni Creator Spiritus"* by Libby Larsen © Oxford University Press Inc. 2002. Assigned to Oxford University Press. Extract reproduced by permission. All rights reserved.

24. *May Sky* music by Libby Larsen. Music © Oxford University Press Inc. 2002. Assigned to Oxford University Press 2010. Music extract reproduced by permission. All rights reserved.

25. "He Never Misses" by Libby Larsen, from *Songs from Letters* © Oxford University Press Inc. 1989. Assigned to Oxford University Press 2010. Extract reproduced by permission. All rights reserved.

26. "A Man Can Love Two Women" by Libby Larsen, from *Songs from Letters* © Oxford University Press Inc. 1989. Assigned to Oxford University Press 2010. Extracts reproduced by permission. All rights reserved.

27. The song cycle, *Songs from Letters*, is based on letters written by Calamity Jane to her daughter. A multimedia work for mezzo-soprano, trombone solo,

and orchestra combines historical narrative, letters, and works of American artist Mary Cassatt. Larsen is also inspired by fictional female characters. The opera *Mrs. Dalloway* is based on the novel by Virginia Woolf, and the song cycle *Margaret Songs* brings to life a character from a short story by Willa Cather.

28. Susan Chastain, "A Conversation with Libby Larsen," *International Alliance for Women in Music Journal* 2 (February 1996): 5.

29. Douglas R. Boyer, "Musical Style and Gesture in the Choral Music of Libby Larsen," *Choral Journal* 34, no. 3 (October 1993): 18. Based on an interview with Larsen on December 26, 1991.

30. Cynthia Green, "Interview with Composer Libby Larsen," *International League of Women Composers Journal*, June 1992, 26.

31. Libby Larsen, "Double Joy," *American Organist* 18 (March 1984): 50.

32. Henry's sixth wife, Catherine Parr, is not included since she outlived the king.

33. Allan W. Atlas, ed., *Anthology of Renaissance Music: Music in Western Europe, 1400–1600* (New York: Norton, 1998), 384.

34. Libby Larsen, composer's preface, *Try Me, Good King: Last Words of the Wives of Henry VIII* (London: Oxford University Press, 2002).

35. She would later rule as "Bloody Mary."

36. Karen Lindsey, Divorced, Beheaded, Survived: A Feminist Reinterpretation of the Wives of Henry VIII (Reading, MA: Addison-Wesley, 1995), 109. The oath also restricted the heir to the throne to a male child born from any of Henry's subsequent marriages.

37. "Katherine of Aragon" by Libby Larsen, from *Try Me, Good King* © Oxford University Press Inc. 2002. Assigned to Oxford University Press 2010. Extracts reproduced by permission. All rights reserved.

38. Anne suffered two subsequent miscarriages.

39. Retha M. Warnicke, *The Rise and Fall of Anne Boleyn: Family Politics at the Court of Henry VIII* (Cambridge, UK: Cambridge University Press, 1989), 226.

40. "Anne Boleyn" by Libby Larsen, from *Try Me, Good King* © Oxford University Press Inc. 2002. Assigned to Oxford University Press 2010. Extracts reproduced by permission. All rights reserved.

41. Carolly Erickson, *Royal Panoply: Brief Lives of the English Monarchs* (New York: Quality Paperback Books, 2003), 177, 181. Edward was a healthy infant, but his health weakened as he grew older. He assumed the throne in 1547 and died of tuberculosis at the age of fifteen. Jane Seymour was in labor for three difficult days before his birth.

42. This anonymous poem, to the writer's knowledge, has not been dated. The flower itself now stands as the traditional heraldic emblem of England.

> I loue the rose both red & white.
> Is that your pure perfite appetite?
> To her talke of them is my delite!
> [J]oyed may we be,
> our prince to se,
> & rosys thre!

43. "Jane Seymour" by Libby Larsen, from *Try Me, Good King* © Oxford University Press Inc. 2002. Assigned to Oxford University Press 2010. Extracts reproduced by permission. All rights reserved.

44. Alison Weir, *Henry VIII: The King and His Court* (New York: Ballantine, 2001), 421. This incident caused Cromwell to fall from the favor of the king. He was executed on grounds of treason and heresy on July 28, 1540.

45. Petronelle Cook, *Queen Consorts of England: The Power Behind the Throne* (New York: Facts on File, 1993), 153.

46. "Anne of Cleves" by Libby Larsen, from *Try Me, Good King* © Oxford University Press Inc. 2002. Assigned to Oxford University Press 2010. Extracts reproduced by permission. All rights reserved.

47. Weir, *Henry VIII*, 429.

48. It was rumored the two were planning to marry before Henry made his interest in Katherine known.

49. "Katherine Howard" by Libby Larsen, from *Try Me, Good King* © Oxford University Press Inc. 2002. Assigned to Oxford University Press 2010. Extracts reproduced by permission. All rights reserved.

50. Photograph used by permission, Philip Little.

APPENDIX A: LIST OF WORKS

Opera/Stage

Moon Door (1976, revised 1980)—full evening performance with slides, tapes, costumes

The Silver Fox (1979)—children's opera; John Olive, libretto

Tumbledown Dick (1980)—comic opera; Vern Sutton, libretto after the play by H. Fielding

Clair de Lune (1984)—chamber opera; Patricia Hampl, libretto

Frankenstein: The Modern Prometheus (1990)—full-length music drama; Libby Larsen, libretto after Mary W. Shelley

A Wrinkle in Time (1991)—opera; Walter Green, libretto

Mrs. Dalloway (1993)—full-length music drama; Bonnie Grice, libretto

Eric Hermannson's Soul (1998)—opera; Chas Rader-Shieber, libretto after Willa Cather

Barnum's Bird (2000)—chamber choral opera; Bridget Carpenter, libretto

Dreaming Blue (2002)—one-act opera with children's chorus, rhythm chorus, and SSA chorus

Picnic (2009)—opera in three acts; 6 soprano, baritone, tenor, contralto, mezzo-soprano, bass, orchestra, and jazz combo; David Holley, text

Orchestra

Weaver's Song and Jig (1978)—chamber orchestra, string band

Pinions (1981)—violin concerto, chamber orchestra

Deep Summer Music (1982)—full orchestra

Overture: Parachute Dancing (1983)—full orchestra

Symphony: Water Music (Symphony no. 1) (1985)—full orchestra

Seven Sneezes (1985)—full orchestra

Coming Forth Into Day (Symphony no. 2) (1986)—soprano, baritone, SATB, full orchestra; various texts

What the Monster Saw (1987)—orchestra, optional slides; adaptation from Frankenstein
Trumpet Concerto (1988)—trumpet, full orchestra
Concerto for Trumpet and Orchestra (1988)—C trumpet, full orchestra
Collage: Boogie (1988)—full orchestra
Concerto: Cold, Silent Snow (1989)—flute, harp, chamber orchestra
Tambourines! (1991)—full orchestra
Symphony no. 3, Lyric (1992)—full orchestra
Piano Concerto: Since Armstrong (1992)—piano, full orchestra
Marimba Concerto: After Hampton (1992)—marimba, full orchestra
Atmosphere as a Fluid System, The (1992)—flute solo, string orchestra, percussion
Overture for the End of a Century (1994)—full orchestra
Ring of Fire (1995)—full orchestra
Happy Birthday to David (1996)—full orchestra
Fanfare: Strum (1996)—orchestra
Blue Fiddler (1996)—full orchestra
Spell on Me That Holy Hour: Overture to Tsvetaeva, A (1997)—full orchestra
Roll Out the Thunder (1997)—full orchestra
String Symphony (Symphony no. 4) (1999)—string orchestra
Solo Symphony (Symphony no. 5) (1999)—full orchestra
All Around Sound (A Young Person's Introduction to Orchestral Sound) (1999)—full orchestra, cued CD; John Coy, text
Still Life with Violin (2000)—violin, full orchestra
Fanfare: Sizzle (2001)—orchestra, no strings
Patterns for Orchestra (2002)—full orchestra
Dreames and Imaginations (2002)—full orchestra
A Brandenburg for the New Millenium (2002)—trumpet, marimba, electric guitar, amplified harpsichord, and string orchestra
Song Concerto (2005)—alto and soprano saxophone and chamber orchestra
Evening in the Palace of Reason (2008)—string orchestra and solo string quartet
Bach 358 (2008)—full orchestra
Ancient Places (2008)—full orchestra

Band/Concert Winds

Grand Rondo: Napoleon Dances the Can-Can with Italy, Hungary, and Poland (1988)—concert band
Sun Song (1991)—concert band
Short Symphony (1996)—concert band
Fanfare: Strum (1996)—orchestra, no strings
Concert Dances (1996)—concert band
Brass Flight (1996)—brass choir
Holy Roller (1997)—solo saxophone, wind ensemble
Hambone (1999)—concert band
Brazen Overture (2000)—brass quintet
Strut (Strut Ole) (2003)—concert band
Fanfare for Humanity (2003)—brass ensemble

River Fanfare (2004)—brass band
Fanfare for a Learned Man (2005)—brass quintet
Introduction to the Moon, An (2005)—symphonic wind ensemble, tuned water glasses, recorded voice, and eight collaborative improvisations

Dance

Tom Twist (1976)—orchestra, narrator, dancer or mime
Ghosts of an Old Ceremony (1991)—full orchestra

Choral

Little Notes on a Simple Staff—SATB, piano; Siv Cedering, text
Garden Wall, A—unison choir, keyboard, Orff instruments, 2 adults, 5 children with speaking roles, congregational singing
Flee We to Our Lord—SATB a cappella; Julian of Norwich, text
Falling—SATB chorus, SATB quartet, SAT trio, trumpet, piano, percussion; James Dickey, text
Eine Kleine Snail Music—SA and contrabass; May Sarton, text
And Sparrows Everywhere—SATB, piano; Keith Gunderson, texts
Dance Set (1980)—SATB, clarinet, cello, percussion, piano
She's Like a Swallow (1981)—SATB, flute, piano; folk song text
Everyone Sang (1983)—SATB, harp, 2 percussion; Siegfried Sassoon, text
Welcome Yule (1984)—TTBB and strings
A Creeley Collection (1984)—SATB, flute, percussion, piano; Robert Creeley, texts
Clair de Lune (1985)—TTBB, tenor solo; Paul Verlaine, text
Songs of Youth and Pleasure (1986)—SATB a cappella; Renaissance text
Coming Forth into Day (Symphony no. 2) (1986)—soprano, baritone, SATB, full orchestra; various texts
Claire de Lune in Blue (1986)—SATB jazz choir, piano
Canticle of the Sun (1987)—SSAAA chorus, finger cymbals, synthesizer, organ; St. Francis of Assisi, text
Settling Years, The (1988)—SATB, woodwind quintet, piano; pioneer texts
How It Thrills Us (1990)—SATB, a cappella; Rainer Marie Rilke, text
Now I Become Myself (1992)—Soprano solo, TTBB a cappella; May Sarton, text
Eagle Poem (1992)—SATB, 4-hand piano; Joy Harjo, text
Deck the Halls (1992)—TTBB, 5 soloists, piano, handbells
Roll Over Beethoven (1994)—SATB, piano
I Just Lightning (1994)—SSAA, percussion; Maria Sabina, text
Choral Welcome, A (1994)—SSAATTBB and keyboard or orchestra; G. Galina, text
Canticle of Mary (1994)—SSA, four-hand piano or chamber orchestra; Magnificat, Gregorian hymnal, text
Today, This Spring (1995)—SA, piano; Emily Dickinson, Charles Wilson, Jan Kimes, texts
Seven Ghosts (1995)—SATB, soprano solo, brass quintet, piano, percussion; twentieth-century biographical texts

Invitation to Music (1995)—SATB, string quintet or string orchestra (or piano); Elizabeth Bishop, text

Fanfare and Alleluia (1995)—SATB, brass, handbells, chimes, organ

So Blessedly It Sprung (1996)—SATB, oboe, viola, harp; twelfth-century poetry, Old English, Adam of St. Victor

Love and Friendship (1996)—SATB; Emily Bronte, text

Eleanor Roosevelt (1996)—2 sopranos, mezzo-soprano, speaker, SATB chorus, clarinet, violoncello, piano, percussion played by chorus; Sally M. Gall, text

Reasons for Loving the Harmonica (1997)—SATB and piano; Julie Kane, text

Love Songs (1997)—SATB, piano; based on love poems by American women poets Muriel Rukeyser, Jeanne Shepard, Bessie Smith, Willa Cather, Angelina Weld Grimke

I Find My Feet Have Further Goals (1997)—SATB unaccompanied; Emily Dickinson, text

Sweet and Sour Nursery Rhymes (1998)—SATB, French horn; Nursery rhyme text

Stepping Westward (1998)—SSA, handbells, oboe, marimba; Denise Levertov, text

Ring the Bells (1998)—SSA chorus (children), piano; M. K. Dean, text

Refuge (1988)—SSAA a cappella; Sara Teasdale, text

Density of Light (1998)—SATB choir, treble choir, brass; Thomas H. Troeger, text

To a Long Loved Love (1999)—SATB, string quartet; Madeline L'Engle, texts

Ten Times Tallis (1999)—SATB, a cappella

Salute to Louis Armstrong, A (1999)—SATB chorus, piano; from the choral suite Seven Ghosts

Here's to an Opening and Upward (1999)—SATB, a cappella; e. e. cummings, text

Day Song (1999)—SSA chorus, a cappella; Libby Larsen, text after F. F. S. Grundtwig

By a Departing Light (1999)—SATB, a cappella; Emily Dickinson, texts

Witches' Trio, The (2000)—SSAA a cappella; William Shakespeare, text

Touch the Air Softly (2000)—SSAA, a cappella; William Jay Smith, text

Sea Change (2000)—SATB a cappella; Martha Sherwood and John O'Donohue, texts

Lover's Journey, A (2000)—Six-voice male a cappella group; James Joyce, William Shakespeare, Goliard poets, text

Lord, Before This Fleeting Season (2000)—SATB, a cappella; Maryann Jindra, text

How to Songs (2000)—SSA children's chorus

Jack's Valentine (2000)—SSAA, a cappella; Aldeen Humphreys, text

May Sky (2002)—SATB, a cappella; Tokuji Hirai, Neiji Ozawa, Reiko Gomyo, Suiko Matsushita, text

Ballerina and the Clown, The (2002)—SSA chorus and harp; Sally Gall, texts

Young Nun Singing, A (2003)—SAA, a cappella; anon., Sor Juana Inés de la Cruz and Idea Vilariño, text

Womanly Song of God, The (2003)—a cappella; Catherine de Vinck, text

Come Before Winter (2003)—SATB, baritone solo, orchestra or piano; Arthur Mampel, text

Jesus, Jesus Rest Your Head (2004)—Two or three-part chorus, solo voice, piano; traditional text

Cry Peace (2004)—SSAATTBB a cappella, text adapted by L. Larsen

Natus Est Emmanuel (2004)—SSSAAA, a cappella; anonymous text from *Piae Cantiones*

Western Songs (2005)—SATB, a cappella; American folk song, text

My Soul Borne Up (2005)—SATB, a cappella; Peter Raatz, text

I Dream of Peace (2005)—SATB, percussion; texts by children of the former Yugoslavia

God So Loved the World (2005)—SATB, a cappella; John 3:16–17, text

Giving Thanks, A Native American Good Morning Message (2005)—SSAA, string quartet; Chief Jake Swamp, text

Thomas Jefferson Alma Mater (2006)—SATB, string orchestra, wind ensemble; M. K. Dean, text

Summer Day, The (2005)—SSAA and string quartet; Mary Oliver, text

Of Music (2006)—SSAA, four-hand piano; Emily Dickinson, texts

Whitman's America (2007)—SATB, a cappella; Walt Whitman, text

Crowding North (2007)—SATB, flute, oboe, bassoon, guitar, violin 1 and 2, viola, violoncello, contrabass; Deborah Larsen, text

Four Mediations of Mechthild of Magdeburg (2007)—SATB chorus, handbells, organ; Mechthild of Magdeburg, text

To Sing (2008)—SSA chorus, piano; Kasey Zitnik, text

Mind You, Now (2009)—SSAA chorus, string quartet or piano; John Ciardi, text

Anthems

I Love the Lord—SATB, organ; Nathan Everett, text

All Shall Be Well—SA choir, soprano, soprano recorder, triangle, keyboard

Double Joy (1982)—SSAATTBB, handbells, organ; Michael Thwaites (adapted), text

Who Cannot Weep, Come Learn of Me (1985)—Mezzo-soprano, tenor, SSA

We Celebrate (1985)—SATB, piano (organ); John Cummins, text

Peace, Perfect Peace (1985)—SATB, a cappella; Isaiah 26:3, Edward Bickersteth, text

I Am a Little Church (1991)—organ; e. e. cummings, text

Pied Beauty (Glory Be to God) (1992)—SATB, 4-hand piano; Gerard Manley Hopkins, text

Mother, Sister, Blessed, Holy (1992)—SATB, 4-hand piano; Gerard Manley Hopkins, text

How Lovely Are Thy Holy Groves (1992)—soprano solo, piano; Chinook psalter, text

Alleluia (1992)—SATB, a cappella

God as Ribbon of Light (1993)—SATB, organ; Sr. Mary Virginia Micka, text

I Will Sing and Raise a Psalm (1995)—SATB, organ; St. Francis of Assisi, text

I Arise Today (1995)—SATB, organ; "St. Patrick's Breastplate" (seventh century), text

Is God, Our Endless Day (1999)—a cappella; Julian of Norwich, text

Psalm 121 (2000)—SSSAAA a cappella; Psalm 121, Patricia Hennings and John Muir, texts.

Anthem: For the Cowboy and the Plains (2009)—SATB chorus, piano; Buck Ramsey, text

Choral with Orchestra

In a Winter Garden (1982)—soprano, tenor, SATB, chamber orchestra; Patricia Hampl, text

Ringeltänze (1983)—SATB, handbells, string orchestra; medieval French, text, translated by Libby Larsen

Coming Forth Into Day (Symphony no. 2) (1986)—soprano, baritone, SATB, full orchestra; various texts

Three Summer Scenes (1988)—SATB, optional youth chorus, full orchestra; William Carlos Williams, Lloyd Frankenburg, Maurice Lindsay, texts

Missa Gaia: Mass for the Earth (1992)—soprano solo, SATB choir, SSA choir (opt.), oboe, strings, 4-hand piano; G. M. Hopkins, Bible, Maurice Kenny, Joy Harjo, text

Song-Dances to the Light (1994)—SA, Orff instruments, full orchestra (or piano)

Choral Welcome, A (1994)—SSAATTBB and keyboard or orchestra; G. Galina, text

Canticle of Mary (1994)—SSA, four-hand piano or chamber orchestra; Magnificat, Gregorian hymnal, text

Hymnal, text

If I Can Stop One Heart from Breaking (2001)—SA, orchestra; Emily Dickinson, texts

I It Am: The Shewings of Julian of Norwich (2002)—soprano, countertenor, baritone, SSAATTBB chorus, orchestra; John Mauropus, Folquet de Marseille, Josephus, Konrad von Wuerzburg, Ratpert of Saint Gall, Theodore of Studite, Mechthild of Magdeburg, Psalms 17, 18, 27, 41, 54, text

Come Before Winter (2003)—SATB, baritone solo, orchestra or piano; Arthur Mampel, text

Praise One (2004)—SATB, SATB chorus favori, orchestra; Psalms 146, 147, 148, 150 adapted by Libby Larsen, text

Nothing That Is, The (2004)—SATB, baritone solo, 3 speaking voices, orchestra; text adapted by Libby Larsen

Sacred Vows (2008)—solo tenor, baritone, narrator, SATB chorus, full orchestra; U Sam Oeur, text

Songs, Sets, and Cycles

Selected Poems of Rilke—soprano, flute, guitar, harp; Rainer Maria Rilke, texts

Fern Hill—tenor solo; Dylan Thomas, text

Saints without Tears (1976)—soprano, flute, bassoon; Phyllis McGinley, text

Lululu's Funeral (1976)—solo voice, prepared piano; Kusano Shimpei, text

Cowboy Songs (1979)—soprano, piano; anon., Belle Star, Robert Creeley, text

Verse Record of My Peonies, A (1980)—tenor, tape, percussion; Masaoka Shiki, text

Three Rilke Songs (1980)—high voice and guitar; Rainer Maria Rilke, texts

Before Winter (1982)—baritone solo, organ; Arthur Mampel, text

Me (Brenda Ueland) (1987)—soprano, piano; Brenda Ueland, text

Late in the Day (1988)—soprano, piano; Jeanne Shepard, text

Songs from Letters: Calamity Jane to Her Daughter Janey 1880–1902 (1989)—soprano, piano (or chamber ensemble); Calamity Jane, text

When I Am an Old Woman (1990)—soprano, piano; Jenny Joseph, text

Perineo (1993)—baritone, piano; Roberto Echavarren, text

Beloved, Thou Has Brought Me Many Flowers (1994)—mezzo-soprano, cello, piano; Elizabeth Barrett Browning, Hilda Doolittle, Rainer Marie Rilke, Percy Bysshe Shelley, texts

Margaret Songs (1996)—soprano, piano; Willa Cather, Libby Larsen, texts

Chanting to Paradise (1997)—soprano, piano; Emily Dickinson, text

Acapelorus (1997)—soprano, string quartet, cued CD; Lewis Carroll and children's original text

Ant and the Grasshopper, The (extracted from *Late in the Day*) (1998)—soprano, piano; Jeanne Shepard, text

Try Me, Good King: Last Words of the Wives of Henry VIII (2000)—soprano, piano; Katherine of Aragon, Anne Boleyn, Jane Seymour, Anne of Cleves, Katherine Howard, texts

My Antonia (2000)—high voice, piano; Willa Cather, text

Love After 1950 (2000)—mezzo-soprano, piano

Lord, Make Me an Instrument (Prayer of St. Francis) (2000)—tenor, piano; St. Francis of Assisi, text

Jazz at the Intergalactic Nightclub (2001)—tenor, piano; Thomas McGrath, text

Hell's Belles (2001)—mezzo-soprano, handbell choir; Tallulah Bankhead, Billy Jean King, Gertrude Stein, nursery rhyme, text

Apple's Song, The (2001)—baritone, piano; Edwin Morgan, text

If I Can Rise from Ashes (2002)—tenor, piano; Michelangelo Buonarroti, text

This Unbearable Stillness: Songs from the Balcony (2003)—soprano, string quartet; Dima Hilal, Sekeena Shaben, text

I Love You Through the Daytimes (2003)—voice, piano; ancient Egyptian, text

De Toda La Eternidad (2003)—soprano, piano; Sor Juana Inez de la Cruz, text

Word from Your Jenny, A (2004)—soprano, piano; Jenny Lind, adapted by Libby Larsen, text

Pig in the House, A (2004)—tenor, piano; Alvin Greenberg, text

Sifting Through the Ruins (2005)—mezzo-soprano, viola, and piano; Hilary North, anon., Alicia Vasquez, Martha Cooper, and Ted Berrigan, texts

Take (2006)—soprano, piano; Margaret Atwood, text

Sey Mir Gegrusst Mein Schmeineindes Klavier (2007)—solo voice, piano; anon., text

Forget-Me-Not (2008)—soprano, tenor, piano; anon., text

Flower, The (2009)—baritone, piano; George Herbert, text

Voice with Orchestra

Songs from Letters: Calamity Jane to Her Daughter Janey 1880–1902 (1989)—soprano, chamber ensemble (or piano); Calamity Jane, text

Sonnets from the Portuguese (1991)—soprano, chamber ensemble (or piano); Elizabeth Barrett Browning, text

Mary Cassatt (1994)—mezzo-soprano, trombone, orchestra and slides; historical narrative and letters of Mary Cassatt, text

Eleanor Roosevelt (1996)—2 sopranos, mezzo-soprano, speaker, SATB chorus, clarinet, violoncello, piano, percussion played by chorus; Sally M. Gall, text

Songs of Light and Love (1998)—soprano, chamber ensemble; May Sarton, text

Notes Slipped Under the Door (2001)—soprano, flute, orchestra; Eugenia Zukerman, text

Raspberry Island Dreaming (2002)—mezzo-soprano, orchestra; Joyce Stuphen, Patricia Hampl, text

Within the Circles of Our Lives (2007) (excerpted from *Missa Gaia* with some alterations in voicings and orchestration)—soprano, baritone and orchestra; Wendell Berry, text

Instrumental

FLUTE

Selected Poems of Rilke—soprano, flute, guitar, harp; texts, Rainer Maria Rilke

Three Pieces for Treble Wind and Guitar (1974)—treble wind, guitar

Aubade (1982)—solo flute

Vive: Celebration for Flute Quartet (1988)

Blue Third Pieces (1996)—flute or clarinet, guitar

Ulloa's Ring (1997)—flute, piano

Barn Dances (2001)—flute, clarinet, piano

Firebrand (2003)—flute/piccolo, violin, cello, piano

Tatterdemalion (2005)—flute, alto saxophone, clarinet, contrabass, percussion, harp, and piano

Slow Structures (2005)—flute, cello, piano

Downwind of Roses in Maine (2009)—flute, B-flat clarinet, and mallet percussion

OBOE

Three Pieces for Treble Wind and Guitar (1974)—treble wind, guitar

Circular Rondo, Canti Breve (1974)—oboe, guitar

Kathleen, As She Was (1989)—oboe, harpsichord

Pocket Sonata (2003)—oboe, alto sax, violin, cello, marimba/vibraphone, piano

CLARINET

Three Pieces for Treble Wind and Guitar (1974)—treble wind, guitar

Corker (1977)—clarinet, one percussion

Song Without Words (1986)—clarinet and piano

Black Birds, Red Hills (1987, revised 1996)—clarinet, viola, piano, optional slides

Slang (1994)—clarinet, violin, piano

Dancing Solo (1994)—clarinet solo

Blue Third Pieces (1996)—flute or clarinet, guitar

Barn Dances (2001)—flute, clarinet, piano

Bally Deux (2001)—2 clarinets, string quartet

Licorice Stick (2002)—clarinet and piano

Yellow Jersey (2004)—2 clarinets

Tatterdemalion (2005)—flute, alto saxophone, clarinet, contrabass, percussion, harp, and piano
Downwind of Roses in Maine (2009)—flute, B-flat clarinet, and mallet percussion

BASSOON

Xibala—bassoon and percussion
Jazz Variations for Solo Bassoon (1977)—bassoon solo

SAXOPHONE

Holy Roller (1997)—saxophone, piano
Bid Call (2003)—cello, alto saxophone
Pocket Sonata (2003)—oboe, alto sax, violin, cello, marimba/vibraphone, piano
Tatterdemalion (2005)—flute, alto saxophone, clarinet, contrabass, percussion, harp, and piano

TRUMPET

Concerto for Trumpet and Orchestra (1988)—C trumpet, full orchestra
Fanfare for the Women (1994)—trumpet solo
Engleberg: Trio for Brass and Organ (2006)—trumpet, horn in F, trombone, organ

TROMBONE

Bronze Veils (1979)—trombone, 2 percussion
Engleberg: Trio for Brass and Organ (2006)—trumpet, horn in F, trombone, organ

TUBA

Concert Piece for Tuba and Piano (1993)—tuba, piano

PERCUSSION

Corker (1977)—clarinet, 1 percussion
Bronze Veils (1979)—trombone, 2 percussion
Pocket Sonata (2003)—oboe, alto sax, violin, cello, marimba/vibraphone, piano
Concertino for Tenor Steel Drum and Chamber Ensemble (2004)—tenor steel drum solo, flute/piccolo, clarinet/bass clarinet, trumpet, trombone, violin, violoncello, piano
Tatterdemalion (2005)—flute, alto saxophone, clarinet, contrabass, percussion, harp, piano
Ricochet (2008)—2 marimbas
Downwind of Roses in Maine (2009)—flute, B-flat clarinet, and mallet percussion

PIANO

Piano Suite (1976)—solo piano
Four on the Floor (1983)—violin, cello, bass, piano
Black Birds, Red Hills (1987, revised 1996)—clarinet, viola, piano, optional slides
Slang (1994)—clarinet, violin, piano
Halley's Dance (1998)—solo piano
Mephisto Rag (2000)—solo piano
Trio: For Violin, Cello and Piano (2001)
Barn Dances (2001)—flute, clarinet, piano
Firebrand (2003)—flute/piccolo, violin, cello, piano
Pocket Sonata (2003)—oboe, alto sax, violin, cello, marimba/vibraphone, piano
Music Boxes (2004)—five-hand piano, storyteller
Gavel Patter (2004)—four-hand piano
Penta Metrics (2004)—solo piano
For Two (2004)—four-hand piano
Tatterdemalion (2005)—flute, alto saxophone, clarinet, contrabass, percussion, harp, and piano
Slow Structures (2005)—flute, cello, piano
Over, Easy (2009)—violin, viola, violoncello, piano
Hardy's Lark (2009)—violin, violoncello, piano

ORGAN

Fantasy on Slane—flute and organ
Sonata in One Movement on Kalenda Maya (1983)—organ solo
Aspects of Glory (1990)—organ solo
Blessed Be the Tie That Binds (1996)—organ solo
Prelude on "Veni Creator Spiritus" (1997)—organ solo
On a Day of Bells (2002)—organ solo
Engleberg: Trio for Brass and Organ (2006)—trumpet, horn in F, trombone, organ

CARILLON

Pealing Fire (2004)—carillon

HANDBELLS

Gathered in God's Presence (2009)—handbell ensemble

STRINGS

Adventures of Wonderboy, The: Issue One—bass, sampler, narrator, cartoons, strings
Scudding (1980)—cello solo
Cajun Set (1980)—guitar, string trio
Black Roller (1981)—flute, oboe, clarinet, bassoon, piano, violin, viola (featured), cello

Four on the Floor (1983)—violin, cello, bass, piano
Up Where the Air Gets Thin (1985)—cello, bass
Juba (1986)—cello, piano
Alauda: Concert Piece for String Quartet (1986)
Black Birds, Red Hills (1987, revised 1996)—clarinet, viola, piano, optional slides
Quartet: Schoenberg, Schenker and Schillinger (1991)—string quartet
Three for the Road (2000)—violin, cello, piano
Viola Sonata (2001)—viola, piano
Trio: For Violin, Cello and Piano (2001)
Firebrand (2003)—flute/piccolo, violin, cello, piano
Bid Call (2003)—cello, alto saxophone
Pocket Sonata (2003)—oboe, alto sax, violin, cello, marimba/vibraphone, piano
Slow Structures (2005)—flute, cello, piano
Quartet: She Wrote (2008)—string quartet
Double String Quartet: J. S. B. (2008)—double string quartet
Over, Easy (2009)—violin, viola, violoncello, piano
Hardy's Lark (2009)—violin, violoncello, piano

GUITAR

Tango—guitar solo
Argyle Sketches—guitar solo
Circular Rondo, Canti Breve (1974)—oboe, guitar
Three Pieces for Treble Wind and Guitar (1974)—treble wind, guitar
Cajun Set (1980)—guitar, string trio
Blue Third Pieces (1996)—flute or clarinet, guitar

MIXED ENSEMBLE

Cajun Set (1980)—guitar, string trio
Black Roller (1981)—flute, oboe, clarinet, bassoon, piano, violin, viola (featured), cello
Four on the Floor (1983)—violin, cello, bass, piano
Black Birds, Red Hills (1987, revised 1996)—clarinet, viola, piano, optional slides
Schoenberg, Schenker and Schillinger (1991)—flute, oboe, viola, cello, keyboard
Slang (1994)—clarinet, violin, piano
Blue Third Pieces (1996)—flute or clarinet, guitar
Child's Garden of Monsters: Dracula's Blues, A (1997)—2 oboes, B-flat clarinet, 1/E-flat clarinet, B-flat clarinet, 2 horns, 2 bassoons
Neon Angel (2000)—violin, cello, clarinet (or saxophone), flute, piano, percussion, cued CD
Book of Rhythms, The (2001)—woodwind quintet, Orff instrumentarium
Barn Dances (2001)—flute, clarinet, piano
Bally Deux (2001)—2 clarinets, string quartet
Firebrand (2003)—flute/piccolo, violin, cello, piano
Bid Call (2003)—cello, alto saxophone
Pocket Sonata (2003)—oboe, alto sax, violin, cello, marimba/vibraphone, piano

Mr. Potter's Pokey (2004)—clarinet, bones, jaw harp, or other percussion

Concertino for Tenor Steel Drum and Chamber Ensemble (2004)—tenor steel drum solo, flute/piccolo, clarinet/bass clarinet, trumpet, trombone, violin, violoncello, piano

Tatterdemalion (2005)—flute, alto saxophone, clarinet, contrabass, percussion, harp, and piano

Engleberg: Trio for Brass and Organ (2006)—trumpet, horn in F, trombone, organ

DOUBLE WOODWIND QUINTET

With Love and Hisses (1985)—double woodwind quintet. A piece which accompanies the silent Laurel and Hardy film Love and Hisses. (Piece may also be performed without film.)

APPENDIX B: DISCOGRAPHY

Aspects of Glory. Diane Meredith Belcher, organ. Pipedreams CDs, PD CD-1003. "Pipedreams Premiers, Vol. 2: A Collection of Music for the King of Instruments."

Aubade. Laurel Ann Maurer, flute. 4Tay Inc. 4081. "Legacy of the American Woman Composer."

Aubade. Eugenia Zukerman, flute. Pro Arte PAC 1086. "Music for Flute."

Beloved, Thou Has Brought Me Many Flowers. Theresa Treadway Lloyd, Toby Blumenthal, Bert Phillips. Albany Records TROY 408. "Barab, Bolcom, Larsen, Previn: Chamber Music."

Beloved, Thou Has Brought Me Many Flowers. Terry Rhodes, soprano; Ellen Williams, mezzo-soprano; Benton Hess, piano; Steven Reis, cello. Albany Records TROY 634. "Grand Larsen-y: Vocal Music of Libby Larsen."

Black Birds, Red Hills. Caroline Hartig, clarinet; assisted by Kevin Purrone, David Harding, Christopher Kachian, and Robert Adney. Innova Recordings ACF 002, American Composers Forum. "Dancing Solo: Clarinet Chamber Music of Libby Larsen."

Black Roller. Minnesota Contemporary Ensemble. Innova Recordings, American Composers Forum. "180 Degrees from Ordinary."

Blue Third Pieces. Duologue (Susan Morris DeJong, flute; Jeffrey Van, guitar). Gasparo Records. "Canyon Echoes: New Music for Flute and Guitar."

Blue Third Pieces. Caroline Hartig, clarinet; assisted by Kevin Purrone, David Harding, Christopher Kachian, and Robert Adney. Innova Recordings ACF 002, American Composers Forum. "Dancing Solo: Clarinet Chamber Music of Libby Larsen."

Blue Third Pieces. Robert D'Ambrosio and Louis Arnold. D & A Enterprises. "Music for Clarinet and Guitar."

Blue Third Pieces. Jan Boland, flute; John Dowdall, guitar. Fleur de Son Classics, FDS 57960. "Red Cedar Collection: American Music for Flute and Guitar."

Canticle of Mary. Las Cantantes; Bradley Ellingboe, conductor. University of New Mexico. Rhode-Kil Records RK 1003. "I Just Lightning."

Canticle of the Sun. Las Cantantes; Bradley Ellingboe, conductor. University of New Mexico. Rhode-Kil Records RK 1003. "I Just Lightning."

Chanting to Paradise. Terry Rhodes, soprano; Ellen Williams, mezzo-soprano; Benton Hess, piano; Steven Reis, cello. Albany Records TROY 634. "Grand Larsen-y: Vocal Music of Libby Larsen."

Claire de Lune in Blue. "The Gregg Smith Singers."

Collage: Boogie. Zubin Mehta, conductor. "American/Soviet Youth Symphony."

Collage: Boogie. Baltimore Symphony Orchestra; David Zinman, conductor. Argo 444-454 "Dance Mix."

Coming Forth Into Day. Linda Russel, soprano; Jubilant Sykes, baritone; Jehan El Sadat, narrator; Phillip Brunelle, conductor. Plymouth Music Series PMS 003. "The Plymouth Festival Orchestra and Chorus and the Bel Canto Singers."

Concert Dances. University of Wisconsin-Madison Symphonic Wind Ensemble; James Smith, conductor. "The Centennial Commissions."

Concert Piece for Tuba and Piano. Mark Nelson, tuba and friends. Produced by Mark Nelson. "Aboriginal Voices."

Corker. Caroline Hartig, clarinet; assisted by Kevin Purrone, David Harding, Christopher Kachian, and Robert Adney. Innova Recordings ACF 002, American Composers Forum. "Dancing Solo: Clarinet Chamber Music of Libby Larsen."

Corker. Dinosaur Annex Music Ensemble; Barbara Cassidy, executive director and production coordinator. "Thirty Years of Adventure 1975–2005."

Cowboy Songs. Nannette McGuinness, soprano; Jan Roberts-Haydon, flute; Sylvie Beaudette, piano. Centaur Records CRC 2461. "Fabulous Femmes."

Cowboy Songs. Eileen Strempel, soprano; Sylvie Beaudette, piano. Centaur Records CRC 2666. "Love Lies Bleeding: Songs by Libby Larsen."

Cowboy Songs. Louise Toppin. Albany Records TROY 385. "Rich, Edwards, Larsen and Others."

Cowboy Songs. Judith Cline, soprano; Michael Sitton, piano. Hollins University. "A Sampler in Song: Art Songs by Women Composers."

Cowboy Songs. Linda Dykstra, soprano; Joan Conway, piano. SPERA Recordings CD-1102-01. "Treasures: Little Known Songs by Women Composers."

Dance Set. "The Gregg Smith Singers."

Dancing Solo. Caroline Hartig, clarinet; assisted by Kevin Purrone, David Harding, Christopher Kachian, and Robert Adney. Innova Recordings ACF 002, American Composers Forum. "Dancing Solo: Clarinet Chamber Music of Libby Larsen."

Dancing Solo. Stefan Harg, clarinet; Katerina Strom-Harg, piano; Kathleen Roland-Silverstein, soprano; Asa Johansson, violin. Rhode-Kil Records RK 1001. "Licorice Stick: Clarinet Chamber Music of Libby Larsen."

De Toda La Eternidad. Bonnie Pomfret, soprano; Laura Gordy, piano. ACA Digital Recording Inc. ACA CM20090. "De Toda La Eternidad, Songs of American Women Composers."

Deep Summer Music. Colorado Symphony; John Kinzie, marimba; Marin Alsop, conductor. Koch International Classics 7520. "Deep Summer Music."

Dreaming Blue. Fox Valley Symphony; Brian Groner, conductor. Rhode-Kil Records RK 1002. "Dreaming Blue: Commemorative Edition."

Dreaming Blue. Terry Rhodes, soprano; Ellen Williams, mezzo-soprano, Benton Hess, piano; Steven Reis, cello. Albany Records TROY 634. "Grand Larsen-y: Vocal Music of Libby Larsen."

Eleanor Roosevelt. Camerata Singers; Floyd Farmer, conductor. New World Records NW 1772. "Roosevelt."

Fantasy on Slane. Lynn Zeigler, organ; Elizabeth A. Sadilek, flute; Kevin Schilling, oboe and bassoon. Calcante Recordings Ltd. "Notes from Iowa."

Four on the Floor. Innova Recordings, American Composers Forum. "The Minneapolis Artists Ensemble."

Hell's Belles. Terry Rhodes, soprano; Ellen Williams, mezzo-soprano; Benton Hess, piano; Steven Reis, cello. Albany Records TROY 634. "Grand Larsen-y: Vocal Music of Libby Larsen."

Holy Roller. Paul Bro, saxophone; Indiana State University Symphonic Wind Ensemble and Faculty Winds. ELF CD 1006. "Symphonies and Such."

How Do I Love Thee? Arleen Auger, soprano; members of the St. Paul Chamber Orchestra and Minnesota Orchestra; Joel Revzen, conductor. Koch International 3-7603-2. "Women of Note."

How It Thrills Us. James Briscoe. Indiana University Press Companion CD. "Contemporary Anthology of Music by Women."

How It Thrills Us. Stephen Cleobury, director. EMI Classics. American Choral Music, CDC 7. "The Kings College Choir."

I Just Lightning. Las Cantantes; Bradley Ellingboe, conductor. University of New Mexico. Rhode-Kil Records RK 1003. "I Just Lightning."

I Thought Once How Theocritus Had Sung. Arleen Auger, soprano; Members of the St. Paul Chamber Orchestra and Minnesota Orchestra; Joel Revzen, conductor. Koch International 7346. "American Dreams: The American Music Sampler, Vol. 2."

I Thought Once How Theocritus Had Sung. Arleen Auger, soprano; Members of the St. Paul Chamber Orchestra and Minnesota Orchestra; Joel Revzen, conductor. Koch International 3 7360-2. "American Songbook: The American Music Collection, Vol. 3."

If I Can Stop One Heart from Breaking. Las Cantantes; Bradley Ellingboe, conductor. University of New Mexico. Rhode-Kil Records RK 1003. "I Just Lightning."

In a Winter Garden. Phillip Brunelle, conductor. ProArte PAD 151. "Plymouth Festival Orchestra and Chorus."

Introit (from Missa Gaia). Oregon Repertory Singers. Koch International 3-7603-2. "Women of Note."

Jack's Valentine. Las Cantantes; Bradley Ellingboe, conductor. University of New Mexico. Rhode-Kil Records RK 1003. "I Just Lightning."

Kathleen, As She Was. Cynthia Green Libby, oboe; Peter Collins, piano. Hester Park CD 7707. "Daystream Dances."

Late in the Day. Patricia Stiles, mezzo-soprano; Graham Cox, piano. Cavalli Records, Bestell Nr. CCD 308. "Vitality Begun."

Licorice Stick. Stefan Harg, clarinet; Katerina Strom-Harg, piano; Kathleen Roland-Silverstein, soprano; Asa Johansson, violin. Rhode-Kil Records RK 1001. "Licorice Stick: Clarinet Chamber Music of Libby Larsen."

Love After 1950. Susanne Mentzer, mezzo-soprano; Craig Rutenberg, piano. Koch International 7506. "The Eternal Feminine."

Margaret Songs: Three Songs of Willa Cather. Terry Rhodes, soprano; Ellen Williams, mezzo-soprano; Benton Hess, piano; Steven Reis, cello. Albany Records TROY 634. "Grand Larsen-y: Vocal Music of Libby Larsen."

Marimba Concerto: After Hampton. Colorado Symphony; John Kinzie, marimba; Marin Alsop, conductor. Koch International Classics 7520.

Mary Cassatt. Sonya Gabrielle Baker, soprano; Vicki Berneking, piano; Jeannie Little, trombone. Murray State University. "She Says, Sonya Gabrielle Baker."

Mephisto Rag. Stefan Harg, clarinet; Katerina Strom-Harg, piano; Kathleen Roland-Silverstein, soprano; Asa Johansson, violin. Rhode-Kil Records RK 1001. "Licorice Stick: Clarinet Chamber Music of Libby Larsen."

Missa Gaia: Mass for the Earth. Karen Leigh, mezzo-soprano; David Heller, piano. Classical Vocal Reprints. "Be Still My Soul: Selections from American Art Song for the Sacred Service."

Missa Gaia: Mass for the Earth. Koch International Classics 3-7279-2HI. "Oregon Repertory Singers."

Missa Gaia: Mass for the Earth. Oregon Repertory Singers. Koch International 3-7603-2. "Women of Note."

My Antonia. Paul Sperry, tenor; Margo Garrett, piano. Albany Records TROY 654. "Larsen/Hagen/Moravec/Cipullo: New American Song Cycles."

Overture for the End of a Century. "Let Music Live: Sounds of the 20th Century."

Overture: Parachute Dancing. Carol Ann Martin, conductor. Leonarda (New York). "Bournemouth Sinfonietta."

Overture: Parachute Dancing. The London Symphony Orchestra; Joel Revzen, conductor. Koch International Classics 3-7370-2-H1. "Water Music."

Pealing Fire. John Gouwens, Carillon. Culver Academies' Bookstore. "The Organ and Carillon of Culver, Vol. 3: A Summer's Night."

Perineo. Bradley Greenwald, baritone; Tim Linker, piano. Innova Recordings, no. 500. "Heartbeats: New Songs from Minnesota for the AIDS Quilt Songbook."

Reasons for Loving the Harmonica. American Boychoir. EMI/Virgin Classics. "Fast Cats and Mysterious Cows: Songs from America."

Refuge. Las Cantantes; Bradley Ellingboe, conductor. University of New Mexico. Rhode-Kil Records RK 1003. "I Just Lightning."

Ring of Fire. The London Symphony Orchestra; Joel Revzen, conductor. Koch International Classics 3-7370-2-H1. "Water Music."

Ringeltänze. Phillip Brunelle, conductor. Plymouth Music Series PMS 002. "The Plymouth Festival Orchestra and Chorus."

Schoenberg, Schenker and Schillinger. Los Angeles Chamber Orchestra. "Tribute to Mozart: Forty Years of Discovery, 1954–1994."

Settling Years, The. The Dale Warland Singers; Dale Warland, conductor. Innova Recordings, American Composers Forum. "Choral Currents."

Slang. Stefan Harg, clarinet; Katerina Strom-Harg, piano; Kathleen Roland-Silverstein, soprano; Asa Johansson, violin. Rhode-Kil Records RK 1001. "Licorice Stick: Clarinet Chamber Music of Libby Larsen."

Slang. The Verdehr Trio. Crystal Records CD940. "The Making of a Medium, Vol. 10."

So Blessedly It Sprung. Ars Nova Singers; Thomas Edward Morgan, conductor. New Art Recordings NAR-005. "Midwinter: Carols in Concert."

So Blessedly It Sprung. The New York Concert Singers; Judith Clurman, conductor. New World Records CD 80592-2. "A Season's Promise."

Solo Symphony. Colorado Symphony; John Kinzie, marimba; Marin Alsop, conductor. Koch International Classics 7520.

Sonata in One Movement. Lynn Zeigler, organ; Elizabeth A. Sadilek, flute; Kevin Schilling, oboe and bassoon. Calcante Recordings Ltd. "Notes from Iowa."

Sonata in One Movement. Hester Park CD 7704. "Summer Shimmer"

Song for a Dance (from Songs of Youth and Pleasure). Yale Glee Club; Jeffrey Douma, director. "Yale Glee Club Song: Live Concert Highlights from 2004 and 2005."

Song Without Words. Caroline Hartig, clarinet; assisted by Kevin Purrone, David Harding, Christopher Kachian, and Robert Adney. Innova Recordings ACF 002, American Composers Forum. "Dancing Solo: Clarinet Chamber Music of Libby Larsen."

Song Without Words. Stefan Harg, clarinet; Katerina Strom-Harg, piano; Kathleen Roland Silverstein, soprano; Asa Johansson, violin. Rhode-Kil Records RK 1001. "Licorice Stick: Clarinet Chamber Music of Libby Larsen."

Songs from Letters. Anne Marie Church, soprano; Linda Sweetman-Waters, piano. Josara Records JR 001CD. "American Art Song Today Alive."

Songs from Letters. Bonnie Pomfret, soprano; Laura Gordy, piano. ACA Digital Recording Inc. ACA CM20090. "De Toda La Eternidad, Songs of American Women Composers."

Songs from Letters. Terry Rhodes, soprano; Ellen Williams, mezzo-soprano, Benton Hess, piano; Steven Reis, cello. Albany Records TROY 634. "Grand Larsen-y: Vocal Music of Libby Larsen."

Songs from Letters. Laury Christie, soprano. University of South Carolina School of Music Commemorative CD. "A Journey in Song, 1981–2004."

Songs from Letters. Scottish Chamber Orchestra; Benita Valente, soprano; Joel Revzen, conductor. Koch International Classics 307481-2-H1. "Libby Larsen."

Songs from Letters. Stefan Harg, clarinet; Katerina Strom-Harg, piano; Kathleen Roland Silverstein, soprano; Asa Johansson, violin. Rhode-Kil Records RK 1001. "Licorice Stick: Clarinet Chamber Music of Libby Larsen."

Songs of Light and Love. Scottish Chamber Orchestra; Benita Valente, soprano; Joel Revzen, conductor. Koch International Classics 307481-2-H1. "Libby Larsen."

Sonnets from the Portuguese. Arleen Auger, soprano; Members of the St. Paul Chamber Orchestra and Minnesota Orchestra; Joel Revzen, conductor. Koch International 3-7346. "American Dreams: The American Music Sampler, Vol. 2."

Sonnets from the Portuguese. Arleen Auger, soprano; members of the St. Paul Chamber Orchestra and Minnesota Orchestra; Joel Revzen, conductor. Koch International 3-7360-2. "American Songbook: The American Music Collection, Vol. 3."

Sonnets from the Portuguese. Arleen Auger, soprano; members of the St. Paul Chamber Orchestra and Minnesota Orchestra; Joel Revzen, conductor. Koch International 3-7248-2. "The Art of Arleen Auger."

Sonnets from the Portuguese. Eileen Strempel, soprano; Sylvie Beaudette, piano. Centaur Records CRC 2666. "Love Lies Bleeding."

Sonnets from the Portuguese. Arleen Auger, soprano; members of the St. Paul Chamber Orchestra and Minnesota Orchestra; Joel Revzen, conductor. Koch International 3-7603-2. "Women of Note."

Stepping Westward. Las Cantantes; Bradley Ellingboe, conductor. Triangulum. "Stepping Westward."

Stepping Westward. Las Cantantes; Bradley Ellingboe, conductor. Rhode-Kil Records RK 1003. "I Just Lightning."

String Symphony. Scottish Chamber Orchestra; Benita Valente, soprano; Joel Revzen, conductor. Koch International Classics 3-7481-2-H1. "Libby Larsen."

Suite for Piano. Jeffrey Jacob, pianist. New Ariel Recordings. "Contemporary American Eclectic Music for the Piano."

Sweet and Sour Nursery Rhymes. The U.S. Air Force Singing Sergeants. "An American Choral Landscape."

Sweet and Sour Nursery Rhymes. Camerata Singers; Timothy Mount, director. Koch International Classics. "Randall Thompson, Libby Larsen."

Symphony no. 3, Lyric. The London Symphony Orchestra; Joel Revzen, conductor. Koch International Classics 3-7370-2-H1. "Water Music."

Symphony: Water Music. Minnesota Orchestra; Sir Neville Marriner, conductor. Nonesuch/Elektra 79147-1. "Water Music."

Symphony: Water Music. The London Symphony Orchestra; Joel Revzen, conductor. Koch International Classics 3-7370-2-H1. "Water Music."

Three Pieces for Treble Wind and Guitar. Annette Heim, flute; Bret Heim, guitar. Nomad Classics. "Celestials: American Music for Flute and Guitar."

Three Pieces for Treble Wind and Guitar. Caroline Hartig, clarinet; assisted by Kevin Purrone, David Harding, Christopher Kachian, and Robert Adney. Innova Recordings ACF 002, American Composers Forum. "Dancing Solo: Clarinet Chamber Music of Libby Larsen."

Today, This Spring. Las Cantantes; Bradley Ellingboe, conductor. Rhode-Kil Records RK 1003. "I Just Lightning."

Touch the Air Softly. Las Cantantes; Bradley Ellingboe, conductor. Rhode-Kil Records RK 1003. "I Just Lightning."

Try Me, Good King: Last Words of the Wives of Henry VIII. Eileen Strempel, soprano; Sylvie Beaudette, piano. Centaur Records CRC 2666. "Love Lies Bleeding: Songs by Libby Larsen."

Ulloa's Ring. Eugenia Zukerman, flute; Lisa Emenheiser, piano. ProArte PaC 1086. "Music for Flute."

Veni, Creator Spiritus. Douglas Cleveland. Gothic 49113. "Celestial Fire."

What the Monster Saw. The Cleveland Chamber Symphony; Edwin London, conductor. GM Recordings GM 2039 CD.

When I Am an Old Woman. Neva Pilgrim, soprano. Leonarda LE 338. "Women's Voices: Five Centuries of Song."

Witches Trio, The. Las Cantantes; Bradley Ellingboe, conductor. Rhode-Kil Records RK 1003. "I Just Lightning."

SOURCES

Atlas, Allan W., ed. *Anthology of Renaissance Music: Music in Western Europe, 1400–1600.* New York: Norton, 1998.

Barbieri, Susan M. "The Language of Strings: Composer Libby Larsen's Music Speaks in American Vernacular." *Strings* (November/December 1999): 70–72, 74, 76, 77.

Boyer, Douglas R. "Musical Style and Gesture in the Choral Music of Libby Larsen." *Choral Journal* 34, no. 3 (October 1993): 17–28.

Chastain, Susan. "A Conversation with Libby Larsen." *Journal of the International Alliance for Women in Music* 2, no. 1 (February 1996): 4–7.

Cook, Petronelle. *Queen Consorts of England: The Power Behind the Throne.* New York: Facts on File, 1993.

Erickson, Carolly. *Royal Panoply: Brief Lives of the English Monarchs.* New York: Quality Paperback Books, 2003.

Green, Cynthia, "Interview with Composer Libby Larsen." *International League of Women Composers Journal*, June 1992, 24–27.

Harg, Stefan. "An Interview with Libby Larsen." *The Clarinet* 30, no. 2 (June 2003): 58–61.

Hartig, Caroline. "Dancing Solo for Solo Clarinet (1994), Libby Larsen." *The Clarinet* 30, no. 1 (December 2002): 6–10.

Kessler, Richard. "Libby Larsen Interview." *NewMusicBox*, February 1999. www.newmusicbox.org/archive/firstperson/larsen/interview2.html.

Larsen, Libby. "A Composer and Her Public: A Mutual Seeking." *Symphony* 35, no. 6 (1984): 34–36.

———. "Double Joy." *American Organist* 18 (March 1984): 50–51.

———. "MENC Vision 2020 Conference Address: Music Instruction for 2020." Available on the composer's website: www.libbylarsen.com/MainFrame.html?page=Resources.html.

Lindsey, Karen. *Divorced, Beheaded, Survived: A Feminist Reinterpretation of the Wives of Henry VIII.* Reading, MA: Addison-Wesley, 1995.

Malitz, Nancy. "Song of the Monster: Libby Larsen Breaks New Ground in *Frankenstein: The Modern Prometheus,* Due for Its Premier in Minnesota this Month." *Opera News*, May 1990, 44–46.

McCutchan, Ann. *The Muse That Sings: Composers Speak about the Creative Process.* New York: Oxford University Press, 1999.

Milhorn, Tina M. "Music and Memoir: Libby Larsen's Settings of First-person Texts by Women: Me (Brenda Ueland); Songs from Letters: Calamity Jane to Her Daughter Janey; Try Me, Good King: Last Words of the Wives of Henry VIII." D.M.A. diss., University of Cincinnati, 2004.

Moorhouse, Linda R. "Libby Larsen." In *A Composer's Insight: Thoughts, Analysis, and Commentary on Contemporary Masterpieces for Wind Band,* edited by Timothy Salzman. Galesville, MD: Meredith Music Publications, 2003.

Romey, Kathy. "Interview with Libby Larsen." Held on June 10, 2002, for the Sixth World Symposium on Choral Music in Minneapolis, MN, August 3–10, 2002. Available on the composer's website: www.libbylarsen.com/resources_icb_2.jpg.

Warnicke, Retha M. *The Rise and Fall of Anne Boleyn: Family Politics at the Court of Henry VIII.* Cambridge, UK: Cambridge University Press, 1989.

Weir, Alison. *Henry VIII: The King and His Court.* New York: Ballantine, 2001.

James Spinazzola

TANIA LEÓN (1943–)

Their story is incredible. They came from different places, just like in this country. Their ancestry was African, Chinese, Spanish, and European—and they were in Cuba, and they were poor. What people had in common was that they were poor. So that is how I grew up: my family, friends, neighbors, and school; there was no separation between people. I talk about these people wherever I go. And now most of them are gone, and the only one left is the one with the direct line to the Africanos, which is my mother. All of the others are dead, but they have been dying in the distance. I have not been there; I've never been at any funeral. They have become spirits in the distance, and that, for me, is very powerful.[1]

Tania Justina León was born on May 14, 1943 in Havana, Cuba, to Oscar León and Dora Ferrán. Her parents were of mixed descent (French, Spanish, African, and Chinese), and she was exposed to numerous cultural influences at an early age. Her family was close-knit and often worked together as a result of their limited financial resources, a situation which León feels had a positive impact on her approach to working as a professional musician.

When you live in a household where there are not many means, everybody collaborates with everybody. There was a time I had to collaborate with my father in order

251

to actually keep the electricity running in the apartment. I learned through him how to put electrical wires together and how to make connections, and so I became his sideman. It was not, "She's a girl; she's not supposed to do this." So by the time I went out in the world, my whole outlook about working with people didn't have that much demarcation per se.[2]

Music was an important part of León's early years, and her aptitude was quickly recognized. At the age of four, her grandmother enrolled her in piano lessons at the Carlos Alfredo Peyrellade Conservatory, where she later studied violin and music theory,[3] and the following year her grandfather purchased her a piano. Her formal training also came at the conservatory; she earned a bachelor's degree in *solfège* and theory in 1961 and another in piano in 1963.[4] During her time at the conservatory, León also began her compositional training; she composed boleros, bossa novas, and short pieces in the style of Cuban popular music. "It's some kind of cultural pride to understand or know what can happen with the local music in all spheres, not only in the popular, but in what we term the serious music," says León. "So therefore, for us to study Chopin and to study [Ernesto] Lecuona,[5] it was on equal terms."[6] Subsequent study came at the National Conservatory in Havana from which she earned a master's degree in music education in 1964.

Following graduation, León remained in Cuba and began a promising career as a concert pianist.[7] Despite her musical success, however, she began to feel isolated and decided to live abroad in order to fully realize her potential. She later stated, "My spirit is not an island spirit. . . . I felt trapped not being able to go elsewhere without a boat."[8] León planned to immigrate to Paris, but serendipity awarded her a free flight to Miami in 1967 through the Freedom Flights program.[9] While it was an exciting opportunity, her departure from Cuba also marked the beginning of the most difficult period of her life.

A few days after arriving in Miami, León settled in New York City, and within her first year, she was asked by a friend to substitute as accompanist for a dance class at the Harlem School of the Arts.[10] The class was conducted by Arthur Mitchell, who was so impressed by her technique and improvisational skills that he offered her a position as rehearsal pianist for the Dance Theatre of Harlem, of which he was founder and director. Less than a year after that, Mitchell appointed León the Dance Theatre's first music director, a post she held from 1969 until 1980. During her eleven-year tenure, León served as pianist, conductor, and composer. She organized the Dance Theatre's music school and orchestra and composed four ballets for the troupe: *Tones* (1970), *The Beloved* (with Judith Hamilton, 1972), *Haiku* (1973), and *Dougla* (with Geoffrey Holder, 1974). She later recalled the importance of her long and fruitful association with the Dance Theatre: "Meeting Arthur Mitchell and . . . the foundation of a company starting from zero—that is what actually has shaped, I think, the Tania that I am right now."[11]

Soon after she began working at the Dance Theatre, León earned a scholarship to attend New York University, where she studied composition with Ursula Mamlok (1928–) and earned two degrees (B.S., 1971; M.S., 1975). She also spent time studying the trombone and bassoon and continued to perform as a pianist, playing with the New York College Music Orchestra in 1967, the New York University Orchestra in 1969, and the Buffalo Symphony Orchestra in 1973.[12] While encouraged by her success, León began to feel that her time was monopolized by the hours she devoted to practicing her technique and began to contemplate a change of career from pianist to conductor.

I study everybody, and that's what I love about conducting—because that's why I study. When I study the most is when I'm conducting something because I'm a total detective, and that's when you see technique. I see the technique, I see ways of coloring; I see personalities, shapes, graphics, architecture, space, culture.[13]

León's conducting career began in 1971, when the Dance Theatre of Harlem participated in the "Festival of Two Worlds" in Spoleto, Italy, accompanied by the Juilliard Orchestra. The decision was made to use live, rather than recorded, music; and though she had no formal training as a conductor, León was encouraged by Arthur Mitchell and Gian-Carlo Menotti to rehearse the orchestra and conduct the performance. She reminisced, "I had never done it in my life. It was my very first time, but I picked up the baton, and I conducted the performance."[14]

This experience sparked León's interest in conducting, and after returning to the United States she began studying with Laszlo Halasz.[15] She then had subsequent training with Vincent La Selva[16] and numerous guest conductors at the Berkshire Music Center at Tanglewood (1978), including Leonard Bernstein and Seiji Ozawa. She also began attending rehearsals of the New York Philharmonic, where for two years she was a guest of Zubin Mehta.

León's reputation grew, and throughout the 1970s she fulfilled numerous engagements as a guest conductor of American and international ensembles, including the Buffalo Philharmonic (1970, 1975); the Symphony of the New World (1974); and the BBC Northern Orchestra (1976). She served as music director for the Broadway production of *The Wiz* (1977–1978), while also helping to organize the Brooklyn Philharmonic Community Concert Series with fellow composers Julius Eastman and Talib Rasul Hakim. This weekly series was initiated at the suggestion of Lukas Foss, who was then music director. Its objective was to introduce the works of minority composers and performers to urban communities in the greater New York City area.[17]

In choosing repertoire, León is an advocate of contemporary music, especially that of Latin American composers. From 1996 to 1997, she was new music advisor to Kurt Mazur and the New York Philharmonic, and she served as Latin American music advisor to the American Composers Orchestra until 2001. Stemming from her work with that organization, she cofounded the American Composers Orchestra *Sonidos de las Americas* (Sounds of the Americas) music festivals. Featuring concerts, symposia, and master classes, the first festival was held in New York City in cooperation with Carnegie Hall and featured the music of Mexican composers. "It began with an old-fashioned fact-finding tour," León recalls, "but our calendar moved at the pace of a good conga—very fast."[18]

After resigning from the Harlem Dance Theatre in 1980, León was able to devote more time to guest conducting. She has since led some of the world's finest ensembles, including the Netherlands Wind Ensemble, the Metropolitan Opera Orchestra, the Kennedy Center Opera House Orchestra, the Beethovenhalle Symphony Orchestra, the National Symphony Orchestra of Johannesburg, the Louisville Symphony, the Leipzig *Gewandhausorchester*, the New World Symphony, members of the New York Philharmonic, and the Symphony Orchestra of Marseille, France.

It was not until the late 1970s that León considered a career as a composer. She was versed in a vast array of musical styles but feared that her diverse approach to composition would not be taken seriously by the critical New York public. "Perhaps I was looking for an entry into the mainstream," she later recalled.[19] In her early works, she searched for a way to separate herself from the influences of indigenous music that she had long studied and admired, and to discover her own compositional voice.

It was after a trip home to Cuba to visit her ailing father that León made a rather sudden and life-altering compositional turn; she began working to combine the Latin American musical influences of her youth, elements of her classical training from the Havana Conservatory and New York University, and the numerous sounds she encountered as a resident of New York City, in order to develop a highly personalized style. This new approach (in which the source sounds are clearly present, yet extremely subtle) began to attract national attention in the 1980s. Her first orchestral work, *Concerto Criollo* (1980), was commissioned by the National Endowment for the Arts, and she was named the resident composer of the Lincoln Center Institute in 1985. Subsequent commissions include those from the American Composers Orchestra (*Kabiosili*, 1988); the Cincinnati Symphony (*Carabali*, 1991); the Meet the Composer program (*Para Viola y Orquestra*, 1994); the NDR Sinfonie Orchester, Hamburg (*Horizons*, 1999); the American Composers Orchestra (*Desde . . .*, 2001); and the State University of New York (*Ácana*, 2008). Among her many chamber music commissions are those from the Da Capo Chamber Players (*Parajota De-laté*, 1988); New York City's Town Hall (*Indígena*, 1991); Ensemble Modern (*Hechizos*, 1995); the Library of Congress (*Fanfarria*, 2000); and the Fromm Music Foundation (*Esencia para Cuarteto de Cuerdas*, 2009).[20]

Tania León is especially well known for her compositions for solo piano, two of which, *Rituál* (1987) and *Mística* (2003), were performed in March 2005 at the Chicago Symphony's *MusicNow* celebration for Pierre Boulez's eightieth birthday. Recent works include *Variacíon*, written in 2004 for Gilbert Kalish (and on commission from the Gilmore International Keyboard Festival); *Tumbao* (2005), commissioned by Elena Riu; and *Para Noah* (2006), written in honor of Noah Creschevsky's sixtieth birthday.

León has also contributed significant works for solo and ensemble voices. Of particular importance is her relationship with the Western Wind Vocal Ensemble, which yielded *De-Orishas* (1982) and *Batéy* (1989); both works were written in collaboration with pianist Michel Camilo. More recent vocal works include *A Row of Buttons* (2002, SA choir), commissioned by the New York Treble Singers, and *Metisse* (2006, SATB chorus and percussion), commissioned by the Commissioning Project. Her first opera, *The Scourge of Hyacinths* (1994), was the result of a commission by the Munich *Biennale*, where it won the BMW Prize as the best new work of opera theater. She also authored the libretto, which was based on a play by the Nobel laureate Wole Soyinka. One aria, *O Yemanja* (*Mother's Prayer*), has become particularly well known; it was recorded in 1998 by Dawn Upshaw and the Orchestra of St. Luke's, conducted by David Zinman. León and Soyinka collaborated again on *Samarkand* (2005), a theater work for narrator, chorus, children's chorus, and mixed instrumental ensemble, which marked the opening of the Shaw Center for the Performing Arts in Baton Rouge, Louisiana, in March 2005.

In 1998, León earned the New York Governor's Lifetime Achievement Award, and in the same year she held the Fromm Residency at the American Academy in Rome. Other awards include those from the American Academy of Arts and Letters, the National Endowment for the Arts, Chamber Music America, the Lila Wallace/Reader's Digest Fund, ASCAP, the Koussevitzky Foundation, the National Women's History Project, the Coalition of 100 Black Women, and the Nathan Cummings Foundation. In 2004, she was featured in a composer portrait concert at Columbia University's Miller Theatre. León holds honorary doctoral degrees from Colgate University, Oberlin College, and the State University of New York, and she has served as visiting professor at Harvard University, Yale University, the University of Michigan, and the Musikschule in Hamburg, among others. She was the Karel Husa Visiting Professor of Composition at Ithaca College (1997–1998), and in 2000 she was named Claire and Leónard Tow Professor at Brooklyn

College, where she has taught since 1985. In 2006, she was awarded the rank of distinguished professor by the City University of New York board of trustees, and in 2007 she received a Guggenheim Fellowship Award in Music Composition.

> *I am tired of all our labels; I am not a feminist, am not a black conductor, and am not a woman conductor. I am nothing that the people want to call me. They do not know who I am. The fact that I am using this physical costume does not describe my energy, does not describe my entity.*[21]

Although she rarely speaks of the challenges she faced early in her career, León acknowledged preconceptions regarding gender and ethnicity in a 1989 interview for *Ebony* magazine: "It's not common for a woman of my skin color to conduct serious music, so I have to know the score inside-out, or work twice as hard as male conductors."[22] She is steadfast in her rejection of the categorization of individuals according to culture or gender, for one cannot embrace a label or category without excluding another, thus becoming inherently limited.

According to León, the term *Afro-Cuban* does not accurately represent the numerous and disparate influences that combined to make Cuban music what it is today; while African characteristics are important, they were joined with music and instruments indigenous to French, Spanish, and Chinese immigrants, as well as native Indians. She said earlier in the interview, "Tell me, when Bizet put the *habanera* in *Carmen*, did he call it Afro-Cuban!?"[23]

> *I speak with an accent, so my music might have an accent, which might not be understood by many people. And if the accent has to be roots or folklore or whatever you want to call it at some point, fine. That's okay. That's how I define this type of situation. I think that labels—going back to the Afro-Cuban thing—are selling short what the whole thing is about.*[24]

Tania León's compositions join contemporary techniques with numerous stylistic elements of Latin American, jazz, and gospel music. This pluralistic approach to composition results in an individual style that defies categorization and yields a self-portrait of the composer. Her background and environment directly affect her compositional process, and her artistry lies in the subtle manner in which these sources inform her music without overshadowing its complexity. Formidable technical demands, contemporary harmonic language, angular melodies with plentiful ornamentation, dense rhythmic layering, nearly constant rhythmic vitality, and colorful orchestration are equally important in her work. She often works from numerous sketches posted on a wall in her studio. After examining them, she formulates a concept for the piece as a whole, and her approach to assembling the work is largely intuitive.

My ideas have to do with my present. . . . They come when I least expect it, in the street, sitting at home, in the car. Ideas start tapping in anywhere, anytime. They wake me up and all of a sudden I'm hearing an entire orchestra playing something. I keep pencil and paper by the bed. Sometimes I write the rhythm, sometimes it's the pitches, sometimes it's complete. It's like making a soup. You're collecting different items before you cook.[25]

Improvisation has been an important part of León's approach to music since her early years in Cuba. She recalls improvising new arrangements of standard melodies such as *Malegueña*; these enjoyable exercises fostered her creativity and laid the foundation for her work as a pianist and composer. And this innate fondness for improvisation also led to her appreciation of jazz, to which she was first exposed with a recording of the pianist Art Tatum soon after arriving in New York City.[26] Throughout her career, León has immersed herself in various styles of jazz and has collaborated with performers such as Paquito D'Rivera and Michel Camilo.[27]

At a glance, the most salient aspect of León's rhythmic vocabulary appears to be her utilization of Latin American rhythms. While such rhythms often permeate her shorter works such as *Tumbao* (2005, piano) and *Bailarín* (1998, guitar), in her more substantial compositions they are used with great discretion; they are generally not presented until late in a piece, and then only for brief episodes. When combined with harmonic and melodic language not indigenous to Latin America, they assume the character of filtered images rather than clear aural pictures.

For me, movement is music. When I hear music, movement materializes, and vice versa. . . . There's dance in it. But to me it's not dance—it's something indigenous and vital that had no connection to dance when I wrote it.[28]

For one example, let us consider the *Four Pieces for Violoncello* (1983), León's first composition after the death of her father. As stated earlier, their last conversation inspired her to begin integrating Cuban influences into her work. The third of the four pieces is marked *Montuno*. The *son montuno* is one of the most recognizable styles of Cuban popular music, primarily due to the prevalence of a few typical piano figures, such as the one shown in figure 6.1.

Figure 6.1. *Montuno* **piano figure**

Montuno's thirty-two measures are unified by a recurring rhythmic motive derived from the *tumbaó*, a fundamental Afro-Cuban string bass pattern. Based on the *son clave*, the *tumbaó*'s pitch content mainly consists of harmonic roots, fourths, and fifths, with other pitches added as improvised passing tones.[29] The *tumbaó* is used as a primary rhythmic and harmonic layer in numerous styles derived from the *son* and *danzón* traditions, including the *cha-cha*, *mambo*, and *montuno* (see figure 6.2).[30]

Figure 6.2.   *Son clave* and· *tumbaó*, centered on C

Although the rhythm of the *tumbaó* permeates León's *Montuno*, it is partially concealed by chromatic melodic material and a lack of clear harmonic centricity. The only authentic presentation of the source material occurs in measures 23 and 24, the final two measures in example 6.1. Clearly centered on B-flat, the passage is preceded by a fifth progression (C-F-B♭) and is reinforced by a reference to the most common chord progression in Afro-Cuban music: I-IV-V. Its authenticity is enhanced by León's instruction for the cellist to knock on the soundboard on the second beat of each measure; this is typically the point at which a conga player in an Afro-Cuban ensemble would insert a rhythmic accent by slapping the instrument with his or her closed hand. Also note that the passage is prepared with a change from *arco* to *pizzicato* in order to produce a more characteristic articulation.

Example 6.1.   *Four Pieces for Violoncello*, III, mm. 15–24[31]

In *Batá* (1985), León evokes the rhythms and textures of the ritual *Batá* drumming of the Yoruban people of West Africa.[32] The piece is 167 measures in length, and the first clear reference to African rhythm is presented in measure 95, with the sudden entrance of a large cowbell.[33] Known as the *cencerro* or *campana grande*, this instrument is one of the most important in Afro-Cuban percussion; here it plays a pattern derived from the basic 6/8 bell pattern present in many African drumming traditions.[34]

Example 6.2a.   Basic Afro-Cuban 6/8 bell pattern

Example 6.2b.   *Batá*, mm. 95–96, cowbell[35]

In the following passage, note the juxtaposition of duple and triple subdivisions, a common characteristic of Afro-Cuban rhythm. This pattern continues until measure 149, and each two-measure repetition is bracketed. The cowbell is joined by the string section, whose running eighth notes have the dual purpose of maintaining rhythmic vitality as well as the pervading sonority, which in this case is a B-flat7 chord. The passage is decorated with accents carefully placed to first strengthen, and then partially obscure, the pulse of the dotted quarter note. Note the tom-tom passage, which initially reinforces the bell pattern but subsequently becomes less regular.

Example 6.3.   *Batá*, mm. 139–149, reduction

Ostinati such as the one seen in example 6.3 are a trademark of León's compositional style; they are used not only as a means of maintaining pulse and tonality, but also as a generator of form, ranging in duration from brief episodes to longer repeated sections marked with a temporal parameter. Regardless of their length, they function in the same manner as Latin American *claves*; a foundational "groove" is established, over which one or more rhythmic layers are superimposed.

In a variation of the same technique, León often writes ostinati designed not to reinforce the pulse but to temporarily suspend it. When combined with a static harmony, the ositnati create the illusion of temporary rhythmic stasis. León compares such passages to the visual image of a bicycle or automobile wheel in motion. At certain rates of speed, the inner part of the wheel often appears to move at a slower rate or even to stand still; however, this does not alter its overall motion. In her music, León freely moves between both parts of this "wheel," but in her conception, the motion is uninterrupted.[36] León's ostinati are often used as transitions, as they create a wash of sound in which individual pitches are not easily discernible and thus project no tonality or centricity. They effectively draw focus away from previous material and anticipate the next event—a kind of aural scene change.

In *Indígena*, León combines both types of ostinati to great effect. (*Indígena* will be discussed in detail later in this chapter.) In one layer, a rhythmic piano ostinato projects D centricity through registral and rhythmic importance; while in a second layer, the violins and viola repeat chromatic, arrhythmic material that is specified to be played *piano* and *sul ponticello*. The soft, shimmering quality of the strings counterbalances the rhythmic vitality of the piano.

Example 6.4.   *Indígena*, m. 21, piano and strings[37]

Rhythm is likewise an important generator of León's melodic material. Syncopation, multiple contrasting subdivisions of the beat, irregular accents, frequent and irregularly placed fermatas, plentiful ornamentation, and hemiola are frequently combined with her characteristically jagged melodic contour. The following passage shows a basic example, in which syncopation is generated simply by note grouping.

Example 6.5. *Parajota Delaté*, mm. 21–24, flute[38]

More complex rhythmic content is typical of León's music, however. The composer frequently combines myriad rhythmic techniques to create rhapsodic, quasi-improvisational melodies. The following excerpts highlight her predilection for complexity within a polyphonic texture; the resulting polyrhythms often project contrasting subdivisions, shown in example 6.6a, or meters, as in example 6.6b. The juxtaposition of simple and compound meters is prevalent (see example 6.6a and 6.6b).

Note that example 6.6b includes four distinct layers: the clarinet has primary melodic material, the piano provides one layer of melodic accompaniment, and the strings contribute two additional layers. The viola and cello reinforce the primary pulse, which in the violins is displaced by one eighth note, and the contrabass alternates between the two accent patterns.[39]

One final characteristic of León's rhythmic language is her usage of the syncopations and cross-rhythms of jazz music. Examples permeate her music and are generally in the form of short rhythmic figures which are repeated to form complete phrases. The passage shown in example 6.7 serves as a transition into the final portion of *Momentum* (1986), for solo

Example 6.6a. *Parajota Delaté*, mm. 41–44

Example 6.6b. *Indígena*, mm. 9–11

piano. It is based on a one-beat rhythmic motive, which is presented on the first and third beats of each measure; on the second beat, its syncopation is accented by placing it over eighth notes in the left hand. Of specific interest is the repetitive tritone movement in the bass (F-B); this is common to León's music (see example 6.7).

The eclecticism of León's compositional style is perhaps most evident in her melodic language. Clear references to melodic characteristics of

Example 6.7. *Momentum*, mm. 30–33[40]

Latin American music and jazz are on equal footing with chromaticism and momentary atonality. Melodic material is drawn from numerous sources, including diatonic, chromatic, whole-tone, octatonic, and blues collections. While lyrical melodies exist—for example, in *Oh Yemanja* (*Mother's Prayer*) from the opera *The Scourge of Hyacinths*—the majority are in the form of short motives or long, improvisatory lines. Jagged melodic contour is generated by extreme intervallic leaps and infrequent use of immediately repeated pitches. Prevalent use is made of major and minor seconds, their inversions (major and minor sevenths), and their equivalents after octave displacement (major and minor ninths). Plentiful ornamentation consists mainly of grace notes, glissandi, flutter tonguing in wind instruments, and tremolos in strings.

One of León's most common melodic practices is octave displacement. In the following excerpt from *Indígena*, a horizontal line utilizing the harmonic root (B), seventh, and lowered seventh scale degrees becomes an angular, disjointed melody.

Example 6.8a. *Indígena*, m. 37, clarinet

Example 6.8b. *Indígena*, m. 37, author's reduction

The technique presented above is often combined with another of León's favored compositional devices: an adaptation of the *acciaccatura*, or "crushed tone." In her treatment, one or more pitches of a tertian harmony are joined by chromatic nonharmonic tones—either simultaneously or as grace notes—and the resulting dissonance significantly alters the character of the passage. An example of this technique was demonstrated in example 6.4; reprinted below, we see that the piano part is centered on D, but in the right hand it is always surrounded by its chromatic and diatonic neighbors.

Example 6.9. *Indígena*, m. 21, piano only

Another example is found in the clarinet in measures 9 through 11 of the same work. The passage can be interpreted as an arpeggiated D7 chord; shown by the dotted slurs, the melody is shaped toward structural pitches, and the others are common natural and altered scalar extensions (the lowered ninth and lowered and natural thirteenth). Here, *acciaccaturas* appear as grace notes that decorate the melody.

Example 6.10.   *Indígena*, mm. 9-11, clarinet (author's markings)

The following passage from the first of the *Four Pieces for Violoncello* is another example of León's careful use of chromaticism in melodic construction. Grounding in E-flat major is reinforced with the registral importance of the harmonic root, carefully placed fermatas, and agogic accents. Moreover, the pitch content is drawn exclusively from the E-flat major scale, with the exception of three chromatic neighbor notes: E, F♯, and B.

Example 6.11.   *Four Pieces for Violoncello*, I, mm. 23–26

Despite their angularity, León's melodies often exhibit long-range contour that reflects chromatic voice leading. Example 6.12 illustrates an overall descending line (marked by dotted slurs) that is masked by angular internal melodic contour. Note the grace notes expanded through octave displacement and their impact on the melodic shape.

Example 6.12.   *Indígena*, mm. 1–2, flute

The melodic influence of jazz is heard to varying degrees in León's compositions, with the most common elements being references to improvisation and usage of the blues scale. Some of her most overtly jazz-inspired work can be found in *Momentum* for solo piano, an interpretation of the blues. The source material is clear in the main theme of the work; E7 is arpeggiated in the left hand, with a subtle reference to a common blues chord progression: I-IV-I-V-I.[41]

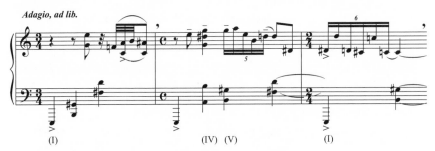

Example 6.13. *Momentum*, m. 35 (author's chord symbols)

Commonly referred to as "blue notes," the third, fifth, and seventh scale degrees are often lowered by a semitone to create dissonance with dominant seventh and minor seventh chords. These pitches, as well as two common altered scalar extensions, the lowered ninth (F) and thirteenth (C) degrees, are prominent in the melody shown above. Note that the lowered third completely replaces the natural third. This is in keeping with jazz performance practice, in which the blue fifth is almost always used in conjunction with the blue third. Also note the presence of *acciaccaturas* (the root is surrounded with its chromatic neighbors, D-sharp and F) and the expansion of semitones through octave displacement.

León has developed a complex harmonic language, and analysis reveals centricity as the main basis of harmonic organization. Striking harmonic complexity in the foreground is achieved through numerous nonharmonic tones, nonfunctional triadic harmonies, frequent tonicization, and the use of numerous collections based on the same centric pitch. Often centricity or tonality is subtly maintained by one instrument or section.

Example 6.14. *Indígena*, m. 28, piano

Common sonorities in León's music include tertian and quartal harmonies and various tonal clusters. She makes frequent use of seventh chords of all types, which are often decorated with altered and unaltered scalar extensions. Certain voicings point to the influence of the piano on her approach to harmonic construction. For instance, the nearly symmetrical chord shown in example 6.15 uses B3 and C4 as its axis; an internal fourth yields F♯ in octaves, and both hands span a major ninth (see example 6.14).

León's approach to structural organization is varied; some of her compositions loosely adhere to traditional formal models, but most are through composed. For one example, her before-mentioned *Four Pieces for Violoncello* is cast in the mold of a four-movement symphony. The opening *Allegro* is the most formal of the four movements; a declamatory motive based on the whole-tone collection sets the tone for the work, both in character and in melodic language. The second movement, "*Lento doloroso, sempre cantabile*," is much slower and more lyrical. The third movement functions as a scherzo; its dancelike quality is immediately evident through León's use of *montuno* as a character marking. Marked *vivo*, the final movement is a tour de force that displays the virtuosity of both composer and performer.

> *I don't like to follow a structure of patterns. They have their merits, but they don't function for the things I want to do. When I compose I assemble materials, and sometimes the material dictates the beginning, the middle, and the end. My most challenging situation with each piece is for it to evolve in a seamless way. Let me explain: At one point I had a fish tank with many fish, and it always fascinated me— the command a fish has in the water. It goes in one direction, and then all of a sudden shoots off in another! It's constantly moving, and it's just amazing. The fluidity is amazing, and that fluidity is what I want to capture with my sounds.*

Tania León's music exhibits careful attention to overall proportion and the balance of contrast and repetition. Her large-scale formal divisions are generally conveyed through typical means, including changes in centricity, thematic material, rhythmic language, tempo, texture, and orchestration. But while the global structure is often clearly articulated, local organization is comparatively ambiguous. Phrases are generally irregular in length and, when repeated, are altered through extension. Melodies are joined through elision and often begin in the foreground, temporarily yielding to secondary material before reemerging in a slightly altered form. Contrasting musical elements are altered at slightly different times. Rhythm is the primary generator of form, typically through unexpected changes and carefully placed silence. This is the signature of Tania León's writing: while her music is carefully structured and proportioned, it is, much like its creator, nearly void of internal boundaries.

A CONVERSATION WITH TANIA LEÓN

Occasionally we have the privilege of interacting with someone who possesses a spirit—a light, if you will—that shines so brightly we can't help but feel enriched by it. That is how I felt after each of the two interviews I had with Tania León. Both took place in New York City, and afterward I walked the streets and listened to the recordings of our conversations, riveted by her seemingly boundless energy, her life-affirming philosophy, her honesty, and, most of all, her musical and personal depth. She speaks quickly and expressively—mainly in English, but with a little Spanish mixed in—and her laugh is infectious. When discussing her music, she rarely speaks about technique; instead, she shares her inspirations and goals, and what each piece means to her. The time I spent with Ms. León led me to a greater understanding and appreciation of her art, and I hope the reader is similarly inspired by the following collection of exchanges.—James Spinazzola

SPINAZZOLA: The weight of your personal story, how you left your homeland to come to America, is not without profundity. Could you talk a bit about how you felt as you began your journey?

LEÓN: When I set foot in Miami, I thought to myself, "What a mess I've made!" I was so afraid—you have no idea—and I thought I had made the biggest mistake of my life. Even my grandmother said, "If you leave, you will never see me again." But it was my only chance to get out of the island, and I had to do it. When you left, you were stripped of your citizenship, so my passport was no longer valid. It was the point of no return. I remember thinking, "What am I going to do!?"

SPINAZZOLA: And you decided to go to New York, which must have been quite a culture shock. What did you do when you got there?

LEÓN: Well, I initially resided in the Bronx with friends of my family. And I began searching for work as a pianist while trying to immerse myself in the city's cultural community. About a year after I arrived in the States, I received word that my grandmother died, and something happened inside of me; I said to myself, "I *have* to do something. I *have* to make something happen." My family gave me the education they never had. I was the first to graduate, the first to come over [to the United States], and so it was a big responsibility. I wanted to honor them, and I want to keep honoring them.

SPINAZZOLA: Your family is very important to you. I can't imagine how it must have felt to leave them behind.

LEÓN: Yes. The last conversation I had with my father before his death proved to be a pivotal moment, both personally and professionally. He told me that he had heard a recording of my music but could not hear *me* in the music. Until that point, I had not considered allowing Cuban musical influences to inform my works. But after that, I felt an explosion inside of me, and I felt the sounds of Cuba, the sounds of my childhood, starting to come back to me.

SPINAZZOLA: Who would you cite as your primary compositional influences? Who inspires you?

LEÓN: Stravinsky is one of my foremost influences, and I've also studied the works of Ligeti, Janáček, Ives, and a number of others.

SPINAZZOLA: Your style is original, but I would agree that it melds various aspects of Stravinsky, in its rhythmic vitality and complexity, and colorful orchestration.

LEÓN: We have a few interesting things in common. Both of us began our careers with music written to accompany dance, and those experiences informed later compositions. In addition, we both remained connected to music of our heritage. Perhaps that has something to do with this connection I feel with him.

SPINAZZOLA: During your studies, would you say you were inspired by the modernists? Have you ever tried your hand at writing serial music, for instance?

LEÓN: I don't typically employ dodecaphonic techniques, no, although I have certainly studied the music of the Second Viennese School. I would say that there is always some level of tonal centeredness within even my most atonal works.

SPINAZZOLA: Let's talk about your creative process. How do you approach a new work?

LEÓN: I often work from sketches, which I sometimes post on a wall in my studio. After examining them, I formulate a concept for the piece as a whole, and then my approach to assembling the work is largely intuitive. I write what I feel.

SPINAZZOLA: Do you compose at the piano?

LEÓN: Fortunately, due to my years as a pianist and my training in solfège, I don't require a piano to compose, but I use it for improvisation and the formulation of ideas.

SPINAZZOLA: You are a very busy woman. How are you able to find time to compose while also maintaining such an extremely full schedule of lecturing and conducting?

LEÓN: I compose everywhere—on the plane, in the hotel, everywhere. Once I settle into a piece, my mind centers on it, and I start collecting materials. If you focus on what you want to do, you are always writing.

SPINAZZOLA: And so you rely upon your innate improvisational abilities?

LEÓN: Yes, but I think it is human nature. It is a part of my compositional process because it is a natural part of the human experience. We are always improvising—when we fight and when we laugh. Even when reading music we are improvising, for that is the essence of interpretation.

SPINAZZOLA: Interesting, and that takes my mind back to jazz; I know you have some experience with that.

LEÓN: Oh, yes! Jazz inspires me. I've seen jazz ensembles and how they play with abandonment—at least that is what we are led to believe. They know the "turns"—the harmonic structure of the piece—but a conversation forms between the different characters. The people that comprise the band have their own voices, and you hear them when they solo. But, whether it is by design or intuition, when they decide to strike a chord together, it's like nails. It is control and fluidity at the same time, and it captivates me. I'm always searching for a way to write music that at times might sound improvised.

SPINAZZOLA: Perhaps the most interesting aspect of your music is its rhythmic vitality; where would you say this comes from? Your upbringing? Your training?

LEÓN: Well, certainly the influence of physical response to the pulse and rhythm of music can be traced to my early years in Cuba, where dance is a common part of everyday life. But I feel that *motion*, not rhythm, is the most important element of my compositional style. It is much like riding a bicycle: in order to sit on a bicycle without falling, one must be in motion, and it is necessary to create forward momentum before riding. So I am endeavoring to maintain constant motion.

SPINAZZOLA: How do you approach the formal design of a piece, in its conception?

LEÓN: I would say that my works are frequently designed to reflect a descriptive or programmatic concept, and as a result, they are often "through-composed." For me, form isn't as important as motion, as the piece's having a sense of moving somewhere.

SPINAZZOLA: *Horizons* is a piece that comes to mind.

LEÓN: Absolutely. *Horizons* is autobiographical; it portrays memories from my early years in Cuba.

SPINAZZOLA: Would you mind sharing some of that story?

LEÓN: When I was a teenager, I used to sit on the *Malecón* and stare at the sunsets; it was like a boardwalk, and many people sat there—couples, kids with their parents. If you live on an island, you do a lot of staring at the horizon! I grew up only eight blocks from the sea, so that was very normal for me, to stare at the sea, always wondering what was on the other side. That inspired the title and design of the piece.

SPINAZZOLA: That's a lovely picture; how do you mean it inspired the design of the work, though?

LEÓN: Yes, well, the beginning is an image of me flying out of the island, and the image is of one bird in a flock. I am flying into the world, and seeing the horizon from a different point of view, from above. I go through hurricanes, et cetera—all of the many things I have gone through emotionally. Then the center of the piece is a quiet moment, introspective. I am looking down at the sea, and nothing is moving. The sound has that quality. Then, more fighting, more struggling! At the end of the piece, before the coda, it is anchored on D. That is blatant. The brass play repeated figures, and there I'm pushing through something, but the voice pushing through is now the clarinet. The bird has now grown, and it is not the same; all of a sudden, the little bird has grown into something bigger. I relate it to the condor, which is one of the national birds in Latin America. Toward the end of the piece, I decided to land in Yucatán; that is the reason for the harp, as harps are so common there. That is one of the only times in my pieces that I arrive in Latin America. The clarinet sings with strange leaps, and it is a bird's song, but a more mature bird.

SPINAZZOLA: Expressing a personal statement through one's work is a daunting task; what would you say to a young composer seeking to do this?

LEÓN: I would say that it's a gradual process. For example, consider early Beethoven. In his early work, we hear seeds of his later masterpieces. He did not change what was uniquely his—he held on to it, and it grew organically. That's what made him who he was.

SPINAZZOLA: How do you approach the teaching of composition? Is there anything specific that you endeavor to impart to your students?

LEÓN: My approach depends on the individual, but with every student, I try to help them locate the *source* of their urge to compose. First we learn to write, and then we use our tools to express ourselves in our own way. The result—be it with words, or with music—should be the manifestation of who we really are. Young composers must discover why they want to create and what they want to say, because the piece is not a mechanical tool, it is a personal statement.

SPINAZZOLA: What are you working on now? Are you busy with a new piece?

LEÓN: Oh, there is so much to do! I'm currently working on a piece for wind ensemble on a commission from the Harvard University Band. It's titled *Cumba Cumbakín*, and it refers to a type of Cuban singing that is like nothing you've ever heard; their voices are extremely versatile and expressive. For example, a group of singers can sound like a full band, as though they are playing instruments.

SPINAZZOLA: That sounds fascinating. Could you describe the piece to me?

LEÓN: Well, parts are neocontemporary; there are references to . . . . Oh, I can't describe it—there are too many elements brewing! It will be a stew! I'm looking forward to hearing it, but immediately after it's finished I need to begin writing my second string quartet, which will be premiered by the Harlem Quartet. Many other projects are also awaiting my attention, so I will constantly be working!

SPINAZZOLA: How do you react to the terminology "woman composer"?

LEÓN: Well, I am a woman; you've got me there! It's interesting. You know, there was a time when we talked about "composers"—not "male composers," "female composers," et cetera. The term *composer* encompasses everybody, and we do not need to go past that. Look, let's assume that we're talking about doctors. Do you discuss women doctors and men doctors? No! My preference is to be called by my name. Forget about the rest—my color, my gender. Our appearance has nothing to do with what's inside, with our spirit. And please understand that adhering to this philosophy has not been easy for me, because this kind of statement has sometimes offended people who believe I should be in one camp or another. Frankly, I don't care, because I believe that human beings should be above all of that. It is an imposition to tell me that I am something, or that I should call myself something. I'm not imposing myself on anyone. I'm simply who I am.

ANALYSIS: *INDÍGENA* (1991)

Tania León's *Indígena* was composed in response to a commission from New York City's Town Hall with support from the Mary Flagler Cary Charitable Trust for the Solisti New York Chamber Players. The work was premiered in 1991 with Ransom Wilson conducting. Approximately eight minutes in duration, it is scored for thirteen instruments: flute, oboe, clarinet in B-flat, bassoon, horn, trumpet in B-flat, piano, two violins, viola, cello, double bass, and one percussionist.[42] The instrumentation of the ensemble was dictated by the performing forces of the Solisti Players, but the length, style, and difficulty of the work were left to the composer's discretion.

León wrote *Indígena* not long after she returned from a visit to Cuba, and the music means to evoke images of her journey through its various programmatic elements. During her visit, she met her young nephew for the first time, and it was he and his youthful spirit that inspired the title of the piece. León recalled, "He was the most indigenous person I met in my family. He was . . . like a mango, like a palm tree." We will see that much of *Indígena* is programmatic, and that this aspect of the work's construction contributed to its formal design.

Indígena's 165 measures are loosely organized in binary form, with its two parts approximately equal in size and duration. The final measure of the work functions as a coda; it is marked to be repeated to total a length of fifteen seconds.

A	**B**	**Coda**
mm. 1-85	**mm. 86-164**	**ca. 15″** ‖
ca. 4 min.	**ca. 3$^{1/2}$ min.**	

Figure 6.3.

The internal proportions of the A section are microcosmic of the whole; it is organized into two subsections and a codetta.

Figure 6.4 illustrates the separation of subsections I and II by a centric shift from G to B. Much of the local formal design is left to analytical interpretation; most of the phrase divisions are not clearly articulated, and changes in texture, tempo, centricity, and instrumental color rarely occur simultaneously. As stated earlier, this seamlessness is an important element of León's compositional style.

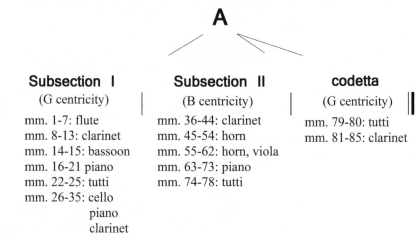

Subsection I	Subsection II	codetta
(G centricity)	(B centricity)	(G centricity)
mm. 1-7: flute	mm. 36-44: clarinet	mm. 79-80: tutti
mm. 8-13: clarinet	mm. 45-54: horn	mm. 81-85: clarinet
mm. 14-15: bassoon	mm. 55-62: horn, viola	
mm. 16-21 piano	mm. 63-73: piano	
mm. 22-25: tutti	mm. 74-78: tutti	
mm. 26-35: cello		
piano		
clarinet		

Figure 6.4.

The first half of *Indígena* employs a presentational strategy, with all of the wind instruments (excluding the trumpet) progressively featured as soloists. Each soloist represents a person León met on her visit to Cuba, and with each passage, she attempted to depict their individual speech patterns and rhythm. Taking this into consideration, it seemed analytically appropriate to divide sections according to changes in solo instruments. The rhythmic break that occurs between measures 14 and 15 can then be interpreted as a temporary pause in the bassoon solo, rather than a formal division. According to León, "The stops are abrupt because that is the way of conversation. You see someone, stop, and then continue the conversation."

The large B section is essentially a digression from the remainder of the work—in form, harmonic and melodic language, rhythm, texture, and mood. Its most notable feature is a prevalence of Afro-Cuban melodic, rhythmic, and instrumental references. In this section, León discontinues the systematic presentation of the wind instruments in favor of a series of extended trumpet solos.[43] A brief interruption by the piano in measures 121 to 126 serves as an interlude and contributes to an allusion to ternary design for the section as a whole. Because G centricity is prominent throughout, the tritone C-sharp centricity of subsection II contributes to formal division and also foreshadows the coda.

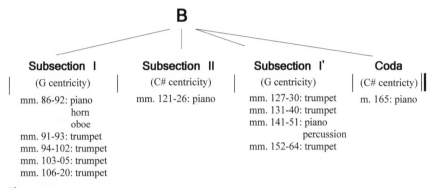

B

Subsection I	Subsection II	Subsection I'	Coda
(G centricity)	(C# centricity)	(G centricity)	(C# centricty)
mm. 86-92: piano	mm. 121-26: piano	mm. 127-30: trumpet	m. 165: piano
horn		mm. 131-40: trumpet	
oboe		mm. 141-51: piano	
mm. 91-93: trumpet		percussion	
mm. 94-102: trumpet		mm. 152-64: trumpet	
mm. 103-05: trumpet			
mm. 106-20: trumpet			

Figure 6.5.

At the surface level, it may appear that the two sections of *Indígena* have little in common; they differ in harmonic construction, melodic content, texture, and mood—and section B begins with almost no preparation. The coda also comes as a complete surprise; as such, it is one of the most effective points in the work. However, further examination reveals León's use of centricity and a carefully maintained tonal progression to join these sections and propel the work forward to its unique conclusion.

The overall form of *Indígena* is principally generated by manipulation of the octatonic collection. Named in 1963 by Arthur Berger,[44] an octatonic scale includes eight pitches in an alternation of minor and major seconds; it can be written to begin with either of those intervals.

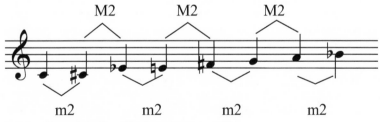

M2   M2   M2

m2   m2   m2   m2

Figure 6.6.   The octatonic collection, starting on C

The collection's symmetry has made it attractive for post-tonal composition; it maps onto itself at four levels of transposition: T_0, T_3, T_6, and T_9 (as does its complement, the diminished seventh chord), and it is limited to only three transpositions. Within this chapter, the three octatonic collections will be labeled in accordance with the system of Joseph Straus; each is identified by its first two pitch classes.[45]

Figure 6.7.   Octatonic collection at three transpositions

Given its inherent tonal ambiguity, one might initially think exclusive use of the octatonic collection in the tonal development of a work would prove difficult. On the contrary, clear tonal implications often result from use of octatonic subsets, which range from traditional tertian harmonies to more conventionally dissonant pitch class sets. If ordered to begin with the semitone, major and minor triads may originate on the first, third, fifth, and seventh degrees of the collection. As triads can be used to reinforce pitch classes, this symmetry can produce a centric conflict. According to Straus, "Sometimes, tritone-related pitch classes are poised against one another, competing for priority."[46]

This centric polarity is exposed in the fundamental structure of *Indígena*. The majority of the work employs G as its centric pitch, but in two places (the middle of the B section and again at the coda) the centricity suddenly shifts to C-sharp. While at first listening it appears to have no preparation, the shift of a tritone highlights the natural division of the octatonic collection; when the collection is transposed to begin on G, C-sharp lies at its center.[47]

Figure 6.8.   Tritone division of Oct^{1,2}

Revisiting the formal chart of *Indígena* with regard to the primary centric pitch of each section, we see that this is important to the fundamental architecture of the piece.

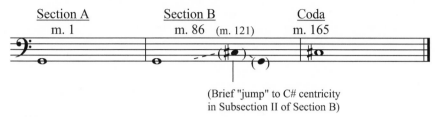

Figure 6.9.

The tritone relationship is further enhanced by examining the G^6 chord that begins section B (m. 86) and the C-sharp^6 chord that concludes the piece (m. 165). A major triad with an added sixth degree, (0358 in prime form) is an octatonic subset; it follows that because these chords are separated by a tritone, when joined together they produce Oct^{1,2}, the predominant collection of the work.

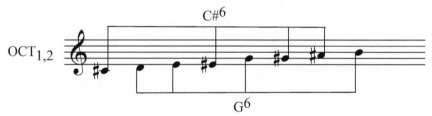

Figure 6.10.

The added sixth chord was a favorite octatonic subset for many twentieth-century composers, including Stravinsky and Messiaen. Stravinsky employed it as a chord of resolution in the "Soldier's March" of *L'Histoire du Soldat* (1918), as well as in the final movement of the *Symphony in Three Movements* (1946), and Messiaen devoted a chapter of his *Technique de Mon Langage Musical* (1956) to added sixth chords. This chord received frequent use in his compositions, often joined by the raised fourth; Messiaen referred to that pentachord as "the typical chord of the second mode of limited transpositions."[48]

According to Joseph Straus, "The diatonic and octatonic collections make a particularly effective pair."[49] As stated earlier, this is especially true in regard to the many diatonic harmonies that are also octatonic subsets. Section A of *Indígena* employs both collections on a structural level. If we consider a bass-line sketch of section A, we readily see that the most important structural pitches reinforce G centricity by arpeggiating a G major triad.

Figure 6.11.   Bass-line sketch of section A

Numerous pitch class sets are generated by the octatonic collection; one of the most often utilized is the octatonic tetrachord 0347, set class 4-17. This set class is often referred to as the major-minor chord or chord of mixed thirds. Composers have found 4-17 useful not only for its unique sound, but also for its transpositional symmetry; as an octatonic subset, it can be transposed at T_3, T_6, and T_9 without introducing any pitches outside of the collection. Stravinsky was one of the many composers fond of this particular sonority, and it is therefore unsurprising to find it functioning as the initial sonority of *Indígena* (see example 6.15).

Although there are five pitch classes involved, the chord is yet identified as a tetrachord, because the F-sharp of the contrabass does not function as part of the sonority, but rather as a means of obscuring G as the foundational pitch. We must recall León's common use of chromatic neighboring pitches as a generator of nonfunctional dissonance.

In the final measures of the work, we see the aforementioned C-sharp⁶ chord in the left hand of the piano part. G^7 and A^7 are not being considered as part of the sonority because of their registral separation, and because in relation to

Example 6.15. *Indígena*, opening tetrachord

the chord tones of G-sharp and A-sharp, they function in the same manner as the F-sharp in the previous example.

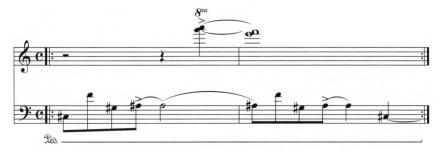

Example 6.16. *Indígena*, final sonority

León's choice of these sonorities also reflects her treatment of tonality and dissonance. Much of the piece is locally atonal, but in the overall progression of the work, dissonance is treated traditionally. The inherent dissonance of the major-minor chord at the outset creates a sense of drama, whereas the conclusion on an added sixth chord projects a relative feeling of finality and resolution.

While theoretical analysis yields important insights into how the piece is constructed, much will arguably go unnoticed by the listener. More recognizable will be the references to jazz in the first half of the work, and to Latin American music in the second half. Section A exhibits the character of improvisation, the melodic inflection of blue notes, and the harmonic and melodic vocabulary of post-bebop jazz. The correlations between bebop, blues, and the octatonic collection should not be ignored. Shown below is the blues scale based on G; note its similarity with Oct[1,2]. Both collections feature the three blue notes, and the octatonic collection includes two altered chord extensions: the lowered ninth and thirteenth.

Figure 6.12.   Blues and octatonic scales in relation to G[7]

Melodic usage of the blues scale in section A of *Indígena* includes the passage shown in example 6.18. This transition begins with an excerpt from the F-sharp major pentatonic collection, briefly alludes to the pervading G centricity, returns to F-sharp pentatonic, and finally employs a fragment of the D blues scale to lead to D centricity in the following measure. The harmonic shift (F#-G-F) is comparable to a jazz improvisational technique commonly referred to as side stepping, or temporarily moving a semitone away from a given chord. Due to the close proximity of the pitches, "the ear can easily relate the line to its actual harmonic base and conceive the logic in the dissonance."[50]

Example 6.17.   *Indígena*, mm. 24–25, reduction

In *Indígena*'s opening flute solo, the combined sound of the G major-minor chord and the melodic material provides further references to jazz improvisational practices. Numerous chromatic passing tones, altered extensions, and the juxtaposition of the natural and lowered third are joined by prevalent octave displacement. Note that the melodic contour highlights important chord tones and extensions; the passage begins on the raised eleventh, falls to the lowered seventh (then the lowered thirteenth), rises to the root, falls to the raised eleventh, rises to the third, and finally resolves on that chord tone in the third measure. This use of "goal tones," as well as the chromatic melodic language of the passage, is quite common in contemporary jazz improvisation.[51]

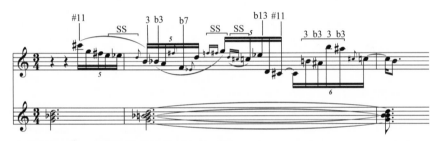

Example 6.18.   *Indígena*, mm. 1–3, reduction

Another example is the solo clarinet in measures 9 through 11, arpeggiating an embellished D⁷ chord. Note the structural importance of the natural and lowered third and fifth and the presence of altered extensions. Numerous grace notes provide another example of León's use of chromatic neighbor tones in melodic construction.

Example 6.19.   *Indígena*, m. 9, clarinet

A final example is demonstrated in the piano, which also has important melodic material in measures 9 through 11. The D centricity of the clarinet solo presented above is reinforced, but with great subtlety. In example 6.21, the dotted slurs follow the persistent alternation between D and D-sharp.

Example 6.20. *Indígena*, mm. 9–11, piano

The second measure (above) highlights a short descending line that is quite reminiscent of post-bebop jazz improvisation; it begins on the dominant and then moves to its tritone substitute.[52] While the passages presented above do not overtly sound like jazz, examination reveals compelling evidence of its influence on León's melodic and harmonic language.

León states that section B of *Indígena* was designed to evoke the sound of a *comparsa*. In current usage, this term refers to an Afro-Cuban street band assembled by city districts or neighborhoods for participation in Carnival celebrations.[53] In addition to energetic music and elaborately choreographed dance routines, *comparsa* members typically wear decorative homemade costumes, carry a banner bearing their name, and compose original songs for the occasion. Instrumental combinations generally feature a lead trumpeter and an ensemble of trumpets and other brasses, various percussion instruments, sometimes the *corneta China*,[54] and many other instruments improvised from household materials, including bells, whistles, frying pans, and tire rims.[55]

Comparsas represent a musical genre called *conga*, which has been adapted for use in Carnival celebrations and become known as *la conga comparsa*. It is played in cut time at fast tempos and features call-and-response passages between the lead vocalist and the other singers, as well as improvised solos by the lead trumpeter. The exact sound of *la conga comparsa* is quite varied, due in part to regional differences (for example the *conga Habanera* and *conga Matanzera*) and to the improvisatory nature of the performances. The crucial constant is its rhythmic foundation which, as with all Cuban rhythms, is found in the *claves*.

The rhythmic concept of the *clave* originated in Africa, but due to the integration of African culture in Latin America, it has influenced the music of nearly all of Central and South America and the Caribbean islands. In Afro-Cuban music, *clave* rhythms have been codified in two patterns:

clave de son and *clave de rumba*, each of which can be played in duple or 6/8 meter. The rhythms are two measures long and are typically repeated without variation. Shown in figures 6.13a and 6.13b are both forms of the *clave de son.*

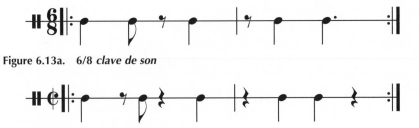

Figure 6.13a. 6/8 *clave de son*

Figure 6.13b. 2/2 *clave de son*

The following example of a *conga de comparsa* is printed in Ed Uribe's book, *Afro-Cuban Percussion and Drum Set.*[56] It is played in time, with a tempo of approximately quarter = 130. In this case, the polyrhythmic texture is built on the foundational *son clave.* Section B of *Indígena* is informed by this layering process, as well as the instruments and their characteristic rhythms.[57]

Figure 6.14. *Comparsa* percussion instruments[58]

The most audible method by which León integrates Afro-Cuban music into section B is in instrumental treatment. In section A, the woodwinds and horn are featured as soloists, but in section B they join the strings in an accompanimental role and are used for their percussive quality in a manner similar to that of Stravinsky. These instruments are given melodic material on only two occasions, and *tutti* rhythms simulate the *comparsa* brass section. The trumpet, which is relatively unimportant in section A, is featured throughout, clearly in reference to the lead trumpeter of the *comparsa*. In like manner, section A features the marimba as the primary percussion, which generally adds to the accompaniment of the piano and strings. But in section B, the marimba is replaced by an assortment of nonpitched percussion. And although León does not employ any of the specific Afro-Cuban instruments shown in figure 6.14, the instruments she uses have similar timbres and employ characteristic rhythms, as shown in figure 6.15.

Afro–Cuban instruments: **Representative *Indígena* instruments:**

timbale   – – – – – – – – – – – – – –   roto toms
congas   – – – – – – – – – – – – – – ·   floor toms
bombo   – – – – – – – – – – – – – – ·   bass drum
sartenes   – – – – – – – – – – – – –   porcelain mugs

Figure 6.15.

At the outset of section B (measure 85), the woodwinds and strings repeat a G major chord in ostinato fashion. This is the first time in the work that G centricity is clearly audible, and it is reinforced by a shift to subdominant C in measures 90 and 91 and the subsequent return to G in measure 92. Harmonically, this provides a clear reference to traditional Afro-Cuban music, which is largely built on I, IV, and V chords. The passage sweeps away the chromaticism of the previous section, creates a change of mood, and serves as an introduction to the trumpet solo. Shown in example 6.21 are the first three measures of the ostinato.

Example 6.21.   *Indígena*, reduction of mm. 86–88, woodwinds and strings

The passage is constructed from four one-beat germinal rhythmic motives and does not exhibit a repetitive pattern. In character, it is informed by the Afro-Cuban *campana*, or cowbell. This instrument has a function similar to the ride cymbal in jazz, playing syncopated rhythmic figures over a steady pulse. In *campana* performance practice, the bell is held loosely in one hand, with the index finger used as a method of dampening the bell to produce open and closed tones; these translate to the accented and unaccented notes shown above. To represent the

Afro-Cuban style with her own devices, León combines characteristic *campana* rhythms with chordal accompaniment, withholds the underlying pulse, and sets the passage in 3/4 time, a meter that is rarely used in Afro-Cuban music.

Apart from the influence of the *comparsa* ensemble, we can readily see the influence of the contemporary timbale-based Afro-Cuban drum set, which allows one person to simulate an entire percussion ensemble. It commonly includes at least two and up to four timbales, a variety of cowbells and cymbals used for ride patterns, a kick bass drum, and a wood block.

The first percussion entrance in section B is in measure 94, where the roto-toms provide an introduction, and then the bass drum "kicks the band."[59]

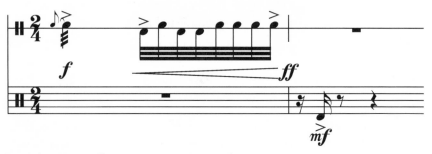

Example 6.22. *Indígena*, mm. 94–95, percussion

The passage above is reminiscent of a characteristic timbale rhythm called the *abanico*, which in Spanish means "fan." The roll evokes the sound of a fan unfolding and leads the ensemble in a new direction.[60] The *abanico* is repeated in measures 106 and 122; both passages also prepare new material.

One last interesting aural effect begins in measure 116, with the entrance of two porcelain mugs. For the remainder of the piece, the mugs maintain rhythmic vitality with a ride pattern, which on an Afro-Cuban drum set would be played on two cowbells of contrasting pitch. The mugs are used to evoke a memory from the composer's childhood, when extemporaneous musical performance was an integral part of her family's daily life. She recalls evenings at a full dinner table when everyone joined in an improvised groove, using tabletop items as percussion instruments; among these were coffee cups played with silverware. This is a final place in this piece, and just one of many in Tania León's music, in which she references strong ties to her family and its importance in her life and career.

CODA

Tania León currently resides in New York State and divides her time between numerous composition projects and a wide range of conducting, teaching, and speaking engagements.[61] Through her work in all of these areas, she has become a distinctive and vital voice in contemporary music. Her method of combining complex musical construction with numerous musical influences, most notably Latin American music and jazz, yields a compositional style that is personal, original, and quintessentially American. Her vision, though, is of a global society in which there are no demarcations of gender or race, and where the contributions of those in the community transcend geographical and social boundaries. León continues to spread that message to audiences throughout the world.

It is because of the place in which I grew up—my family, friends, neighbors, and school; there was no separation between people. Therefore, leaving Cuba and coming into the world and seeing all of this disturbing behavior from people—it is something I have never been able to comprehend. That began when I first came to this country. Martin Luther King Jr. was still alive and walking the streets, and I saw his assassination; I saw Robert Kennedy's assassination; it was the midst of the Vietnam War. Everything was happening. And being in New York, which to me is one of the most exciting places in the world, because everybody is here; my point is that, because everybody's here, we have to do something about getting along.

NOTES

1. Tania León, interview by author, audio recording, New York, NY, August 4, 2009. Unless otherwise cited, all quotations and other information are from direct correspondence or interview between the author and the composer, and permission for their usage has been granted by the composer. Photo used by permission, Michael Provost.

2. Tania León, "What Is American Music?" interview by Frank J. Oteri, *NewMusicBox* 1, no. 4, August 4, 1999, www.newmusicbox.org/page.nmbx?id=04fp00/ (accessed May 24, 2005).

3. K. Robert Schwarz, liner notes to *Indígena*, Continuum, Tania León, director, Composers Recordings CR1662, 1994.

4. Donna Jean Reiner, "The Colors of Culture: Characteristics in Selected Works of Tania Justina León" (Ph.D. diss., Union Institute, 2000), 38.

5. Lecuona (1896–1963) was a Cuban composer and pianist who was educated at the National Conservatory in Havana. He is known for his salon piano pieces and many of his songs, though he also composed music in a more formal style.

6. León, "What Is American Music?"

7. León also earned a degree in accounting and business administration from Havana University (1965), in the event that her hopes for a performing career did not come to fruition.

8. León, "What Is American Music?"

9. The Freedom Flights program was begun by the administration of President Lyndon B. Johnson. Between 1965 and 1971, it provided free travel to Miami for 250,000 Cubans refugees. Tickets were awarded through a drawing similar to a lottery.

10. Reiner, "The Colors of Culture," 41.

11. León, "What Is American Music?"

12. Reiner, "The Colors of Culture," 40.

13. Tania León, interview by Jenny Raymond.

14. Anne Lundy, "Conversations with Three Symphonic Conductors: Dennis DeCoteau, Tania León, Jon Robinson," *Black Perspective in Music* 16, no. 2 (Autumn 1988): 217.

15. Halasz (1905–2001) was the first music director of the New York City Opera Company.

16. La Selva joined the faculty of the Juilliard School in 1969, and he founded the New York Grand Opera Company in 1973.

17. Reiner, "The Colors of Culture," 43.

18. Octavio Roca, "Sonidos de las Americas: Mexico—the Sound of America," *Symphony* 45, no. 3 (May/June 1994): 38.

19. Schwarz, liner notes for *Indígena*.

20. Tania León, composer's homepage, January 6, 2006, www.tanialeon.com (August 1, 2009).

21. Lundy, "Conversations," 219.

22. Dalton Narire, "The Maestros," *Ebony* 46, no. 4 (February 1989): 62.

23. Tania León, interview by Jenny Raymond.

24. Tania León, interview by Jenny Raymond.

25. Philippa Kiraly, "Musical Melding," *Symphony* 42, no. 5 (1991): 29.

26. Tania León, interview by Frank J. Oteri. Art Tatum (1910–1956) was a pianist who mastered the "stride" style prevalent in New York City in the early decades of the twentieth century.

27. Born in Cuba in 1948, Paquito D'Rivera is a Grammy-winning clarinetist, saxophonist, and composer. Michel Camilo (1954–) is a native of the Dominican Republic and is one of the most respected living jazz pianists and composers. Among his many honors are two Latin Grammy Awards.

28. Kiraly, "Musical Melding," 29.

29. In Latin American music, *claves* refers not only to the instrument, but to standard, foundational rhythmic patterns over which numerous rhythmic layers are superimposed.

30. The *son* is the most influential style of Afro-Cuban popular music. Its inception has been traced to integration of Spanish and African music in the eastern Cuban province of Oriente and is now acknowledged as a national style. The *danzón* also developed in Oriente, which in the late 1700s became populated with Haitian immigrants who were largely of French descent. The gradual adaptation of the French *contredanse* led to the *danza*, then the *habanera*, and finally to the *danzón*.

31. Excerpts from *Four Pieces for Violoncello* by Tania León © 1983 Southern Music Pub. Co. Inc. Used by permission. All rights reserved.

32. *Batá* drums are two headed and hourglass shaped. In Yoruban religious rituals called *santeria* ceremonies, the drums are used to contact deities called *orichas*.

33. The Afro-Cuban cowbell is a descendant of the *guataca*, which is the blade of a garden hoe struck with a large nail or metal spike.

34. Ed Uribe, *The Essence of Afro-Cuban Percussion and Drum Set* (Miami: Warner Bros., 1996), 35.

35. Excerpts from *Batá* by Tania León © 1985 Southern Music Pub. Co. Inc. Used by permission. All rights reserved.

36. Uribe, *The Essence*, 35.

37. Excerpts from *Indígena* by Tania León © 1994 Southern Music Pub. Co. Inc. Used by permission. All rights reserved.

38. Excerpts from *Parajota Delaté* by Tania León © 1991 Southern Music Pub. Co. Inc. Used by permission. All rights reserved.

39. The harmonic basis of this passage is discussed in examples 50 and 51.

40. Excerpt from *Momentum* by Tania León © 1984, 1986 Southern Music Pub. Co. Inc. Used by permission. All rights reserved.

41. The tonic chord in the blues is generally a dominant seventh chord.

42. Percussion instruments include two tom-toms, two roto-toms, two porcelain mugs, marimba, bass drum, and shaker.

43. The programmatic nature of this textural change will be discussed later in this chapter.

44. Arthur Berger, "Problems of Pitch Organization in Stravinsky," *Perspectives of New Music* 2, no. 1 (Fall/Winter 1963): 11.

45. Joseph Straus, *Introduction to Post-Tonal Theory*, 2nd ed. (New Jersey: Prentice Hall, 2000), 120.

46. Straus, *Introduction to Post-Tonal Theory*, 125.

47. This reveals another parallel with Stravinsky, who often exploited this tritone relationship. The reader is referred to pp. 18–26 of Arthur Berger's article, "Problems of Pitch Organization in Stravinsky," *Perspectives of New Music* 2, no. 1 (Fall/Winter 1963), for a description of octatonic tritone polarity in *Les Noces*.

48. Olivier Messiaen, *Technique de mon langage musical*, trans. John Satterfield (Paris: Leduc, 1956), 48.

49. Straus, *Introduction to Post-Tonal Theory*, 123.

50. Mark Levine, *The Jazz Theory Book* (Petaluma, CA: Sher Music, 1995), 187.

51. This correlation may be clearly illustrated by comparing León's flute solo with excerpts of solos by the saxophonist John Coltrane and the trumpeter Miles Davis.

52. Tritone substitution is common in post-bebop jazz improvisation. Basically, for any dominant sonority, one can substitute its tritone. This yields additional scalar material for the soloist, a more interesting harmonic progression, and often smoother voice leading. For example, a ii-V-I progression in G would typically be Em7-A7-D; a "tritone sub" results in chromatic root movement: Em7-E♭7-D.

53. Robin Moore, *Nationalizing Blackness: Afrocubanismo and Artistic Revolution in Havana, 1920–1940* (Pittsburgh: University of Pittsburgh Press, 1997), 62.

54. The Chinese cornet is a double-reed instrument similar to the oboe; it was introduced in Cuba by Chinese immigrants who arrived in that country in the mid-1800s.

55. Moore, *Nationalizing Blackness*, 64.

56. Uribe, *The Essence*, 191.

57. It is important to remember that actual *conga de comparsa* rhythms are quite varied as a result of regional differences and the improvisational techniques of individual performers.

58. The *conga, rebajador, salidor,* and *quinto* are *conga* drums of different sizes. In performance, their rhythms are colored with complex playing techniques including open and closed tones, slaps, and palm tones.

59. The technique of "kicking" the band is common to both jazz and Latin big band drummers. Usually on a bass or snare drum, the "kick" lends a more percussive attack to an ensemble entrance.

60. Uribe, *The Essence*, 117.

61. Photo used by permission, Michael Provost.

APPENDIX A: LIST OF WORKS

Opera

Scourge of Hyacinths full opera (1999), chamber opera (1994)
    Libretto by T. León, based on a play by Wole Soyinka
    M, 3T, 3Bar, B, 3 spkrs; 1(A fl, pic)-1(E♭, b cl)-A sax(T sax)-1(cbn); 1-1(cnt)-T tbn-0;
    3 perc, pf; solo str
    Commissioned by the Munich Biennale for New Music Theater; full orchestra edition premiered by the Grand Théâtre de Genève, Switzerland
    (duration ca. 90 minutes)

Ballet

Tones (1970)
  2-2-1-0; 1-0-1-1; timp, 2 perc, pf, str
  Commissioned by the Dance Theatre of Harlem
  (duration ca. 18 minutes)
The Beloved [with Judith Hamilton] (1972)
  fl, ob, cl, bn, pf, vc, db
  For the Dance Theatre of Harlem
  (duration ca. 10 minutes)
Haiku (1973)
  fl, bn, 5 perc
  Commissioned by the Dance Theatre of Harlem
  (duration ca. 25 minutes)
Dougla [with Geoffrey Holder] (1974)
  2 fl, perc
  For the Dance Theatre of Harlem
  (duration ca. 20 minutes)
Belé [with Geoffrey Holder] (1981)
  Solo pf, perc, str
  For the Dance Theatre of Harlem
  (duration ca. 15 minutes)
Inura (2009)
  Voices (SATB), strings, percussion
  Commissioned by Brandon Fradd for Dance Brazil
  Premiered March 19, 2009, at the Skirball Center, New York City
  (duration ca. 40 minutes)

Mixed Genre

Drummin' (1997)
  fl (pic)-cl (b cl)-sax (sop/alto/tenor); bn (contra bn)-hn-2 tpt-tbn; 2 perc-trap set;
  pf (synth); vn-va-vc-db (b gtr); ethnic percussion ensembles
  Co-commissioned by Miami Light Project, Miami-Dade Community College,
  Arizona State University, and the New World Symphony
  (duration ca. 60 minutes)
Duende (2003)
  Baritone; 3 bata drums; 4 percussionists
  Commissioned by Fest der Kontinente, Berlin, Germany, in honor of the eighti-
  eth birthday of Gyorgy Ligeti
  (duration ca. 18 minutes)
Samarkand (2005)
  Text by Wole Soyinka
  Speaker, SATB, children's chorus, A fl/sax, 2 perc, 3 bata drums, pf, 2 vc
  Commissioned by *Southern Crossroads* in celebration of the opening of the Shaw
  Center for the Arts, Baton Rouge, Louisiana
  (duration ca. 60 minutes)

Orchestra

Concerto Criollo (1980)
Solo timp, solo pf; 2-2-2-2; 4-4-3-0; perc; str
Commissioned by the National Endowment for the Arts
(duration ca. 20 minutes)

Batá (1985, rev. 1988)
2(pic)-2(eh)-2(b cl)-2; 2-2-2-1; 2 perc, hp, pf, cel; str
Commissioned by the Bay Area Women's Philharmonic
(duration ca. 7 minutes)

Kabiosile (1988)
Solo pf; 2(pic)-2(eh)-2(b cl)-2(cbn); 4-2-3-0; timp-2 perc; str
Commissioned by the American Composers Orchestra
(duration ca. 8 minutes)

Carabalí (1991)
2(pic)-2,eh-2,b cl-2,cbn; 4-3-3-1; timp-3 perc, hp, pf, cel; str
Commissioned by the Cincinnati Symphony Orchestra
(duration ca. 17 minutes)

Para Viola y Orquestra (1994)
Va solo; 2(pic, A fl)-2-2(b cl)-2(cbn); 2-2-1-0; timp-2 perc, cel; str
Commissioned by Meet-the-Composer/Reader's Digest Commissioning
Program
(duration ca. 18 minutes)

Seven Spirituals (arr. Ryan, orch. León) (1995)
Bar solo (or B Bar); 2(pic)-1-1-1; 2-2-1-1; 2 perc, pf, str
For the Leipzig Gewandhaus Orchestra
(duration ca. 20 minutes)

Horizons (1999)
Commissioned by the NDR Sinfonie Orchester, Hamburg, and Hammoniale
Festival der Frauen, Germany
(duration ca. 10 minutes)

Desde . . . (2001)
2(pic)-2(eh)-2(b cl)-2(cbn); 4-2-3-0; timp-2 perc; str
Commissioned by the American Composers Orchestra with support from the
Koussevitsky Music Foundation Inc.
(duration ca. 18 minutes)

Didn't My Lord Deliver Daniel (arr. León) (2005)
Bar solo; 3-2-2-2; 2-2-3-0; timp; str
Commissioned by the Albany Symphony Orchestra with support from Paul
Underwood
(duration 3 minutes)

Ácana (2008)
2(pic)-2-2(b cl)-2; 2-2-1; 2 perc, pf; str
Commissioned by the Research Foundation of the State University of New
York–Purchase College and Orpheus with support from the New York State
Music Fund
Premiered by Purchase College, February 29, 2008, and Orpheus, April 1, 2008,
Carnegie Hall, New York City
(duration ca. 13 minutes)

Band/Wind Ensemble

Alegre (2000)
2 fl (ob may substitute for fl 2), 2 cl in Bb, alto sax, tsax, 2 tpt in Bb, trbn, bar,
tuba, perc (4 players: 2 bongos, 4 toms, maracas, bd)
Commissioned by the American Composers Forum for New Band Horizons
(duration ca. 3 minutes)

Mixed Chamber Ensemble

Pet's Suite (1980)
fl, pf
Commissioned by Composers' Forum
(duration ca. 20 minutes)
Permutation Seven (1981)
fl, cl, tpt, perc, vn, vc
Commissioned by the Lincoln Center Institute
(duration ca. 15 minutes)
Ascend (1983)
4 hn, 4 tpt, 3 tbn, tba, 3 perc
Commissioned by the Queens Symphony
(duration ca. 3 minutes)
String quartet
Commissioned by the Fromm Music Foundation for the Del Sol Quartet
Premiered on May 8, 2009, at Presidio Chapel, San Francisco, CA
(duration ca. 18 minutes)
A La Par (1986)
pf, perc
Commissioned by the Whitney Museum
(duration ca. 13.5 minutes)
Elegia a Paul Robeson (1987)
violin, cello and piano
Parajota Delaté (1988)
Commissioned by the Da Capo Chamber Players, 1988
fl, cl, vn, vc, pf
For the Netherlands Wind Ensemble, 1990
fl, ob, cl, bn, pf
(duration ca. 4.5 minutes)
Indígena (1991)
fl, ob, cl, bn, hn, tpt, pf, perc, 2 vn, va, vc, cb
Commissioned by New York City's Town Hall
(duration ca. 8 minutes)
Crossings (1992)
hn, 4 tpt, 4 tbn, tuba
Commissioned by the City University of New York
(duration ca. 1 minute)
Arenas d'un Tiempo (1992)
cl, vc, pf

Commissioned by the New York State Music Teachers Association
(duration ca. 12 minutes)

Ajiaco (1992)
electric guitar and piano
Commissioned by the Schanzer/Speach Duo
(duration ca. 7 minutes)

Son Sonora (1993)
fl, gui
Commissioned by Duologue
(duration ca. 15 minutes)

sin normas ajenas (1994)
fl(pic), ob, cl; pf, 2 perc; 2 vn, va, vc
Commissioned by the U.S.-Mexico Fund for Culture
(duration ca. 7 minutes)

Tau (1995)
electric oboe, electric bass, electronic keyboards
Commissioned by First Avenue

Hechizos (1995) 15:00
fl/pic, ob, cl(A and B-flat), b cl/sop sax/ten sax; hn, tpt(B-flat), tbn; 2 perc, pf/
cel/hpsd, gui; vn, va, vc, cb
Commissioned by Ensemble Modern
(duration ca. 15 minutes)

De Color (1996–1997)
vn, mar
Commissioned by Marimolin

Saóko (1997)
For the Meridian Arts Ensemble
brass qnt
Commissioned by the South Florida Composers Alliance/Center for Cultural
Collaborations International
(duration ca. 9 minutes)

Entre nos (1998)
cl, bn, pno
Commissioned by Trio Neos
(duration ca. 12 minutes)

Satiné (2000)
2 pianos
Commissioned by Mirta Gomez
(duration ca. 7 minutes)

Fanfarria (2000)
4 tpt, 2 tbn, bass tbn, 1 perc (lg sus cym, tamburo ten, med bass dr, lg bass dr)
Commissioned by the Library of Congress for the Copland Centennial Celebration
(duration ca. 3 minutes)

De Memorias (2000)
fl, ob, cl, hn, bn
Commissioned by the Mexico City Woodwind Quintet with support from the
Mexico/U.S. Fund for Culture

(duration ca. 9 minutes)
Caracol (2000)
>vn, va, vc, perc, pno
>Commissioned by the Manchester Music Festival
>(duration ca. 7.5 minutes)

Toque (2006)
>cl, alto sax, pno, 2 perc, vn, db
>Commissioned and premiered by Opus 21
>(duration ca. 8 minutes)

Raices (Tabla Raza) (2007)
>fl, vn, voice, pno, double bass, tabla solo, 2 perc
>Commissioned by Latin Fiesta with support from the Philadelphia Music Project, Pew Charitable Trust
>Premiered September 22, 2007, Philadelphia, PA

Alma (2007)
>fl, pno
>Commissioned by the Bay Paul Foundation as part of the Flute Book for the Twenty-first Century developed through Meet the Composer's New Music, New Donors Initiative
>Premiered March 29, 2007, by Marya Martin at the Weill Recital Hall, New York City
>(duration ca. 8 minutes)

Ancients (2008)
>2 sop, fl, cl, perc, va, vc
>Commissioned by Carolina Performing Arts for Terry Rhodes
>Premiered March 27, 2008, Chapel Hill, NC

Instrumental Solo

Four Pieces for Cello Solo (1983)
>(duration ca. 12 minutes)

¡Paisanos Semos! (1984)
>Guitar
>(duration ca. 4.5 minutes)

Momentum (1984)
>Piano
>Commissioned by the Women Composers Congress (Mexico)
>(duration ca. 7.5 minutes)

Rituál (1987)
>piano
>Commissioned by Affiliate Artists Inc.
>(duration ca. 7 minutes)

Bailarín (1998)
>guitar
>Commissioned and premiered by David Starobin
>(duration ca. 4 minutes)

Axon (2002)

violin and interactive computer
Commissioned for ISCM, Hong Kong, and premiered by Mari Kimura
(duration ca. 12 minutes)
Mistica (2003)
  piano
  Commissioned and premiered by Ursula Oppens
  (duration ca. 12 minutes)
Variación (2004)
  piano
  Commissioned by the Gilmore Festival
La Tina (2004)
  piano
  Commissioned by the Lucy Moses School
  (duration ca. 3 minutes)
Hebras d' Luz (2004)
  electric viola
  Commissioned and premiered by Martha Mooke
  (duration ca. 8 minutes)
Tumbao (2005)
  piano
  Commissioned by Elena Riu
  (duration ca. 3 minutes)
Para Noah (2006)
  piano
  Written in honor of Noah Creschevsky's sixtieth birthday
  (duration ca. 1 minute)
Abanico (2007)
  violin, interactive computer
  Commissioned by the University of Maryland for Airi Yoshioka
  Premiered May 9, 2007, at the America's Society, New York City

Vocal Ensemble

El Manisero [Simons, arr. León] from "Two Cuban Songs"
  12 solo voices (SSSAAATTTBBB)
  Commissioned by Chanticleer
  (duration ca. 3 minutes)
Drume Negrita [Grenet, arr. León] from "Two Cuban Songs"
  12 solo voices (SSSAAATTTBBB)
  Commissioned by Chanticleer
  (duration ca. 3 minutes)
Namiac Poems (1975)
  Voices and mixed ensemble
  Written for New York University Contemporary Ensemble
Spiritual Suite (1976)
  Narrator, 2 sopranos, chorus and amplified ensemble
De-Orishas (1982)

Text by Betty Neals
2 sopranos, countertenor, 2 tenors, bass
Commissioned by the Western Wind Vocal Ensemble
(duration ca. 11 minutes)

Heart of Ours—A Piece (1988)
Texts by R. Sandecki, American Indians
T solo, men's chorus; fl, 4 tpt, 2 perc
Commissioned by the Vietnam Veterans' Theater Company
(duration ca. 8 minutes)

Batéy [with Michel Camilo] (1989)
Text by T. León, M. Camilo
2 sopranos, countertenor, 2 tenors, bass
Commissioned by the Western Wind Vocal Ensemble
(duration ca. 30 minutes)

Sol de Doce (1997)
Text by Pedro Mir
12 solo voices (SSSAAATTTBBB)
Commissioned by Chamber Music America
(duration ca. 7 minutes)

May the Road Be Free (1999)
Text by John Marsden
Children's chorus and percussion
Commissioned by Lincoln Center for the Tree Lighting Ceremony (New York)
(duration ca. 4 minutes)

Rezos (2001)
Text by Jamaica Kincaid
SATB choir
Commissioned by Terry Knowles and Marshall Rutter to honor Grant Gershon, music director, Los Angeles Master Chorale
Premiered March 8, 2003, Los Angeles, CA
(duration ca. 12 minutes)

A Row of Buttons (2002)
Text by Fae Myenne Ng
SA choir
Commissioned by the New York Treble Singers
(duration ca. 4 minutes)

Metisse (2006)
SATB chorus, perc
Commissioned by the Commissioning Project

Vocal Solo

Pueblo Mulato (1987)
Three Songs on Poems by Nicolás Guillén
S, ob, gui, db, perc, pf

Commissioned by the Cornucopia Chamber Ensemble
(duration ca. 12 minutes)

To and Fro (1990)
Four Songs on Poems by Alison Knowles
Med vocalist, pf
Commissioned by the International Society for Contemporary Music
(duration ca. 8.5 minutes)

Journey (1990)
High vocalist, fl, hp
Commissioned by the Jubal Trio
(duration ca. 6 minutes)

"Or like a . . ." (1994)
Text by John Ashbery
Bar, vc, perc
Commissioned by WNYC
(duration ca. 15 minutes)

Singin' Sepia (1996)
Five songs on poems by Rita Dove
S, cl, vn, pf four hands
Commissioned by the Continuum Ensemble
(duration ca. 12 minutes)

Turning (2000)
Song cycle for Sop, Pno and Vc
Commissioned for the Ann and Richard Barshinger Center for Musical Arts in Hensel Hall, Franklin and Marshall College
(duration ca. 15 minutes)

Ivo, Ivo (2000)
Text by Manuel Martin
Sop, cl, b cl, va, vc, db
Commissioned and Premiered by Sequitur, Joe's Pub at the Public Theater, New York
(duration ca. 5 minutes)

At the Fountain of Mpindelela (2000)
Commissioned and Premiered by the National Musical Arts program, "Africa Spirit Ascending," in honor of Nelson Mandela, Kennedy Center, Washington, DC
(duration ca. 14 minutes)

Canto (2001)
Song cycle for Bar, cl (Bb/b cl), mar, vc, pf
Commissioned by Mutable Music for Thomas Buckner
(duration ca. 15 minutes)

Love After Love (2002)
Text by Derek Walcott
Soprano and marimba
Commissioned by Mary Sharp Cronson, Works and Process
Premiered by Elizabeth Farnum at the Guggenheim Museum
(duration ca. 9 minutes)

Atwood Songs (2007)
   Poetry by Margaret Atwood
   Soprano and piano
   Commissioned with support from the Hanson Institute for American Music
   and the Syracuse University College of Arts and Sciences
   (duration ca. 8 minutes)

Theater

Maggie Magalita (1980)
   Incidental music to the play
   fl, cl, vc, 2 perc, pf, gui
   Text by Wendy Kesselman
   Commissioned by the Kennedy Center for the Performing Arts
   (duration ca. 25 minutes)
The Golden Windows (1982)
   A play in 3 acts
   Text by Robert Wilson
   fl(pic, a fl), ob(Eh); tpt; perc-hpsd-pf; str
   Commissioned by Byrd Hoffman Foundation(duration ca. 30 minutes)

APPENDIX B: DISCOGRAPHY

A La Par. Peggy Benkeser and Laura Gordy. ACA Digital Recordings CM20064. "A City Called Heaven." 2003.

A La Par. Kane Richeson and Kathleen Murray. Composers Recordings CRI 823. "A La Par."

A La Par. Chris Lamb and Virginia Perry Lamb. Composers Recordings CRI 622. "Indígena." 1994.

A La Par. Edith Salmen and Dieter Lallinger. Castigo 02419. "Percussion." 2004.

Allegre. American Composers Forum, (www.bandquest.org: promotional recording). "Bandquest."

Arenas d'un Tiempo. Speculum Musicae. Bridge Records 9231. "Tania León: Singin' Sepia." 2008.

Axon. Mari Kimura, violin. Bridge Records 9231. "Tania León: Singin' Sepia." 2008.

Batá. Louisville Orchestra; Lawrence Leighton Smith, music director. First Edition Recordings LCD 010. "First Edition Recordings." 1995.

Bailarín. David Starobin, guitar. Bridge Records 9231. "Tania León: Singin' Sepia." 2008.

Batéy. The Western Wind. Composers Recordings CRI 662. "Indígena." 1994.

Batéy. The Western Wind. Western Wind WW 2001. "Blessings and Batéy." 1993.

Carabalí. Louisville Orchestra; Lawrence Leighton Smith, music director. First Edition Recordings LCD 010. "First Edition Recordings." 1995.

Ciego Reto. Paquito D'Rivera & Brooklyn String Orchestra. Universal Music Latino 2453607112. "La Habana-Rio Conexión." 2005.

De Memorias. Mexico City Woodwind Quintet. Urtext Records JBCC 051. "Visiones Panamericanas." 2002.

De Orishas. The Western Wind. Newport Classic NPD 85507.

Entre Nos. Trio Neos. Quindecim Recordings QP 043. "Mujeres de las Americas, Music of Women of the Americas."

Horizons. NDR Sinfonie Orchester; Peter Ruzicka, conductor. Bridge Records 9231. "Tania León: Singin' Sepia." 2008.

Indígena. Continuum; Tania León, conductor. Composers Recordings CRI 662. "Indígena." 1994.

Journey. Jubal Trio. Composers Recordings CRI 738. "Jubal Songs." 1997.

Momentum. Nanette Kaplan Solomon. Leonarda Records LE 334. "Character Sketches." 1995.

Oh Yemanja (Mother's Prayer). Dawn Upshaw & Orchestra of St. Luke's; David Zinman, conductor. Nonesuch 79458-2. "World So Wide." 1998.

Paisanos Semos. Ana Maria Rosado. Albany Records TROY 087. "We've Got (Poly) Rhythm." 1995.

Parajota Delaté. Continuum. Composers Recordings CRI 662. "Indígena." 1994.

Pueblo Mulato. Voces Americanas. Composers Recordings CRI 773. "Voices of Change." 2001.

Rituál. Karen Walwyn. Albany Records TROY 266. "Dark Fires." 1997.

Rituál. Clemens Leske. Composers Recordings CRI 662. "Indígena." 1994.

Rituál. Martha Marchena. Albany Records TROY 242. "Sonoric Rituals." 1997.

Satiné. Quattro Mani. Bridge Records 9231. "Tania León: Singin' Sepia." 2008.

Singin' Sepia. Continuum. Bridge Records 9231. "Tania León: Singin' Sepia." 2008.

Tumbáo. Elena Riu. Somm Recordings 237. "Salsa Nueva." 2005.

SOURCES

Arnold, Ben. "Momentum, for Solo Piano." *Notes* 44, no. 3 (March 1988): 581–582.

Berger, Arthur. "Problems of Pitch Organization in Stravinsky." *Perspectives of New Music* 2, no. 1 (Fall/Winter 1963): 11–42.

Briscoe, James R., ed. *Contemporary Anthology of Music by Women.* Bloomington: Indiana University Press, 1997.

Brooks, Iris, ed. "An American in Paris and Other Expatriate Composers Speak Out." *Ear* 1, no. 4 (October 1989): 28–24.

Clark, Walter Aaron. "Recording Reviews—Tania León: *Indígena.*" *American Music* 15, no. 3 (Autumn 1997): 421–422.

Cook, Nicholas. *A Guide to Musical Analysis.* New York: Norton, 1987.

Edwards, J. Michele. "North America Since 1920." In *Women and Music: A History*, ed. K. Pendle. Bloomington: Indiana University Press, 1991. www.netlibrary.com/urlapi.asp?action=summary&v=1&bookid=546/ (accessed October 12, 2005).

———. "Tania León." *Grove Music Online*, ed. L. Macy. http://80-www.grovemusic.com.libezp.lib.lsu.edu/ (accessed May 24, 2005).

Euba, Akin. *Yoruba Drumming: The Dúndùn Tradition.* W. Germany: E. Breitinger, Bayreuth University, 1990.

Forte, Allan. *The Atonal Music of Anton Webern*. New Haven: Yale University Press, 1998.

Gann, Kyle. "Music: Life after Minimalism." *The Village Voice* 37, no. 88 (June 9, 1992): 88.

Handy, D. Antoinette. *Black Women in American Bands and Orchestras*. 2nd ed. Lanham, MD: Scarecrow Press, 1981. www.netlibrary.com/urlapi.asp?action=summary&v=1&bookid=3025 (accessed October 14, 2005).

Kiraly, P. "Musical Melding." *Symphony* 42, no. 5 (1991): 29.

León, Tania. "Remaking American Opera." *Institute for Studies in American Music Newsletter* 24, no. 2 (1995): 1–2.

León, Tania. "What Is American Music?" Interview by Frank J. Oteri. *NewMusicBox* 1, no. 4 (August 4, 1999). www.newmusicbox.org/page.nmbx?id=04fp00/ (accessed May 24, 2005).

———. "Tania León Home Page." January 6, 2006. www.tanialeon.com (accessed August 1, 2009).

———. Interview by the author. Digital audio recording. New York, NY, December 13, 2005.

———. Interview by the author. Digital audio recording. New York, NY, August 4, 2009.

León, Tania, Laurie Anderson, Meredith Monk, and Pauline Oliveros. *The Sensual Nature of Sound*. New York: Michael Blackwood Productions, 1993. Videocassette, OCLC: 29374076.

León, Tania, Elinor Armer, Victoria Bond, Janice Giteck, Libby Larsen, Marsha Mabrey, and Pauline Oliveros. *American Women Conductors and Composers in Performance*. Eugene: University of Oregon, 1987. Videocassette, OCLC: 36297750.

Leonard, Kendra Preston. "Music Reviews: Short Works for Cello by Augusta Read Thomas: *Spring*, Tania León: *Four Pieces*, Barbara Heller: *Lalai*, and Diana Burrell: *Heron*." *Notes*, 2nd ser., 57, no. 3 (March 2001): 757–759.

Levine, Mark. *The Jazz Theory Book*. Petaluma, CA: Sher Music, 1995.

Liebman, David. *A Chromatic Approach to Jazz Harmony and Melody*. Rottenburg, Germany: Advance Music, 1991.

Lundy, Anne. "Conversations with Three Symphonic Conductors: Dennis DeCoteau, Tania León, Jon Robinson." *The Black Perspective in Music* 16, no. 2 (Autumn 1988): 213–226.

Mandel, H. "Tania León: Beyond Borders." *Ear* 13 (December 1988/January 1989): 12–13.

Manuel, Peter, ed. *Essays on Cuban Music: North American and Cuban Perspectives*. Lanham, MD: University Press of America, 1991.

Messiaen, Olivier. *Technique de mon langage musical*. Translated by John Sadderfield. Paris: Leduc Publications, 1956.

Moore, Robin. *Nationalizing Blackness: Afrocubanismo and Artistic Revolution in Havana, 1920–1940*. Pittsburgh: University of Pittsburgh Press, 1997.

Narire, Dalton. "The Maestros." *Ebony* 46, no. 4 (February 1989): 54–62.

Papp, Joseph. *Portrait of the Artist*. New York: WNYC-TV, 1987. Videocassette, OCLC: 56042242.

Reiner, Donna Jean. "The Colors of Culture: Characteristics in Selected Works of Tania Justina León." Ph.D. diss., Union Institute, 2000.

Roca, Octavio. "Sonidos de las Americas: Mexico—The Sound of America." *Symphony* 45, no. 3 (1994): 38–44.

Rosenberg, Robert, Maria Peralta, and Moe Foner, eds. *Women of Hope: 12 Ground-Breaking Latina Women*. Princeton, NJ: Films for the Humanities, 1996. Videocassette, OCLC: 35746955.

Schuller, Gunther. *Early Jazz*. New York: Oxford University Press, 1968.

Schwarz, K. Robert. Liner notes for *Indígena*. Continuum, Tania León, director. Compact Disc, Composers Recordings: CR1662.

Straus, Joseph N. *Introduction to Post-Tonal Theory*. 2nd ed. New Jersey: Prentice Hall, 2000.

Sulsbrück, Birger. *Latin-American Percussion: Rhythms and Rhythm Instruments from Cuba and Brazil*. Copenhagen: Den Rytmiske Aftenskoles Forlag/Edition Wilhelm Hansen, 1986.

Telgen, Diana, and Jim Kamp, eds. *Latinas!: Women of Achievement*. Detroit: Visible Ink Press, 1996.

Uribe, Ed. *The Essence of Afro-Cuban Percussion & Drum Set*. Miami: Warner Bros. Publications, 1996.

Walker-Hill, Helen. *Piano Music by Black Women Composers: A Catalog of Solo and Ensemble Works*. New York: Greenwood Press, 1992.

Michael K. Slayton[1]

CINDY McTEE (1953–)

I have become increasingly aware of the ways in which my music reflects or comments upon my personality and my experience. Some would say, "well, of course; art reflects life." But in my case anyway, it took some time to acquire the necessary technical skills and to find a path past the influence of teachers, colleagues, and other music to a place from which a more genuine expression could emerge. Getting older has a few benefits, and this is one: the ability to see oneself more clearly and to express oneself more honestly with each passing day. . . . I would like to advocate for composing in circles rather than in straight lines, looking backwards and sideways for inspiration as we move forward, embracing our ethnicity, our gender, our history, studying old music as well as new, slowing down, noticing the environment in which we live, and mirroring ourselves as we write.[2]

Cindy McTee is a composer who is equally at home in the concert hall, the computer music lab, and the classroom. Most of her compositions are for orchestra, symphonic band, or instrumental chamber ensemble, including electroacoustic (live-tape) pieces. From 1984 until her retirement in 2010, McTee was a member of the composition faculty at the University of North Texas (UNT) in Denton, a large school with strong programs in jazz, band performance, and teacher education, as well as composition. Her works have been commissioned by the symphony orchestras in Dallas, Houston,

299

Amarillo, and Detroit, the National Symphony Orchestra in Washington, D.C., the Dallas new music ensemble Voices of Change, and a number of other chamber music groups and solo recitalists. Press reviews of orchestral premieres, along with other performances, interviews, and preconcert publicity help make her work known to a wider public. McTee's pieces for symphonic band (wind symphony/wind ensemble), most of them arrangements of her orchestral music, and most of them available on recordings, have been commissioned by the College Band Directors National Association, the Big Eight Band Directors Association, and related professional organizations. Several high school and university band directors and graduate students in wind conducting, at UNT and elsewhere, have published studies of her band works.

McTee's distinguished academic career has shaped her successful composing career. Her faculty appointment in 1984 was to North Texas State University, which became the University of North Texas five years later. She was promoted to full professor in 1995 and chaired the division of composition studies for a total of five years until 1998. In 2000, her achievements as composer and teacher were recognized in her appointment as a Regents Professor, a UNT program for outstanding faculty members at the rank of professor who teach introductory courses in return for additional salary. Today, UNT's music program is among the largest in the United States. In the 2008–2009 academic year, the College of Music enrolled just over 1,600 students, one-third of them master's and doctoral students; composition majors numbered 75, taught by seven composition faculty members.

Owing perhaps to her teaching and other academic responsibilities, or to the extraordinary level of care she puts into each new work, McTee has published a relatively small catalog. Some years she has completed nothing at all, other years a single new title or the band arrangement of an earlier orchestral work. Essentially self-published and self-promoted, she uses two companies to print and sell her music, Rondure Music Publishing and Lauren Keiser Music Publishing, but neither represents her in the professional world. She maintains her own extensive website where she lists her works alphabetically, chronologically, and by genre, together with information on timing and instrumentation, important performances, her program notes for each piece, and excerpts from reviews.

Though many of McTee's compositional procedures might also be found in music of her contemporaries, her sources of inspiration are hers alone. She writes articulately about the origins of her ideas; certain things she encounters—a painting, a book, a sound—can invite musical exploration. She relates her attraction to movement and gesture to her love of ballroom dancing. She quotes from music of other composers, including J. S. Bach, Maurice Ravel, Igor Stravinsky, Charles Ives, Krzysztof Penderecki, Samuel Barber, and Jerome Kern. She uses musical ideas from American jazz and popular song traditions. McTee likes "the repetitive sounds of finely crafted machinery," sounds she knows well as a sports car enthusiast and, upon occasion, amateur racing driver. She is inspired by visual art that suggests motion and rest; she likes correspondingly dramatic musical contrasts of sound and silence. She writes music that is meant to feel like looking out from inside a race car, applying a race driver's maxim to music composition: "Stay on the brakes or on the accelerator pedal. Never coast."[3] She describes creating "images" in music and is intrigued by the idea that time is the "space" that contains music. Computer music, she finds, changes time as well as sounds. Her reading about Albert Einstein's theories of relativity and the time-space continuum leads her toward further innovative musical constructions.

In short, McTee is part composer, part engineer, part experimental physicist. Music that is well crafted is like a well-engineered, finely tuned machine operated by a skillful driver. Further, she believes music can suggest interplays of time and space such as Einstein envisioned. Using music to demonstrate physical laws puts her solidly within the Western tradition of science-based musical thought, from the "harmony of the spheres" of Pythagoras, Boethius, Descartes, Kircher, and others, through Rameau and his "natural principle" of the major triad in the overtone series, through Helmholtz and "resonance" theory, and on to today. For McTee, earthly human music suggests phenomena of our Einsteinian universe. Beauty is not simply something lyrical or sweet; beauty is in balance—the natural with the mechanical, the physical with the psychological.

> *It's hard to imagine life without polarities. Can we know the true meaning of joy without grief, or the value of light without darkness? Juxtapositions of disparate elements in music have always interested me as well. . . . Creative energy is born of the union between opposites. Interesting challenges occur when one attempts to integrate those materials which on the surface appear to be quite different. Growth happens as a result.*[4]

It perhaps goes without saying that McTee enjoys the technicalities of composing. "I write music because sound fascinates me. But I also find delight in the more intellectual parts of composing, in creating intricate patterns of pitch and rhythm."[5] Inspired by the work of the Swiss psychiatrist Carl G. Jung, she is intrigued by how the musical unconscious can assert itself through improvisation during the compositional process. McTee finds creative energy in juxtaposing, illuminating, and resolving disparate musical styles, techniques, tempos, and other elements. When appropriate, she uses, in various combinations, techniques such as indeterminacy (chance), twelve-tone rows, octatonic scales and harmonies, quartal harmony, metric modulation, passacaglia, palindrome, extended instrumental techniques, and polymetric spatial notation—the contemporary tool chest. A creative, innovative composer-engineer-physicist, she chooses her words to suit her audience.

> *Elaborate theoretical systems can be found in my work, and they are always employed as a means to an end. I can think of two reasons why I might feel the need to explain my music in theoretical terms: first, to provide the listener with information designed to enhance the experience of hearing a work for the first and possibly the last time; and second, to share my pride in the work's less obvious but essential (and hopefully elegant) structural processes.*[6]

McTee's special combination of interests results from her particular musical background. A native not of Texas but of Washington State, she was born in Tacoma, a port city on Puget Sound, on February 20, 1953, and grew up in the town of Eatonville, a small rural community about thirty miles southeast of Tacoma in the foothills of Mt. Rainier. Family car trips throughout the spacious wilderness of the western states contributed to her appreciation of large open areas—in music as in visual design. She was constantly surrounded by music. Her mother, a schoolteacher, played clarinet and tenor saxophone; her father, who was the service manager at the Chevrolet dealership in Eatonville, played the trumpet. And, to make a little extra money on the weekends, they formed their own small dance band with a drummer, an alto saxophone player, and a pianist. McTee began piano studies at the age of six with local pianist Bea Melvin, who strongly encouraged improvisation.

> *Mrs. Melvin was not classically trained as far as I know, but a masterful performer of popular music from the 1930s and 1940s. Her teaching method included requiring that I play a small number of pieces differently each time I returned for a lesson. I credit her with having given me my first opportunity to compose, although it wasn't until much later that I actually put notes on paper.*

Through her parents and her piano teacher, McTee's repertoire largely consisted of popular music of the 1940s and 1950s. She remembers being taken to her parents' dance band rehearsals instead of being left with a babysitter; she has fond memories of hearing tunes like *Night and Day*, *Misty*, and *Autumn Leaves*. Her mother gave her saxophone lessons and taught her to transpose from sheet music. "When I attended my first band rehearsal in fifth grade," McTee remembers, "I continued to transpose. You can imagine the result." As she went through school, she played saxophone in various jazz bands.

> *Actually, throughout my childhood, I thought I would grow up to be a visual artist. As a youngster, I spent much more time drawing and painting than practicing*

the piano. But looking back, I recognize early signs of my fascination with sound. I remember quite vividly some experiments that got me into trouble, for example, playing inside my grandmother's grand piano and improvising piano accompaniments during high school choir concerts. I wasn't considered to be an ideal music student because I found it very difficult to play exactly what other composers wrote. Improvising—that is, composing spontaneously—was much more interesting to me.

After high school, McTee attended Pacific Lutheran University (PLU) in Tacoma, majoring in music theory and composition; her major professors were David Robbins and Thomas Clark. Learning the repertoire and theoretical systems of the classical concert tradition was a new experience for her. For many years, she continued to think of her academic training in classical music as somehow more significant than her performing and improvising skills.

Toward the end of her junior year, in 1974, her life changed dramatically when her talent attracted the attention of the famed Polish composer Krzysztof Penderecki (1933–), who visited the PLU campus for a week of concerts and other activities. Following a performance of student composers' works, Penderecki invited McTee to spend a year with his family in Cracow, where in return for composition lessons, she would teach English to his two children. McTee spent the 1974–1975 academic year in Cracow, studying composition with Penderecki and orchestration and counterpoint with Marek Stachowski and Krystyna Moszumanska-Nazar at the Higher School of Music. Working with Penderecki, whose innovations in sound and notation were being emulated by composers throughout the world, had lasting influence on McTee.

Penderecki taught me much more than music—he taught me a way of life. I learned about commitment, professionalism, and the benefits of hard work. I learned the value of having a supportive teacher—his frequent encouragement of my work did much to bolster my confidence. He also taught me an appreciation for old things: antique clocks, Renaissance painting, medieval architecture, and Gregorian chant. I know of no one more musically courageous than Krzysztof Penderecki. He has always composed exactly what his muse dictates, writing with honesty and conviction, directly from the heart.

In December 1975, McTee graduated from Pacific Lutheran University with a bachelor of music degree. Penderecki was teaching at the Yale School of Music in New Haven, Connecticut, and McTee entered the master of music degree program there. Besides Penderecki, she studied with Jacob Druckman (1928–1996) and Bruce MacCombie (1943–). She took a jazz composition class taught by the Canadian saxophonist and composer David Mott; she listened to jazz recordings, especially bebop. She wrote a piece for jazz band and titled it after her hometown, *Eatonville* (1976, withdrawn). Through a student exchange program, she spent a semester studying German at the Eberhard-Karls Universität in Tübingen. One work from her Yale years, *Chord* (1977), for solo flute, remains in her list of published works; here her intention was to create different counterbalanced textures—pure or noisy, thin or thick, a single tone or a chord—through the use of extended flute techniques. The multiple sonorities are arranged into patterns which retrograde at the work's midpoint, creating a palindrome. The virtuoso flutist Robert Dick premiered the work in New Haven in 1977.

After receiving her M.M. degree in 1978, McTee entered the Ph.D. program at the University of Iowa, where she was a student of Richard Hervig (1917–). She completed the degree in 1981 and was appointed to a one-year position as assistant professor at her undergraduate alma mater; she stayed on for two more years as an adjunct professor and composer in residence. She has published two of her pieces from those years, both of them vocal works—*Psalm 100* (1982), for choir, and *Songs of Spring and the Moon* (1983), for solo soprano and instrumental chamber ensemble. McTee moved to Denton in 1984, and two years later she married Paul Hebda, a musicologist and attorney. They divorced in 1996.

McTee received her advanced education during the height of the women's movement, when opportunities in music composition, including music technology, began to expand. She established her career during tumultuous times when social and cultural expectations for women and men alike were undergoing many changes. Clearly McTee has not been inhibited by gender stereotypes in living her life. She honors not only her mother's dedication to teaching but also her father's knowledge of automobiles. She does not hesitate to write band music or computer music, musical genres that previous generations might have considered male pursuits—although perhaps not as male as automobile racing.

For a long time, McTee avoided talking about gender issues at all, and she remains fairly uninterested in gender as a political issue. She has thought deeply, however, about how such matters affect her creativity. In 1999, she was invited to address the Research on Gender and American Music Interest Group of the Sonneck Society; her remarks were published in the society's bulletin. She recalls being ridiculed as a "tomboy" during her childhood in the 1950s and 1960s.

> In trying to explain my own gender experience, I would like to begin with the time "when I was a boy." How's that for a gender-bending notion! Actually, I have borrowed the phrase from the title of a popular song by Dar Williams, a young woman with an impressive following. "When I Was a Boy" speaks of passion: the passion of a little girl to fly and imagine with Peter Pan, the passion to be athletic, and the desire to be free of inhibition. . . . Williams's song describes my childhood. I, too, was a "kid that you would like, just a small boy on her bike."[7]

She wonders, now that gender stereotypes are no longer so strong, whether girls still fear ridicule should they join the "ranks of boys" as composers or jazz instrumentalists; do young women think such pursuits might "neutralize" their femininity? She notes that as a composer she perceives the feminine-masculine divide as a split between her personal experience and her academic study, the subjective and the objective. "When I was working on my master's degree at Yale, I remember having felt completely unwilling as a composer to draw upon the subjective, feminine parts of myself. For me, composing music was about the reasoned manipulation of materials into patterns whose logic could not be questioned." She recalls that, as a young professional in the 1980s, she sought acceptance by the men whose work she admired by trying to "blend in." To the Sonneck Society in 1999, she described as her goal an "integrated" personality, a mixture of intuition and craft, subjective and objective, feminine and masculine.

> I have rediscovered the value of subjectivity in art. I say "rediscovered" because I believe it was from a place of subjectivity that I began to compose music. Could it be that years of education eclipsed an important aspect of my muse? Now, I feel most comfortable integrating "feminine" subjects with "masculine" objects. I try to balance spontaneity with formality. I even accept that music allows us to experience our bodies through its sounds and rhythms.[8]

Referring to John Gray's 1992 book *Men are from Mars, Women Are from Venus*, she asks, "Is there not a planet out there for those who wish to adopt the best traits of both sexes? I hope it's Earth." Integration and reconciliation, not only of gender differences, is basic to McTee's thinking.

> The frequent use of circular patterns, or ostinati, offers both the possibility of suspended time and the opportunity for continuous forward movement. Carefully controlled pitch systems and thematic manipulations provide a measure of objectivity and reason, while kinetic rhythmic structures inspire bodily motion. Discipline yields to improvisation, and perhaps most importantly, humor takes its place comfortably alongside the grave and earnest.

In her works of the 1970s and 1980s, McTee's music was more about structure than about extramusical ideas. *Psalm 42: Threnody* (1984), for voice and organ, was commissioned for performance in 1985 at a J. S. Bach bicentenary concert in Tallahassee, Florida, so McTee decided to use Germanic devices, including the B-A-C-H motive and a twelve-tone *passacaglia*. Three years later, in *Images* (1987), for horn and piano, recorded on a 1996 CD, each of the five movements suggests a specific visual image, as McTee explains in her program note. Movement I, "The Beginning of Time," is a dodecaphonic canon which, through the employment of nonretrogradable rhythms, projects an image of Olivier Messiaen's *Quartet for the End of Time.*

Example 7.1.   *Images,* I, "The Beginning of Time," mm. 1–4[9]

Movement II, "The Unanswered Question," is a musical dialogue utilizing the pitches of the doubly diminished (octatonic) scale and including melodic images of Ives's work by that name. In referring to "the doubly diminished scale," a scale that alternates intervals of a whole step and a half step, McTee combines terms from classical music theory ("octatonic") and jazz theory ("symmetric diminished").

Movement III, "Infinite Night," uses the same twelve-tone row as the first movement and projects an image of McTee's earlier work through the simultaneous presentation of periodic and aperiodic (measured and unmeasured) rhythms. Movement IV, "Circles," which uses pitch material similar to that of the second movement, is indeterminate with respect to form. Performers choose from various short motifs according to a set of instructions, and resulting repetitions suggest circular "images." Movement V, "The End of Time," is virtually identical to movement I.

McTee expanded upon the idea of performer's choice in the fourth movement of *Images* in *Circle Music I–IV* (1988), scored for piano with viola (I), flute (II), bassoon (III), or horn (IV).

Circle Music *is indeterminate with respect to form, requiring the performers to make spontaneous decisions as to which of approximately fifteen musical fragments will be heard at any given moment. The order of events and the resulting relation-*

ships between the two parts are therefore different each time the piece is performed. Continuity is achieved by occasional imitation between the parts as well as the consistent use of the octatonic scale (C, C♯, D♯, E, F♯, G, A, B♭) and a recurring C-major triad in the bass register of the piano.

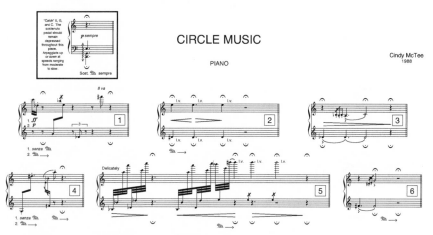

Example 7.2. *Circle Music I*, p. 1, piano[10]

Computer music has become one of McTee's favorite media; like many women of her generation, she turned to it after composing successfully for traditional instruments. At UNT, she worked in the Center for Experimental Music and Intermedia (CEMI), founded in 1982 by the composer and computer music advocate Larry Austin, who directed the studio for most of the next fourteen years. By the late 1980s, the introduction of more affordable and accessible technology such as the Apple Macintosh personal computer and the MIDI (musical instrument digital interface) synthesizer presented new possibilities.[11] McTee's first computer piece, *Metal Music* (1989), arose from her interest in teaching students about the new technology.

> In 1988, I recommended the purchase of two Macintosh computers for CEMI and suggested I use them to teach a restructured Introduction to Electroacoustic Music. The idea met with resistance from some who questioned the validity of a machine that smiled when turned on, was named after a fruit, and was operated by a mouse. Nonetheless, two Macs were eventually purchased along with some Yamaha tone generators and MIDI software. Since there was little music at the time for the Mac, I created Metal Music as a learning model, attempting to make the most out of limited musical materials; for example, of the work's sixteen different metallic sounds, eleven are derived from a single "source voice."

Ten minutes long, *Metal Music* has five sections of synthesized sounds, mainly percussive metal sounds—"Bins and Bells" (the sounds of large bowed bells), "Kettles and Cans" (canonic treatment of nonretrogradable rhythms), "Tins and Tanks" (three-part metallic polyphony), "Buckets and Bolts" (octatonic melodies in various permutations with the sounds of large bowed bells), and "Pots and Pans" (the beating of metal drums). The work is included on volume 9 of the series "The Composer in the Computer Age," issued by the Consortium to Distribute Computer Music (CDCM), which Larry Austin founded in 1986.

The first orchestral piece in McTee's catalog is *Circuits* (1990), written for the Denton Chamber Orchestra. It is also her first band piece (aside from an early student work, *Sonic Shades*, withdrawn). She arranged *Circuits* for wind ensemble for performance in 1991 in Kansas City, Missouri, at the College Band Directors National Association (CBDNA) "Golden Anniversary" National Conference. McTee's experience as a saxophonist and band member makes her quite comfortable with the medium, and she also recognizes certain advantages in writing band music. "For one thing, [student] bands have more rehearsal time than [professional] orchestras; for another, CBDNA conventions feature premiere performances, demonstrating members' interest in new music."[12]

Six minutes long, *Circuits* is frequently performed in both instrumental versions and is invariably well received. In her program note, McTee explains that the title refers to several important aspects of the work: "a strong reliance upon circuitous structures such as ostinati, the use of a formal design incorporating numerous recurring short sections, and an unrelenting, kinetic energy achieved through the use of sixteenth notes at a constant tempo of 152 beats per minute." She also mentions "jazz elements" in the work, and a "playful manipulation of musical materials using syncopation, sudden transposition, and juxtaposition." Brian Alber, in a 2007 article in the *Journal of Band Research*, finds that the rhythmic cells in *Circuits* are layered, usually treated as ostinati, but often manipulated "through specific styles such as bebop and bitonality."[13] Other writers find evidence of octatonicism in the rhythmic cells (see example 7.3).

In 2000, after a performance by the Houston Symphony, Charles Ward in the *Houston Chronicle* described *Circuits* as "a charging, churning celebration of the musical and cultural energy of modern-day America." Mentioning "repetitive ideas reminiscent of Steve Reich" and "walking bass lines straight from jazz," he writes that the work aptly illustrates "the electric, almost convulsive nature of American society near the start of the 21st century."[15] Although the composer likes this description and often quotes it, she does not usually attribute her music to any specific location or even a sense of place, and she has been somewhat surprised by references to her music's American sound.

> *"Americanism" might have to do with the simultaneous presentation of several different ideas—something I owe Ives. For instance, there are passages in my music in which both twelve-tone and octatonic structures live side by side. Dichotomies are*

Example 7.3. *Circuits*, mm. 42–46[14]

also found in my treatment of rhythm where a steady, regular pulse in one or more voices accompanies a tune that moves fluidly over top. I suppose this technique might be informed by jazz as well where the rhythm section chugs away "in time" and solo players improvise freely.

Continuing her work with computer music, McTee returned to Poland in 1990 as Senior Fulbright Lecturer in Computer Music at Cracow's

Academy of Music. Two years later at UNT, she completed two more computer pieces, *Études* and *"M" Music* (both 1992). *Études* is a twelve-minute composition for alto saxophone and computer music on CD; McTee dedicates the work to Debra Richtmeyer, a saxophonist and former UNT faculty member. Two of the work's three movements, "Night Song" and "Tex-Mix," are from a larger piece entitled *Eight Études* (1991, withdrawn), for four instruments and computer music on CD, commissioned by the National Music Honor Society, Pi Kappa Lambda. The remaining movement, "Circuits," is a transcription of her 1990 orchestral piece by the same name.

"M" Music is in seven short movements with intriguing titles—"Tex-Mix," "Filigree," "Orange Blossom," "Baroque Bypass" (with borrowings from J. S. Bach), "Dry Ice," "Filigree," and "Night Song." The first and last movements feature Richtmeyer on alto saxophone, as in *Études*. Realized at the computer music studios of the Academy of Music in Cracow, and at UNT's CEMI, *"M" Music* was heard at the Annual Conference of the Society for Electro-Acoustic Music in the United States (SEAMUS) in 1993, and at the Bourges Twenty-fourth International Festival of Electroacoustic Music in 1994; it is included on volume 18 of the CDCM series of recordings. Like *Metal Music*, the work was created with a Macintosh computer and commercially available MIDI sequencing software; several movements were created with an algorithmic application for the Macintosh called "M" and three Yamaha tone modules.[16] Robert Cummings in the *Computer Music Journal* describes the last movement as "haunting in its otherworldly saxophone theme and chime-like harmonies."[17]

Example 7.4. *"M" Music,* **"Night Song," p. 1**

Composing computer music had a huge impact upon McTee's writing for traditional instruments. "My hearing was sharpened; I became much more attentive to nuances of attack, sustain, and decay; I was able to imagine new textures and timbres; and I could also hear more details of pitch and rhythm, as if looking at sound and time through a microscope." Writing for computer also changed her ideas about musical time.

Computers allow us to effectively "stop" sound, to capture, store, modify, and to play back sounds, thereby changing our relationship with time. I am particularly fascinated by the interplay between the kind of time embodied by prerecorded computer music (fixed and machinelike) and the kind of time represented by live performance (approximate and human).

McTee began to find inspiration in things other than musical sounds and structures during the 1990s. For instance, *The Twittering Machine* (1993), a thirteen-minute piece for chamber orchestra or chamber ensemble, refers in its title to the Swiss painter Paul Klee's famous *Twittering Machine* (1922), which shows four bird-shaped objects shackled atop a primitive crankshaft. Parodying the artistic movement called futurism and its glorification of machines, Klee imagines a machine for creating birdsong that would produce horrible sounds as the mechanical birds were rotated. McTee likes machines and appreciates the comical apparatus; she translates Klee's biting humor into musical humor in the form of repeated structures and denied expectation. "Rhythms are displaced, passages are suddenly transposed or textures juxtaposed," the composer explains. Further, just as Klee's picture conveys dangers that might befall the birds, so the music contains "many large silences, or musical holes, that the players risk falling into if they're not attentive." And she wants the piece to "dance"—to convey movement and engage both mind and body (see example 7.5).

Commissioned by the Barlow Endowment for Music Composition, *The Twittering Machine* was first performed by the Pittsburgh New Music Ensemble, conducted by David Stock. The version for wind ensemble, *California Counterpoint: The Twittering Machine*, for the CBDNA, Western and Northwestern divisions, is five minutes shorter than the orchestral version; the reference to California recognizes the California conductor Mitch Fennell, who organized the commission.

McTee also wrote two smaller works in 1993, *Capriccio per Krzysztof Penderecki*, for solo violin, and *Stepping Out*, for flute accompanied by hand claps, claves, or other percussion—an unusual instrumentation. The *Capriccio*, written in celebration of Penderecki's "inspired music, his dedicated teaching, and his sixtieth birthday," was premiered in Cracow in 1994; in 2008, a revised version was performed in honor of Penderecki's seventy-fifth birthday (see example 7.6).

Example 7.5. *The Twittering Machine,* mm. 391–394[18]

Example 7.6. *Capriccio per Krzystof Penderecki*, mm. 22–31[19]

McTee's first piece originally conceived for concert band is *Soundings* (1995), a fifteen-minute work in four movements, commissioned by the Big Eight Band Directors Association and performed in 1997 at the CBDNA national conference in Athens, Georgia, as well as at the World Association for Symphonic Bands and Ensembles conference in Schladming, Austria. The second movement, "Gizmo," reflects the composer's fascination with "gadgets, motoric rhythms, and the sound of major sevenths." In the fourth movement, "Transmission," McTee transmits musical information using metric or temporal modulation, a process analogous to the one executed by the driver of an automobile using the transmission and smoothly shifting gears to change engine speed (see example 7.7).

In 1996, McTee completed two pieces. *Changes*, for cello and bass, features music that shifts from one historical style to another, always returning to tonal, two-part melodic passages based on chord changes in the Oscar Hammerstein–Jerome Kern song, *All the Things You Are*. The piece was performed at the American String Teachers Association national convention in Kansas City, Missouri (see example 7.8).

In *Einstein's Dreams*, for flute, clarinet, violin, cello, vibraphone, and piano, the composer begins to explore relative time, using the 1993 book of the same name by the American physicist Alan Lightman. McTee was awarded a composers' fellowship from the National Endowment for the Arts, which allowed her to take a leave from teaching to compose the piece, subsequently premiered in Dallas by Voices of Change. The seven movements depict Einstein's ruminations (as imagined by Lightman)

Example 7.7.   *Soundings*, IV, "Transmission," mm. 482–488[20]

Example 7.8. *Changes*, mm. 26–33[21]

on the nature of time while he was developing his theories. In the first movement, "Timescape," based on Lightman's story of a world in which time flows at different speeds in different locations, McTee requires each instrumentalist to perform independently of the rest. In "One Modulation of Light," which lasts less than a minute, time is compressed. The final movement, "Perfect Succession," consists of a single strand of quickly moving sixteenth notes, inspired by Lightman's portrayal of a world where "time is visible in all places . . . each increment of time marching after the other in perfect succession" (see example 7.9).

McTee continues to explore ideas of space and time in *Timepiece* (2000), for orchestra; *Einstein's Dream* (2004), for string orchestra, percussion, and computer music; and *Finish Line* (2005), for orchestra.

Timepiece, commissioned by the Dallas Symphony Orchestra (Andrew Litton, conductor) for the orchestra's centenary season, begins slowly, before time (in McTee's words), in a womblike, subjective holding place. Then a clocklike pulse emerges and provides the driving force behind a sustained, highly energized second section of about six minutes. McTee also arranged *Timepiece* for performance by the North Texas Wind Symphony (see example 7.10).

In January 2001, McTee began a one-semester sabbatical leave from UNT to write a "symphonic-length piece" on a commission from the National Symphony Orchestra (Leonard Slatkin, music director). A few months later, she had the good fortune to be awarded a John Simon Guggenheim Memorial Foundation Fellowship, which allowed her what she called the "luxury" of a two-semester leave, through December. Under normal circumstances, McTee does the majority of her composing in the

Example 7.9. *Einstein's Dreams*, VII, "Perfect Succession," mm. 1–10[22]

summer, when she isn't teaching. "I need long, uninterrupted chunks of time to write," McTee told an interviewer. "I like to unplug the phones and go into hibernation."[24] The commissioned work, *Symphony no. 1: Ballet for Orchestra*, is analyzed in detail later in this chapter.

More than ten years after *Études* and *"M" Music*, in 2003 McTee was able to return to computer music through a grant from the American

Example 7.10. *Timepiece*, mm. 72–80, selected instruments[23]

Academy of Arts and Letters, which allowed her to purchase the necessary hardware and software. *Einstein's Dream*, McTee's second commission from the Dallas Symphony, combines computer music with string orchestra and percussion so that the audience will experience "a new sense of space-time" as they hear the "seen" (the orchestral layers) folded into the "unseen" (the computer music). The work's title refers to Einstein's dream of finding a "theory of everything," a simple mathematical equation that would explain all natural interactions—gravity, electromagnetic force, fundamental particles, everything. (Physicists still debate the concept.) In *Einstein's Dream*, McTee uses a new technique she calls "time stretching," which she describes as "loosely analogous to the way in which Einstein's equations of relativity predict that gravity—the warping of space-time by matter—not only stretches or shrinks distances, but also appears to slow down or dilate the flow of time."[25]

> *Attracted to the immediacy, risk, and excitement of live performance, I also enjoy the distance, safety, and control of prerecorded computer music. I think the great tradition and refinement of orchestral music beautifully complements the futuristic "rough edges" of electronic music. I was very much aware of boundaries crossed when, in composing* Einstein's Dream, *the computer music grew out of the orchestral music and vice versa, the two mediums modulating and merging with one another to represent multiple meanings and multiple temporalities.*

For the computer music, McTee recorded metallic sounds—bowed cymbals, chimes, flexatone—and the voice of the Dallas Symphony's artistic administrator, Victor Marshall, reading from Einstein's writings; she used audio processing software to construct the computer music from these sounds. The piece was scheduled for performance during 2005, which was the World Year of Physics, as well as one hundred years after Einstein published three pivotal papers in 1905. The work is in seven sections, played without pause; section titles are printed in the score: (1) "Warps and Curves in the Fabric of Space and Time," (2) "Music of the Spheres," (3) "Chasing After Quanta," (4) "Pondering the Behavior of Light," (5) "The Frantic Dance of Subatomic Particles," (6) "Celestial Bells," and (7) "Wondering at the Secrets." Woven through the piece is the Lutheran chorale *Wir glauben all' an einen Gott* (*We All Believe in One God*), transposed to the key of E for Einstein.

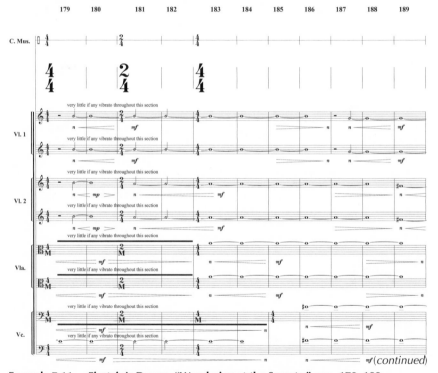

Example 7.11. *Einstein's Dream*, "Wondering at the Secrets," mm. 179–189

According to advance publicity about the premiere, the conductor was concerned about coordinating the strings and percussion with the computer track. To solve this problem, McTee devised a system of polymetric spatial notation for the orchestral parts, using ideas from Jacob Druckman and others. Indications of 2/M, 3/M, 4/M, and so on (*M* for metronome) are used for the periodic (metered, measured) parts, and 1/X, 2/X, 3/X, and so on for the aperiodic parts.

> *The coordination of spatially notated music, while not so problematic in a chamber music setting, presents unique challenges in a conducted environment. I first learned about this while watching Penderecki conduct his orchestral music from the 60s—I observed that a great deal of valuable time was spent talking about who should play what when. Also, I noticed that it was easy to get lost in the long sequences of single-beat, conducted patterns typical of music presented against a spatial grid. . . . The 2/M, 3/M, 2/X, 3/X, etc. meters seem to integrate nicely into the context of 2/4, 3/4; the meaning of the "numerator" remains the same no matter what, and players tend not to get lost. When the DSO rehearsed* Einstein's Dream *for the first time, conductor Andrew Litton spent about three minutes explaining the system, and then played the work (CD music too) from beginning to end without a single stop!*[26]

In *Einstein's Dream*, McTee again takes advantage of the freedom found in octatonicism. The piece exhibits extensive usage of the scale, in both melodic and harmonic fashion. Example 7.12 shows a series of triads whose notes are organized in a repeated pattern of two falling major thirds and a falling minor third, eventually yielding all twelve tones. A violin solo, based on the trumpet tune from Ives's *The Unanswered Question*, is heard over top of these triads. The pitches of this violin tune are drawn from the octatonic scale, which of course contains major triads, among other sonorities. As the triads shift, so does the compatible scale. The specific interrelations between octatonic and dodecaphonic materials in McTee's music will be examined in more detail later in this chapter.

In her next orchestral work, *Finish Line* (2005), McTee returns to the high-speed world of automobile racing. Her reference point is the Italian Futurist artist Giacomo Balla and his paintings that suggest the transformation of landscape by the passage of a speeding automobile; the title of one of Balla's works in particular, *Abstract Speed + Sound*, suggests to McTee that Balla "sought to render on canvas the whirling noise of the automobile itself."

> *It is probably safe to say that futurist thought lay part of the groundwork for what we now call postmodernism, a set of ideas that blurs the distinction between high and low art, often a feature of my music with its genre mixing and reliance upon parody and humor. I make no apology for the inclusion of elements in my work which point to the vernacular (jazz, for example) or which reflect parts of my world not generally associated with "serious" art, such as sports cars!*

The seven-minute work is in three sections and features repeated ostinati to convey speed, contrasted with slower sections; bits of Stravinsky's *Rite of Spring*, a work contemporaneous with futurist art, add pulsating

Example 7.12. *Einstein's Dream,* **"Pondering the Behavior of Light," mm. 47–54**

energy. At one point, McTee creates a "temporal transformation process [commonly referred to as metric modulation] analogous to gear shifting, where the speed, or RPM, of the engine modulates smoothly to a new frequency," as in *Soundings.* The next year, McTee arranged *Finish Line* for the University of Washington Wind Symphony. The title of the piece has a personal meaning for the composer (see example 7.13).

> *In 1996, I bought a 3-series BMW with a manual transmission. I spent the next several years going to driving schools and participating in autocross racing and long-distance "performance" driving with the local BMW and Porsche auto clubs. Racing is about taking risks—it is about testing one's limitations as well as the limitations of one's vehicle. Likewise, writing music requires the courage to explore uncharted and uncertain territory.*

Solstice for trombone and orchestra (2007) was commissioned by the Houston Symphony, conducted by Hans Graf, to feature its principal trombonist, Allen Barnhill. First performed in January 2008, the twenty-minute

Example 7.13. *Finish Line*, mm. 52–59, woodwinds

work is in three continuous movements; the orchestral score calls for brass, percussion, and strings, but no winds. McTee chose the title, from the Latin *sol* (sun) and *sistere* (to stand still), on June 21, 2007, the summer solstice. The music contrasts movement and stasis, light and shadow, the bright major third and the dark minor third (see example 7.14).

Citing her interest in Jungian psychology, McTee notes that "I am very motivated by the compulsion to resolve opposites. *Solstice* therefore both dances and sings, celebrates and mourns, illuminates and darkens." Composing in her usual way, starting with small things—"germs," she calls them—she sent Barnhill her bits of music to evaluate, and eventually put them all together. Charles Ward (*Houston Chronicle*) liked *Solstice* even better than he liked *Circuits*. He heard elements of "free jazz" at times in Barnhill's solo and, in the middle movement, chords "straight from the world of jazz ballads."

Bricolage (2008), for flute and computer music, was written for Mary Karen Clardy to perform at the National Flute Association Convention in Kansas City, Missouri. The computer music is derived from sounds produced by prepared piano, and McTee intends the piece to have a sur-

Example 7.14.   *Solstice,* mm. 637–646, selected instruments

realistic and improvisatory character. The word *bricolage* (from the French *bricoler,* "to tinker or fiddle") means to create art from materials at hand, not necessarily musical instruments.

In 2009, McTee won the Elaine Lebenbom Memorial Award for Female Composers, which supports the creation of an original orchestral work for performance by the Detroit Symphony Orchestra (Leonard Slatkin, conductor). *Double Play,* scheduled for performance in June 2010, has two movements, "The Unquestioned Answer" (2009) and "Tempus Fugit" (in process), which may be performed separately. "I was very interested in creating a structure that presented a counterpoint of ideas," recalls McTee, "but I also wanted to produce something of beauty in response to an answer (a firmly held belief) that could not be questioned."

Cindy McTee's upbringing as a musician who was encouraged to improvise—encouragement which instilled in her a deep affinity for bebop and jazz music—has certainly made an impact on her mature compositional style and creative mindset. She has developed improvisation as a major compositional skill, as a way to tap the unconscious. For McTee, there is a balance to be obtained in music: between the subjective and the objective, between organization and freedom. Coupled with her deep interest in mechanics, physics, time-space, and the cosmos, the improvisatory liberty of her youth has manifested itself in maturity as carefully crafted yet unbounded precision—all things in balance, working together to create her distinctive sound.

A CONVERSATION WITH CINDY McTEE

For years, I had taught the music of Cindy McTee in various university classes, specifically in lectures concerning correlations between visual art and music. And I had often wondered about this woman who had sparked such enriching conversations with her Twittering Machine—*this woman who had so effortlessly connected with Klee's stark mechanical vision of futurist thought. I wanted to ask her what she imagined the four little birds were trying to say—since they sing with her voice. And so when I heard she was to be in Nashville for a performance of* Einstein's Dream *with Leonard Slatkin and the Nashville Symphony Orchestra, I couldn't miss the opportunity to invite her to dinner. We began our conversation that night, and it has continued over the past year. Cindy McTee is one of those people for whom postmodernism is such an easy fit you forget she's wearing it. You forget you are engaging a brilliant contemporary thinker; the focus of any conversation will inevitably turn outward, toward the art itself. Her humility manifests itself in complete accessibility to her intimate inner world—a world of race cars, mechanical engineering, bebop, and Jungian psychology. Yet all these things somehow find balance in Cindy McTee's world—just four birds on a wire. We are left to wonder what would happen if the crank were turned.—Michael Slayton*

SLAYTON: You come from a musical family. Could you talk just a bit about your earliest experiences?

McTEE: Yes. My mother was a very skilled musician, who at the age of fourteen studied with the Seattle Symphony's principal clarinetist. She also played saxophone. My father played trumpet. I have fond memories of hearing their band play on the weekends. And of course, because of Mrs. Melvin, I grew up improvising at the piano. In high school, I played piano for the choir, and even when we sang Brahms, I continued to improvise—much to the director's displeasure. I was presumptuous enough to think I knew better than Brahms! Now, of course, I hope those who play my music will have greater respect for what's on the page than I did. But I highly recommend that children be encouraged to play both classical and popular music—classical for the discipline and popular because it encourages spontaneity—balance is good.

SLAYTON: In what ways do you think your experiences growing up in the northwest have affected you as a musician?

McTEE: I often say jokingly that I grew up in a tent, since I spent many weekends and summer vacations camping with my family. Even now, I return to Washington State at least once per year, first of all to see my family, but secondly to see mountains and oceans and trees—to experience nature's perfection, peace, and beauty. I believe these many encounters with the absolute best nature has to offer—the wildflowers and glaciers of Mt. Rainier National Park and the tide pools and rain forests of the Olympic Peninsula—those things have fed my musical soul in significant ways. Growing up in a small town in the northwest, I didn't have many opportunities to hear live music and in fact didn't hear an orchestra play in concert until I went to college. But my father was an audiophile of sorts. He built his own hi-fi system in the fifties and collected some orchestral recordings of Tchaikovsky, Gershwin, Respighi, and others. I remember putting myself to sleep by imagining my own orchestral music after listening to his records. My parents, Jaquelin and Charles McTee, still live in the house in which I grew up in Eatonville. My sister, Christy, and her family live not far from there.

SLAYTON: Who or what do you listen to now?

McTEE: I listen to jazz. I listen to the repetitive sounds of finely crafted machinery. I listen to Igor Stravinsky, John Coltrane, Jacob Druckman, Maurice Ravel, John Adams, and Sarah McLachlan. I listen to everything.

SLAYTON: I think it's interesting that you include "finely crafted machinery" on your listening list. Would you explain that?

McTEE: I find satisfaction in putting an analog watch up to my ear (although these sorts of timepieces are fast disappearing) or listening to the distinctive sound of a Harley-Davidson. The repetitive, interlocking whirs, ticks, and pops have found their way into my music, mostly in the form of ostinati, pulse-based rhythms, and hocket. Perhaps I'm drawn to these sounds and textures because they represent order, precision, integration, and predictability. However, their musical application is most meaningful, I think, in a context that also includes disorder, flexibility, independence, and surprise. I really enjoy making music that juxtaposes disparate elements. Much of my recent thinking about music is informed by the writings of Carl G. Jung, who felt that creative energy sprang from the tension between opposites. He also became preoccupied with abstract, circular patterns symbolizing synthesis and reconciliation.

SLAYTON: Does this account for your use of the term "circular music"?

McTEE: Probably. The circle has become an important element in my work; it shows up in the frequent use of circular patterns, or ostinati. And my music constantly references previous materials—moving forward, circling back, creating rounded formal shapes. There is, of course, nothing new about this. We once called it "recapitulation"!

SLAYTON: You've often mentioned the profound effect Penderecki had on you and your music. Can you talk a bit about the origins of your experience with him?

McTEE: In the spring of 1974, when I was a junior composition major at Pacific Lutheran University, Mr. Penderecki was the featured guest composer at our festival of contemporary music. Following a concert of student works, he invited me to spend a year with his family in Poland. At first I didn't believe he was serious, and I was also a bit apprehensive about the idea of living behind the Iron Curtain. But several months later, at the age of twenty-one, I flew to London, took the train to Paris for a few days of sightseeing, and continued the journey by train to Cracow.

SLAYTON: What was the time there like? Do you think it has affected your mature compositional decisions?

McTEE: Lessons with Penderecki were conducted informally, generally at the family dining-room table. I studied orchestration, twentieth-century techniques, and sixteenth- and eighteenth-century counterpoint at the Cracow Academy of Music. He insisted I devote a large portion of my time to writing counterpoint exercises because, as he put it, "American schools don't require enough counterpoint." Most of my instruction was given in the form of private lessons conducted in English—an arrangement that suited everyone since I spoke very little Polish. And the academy's professors were more than happy to practice their English. In those days, of course, there were relatively few foreigners behind the Iron Curtain. As far as specific musical influences are concerned, I can say that my current interest in expressing humor through music may be attributable to Penderecki. When thinking of his music, most people probably recall *Threnody*, the *St. Luke Passion*, the *Dies Irae*, and other solemn works. However, there are also several capriccios and a comic opera. I think Penderecki may have given me the courage to break away from the notion that modern music needs always to express serious modes of thinking and feeling—what a wonderful role model.

SLAYTON: How would you describe your creative processes?

McTEE: I work in various ways. Each piece teaches me something new about the creative process. Where does music come from? What provides the initial inspiration? Does a lightning bolt strike? That sudden flash of realization certainly does occur from time to time, but generally, ideas are the result of continuous hard work. They come gradually. They emerge. They evolve. And most often, they are connected to a physical gesture. . . . Sometimes I begin by conceptualizing the larger aspects of form and content and then create the infrastructure. But most often I work much more organically, starting with smaller ideas, which I call "germ seeds" or sound objects—a single sonority or a sequence of short melodic-rhythmic events. And then I let the larger gestures and textures evolve or grow out of these materials.

SLAYTON: Regarding harmonic language, in what ways have you been drawn to techniques for pitch generation, such as serialism, indeterminacy, and the like?

McTEE: I have used both serial and chance techniques in my music, but these procedures are always employed as a means to an end. I never start with a technique. I start with a breath, a feeling, or a physical gesture. We all spend a great deal of time creating elegant compositional tools and complex technologies to help us compose. Sometimes they produce music we would not have otherwise invented. That can be a good thing. But we must be careful to establish ownership of those musical materials that come to us via these objective methods. And we must always, in the end, consult our muse when making decisions about which materials to keep.

SLAYTON: Can you talk a little about your jazz influences?

McTEE: I started to play jazz piano and saxophone in high school. When I went to Europe, I could only take one suitcase, so the saxophone stayed at home. But as a master's degree student at Yale, I took a jazz composition class from David Mott and became especially interested in composers from the bebop era. I worked hard at jazz piano and was very proud of the fact that I was finally able to play *Giant Steps* up to tempo! I gradually let jazz performance go, but jazz resurfaced in my music with the composition of *Circuits* in 1990.

SLAYTON: You say it resurfaced; does that mean it was a subconscious phenomenon?

McTEE: I think so, yes. I stopped doing jazz in one place, and it found its way back into another; *Circuits* was the piece where it first emerged, I think.

SLAYTON: What personal and professional challenges would you say confront you as a composer?

McTEE: First on my list is the encounter with the blank page—finding form in a chaotic sea of infinite possibilities. Next, I would say finding a quiet, private environment within which to imagine sound. I need large blocks of uninterrupted time for a focused and meaningful encounter with the materials. I would definitely add to this the difficulty in negotiating relationships as a person whose profession requires seclusion. I was in school until I was twenty-eight, married at thirty-three, and divorced at forty-three with no children. I've lived alone for most of the last twelve years—coincidentally, my most productive years.

SLAYTON: And there is the challenge of building a career.

McTEE: This is often a difficulty, yes. Asserting oneself as an individual—finding the courage to be authentic in a culture that pretty much encourages conformity—isn't an easy thing to do. We face the added challenge of trying to find a public that truly believes in the value of new music. As artists, most of us want to communicate thoughts and feelings that are about the emotional, intellectual, and spiritual relationship we have with our present. I have absolutely no interest in writing music that sounds like Bach or Mozart, although many people think that's what living composers should do. And then, on the back side, many composers struggle with their own psyche: finding humility when hundreds stand and cheer following a performance, or surviving the scathing review in the newspaper. Both experiences are extraordinarily powerful—the former might lead to grandiosity, the latter to depression and anxiety. Resolving the inner conflict between commitment to one's ideas and doubt as to their worth is a real challenge. It's possible to get caught up in that troublesome loop and not produce. And then there is the challenge of reconciling arts administrators' worries over the box office with the need for genuine artistic expression. Writing music for hire can change the nature of the artistic encounter. It can take artists outside of themselves as they respond to expectations. And it can pressure them to finish by an arbitrary deadline.

SLAYTON: Do you think these challenges are heightened or lessened in any way by an academic appointment?

McTEE: I think it presents *new* challenges, actually. Those of us who are employed by universities sometimes face the challenge of having to convince administrators that analysis and reason are no more valuable than intuition and emotion—that, along with finding ways to lessen the soul-killing effects of endless committee meetings, memos, and reports. We also commonly find ourselves having to placate our students' parents who worry about their sons and daughters finding gainful employment in the arts.

SLAYTON: So in the face of all these challenges, why do you compose?

McTEE: There are many reasons, of course, and some undoubtedly remain unknown to me. But I would say I write music because I enjoy the process. I quite literally find joy in the doing. Composing is an adventure, and I learn from it. In each new piece, I explore uncharted territory, pushing beyond the experience of my previous work. I feel changed by it and invigorated by a positive response from persons who are touched by my music. I write music because sound fascinates me and because I feel I have something to say; I am apparently presumptuous enough to believe that the Mozarts and Stravinskys have not said it all.

SLAYTON: It seems you rather relish these challenges.

McTEE: Challenges are fun! Composing is very difficult for me, actually, and I labor over each note. Part of that labor is born out of my desire to be careful and thorough, so I work slowly and deliberately. I am trying to coax disparate ideas and materials into a state of harmony and balance. The integration and reconciliation of opposing elements have become important aspects of my work; carefully controlled pitch systems and thematic manipulations provide a measure of objectivity and reason, while kinetic rhythmic structures inspire bodily motion. Discipline yields to improvisation, old music finds its way into a new context, and perhaps most importantly, humor takes its place comfortably alongside the grave and earnest. But of all the things I can say about motivation, I think the most powerful driving force can best be explained as emanating from the quest for perfection, especially aesthetic perfection.

SLAYTON: This might be difficult to answer, but I've heard you talk about the "physicality of composing"; for you, what does it *feel like* to compose?

McTEE: I feel a strong parallel between acts of creation and procreation. I've often observed that libidinal energy fuels my muse, something Freud's theories of sublimation apparently support. A poet by the name of Richard Blackmur wrote an essay called "Language as Gesture," and in it he says, "We feel almost everything that deeply stirs us as if it were a gesture, the gesture of our uncreated selves." That statement closely parallels my own experience of making music, that the impulse to compose often begins as a rhythmical stirring and leads to a physical response—tensing muscles, gesturing with hands and arms, or, quite literally, dancing.

SLAYTON: So for you there is an actual visceral response?

McTEE: Yes! It is interesting, too, that we use the word *movement* to designate the sections within a larger musical composition. Physical activity can also help to unshackle the muse. My house is never cleaner than during extended periods of work on a new piece. That's because, to be productive, I need both moments of intense engagement and moments when the conscious brain is distracted by doing something like scrubbing a floor. It seems that revelation and insight almost always happen during times of transition between focused and unfocused attention. Depak Chopra describes a similar gap experience when he talks about a space between thoughts or a contact point between our mind and the "quantum field of all possibilities."

SLAYTON: And then what does it feel like to listen to a performance, especially a premiere?

McTEE: Sometimes the experience is very moving. During performances of the *Adagio* from my *Symphony no. 1* with the National Symphony Orchestra, I remember experiencing goose bumps. The phenomenon of goose bumps has always interested me, and I have tried for a long time to figure out what makes it happen. In this case, I am quite sure it occurred in response to the way in which the music was communicated by me to the conductor, Leonard Slatkin, through him to the orchestra, and then back to me, full circle. The beauty I felt came not so much from the music itself, but from the realization that a great many people were communicating with and through one another to create an experience that transcended my score—thus the goose bumps. It was *their* music too. I shed a tear during rehearsal one day and remember saying in a note to Leonard that never before had I been so completely understood. I felt heard and known and fulfilled.

SLAYTON: Let's turn to the practical aspects of your work for a moment. How do you approach the "head to paper" process? Do you write at the piano? Do you use the computer for notation?

McTEE: My work generally begins with pencil and paper but is completed at the computer using *Finale*. Computers, unfortunately, don't teach us much about *seeing* music. Quarter rests, clefs, and other symbols magically appear—but do they appear always in the right place? Or should they be used at all? These are questions a computer cannot always provide the right answers to. This is why I often encourage my students to use a pencil and paper for a while. A composer who has first experienced drawing music will generally be much more attuned to issues of graphic efficiency and notational sophistication.

SLAYTON: Do you find inspiration through sounds the computer can generate?

McTEE: Yes. Although I prefer to have complete silence in order to fully imagine *new* sound, I also enjoy having high-quality samples of acoustic instruments available to me during the creative process. If the quality of the audio materials is high, and dynamics and articulation are adjusted appropriately, much can be learned prior to the first rehearsal about balance, timbre, and texture. But by far the greatest benefit to me in hearing the computer play my music is this: the computer allows me to step back as if I were a member of the audience and to experience my music's effect on time. Imagined time is so different from real time, and therefore I value the objective perspective that computer playback provides. Some people question the use of machines to make music. But I would likewise question whether or not an instrument like the piano, with its elaborate mechanism of moving parts, is any less a machine than a computer. Perhaps our attitude toward computers would be more forgiving if we talked about them in musical terms, as instruments to be played rather than as machines to be used. We don't, after all, call pianists "piano users."

SLAYTON: That leads naturally to a question about your pure computer music, such as *"M" Music* or *Études*: what advantages do you find in working with digital media?

McTEE: I think experience with computer music can't help but change the way composers hear and assemble sounds. The computer enables us to examine sounds as if hearing them through a microscope and to manipulate them with a high degree of control over even the smallest details. That experience then has the potential to inform the ways in which composers work with acoustic instruments. We ask different questions as a result. Our hearing is sharpened. We pay more attention to subtle timbral changes. We are perhaps also more attuned to the location of sounds in space. And sometimes we try to *emulate* electronic sounds, thus inspiring us to create entirely new sounds for acoustic instruments. There is always, however, the danger that our technology will become an end in itself. It would be unwise, I think, to trust that the authors of music software applications necessarily know best, or to believe that the barriers imposed by computer software cannot be breached. I think we have to be careful, as "players" of computers, to see beyond what they reveal to us.

SLAYTON: How do you react to the terminology "woman composer"?

McTEE: I usually turn that around and say, "I'm a composer who happens to be a woman." I mean, has anyone ever heard the term "man composer"? Or do you think you can identify the gender of a composer by listening? I do think gender *matters*—just like *everything* matters. My experiences as a woman must certainly color my musical world in some way.

SLAYTON: Would you say that gender issues have been a contributing factor, positive or negative, in your career?

McTEE: Well, I can say that I am lucky not to have felt the sting of discrimination as a composer. I acknowledge that it exists, find it absolutely deplorable, and feel great compassion for those who have been treated unfairly. And although I do not often participate in musical organizations which support women in particular, I do realize that I am the beneficiary of important work by other women and men whose dedication to feminist issues has increased awareness and created opportunity.

SLAYTON: Do you think any of this has affected the way you approach teaching composition, especially to young women?

McTEE: Composing is a psychological process but is almost never treated as such in music schools. Getting inside the hearts and psyche of my students as they struggle with their own personal approach to making art is one of the things that interests me most about teaching. I value traditional teaching as much as anyone, and I know the students need it. But is there not also a place for the kind of teaching that focuses on more subjective ways of approaching and guiding the compositional experience? Students who bring their creations to me for evaluation often feel quite insecure, so I must be careful to "do no harm." On the other hand, I must attempt to offer honest responses and constructive criticism. I try hard to balance affirming remarks with those that instruct about the need for change. I don't know that my approach is any different for female students. I try to encourage a full range of music expression—assertive and introspective, intellectual and emotional—from both men and women.

SLAYTON: Critics have described your music in several ways: as distinctly "American," as "having clarity," et cetera. How would *you* describe your own musical effect?

McTEE: Well, although I have never made a conscious attempt to create "American" music, I would have to agree with those who have said that my musical style generally does reflect my American roots more than my European-based training. Ever since the industrial revolution, we Americans have embraced science and technology as a major part of our national identity. As an American artist, I feel I've responded to the nervous energy of our modern, mechanized cities. It also occurs to me that use of the octatonic scale may be a holdover in my ear from my experience playing and listening to jazz. I've also heard listeners talk about the "clarity" of my textures. I think that results from the desire to compose economically and not to waste notes. Complexity, by itself, is not a virtue!

SLAYTON: In our recent history, "new music" has unquestionably suffered in the concert halls. Why do you think this is true? And is it changing?

McTEE: Well, difficulty understanding new music is also exacerbated by a lack of exposure to it. The taste for new music must be acquired. Like so many good things, it is not enough to hear a piece once, or to hear new music only occasionally. The language of new music is for most people like Chinese is to me. I don't understand Chinese because I haven't studied it and because I haven't heard it very much. But Chinese does, of course, communicate meaningfully. Likewise, new music can communicate in a meaningful way to those who understand its language. Perhaps the reputation is poor because there is so much bad new music out there, some of mine included! But this has been the case throughout history. Composers, as all artists, must take risks if they are to discover and develop. Some of their experiments will fail. We must be patient. We must be willing to give new music a hearing. We *need* new music—just as we need new books and new art—to reflect who we are as a society, to provide a lens through which following generations can know and understand who we were in this time and place.

SLAYTON: Do you consciously consider the audience when writing a new piece?

McTEE: Yes, but I do not consciously attempt to make people feel one way or the other. I do not presume to have that power. I make music for others to receive in a manner of their own choosing. What people understand from my music is up to them. As narcissistic as this may sound, my music must be entirely about me and the world I'm responding to. The interpretation, of course, remains open.

SLAYTON: What is the most interesting response you've ever gotten from a listener?

McTEE: [long pause] Well, not long ago, somebody said to me, "Listening to your music makes me want to have sex with you" [laughter]. We laughed and pontificated about possible commercial applications— maybe I could sell my music as an aphrodisiac or something.

SLAYTON: What outside interests have informed your compositional style?

McTEE: In the late 1990s, while waiting in a doctor's office, I noticed a stack of phone books in the corner and picked up a copy of the yellow pages. It opened to an advertisement for the Arthur Murray Dance Studio. Having grown up with dance music from the forties and fifties, I had always wanted to learn the fox-trot, the waltz, and other ballroom dances. So I made the trek from Denton to Dallas several times per week for individual lessons and group classes, and I even participated in a few pro-am competitions. I discovered that doing ballroom dancing was very much like playing jazz, where there is an agreed-upon language within which improvisation takes place. We can relate to music in various ways: on an intellectual level, an emotional level, a spiritual level, and a physical level—mind, heart, soul, and body. Dance helped me to get in touch with the physical aspects of music—breath, tension, and release—and it helped me tap into my intuition and connect musical time and space in ways I am only just beginning to understand.

SLAYTON: And of course there is auto racing.

McTEE: Ha! Yes! I've always had an interest in automobiles—something I likely inherited from my father, who was a very capable mechanic. I've stopped the racing, but I still enjoy driving. In 2005, I took my BMW Z4 on a six-thousand-mile trip from Denton to Los Angeles, hugged the coast along Highway 1 to the Oregon-Washington border, and then continued on to Seattle and returned home via the Colorado Rockies and Santa Fe. It was a glorious ride. And the correlations between music and racing are numerous. An orchestra is a bit like a finely crafted automobile with its many interconnected, moving parts all speeding toward the finish line. I often use repeated fragments (ostinati), a steady pulse, and a spirited tempo to portray the mechanized agitation of machines. And sometimes I employ a seamless, temporal transformation process (metric modulation) analogous to gear shifting, where the speed, or RPM, of the engine modulates smoothly to a new frequency. Racing is about taking risks—it is about testing one's limitations as well as the limitations of one's vehicle. Likewise, writing music requires the courage to explore uncharted and uncertain territory.

SLAYTON: Okay, so what are the four little birds trying to say?

McTEE: [laughs] They're saying, "Hang on!" I was especially attracted to the painting's biting humor—imagine what would happen if the crank shaft were turned! In that piece, I make attempts at humor through the use of repeated structures and denied expectation—rhythms are displaced, passages are suddenly transposed or textures juxtaposed. There are also elements of danger in the painting—arrows piercing some of the birds, a gaping hole or ditch the birds might fall into, and the presence of an exclamation mark, a recurring symbol in Klee's work, meant to suggest impending doom. The danger elements in my piece consist of large silences, musical holes the players risk falling into if they're not attentive. I first got to know Klee's work as a student at Yale where I saw images of his paintings projected during a performance of Gunther Schuller's *Seven Studies on Themes of Paul Klee*. I identified with his interest in both music and art—and of course as a child I thought I would grow up to be a painter.

SLAYTON: Where do you see art music heading in the twenty-first century?

McTEE: I think we've benefited from the experience of highly "rational" approaches and have moved beyond them to make music with well-defined, individual signatures rooted in emotion and intuition. What I fear most about the use of complex systems is that their orderliness and rationality may prevent us from connecting with the more intuitive, irrational, and ultimately more interesting aspects of who we are. I hope we will continue to seek connection with ourselves and what makes us interesting as individuals.

SLAYTON: And where are *you* headed?

McTEE: That's a good question. Change is all around. Artists, of course, respond to an ever-changing world and are also changed by the experience of making art. I really can't predict what's around the corner, but I do know that each piece takes me to a place I've not been before. I know this: I look forward to the journey.

ANALYSIS: *SYMPHONY NO. 1: BALLET FOR ORCHESTRA* (2002)

Music is said to have come from dance—from the rhythmic impulses of men and women. Perhaps this explains my recent awareness of the inherent relationships between thought, feelings, and action—that the impulse to compose often begins as a rhythmical stirring and leads to a physical response—tensing muscles, gesturing with hands and arms, or, quite literally, dancing.

Cindy McTee's *Symphony no. 1: Ballet for Orchestra* marks a pivotal moment in her career. She had decided she wanted to compose a large, multimovement work, something new for her. Most of her previous works were short, programmatic offerings, typically under ten minutes in length; at the time, she had only two pieces—*Soundings* and *Einstein's Dream*—that were fifteen minutes or more. The *Ballet for Orchestra*, then, at thirty minutes in length, was new territory for her, and the work remains the largest in her catalog. As the word *ballet* in the title indicates, McTee's inspiration here is the dance, as a focal point for the "kinesthetic-emotional awareness" she began to define in *Circuits* (1990). Beyond that, she now turns from a scientific or mechanical catalyst to a literary one and prefaces each of the four movements with a verse of English poetry that celebrates dance.

When she was commissioned by the National Symphony Orchestra in 2001, she had already been planning to use a sabbatical semester to compose her "symphonic-length piece"; fortune allowed her the full year through a Guggenheim fellowship. McTee dedicated the *Ballet for Orchestra* to Leonard Slatkin, who conducted its premiere at the Kennedy Center for the Performing Arts in Washington, D.C., on October 24, 2002, and at Carnegie Hall six days later. Allan Kozinn called the work "a four-movement tour of dance forms through which philosophically broader materials are woven."[27]

Each of the *Ballet's* four movements carries a descriptive title, drawn from the poetic verse that prefaces it: "Introduction: On with the Dance," "Adagio: Till a Silence Fell," "Waltz: Light Fantastic," and "Finale: Where Time Plays the Fiddle." In 2004, McTee was commissioned to arrange the *Ballet for Orchestra* for performance by the Honor Band of America Symphonic Band. The resultant work, *Ballet for Band*, was premiered in Indianapolis, Indiana, with Eugene Corporon conducting. Because the symphony's *Adagio* movement requires the sustained sound of stringed instruments, McTee omits that movement from the band version.[28]

True to McTee's vision, the *Ballet for Orchestra* is an important work, probably her most important work to date; it has been treated to numerous repeat performances since its inception. The focus of this analysis will later turn toward detailed investigation of specific traits central to McTee's compositional style, each of which is prominently featured in the *Ballet*, but first let us consider the work as a comprehensive whole.

The preface to movement I, "Introduction: On with the Dance," comes from Lord Byron's *Childe Harold's Pilgrimage* (1812–1818): "On with the dance! let joy be unconfined! / No sleep till morn, when Youth and Pleasure meet / To chase the glowing hours with flying feet . . ." The movement is "inspired by the opening theme of Beethoven's Symphony no. 5; a three-note motif outlining the interval of a minor third (C-E♭-C) is developed and expanded to also include the interval of a major third (C-E♭-C♭)." This three-note motive indeed pervades the first few pages of the score, clearly setting the stage for later development. "There is almost nothing I believe in more than making the most out of the least," says the composer. "I've always been envious of Beethoven's ability to make so much out of so very little." The motive's inherent construction as [03e] (3-11[t11]) naturally leans toward the octatonic collection. McTee's keen usage of octatonicism in this piece will be discussed later, but example 7.15 will illustrate the way successive iterations of McTee's three-note "germ seed" opens a door.[29]

Movement II, "Adagio: Until a Silence Fell," quotes Alfred Lord Tennyson, "All night have the roses heard / The flute, violin, bassoon; / All

Example 7.15. *Ballet for Orchestra*, I, mm. 25–34, strings

night has the casement jessamine stirr'd / To the dancers dancing in tune; / Till a silence fell with the waking bird, / And a hush with the setting moon" ("Maud," 1855). This movement represents the heart of the piece for McTee. She has often said it is one of her personal favorites among her own works. Originally an organ piece entitled *Agnus Dei* (1998), the music was reconceived for string orchestra years later, to honor the memory of those who died in the attacks on New York City on September 11, 2001.

> *In the wake of September 11, I thought a lot about courage: the courage exhibited by those who entered burning buildings; the courage it took to deal with immeasurable anger and grief. I thought too about creative courage and felt a renewed commitment to exposing my true artistic self. And so I decided to re-connect with some music I had written several years before—music which, at the time, seemed almost too private to share. Its message was one of both vulnerability and strength. It was inquiring. It mirrored me, just as I was, for better or worse, and it was completely heartfelt.[30]*

A scant five pages in length, McTee's sorrowful, elegant dirge strikes a reverberating chord that has a demonstrated lasting effect. She brings a tapestry approach to her *Adagio*, weaving a melodic theme from Penderecki's *Polish Requiem* together with occasional references to Barber's *Adagio for Strings*, itself a work often associated with death after its poignant use in Oliver Stone's Vietnam war film *Platoon* (1986). The *Adagio* found a permanent home in the *Ballet for Orchestra*, although the composer arranged a version for string quartet one year later (2003).

The third movement, "Waltz: Light Fantastic," is titled after John Milton's "Come and trip it as ye go / On the light fantastic toe," from "L'Allegro" (1645). Comparatively optimistic, though with a remnant tinge of wariness, the waltz is almost entirely driven by ostinato. It perpetuates itself forward like a great hulking machine, eagerly grinding its gears in counterbalance to the gravity of the *Adagio*. Representative of a classical scherzo, the movement is short and light, dancing in the customary triple meter. Mc-Tee's multiple ostinati are the building blocks for the dance.

> *The third movement is a dance—in this case a quick waltz inspired by a memorable performance of Ravel's* La Valse *in 2000 by the Rhode Island Philharmonic Orchestra under Larry Rachleff. A rising half-step motif in the bass lightens the effect of the falling half-step motive heard in the previous movement.*

Much of the energy of this waltz comes from McTee's hocketlike approach to the instrumentation. The *tutti* moment is rare here; more likely is the quick vacillation of rhythmic-melodic cells, rocketing around the orchestra—individuals working together to complete the whole. Example 7.16 illustrates this effect as it plays out in the string section.

Example 7.16. *Ballet for Orchestra*, III, mm. 60–68, strings

Movement IV, "Where Time Plays the Fiddle," takes its title from Henry Austin Dobson's "Cupid's Alley" (1876): "A whisper, a glance, / "Shall we twirl down the middle?" / O, Love's but a dance, / Where Time plays the fiddle!" This last movement of the *Ballet for Orchestra* is constructed with motives consisting of minor and major thirds, as well as various jazz elements, which will be discussed later in this analysis. But perhaps the most intriguing thing about this movement is McTee's employment of distinct references to Stravinsky's *Rite of Spring* "at several points along the way"; specifically, she incorporates motivic elements from *Les Augures Printaniers: Danses des Adolescentes* (see examples 7.17a and 7.17b).

The Stravinskian motives are heard underlying much of the music of the fourth movement, usually as ostinati. Finally, "material from the beginning of the piece returns and a final statement of the opening motif (C-E♭-C) provides closure."

Any attempt to codify McTee's compositional methodology for the *Ballet for Orchestra* must begin with the amalgam of inspirational sources that comprises the composer's compositional inner self. This chapter has identified many such sources, including her background in improvisation and jazz, her fascination with fine machinery and racing, and her musical

Example 7.17a. Stravinsky, *The Rite of Spring*, "The Augurs of Spring," mm. 8–13

Example 7.17b. McTee, *Ballet for Orchestra*, IV, mm. 19–29, selected instruments

representation of contemporary thought. She is a composer who is as interested in the scientific, evolutionary nature of musical processes as she is in unabashed expression of the heart.

The *Ballet for Orchestra* portrays McTee's inner self most clearly in three stylistic areas or categories. The first category is harmonic and melodic, namely, her characteristic admixture of octatonic and dodecaphonic pitch class arrays in the *Ballet*'s overall sound. The second area encompasses matters she considers subjective and close to her heart—jazz, bebop, and improvisational influences. The third consists of her special union of ostinati and *grandes lignes*. An analysis of the *Ballet* must take inventory of the ways in which each stylistic category informs McTee's creation process.

Admixture of Octatonic and Dodecaphonic Pitch Class Arrays

Though any eight-note scale is technically "octatonic," the special arrangement of alternating semitones and whole tones that yields set class 8-28 has garnered enough particular attention in musicians' circles to warrant its delineation as *the* octatonic scale. From Rimsky-Korsakov to Stravinsky, Liszt to Bartók, Debussy to Messiaen, Ives to Coltrane, composers have been exploring the intrinsic possibilities of this scale for well over a century.

To understand McTee's inventive treatment of octatonicism, we must first observe how the three versions/transpositions of the scale interrelate. Beginning with pitch classes 0 and 1 (C and C$\sharp$/D$\flat$) and continuing a pattern of alternating whole-tone and semitone intervals yields set class 8-28 in its prime form: 0134679t ($8\text{-}28^{t0}$). For purposes of this analysis, we will refer to this array as Oct^0. Transposition of the prime form by a semitone yields the second version of the scale: 124578te ($8\text{-}28^{t1}$); we will refer to this array as Oct^1. Transposition up another semitone yields the third possible version: 235689e0 ($8\text{-}28^{t2}$). This third version is also attained by beginning with pitch classes 0 and 2 and continuing the pattern forward (0235689e). We will refer to this array as Oct^2. Regardless of beginning pitch class or initial interval class, the octatonic array will always reduce to one of these three versions; hence, Messiaen's delineation of it as one of the "modes of limited transposition."

While McTee readily engages with each of the different versions of the octatonic scale in her music, octatonicism itself is not always the driving force behind her procedures in the *Ballet for Orchestra*; rather, the *interconnection* between the octatonic and dodecaphonic collections is often what is of special interest to her. As an illustration of her approach, let us consider how one small chromatic "shift" from any of the three versions of the octatonic scale to any other version of the scale will quickly yield the twelve-note aggregate, with minimal repetition of pitch classes (see figure 7.1).

Many of the serpentine melodies that slither through the textures of the *Ballet for Orchestra* are derived from this sort of octatonic shifting. The language, therefore, is often difficult to pin down as being either dodecaphonic or octatonic. McTee has unsurprisingly found a way to balance the two. The resultant sound is simply "McTeean." A few notable examples from the score will demonstrate her various methods of using octatonic shifting to achieve this sound (see examples 7.18a–c).

Figure 7.1.

Octatonic harmony can get old quickly—perhaps because the structures are characteristically symmetrical. So I break them up with sections of twelve-tone music. I should also mention that I very rarely use all the pitches of a twelve-tone row, preferring to let it, too, remain incomplete. It feels right, from time to time, to use but a part of it, thereby introducing an element of asymmetry.

Incomplete or "asymmetrical" aggregate rows are another hallmark of McTee's compositional style, and there are several examples found in the *Ballet for Orchestra*. In this work she employs both complete and incomplete aggregate rows to counterbalance octatonicism, thereby celebrating their foggy relationship. The *Adagio* provides the clearest illustrations of McTee's dodecaphonic asymmetry; here we find myriad passages in which octatonic and dodecaphonic elements are starkly juxtaposed. Other times, the entirety of the texture seems to be focused on the irregularity of the "teasing" incomplete aggregates. Such is the case in example 7.19, from the middle of the movement.

One of the reasons I like to use pitch aggregates of fewer than twelve notes is to make modulation possible. In a twelve-tone environment, of course, there are never any "new" notes. It's therefore more difficult, for me anyway, to create a sense of movement from one tonal region to another when using the entire chromatic collection of pitches. Modulation requires space.[31]

The first movement features a similar methodology, but with a slight twist. Here the aggregate rows are coming quickly, following one after another in the bass instruments, at times following so closely as to blur

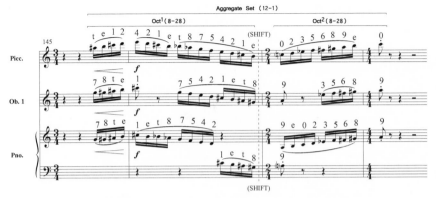

Example 7.18a. *Ballet for Orchestra*, I, mm. 145–148, selected instruments (author's markings)

Example 7.18b. *Ballet for Orchestra*, II, mm. 46–54, selected instruments (author's markings)

Example 7.18c. *Ballet for Orchestra*, IV, mm. 166–173, selected instruments (author's markings)

Example 7.19 *Ballet for Orchestra*, II, mm. 66–70

the line between them. McTee often leaves out a pitch class here or there, thereby placing eleven-note rows alongside twelve-note rows: a different approach to dodecaphonic asymmetry.

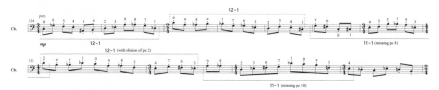

Example 7.20. *Ballet for Orchestra*, I, mm. 124–134, contrabass (author's markings)

It would be irresponsible for the analyst to suggest that McTee is necessarily *consciously* aware of the complex intertwining between octatonic and dodecaphonic forces in this piece, or any of her works. McTee is careful to point out that so much of musical creation for her is about feel, gesture, natural genesis, and evolution. But the level to which any composer is theoretically conscious of his or her own creations is rather beside the point. McTee well understands the octatonic and dodecaphonic collections, and she purposefully employs those materials in this piece, but she does so *in her own way*. And so, at the end of the process, as cognitively aware or mystical as it may have been, the listener is the recipient of an inspired, imaginative, highly intuitive admixture of known theoretical elements, resulting in a musical work that undeniably belongs to its creator. Hasn't that been the case with composers for centuries?

Jazz, Bebop, and Improvisational Influences

Cindy McTee spent much of her youth surrounded by the sounds of popular music from the 1940s and 1950s. Her earliest childhood musical experiences were improvisational. She claims to have a virtually inborn love of bebop. Such important influences could not avoid making their way into her mature catalog, and works such as *Circuits* and *Einstein's Dream* have evidenced the significance of early life experiences to the composer's contemporary existence. In the *Ballet for Orchestra*, we find McTee utilizing a savvy blend of jazz idioms and postmodernist technique, fully embracing her current compositional career while riffing on themes of her youth.

We have thus far understood the octatonic collection as a technique of classical theory, a special collection of alternating interval classes resulting in set class 8-28. But to ignore the scale's roots in jazz music would be an unfortunate oversight; in fact, many believe octatonicism was birthed entirely from jazz. In jazz theory, the octatonic scale is typically referred to as the diminished scale or symmetric diminished scale, due to its inherent construction as the interlocking of any two of the three possible fully diminished seventh chords.

The Three Possible Diminished-Seventh Chords:

The Combination of Any Two:

Figure 7.2.

Jazz musicians frequently employ the half-whole diminished mode or its partner, the whole-half diminished mode, in improvisation. The whole-half diminished mode (meaning the symmetric diminished scale beginning with the whole tone) is commonly used in conjunction with a diminished harmony—for instance, any diminished seventh chord. The half-whole mode is typically played over a dominant harmony. In figure 7.3, we see here how effortlessly it overlies a G^{7m9} chord.

Figure 7.3.

There is a longstanding and well-documented tradition of composers making direct connection between music for the concert hall and music of the jazz hall: Copland's *Music for the Theatre, Clarinet Concerto,* and *Piano Concerto;* Gershwin's *Rhapsody in Blue;* Bernstein's *Prelude, Fugue, and Riffs;* Stravinsky's *Ebony Concerto.*[32] McTee's jazz influences are certainly reflected in her harmonic and melodic choices—including the octatonic elements already discussed—but she also draws on rhythmic components, walking bass lines, and even shout-chorus interruptions to make her connections.

While specific references to jazz in the *Ballet for Orchestra* are rarely overt, idiomatic underpinnings are undeniable. Near the end of movement IV, "Where Time Plays the Fiddle," McTee features a walking *pizzicato* bass line with accompanying swing rhythms, while parallel harmonies in the winds and brass are overlain with jazz-influenced melodic material. The bass line serves the same purpose here as it would in any jazz ensemble: as a rhythmic and harmonic background for faster moving, improvisational, bebop-influenced passages in the winds.[33]

Example 7.21. *Ballet for Orchestra,* **IV, mm. 174–180, selected instruments**

In this piece and others, McTee tends toward another jazz idiom: full-ensemble interruptive gestures, akin to the idea of the shout chorus. McTee often uses these interruptive moments to demarcate a musical change, whether in material, texture, or mood. Example 7.22 illustrates an example of a shout-chorus interruption, a brief moment indicative of the jazz style from perspectives of style, articulation, and vertical structure (see example 7.22).[34]

But McTee also uses well-placed interruptive moments to purposefully thwart a listener's expectations; the decisive displacement of a note or rest, or a sudden transposition, seeks to create an element of humor in her music. "I think humor comes out in the rhythm," says the composer. "There are moments of expectation denied, or use of silence that creates surprise." The fourth movement provides a good illustration. After a full bar of rest in measure 267, a transposed repetition immediately follows; McTee then continues with an unexpected extension of the material heard before the interruption. Moments like this one are prevalent in her writing: an expectation is denied by a sudden interruption, followed by extension of a previously truncated thought (see example 7.23).

Ostinato and La grande ligne

From the isorhythmic motets of the fourteenth century to Mendelssohn's op. 119 to *Einstein on the Beach*, repetition has been used to create musical motion. Techniques of *perpetuum mobile* seek to create sustainability of interest in rhythmic activity, often suspended in harmonic stasis. For McTee, whose longtime fascination with fine machinery informs her writing, clockwork repetition is a motivator of ideas, typically coming in the form of small, whirring cells of music presented in ostinato fashion. But as we might expect, her approach to ostinato is Darwinian; rarely does she preserve any one repeating idea for more than a few measures before altering it. In other words, for McTee, ostinato is often an evolutionary process.

> *Someone described my music as postminimal because it makes frequent use of repetition and ostinato. But the repeated ideas are generally modified after just a few iterations; a note will be left out, a silence inserted, two eighth notes replaced by a dotted eighth-sixteenth, or a pitch displaced by an octave.*

In much of what she terms her "dance music" (as opposed to her "song music"), McTee links chains of ostinati together, causing the listener to actually develop an aural expectation of evolving musical events. Doing this helps McTee move a piece forward in time, her chugging, machine-like rhythmic patterns and figures creating the sense of constant background pulse. Evolution and rhythmic precision are musical soul mates in McTee's compositions; the two necessarily coexist. It is a symbiotic

Example 7.22. *Ballet for Orchestra,* I, mm. 196–203

Example 7.23. *Ballet for Orchestra*, IV, mm. 264–272, selected instruments

relationship, a relationship of exactness and motion that provides the framework for her larger musical structures and goals.

> *Often when something in the background is moving in a predictable way—aligned with a steady pulse—there is a melodic line floating over top using rhythms that are more freely designed. So you get this tension from those things which are grounded, predictable, and machinelike against other things that are more fluid and lyrical.*

An additional layer in McTee's music is the presence of an extended melodic line, frequently found superimposed over iterations of an ostinato. The concept is akin to Boulanger's well-documented idea of *la grande ligne*, a staple of her teaching. Howard Pollack writes, "Boulanger particularly emphasized *la grande ligne* (the long line), a sense of forward motion . . . the feeling for inevitability, for the creating of an entire piece that could be thought of as a functioning entity."[35] A few thoughts from Alfred W. Cochran may also be an aid to understanding the way McTee approaches the concept:

> Scores which, to me, are most effective possess . . . the long line of logical inevitability in music. This quality can be present in a score regardless of its particular external shape or form. It arises as a result of the accumulation of specific, related musical occurrences; but, one's recognition of its presence is often quintessentially subjective. Its value lies in direct proportion to its ability to impart a sense of cohesiveness to the musical flow, the realization of which by the listener need not be apparent at the conscious level. . . . It touches upon some of the broader and more provocative aspects of what music is and is not, how one perceives the passage of time within a musical

context, the role of musical dynamism or its absence, ways that structural form and tonal organization function in music, what the concept of development in music is, and what the various roles and functions of musical rhythm are at various levels of a composition.[36]

McTee considers her own adaptation of the *grande ligne* idea to be a musical personification of her introspective, lyrical "song music." She believes that the simplicity of a song voice adds to overall clarity in her large ensemble works, as a listener's ear will be naturally drawn to the long, lyrical musical lines and away from the fast-moving and ever-evolving ostinato patterns.[37] We may look to the *Ballet for Orchestra* for significant illustrations of McTee's innovative approach. As stated earlier, the virtual entirety of "Waltz: Light Fantastic" is constructed with repeating patterns. The movement features a singular three-beat waltz ostinato, presented in familiar hocket fashion; this pattern is frequently decorated with various other repetitive figures drawn from the orchestra.

Example 7.24. *Ballet for Orchestra*, III, mm. 48–56, selected instruments

The pattern continues, sometimes shifting pitch classes but always retaining rhythm and contour, through all but 17 of the movement's 187 measures. Near the end of the movement, a stirring *grande ligne* rises from the violins and viola (see example 7.25).

An extraordinary passage from the first movement provides a microcosmic example of practically all of the style characteristics heretofore identified. It features an ostinato chain, which begins in the second violins and violas and slowly evolves, moving around to other instruments, adding or subtracting pitches or beats, becoming increasingly active. There are several strategically placed interruptions in the evolutionary

Example 7.25.   ***Ballet for Orchestra*, III, mm. 131–144, selected instruments**

process, and we should further note the abrupt octatonic shift from Oct^0 to Oct^1 (and back again) in measures 68 to 72. Finally, superimposed over all of this activity sing the horns and trombones: McTee's lyrical voice, *la grande ligne* (see example 7.26).

Taking into account the musical depth of the above passage, perhaps it is easy to understand why McTee's *Ballet for Orchestra* has been praised by performers, critics, conductors, and composers around the world. Touted for its frenetic energy and perpetual motion, it is equally appreciated for its long, engaging melodic lines. The *Ballet*'s jazz, bebop, and popular music-inspired elements balance themselves with dodecaphony, creating an admixture of harmonic languages and an amalgam of musical worlds.

Balance—this is McTee's *Urlicht*. Throughout her life she has sought to bring things into equilibrium—levity and gravity, darkness and light, motion and stasis, freedom and precision. And here is a woman whose work reflects her persona. She has always known there must be balance in both art and human existence. She asks herself good and tough questions, takes bold and important steps, and challenges the notion of what it means to be "a composer who happens to be a woman." All of these questions, steps, and challenges have helped forge Cindy McTee's oeuvre into a beacon example of the twenty-first century American sound. The *Ballet* is just one example; there will be others. And as she moves forward into a new chapter of life, it is likely that McTee will continually look back, everything in circles, to reflect upon the journey that brought her here—a journey that coincidentally began with a question of balance, when she was "just a small boy on her bike," looking for a place to ride.

Example 7.26. *Ballet for Orchestra*, I, mm. 48–90, strings and horn

CODA

One of America's most imaginative and innovative composers, Cindy McTee continues to travel, write, study, and influence the world around her. Though retired from teaching, she is regularly booked as a guest speaker, presenter, or composer in residence. The year 2010 will see performances of *Ballet for Band* (University of Washington Wind Ensemble—Tim Salzman, conductor); *Adagio* (Plymouth Philharmonic Orchestra—Steven Karidoyanes, conductor); *Double Play* (premiere); and *Symphony no. 1: Ballet for Orchestra* (Detroit Symphony Orchestra—Leonard Slatkin, conductor). Perpetuating his remarkable reputation as a champion and promoter of new orchestral music, and demonstrating his obvious affinity for McTee's works, Maestro Slatkin is also slated to conduct performances of *Double Play* and *Einstein's Dream* in 2011.[38]

Current compositional projects include completion of *Double Play* for orchestra, commissioned by the Detroit Symphony Orchestra and

Leonard Slatkin in honor of Elaine Lebenbom, a composer, poet, artist, teacher, and lecturer who died in 2002. McTee will subsequently create a version of the work for symphonic winds, scheduled for first performance in the fall of 2010 by Texas's Lone Star Wind Symphony, under the direction of Eugene Migliaro Corporon.

McTee's own words from the preface of the score for *Double Play* aptly summate her approaches to the two movements of the piece ("The Unquestioned Answer" and "Tempus Fugit"), and to the larger philosophical ideals this chapter has brought to the fore:

> *I have always been particularly attracted to the idea that disparate musical elements— tonal and atonal, placid and frenetic—can not only coexist but also illuminate and complement one another. . . . As in Ives'* Unanswered Question, *my* Unquestioned Answer *presents planes of highly contrasting materials: sustained, consonant sonorities in the strings intersect to create dissonances; melodies for the principal players soar atop; and discordant passages in the brass and winds become ever more disruptive. . . .* Tempus Fugit, *Latin for "time flees" but more commonly translated as 'time flies,' is frequently used as an inscription on clocks. My* Tempus Fugit *begins with the sounds of several pendulum clocks ticking at different speeds. . . . Jazz rhythms and harmonies, quickly-moving repetitive melodic ideas, and fragmented form echo the multifaceted and hurried aspects of twenty-first-century American society.*

As this book chapter is finding its conclusion, Cindy McTee is on a plane to Europe, having just finished her last semester of teaching after twenty-six years of service. Time flies, indeed. For this composer, who is listening to the simultaneous ticking of myriad clocks, the future is both uncertain and certain: uncertain in that superficial "what next" sort of way, but certain in the way of the "harmony of the spheres," those synchronous wheels spinning out the illusion of linear time. McTee will undoubtedly continue to listen to that mystical harmony—to the world around her, to the cosmos—and the music yet to come will surely reflect the attunement.

NOTES

1. With admiration and gratitude, I acknowledge the research and pertinent biographical information contributed to this chapter by Deborah Hayes. I thank her profusely for her assistance.

2. Cindy McTee, from a live presentation about her *Symphony no. 1: Ballet for Orchestra*. Unless otherwise cited, all quotes and personal information are from direct correspondence or conversation with the composer.

3. Letter from McTee to David Fullmer, July 5, 1998, quoted in Fullmer, "Cindy McTee," in *A Composer's Insight: Thoughts, Analysis and Commentary on Contemporary Masterpieces for Wind Band*, ed. Timothy Salzman (Galesville, MD: Meredith Music Publications, 2003), 1:108.

4. Cindy McTee, in an interview with Lucinda Breeding, "Unlikely Ideas Fuse in Symphony: UNT Composer Draws on Beethoven, Jazz, 9-11," *Denton Record Chronicle*, 2002.

5. Letter from McTee to David Fullmer, July 5, 1998, quoted in Fullmer, "Cindy McTee," 108.

6. Cindy McTee, "Matter—Viewpoint [Statement on Music Theory]," *NewMusicBox*, April 1, 2003, www.newmusicbox.org/page.nmbx?id=48hf07.

7. McTee, "Gender and Music Composition: A Personal Perspective," *Society for American Music Bulletin* (published as *Sonneck Society Bulletin*) 25, no. 2 (Summer 1999), http://american-music.org/publications/bullarchive/McTee.html.

8. McTee, "Gender and Music Composition." She repeats this statement in a recent interview by Ralph Hartsock, *Journal of the International Alliance for Women in Music* 15, no. 2 (Fall 2009), 3.

9. Used by permission. © 1987 Norruth Music Inc. Copyright assigned 2008 to Keiser Classical (BMI). All rights reserved. International copyright secured.

10. Used by permission. © 1988 Norruth Music Inc. Copyright assigned 2008 to Keiser Classical (BMI). All rights reserved. International copyright secured.

11. Elizabeth Hinkle-Turner, *Women Composers and Music Technology in the United States: Crossing the Line* (Aldershot, Hants, England; Burlington, VT: Ashgate, 2006), 44–46, 110.

12. Cindy McTee, telephone conversation with David Fullmer, June 1, 1998, quoted in Fullmer, "Cindy McTee," 109.

13. Brian Alber, "The Evolution of Melodic Construction in Three 20th-Century Wind Band Works," *Journal of Band Research* 43, no. 1 (Fall 2007), 74. When Alber's article was published, he was director of instrumental music at Plattsmouth (Nebraska) High School and had recently completed graduate studies at the University of Nebraska at Lincoln.

14. Used by permission. © 1990 Norruth Music Inc. Copyright assigned 2008 to Keiser Classical (BMI). All rights reserved. International copyright secured.

15. Ward's review is quoted on McTee's website.

16. According to Hinkle-Turner, *Women Composers and Music Technology*, 110, the MIDI instruments include the Yamaha DX-7 and TX81Z sound modules, which employ John Chowning's FM synthesis and so feature timbres similar to those of analog synthesizers.

17. Robert Cummings, review of *"M" Music*, Centaur Records CRC 2213, in *Computer Music Journal* 21, no. 2 (Summer 1997).

18. Used by permission. © 1993 Norruth Music Inc. Copyright assigned 2008 to Keiser Classical (BMI). All rights reserved. International copyright secured.

19. Used by permission. © 1993 Norruth Music Inc. Copyright assigned 2008 to Keiser Classical (BMI). All rights reserved. International copyright secured.

20. Used by permission. © 1995 Norruth Music Inc. Copyright assigned 2008 to Keiser Classical (BMI). All rights reserved. International copyright secured.

21. Used by permission. © 1996 Norruth Music Inc. Copyright assigned 2008 to Keiser Classical (BMI). All rights reserved. International copyright secured.

22. Used by permission. © 1996 Norruth Music Inc. Copyright assigned 2008 to Keiser Classical (BMI). All rights reserved. International copyright secured.

23. Used by permission. © 2000 Norruth Music Inc. Copyright assigned 2008 to Keiser Classical (BMI). All rights reserved. International copyright secured.

24. Cindy McTee, "Radar—News [Statement on Guggenheim award]," *New-MusicBox*, May 1, 2001, www.newmusicbox.org/article.nmbx?id=1275.

25. Some of McTee's explanations from her program note are also published in her article "Einstein's Legacy: Music Composition," *Imagine* 13, no. 1 (September/October 2005): 5–6, http://cindymctee.com/misc_folder/imagine_ED.htm. *Imagine* is the magazine of the Johns Hopkins University Center for Talented Youth, written for grades seven through twelve.

26. "Cindy McTee's Approach to Meter in the Case of Conducted, Spatial Music" (paper distributed to students in orchestration class, University of North Texas, 2008).

27. Allan Kozinn, "Leonard Slatkin's Gamble on the Road Less Traveled," *New York Times*, November 4, 2002.

28. Dr. Nicholas Enrico Williams, assistant director of wind studies at UNT, and colleague and friend to McTee, has written about the *Ballet for Band* (along with others of her band works). His D.M.A. dissertation, "Primary Stylistic Characteristics of Cindy's McTee's Music as Found in *Timepiece, Ballet for Band*, and *Finish Line*," provides specific insights into the disparate scoring between the orchestra and band versions of the *Ballet*.

29. McTee's use of octatonic elements in this work is the subject of a UNT master's thesis by Jennifer Weaver: "Structural Octatonicism in Cindy McTee's *Symphony no. 1: Ballet for Orchestra*" (master's thesis, University of North Texas, 2007).

30. McTee, interview with Lucinda Breeding.

31. McTee, live presentation about *Symphony no. 1: Ballet for Orchestra*.

32. Nicholas E. Williams, "Primary Stylistic Characteristics of Cindy's McTee's Music as Found in *Timepiece, Ballet for Band*, and *Finish Line*" (D.M.A. diss., University of North Texas, 2009).

33. Williams, "Primary Stylistic Characteristics."

34. Williams, "Primary Stylistic Characteristics."

35. Howard Pollack, *Aaron Copland* (New York: Henry Holt, 1999), 15.

36. Alfred W. Cochran, "The Spear of Cephalus: Observations on Film Music Analysis," *Indiana Theory Review* 11 (1990): 70.

37. Williams, "Primary Stylistic Characteristics."

38. Cindy McTee, composer website.

APPENDIX A: LIST OF WORKS

Orchestra

Circuits (1990)—full orchestra
The Twittering Machine (1993)—chamber orchestra
Timepiece (2000)—full orchestra
Adagio (2002)—string orchestra
Symphony no. 1: Ballet for Orchestra (2002)—full orchestra

Einstein's Dream (2004)—string orchestra, percussion, and CD
Finish Line (2005)—full orchestra
Solstice (2007)—trombone with orchestra
Double Play (2009)—full orchestra
Tempis Fugit (2010)—full orchestra
The Unquestioned Answer—full orchestra

Band

Circuits (1990)—wind ensemble version
California Counterpoint: The Twittering Machine (1993)—wind ensemble version
Soundings (1995)—band
Timepiece (2001)—wind symphony version
Ballet for Band (2004)—band
Finish Line (2006)—wind symphony

Chamber Ensemble

Chord (1977)—flute
Songs of Spring and the Moon (1983)—chamber ensemble
Psalm 142: Threnody (1984)—voice and organ
Images (1987)—horn and piano
Circle Music I (1988)—viola and piano
Circle Music II (1988)—flute and piano
Circle Music III (1988)—bassoon and piano
Circle Music IV (1988)—horn and piano
Études (1992)—alto saxophone and computer music on CD
Capriccio per Kzrysztof Penderecki (1993)—violin
Stepping Out (1993)—flute and percussion
The Twittering Machine (1993)—chamber ensemble
Changes (1996)—violoncello and bass
Einstein's Dreams (1996)—chamber ensemble
Agnus Dei (1998)—organ
Adagio (2003)—string quartet
Fanfare for Trumpets (2004)—two trumpets or trumpet ensemble
Fanfare for Trombones (2007)—two trombones or trombone ensemble
Bricolage (2008)—flute and computer music on CD

Choral

Psalm 100 (1982)—mixed choir

Electroacoustic

Metal Music (1989)—computer music on CD
"M" Music (1992)—computer music on CD
Études (1992)—alto saxophone and computer music on CD
Einstein's Dream (2004)—string orchestra, percussion, CD
Bricolage (2008)—flute and computer music on CD

APPENDIX B: DISCOGRAPHY

Ballet for Band. North Texas Wind Symphony. Klavier Records K 11144. "Allegories." 2004.

Ballet for Band. North Texas Wind Symphony. GIA Publications CD-746. "GIA Composer's Collection: Cindy McTee." 2008.

California Counterpoint: The Twittering Machine. North Texas Wind Symphony. GIA Publications CD-746. "GIA Composer's Collection: Cindy McTee." 2008.

California Counterpoint: The Twittering Machine. North Texas Wind Symphony. Klavier Records K 11070. "Tributes." 1995.

Circuits. Cincinnati College Conservatory of Music Wind Symphony. GIA Publications CD-746. "GIA Composer's Collection—Cindy McTee." 2008.

Circuits. Cincinnati College-Conservatory of Music Wind Symphony. Klavier Records K 11042. "Memorials." 1992.

Circuits. University of Florida Wind Ensemble. Mark Records 2245-MCD. "Wind Tracks."

Études. Arizona University Recordings AUR CD 3128. "America's Millennium Tribute to Adolphe Sax, Vol. 11." 2007.

Études. Mark Records 1806-MCD. "Light of Sothis." 1995.

Fanfare for Trumpets. University of North Texas. GIA Publications CD-746. "GIA Composer's Collection—Cindy McTee." 2008.

Fanfare for Trumpets. Crystal Records CD 763. "Unconventional Trumpet." 2004.

Finish Line. Showa Wind Symphony. CAFUA Records CACG-0112. "Finish Line." 2008.

Finish Line. University of North Texas. GIA Publications CD-746. "GIA Composer's Collection: Cindy McTee." 2008.

Images. Encore Music 8913509EC. "Music for Horn and Piano by Women Composers." 1996.

"M" Music. Centaur Compact Discs CRC 2213. "CDCM Computer Music Series CD, Vol. 18." 1994.

Metal Music. Centaur Compact Discs CRC 2078. "CDCM Computer Music Series CD, Vol. 9." 1994.

Soundings. University of North Texas. GIA Publications CD-746. "GIA Composer's Collection: Cindy McTee." 2008.

Soundings. New World School of the Arts Wind Ensemble. Mark Records 2669-MCD. "Midwest Clinic 1997: New World School of the Arts Wind Ensemble." 1997.

Soundings. University of Georgia Wind Symphony. Mark Records 2871-MCD. "The Riddle of the Sphinx." 1999.

Soundings. North Texas Wind Symphony. Klavier Records K 11084. "Wind Dances." 1997.

Stepping Out. Jessica Johnson, Payton MacDonald. Equilibrium CD-05. "Verederos: Music for Flute and Percussion." 1997.

Timepiece. University of North Texas. GIA Publications CD-746. "GIA Composer's Collection: Cindy McTee." 2008.

Timepiece. Plano East Senior High Wind Ensemble. Mark Records 4013-MCD. "Midwest Clinic 2001: Plano East Senior High Wind Ensemble." 2001.

Timepiece. North Texas Wind Symphony. Klavier Records K 11122. "Time Pieces." 2001.

Timepiece. Showa Wind Symphony. CAFUA Records CACG-0032. "The Warriors." 2002.

SOURCES

Alber, Brian. "The Evolution of Melodic Construction in Three 20th-Century Wind Band Works." *Journal of Band Research* 43, no. 1 (Fall 2007): 63–78.

Fullmer, David Charles. "A Comparison of the Wind Band Writing of Three Contemporary Composers: Karel Husa, Timothy Broege, and Cindy McTee." D.M.A. dissertation, University of Washington, 2003.

———. "Cindy McTee." In *A Composer's Insight: Thoughts, Analysis and Commentary on Contemporary Masterpieces for Wind Band*. Vol. 1. Edited by Tim Salzman. Galesville, MD: Meredith Music Publications, 2003.

Hinkle-Turner, Elizabeth. *Women Composers and Music Technology in the United States: Crossing the Line*. Aldershot, Hants, England; Burlington, VT: Ashgate, 2006.

Hollinger, Diana. "Teacher Resource Guide: *Timepiece* by Cindy McTee." In *Teaching Music through Performance in Band*. Vol. 4. Edited by Richard Miles. Chicago: GIA Publications, 2002.

McInturf, Matthew. "Teacher Resource Guide: *Circuits* by Cindy McTee." In *Teaching Music through Performance in Band*. Vol. 3. Edited by Richard Miles. Chicago: GIA Publications, 2000.

———. "Teacher Resource Guide: *Soundings* by Cindy McTee." In *Teaching Music through Performance in Band*. Vol. 2. Edited by Richard Miles. Chicago: GIA Publications, 1998.

McTee, Cindy. Composer website. www.cindymctee.com.

———. "Einstein's Legacy: Music Composition." *Imagine* 13, no. 1 (September/October 2005): 5–6. http://cindymctee.com/misc_folder/imagine_ED.htm.

———. "Gender and Music Composition: A Personal Perspective." *Society for American Music Bulletin* (published as *Sonneck Society Bulletin*) 25, no. 2 (Summer 1999). http://american-music.org/publications/bullarchive/McTee.html.

———. Interview by Ralph Hartsock. *Journal of the International Alliance for Women in Music* 25, no. 1 (Fall 2009): 1–3.

———. "Matter—Viewpoint [Statement on Music Theory]." *NewMusicBox*, April 1, 2003. www.newmusicbox.org/page.nmbx?id=48hf07.

———. "Radar—News [Statement on Guggenheim award]." *NewMusicBox*, May 1, 2001. www.newmusicbox.org/article.nmbx?id=1275.

Trachsel, Andrew. "Teacher Resource Guide: *Ballet for Band* by Cindy McTee." In *Teaching Music through Performance in Band*. Vol. 5. Edited by Richard Miles. Chicago: GIA Publications, 2004.

———. "Teacher Resource Guide: *California Counterpoint: The Twittering Machine* by Cindy McTee." In *Teaching Music through Performance in Band*. Vol. 6. Edited by Richard Miles. Chicago: GIA Publications, 2007.

Weaver, Jennifer L. "Structural Octatonicism in Cindy McTee's *Symphony no. 1: Ballet for Orchestra*." Master's thesis, University of North Texas, 2007.

Williams, Nicholas Enrico. "Primary Stylistic Characteristics of Cindy's McTee's Music as Found in *Timepiece*, *Ballet for Band*, and *Finish Line*." D.M.A. diss., University of North Texas, 2009.

Sharon Mirchandani

MARGA RICHTER (1926–)

Composing is my response to a constant desire to transform my perceptions and emotions into music. Everything that touches me, everything I become aware of as beautiful, or mysterious, or painful, or joyful, or unknowable becomes an immediate or eventual source of inspiration. Music is the way I speak to the silence of the universe.[1]

Marga Richter has composed over one hundred works, in nearly every genre. Though she is most recognized for her orchestral and chamber music, her many songs and choral pieces (along with her opera *Riders to the Sea*) have received uniform acclaim. Richter's style is eclectic, independent of any one system or approach; she composes intuitively. She has drawn inspiration from myriad and diverse sources: European composers, from Handel to Shostakovich; American choreographers; American, Chinese, Irish, and Japanese poets; Indian classical music; nature; and paintings and photographs. Her music expresses typically romantic moods of beauty, longing, and poignancy, but in a contemporary style. The modal patterns found within Richter's scores often result in sonorities that are tonal but dissonant, emphasizing seconds and sevenths. She makes much use of ostinato (at times creating a minimalist effect), employs a variety of contrapuntal techniques, and primarily centers her focus on the melodic over the harmonic. Richter occasionally reuses material from her earlier works in new compositions, a trait partially a result of her training with Vincent Persichetti, and she has been known to incorporate quotations from European compositions, with smooth transitions from her original material into and out of the borrowed passage. Many of her pieces are single-movement structures with free-flowing forms, often roughly designed in the manner of theme and variations and cultivating an improvisatory slant. With such a profusion of compositional tools ready at her disposal, it is no surprise Marga Richter has steadily risen to become one of America's preeminent musical matriarchs.

Florence Marga Richter was born in Reedsburg, Wisconsin, the heart of the American midwest; she is the middle of the three children of American soprano Inez Chandler. Her father, Paul Richter, was a German soldier from Einbeck, Germany, who had sought out Ms. Chandler after hearing her sing in the local opera house. Marga never actually met her paternal grandfather, Richard Richter, a composer and orchestra conductor in Kassel, Germany. The composer clearly remembers her father's listening to the radio broadcasts of the Metropolitan Opera on Saturday afternoons; if the opera was by Wagner, he would insist on absolute silence throughout the house in order to hear the performance unblemished.

The influence of Marga's mother was quite important to her early musical development. After an opera tour in Europe, Ms. Chandler returned with her husband to the midwest, where she taught private voice lessons and was the soloist in the local Christian Scientist church.[2] Marga was therefore exposed to a rich variety of vocal repertoire, as her mother regularly sang Brahms's *Lieder*, hymns, and other vocal repertoire in the home; Inez Chandler supported her daughter's musical endeavors in every way, instilling in young Marga the idea that the future held no boundaries.

> *I started composing when I was about ten. I would just do it when nobody was around, and I still have to have nobody around because I do it audibly, at the piano.*[3]

During these impressionable years, Marga Richter studied the standard European piano repertoire. And she composed a number of short songs, though she had no composition teacher. The first public performance of her music came in 1941, when she was fifteen years old. She and her mother performed her *Jabberwocky*, a setting of Lewis Carroll's popular poem, at the high school in Robbinsdale, Minnesota.

Though it is Richter's earliest extant work, *Jabberwocky*, which is scored for singer-speaker and piano, contains many of the elements she has consistently appropriated throughout her life: chromaticism, free use of dissonance, rhythmic energy and clever rhythms, ostinato-based forms, and dramatic pacing. Following a brief introduction, a repeated augmented octave (E♭-E) suggests the image of the Jabberwock; perfect fifths and perfect fourths, followed by minor ninths and minor seconds, create dissonant but recognizable patterns; and the piece ends on a diminished octave (E-E♭) that mirrors the earlier augmented one. In some phrases, the singer may find the melody imbedded in the piano part; for others, the singer may simply speak the poem, *Sprechstimme*-style, as the piano burbles its suggestive accompaniment.

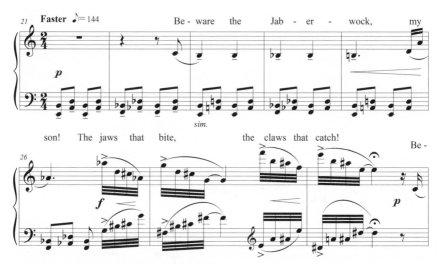

Example 8.1. *Jabberwocky*, mm. 21–28[4]

In the summer of 1941, Richter won a scholarship to attend a piano master class in Minneapolis given by the Polish pianist Countess Helena Morsztyn (Morsztyn had studied with Theodor Leschetizky, who had studied with Carl Czerny). When Morsztyn returned to Minneapolis the following summer, Richter not only reattended the class, she also took private lessons from Morsztyn in preparation for a solo recital to be given that October in Minneapolis. Morsztyn encouraged Richter to come to New York City, offering to take her on as a permanent student, and in 1943, Richter's family moved to New York for that purpose.

During that year, at the age of seventeen, Richter composed *Ballet of the Pixilated Penguins*, for piano solo. Her close friend, Lenore Engdahl, played the piece on her first New York piano recital the following year. *Penguins* exemplifies a playful side the composer has maintained her whole life. Richter possesses a charming, if mischievous, inclination toward titles with double meanings, signing and dedicating her works with special nicknames, and utilizing musical elements to create humor and surprise in many of her compositions. *Penguins*, for example, which is signed *Pengy*, features a syncopated left-hand ostinato that mimics the quirky movements of the penguins, and a chromatically inflected right hand with impetuous "pecking" interspersed with sweeping melodic gestures.

Example 8.2. *Ballet of the Pixilated Penguins,* mm. 9–14[5]

Other interesting figurations in this work include repeated chromatic triplets, chromatic scales a half step apart in each hand, and sixteenth-note passages presented in four simultaneous octaves. After Engdahl played the piece for Leopold Stokowski, the famed conductor remarked, "Tell her never to study composition. She will lose something very unique and fresh."[6]

In 1945, Richter entered the Juilliard School of Music as a piano major under Rosalyn Tureck.[7] Unfortunately, at the end of Richter's freshman year, Tureck resigned from teaching at Juilliard to devote her career solely to concertizing. She did, however, offer to continue teaching two students privately, and Richter was chosen as one of them. Richter was delighted to be given the opportunity to continue her lessons with Tureck, but in order to remain at the school, she officially changed her major to composition in the fall of 1946.[8]

> *What she [Tureck] taught me about rhythm was a revelation. She stressed the importance of lightly accenting the first beat of the metrical unit and creating tension in a phrase by understanding and projecting the rhythmic structure. In addition, we were taught to incorporate an infinitesimal pause between the beats (the "agogic accent") which creates great rhythmic excitement and interest. This gave me an ingrained sense of rhythm and meter which has greatly influenced my composing.[9]*

Embarking on this new direction in her musical life, Richter submitted a few works to the composition department as part of her application.

She was accepted, becoming one of the few female composition majors at Juilliard (and later, the first female to graduate with a master's degree in composition).[10] Richter studied with William Bergsma for one year (1946–1947), after which Bergsma left the school. (He later returned and became the associate dean.) Richter began studies with a new professor, Vincent Persichetti.

> *I submitted that* [Ballet of the Pixilated Penguins] *and a couple of other small piano pieces, and a couple of songs, I guess—and again, I was lucky, because years later they would never have let me in on that. Kids today, they're seventeen and they're writing symphonies, and they have all the synthesizers. They just are really worldly. It's all so fast now. We were slower. It was more fun then. So that's how I became a composer, just because of that.*

Persichetti's compositional style relied heavily on counterpoint and thorough exploitation of modern musical vocabulary with great stylistic freedom; his music deftly merged varying approaches, from diatonicism to atonality, and he stood at the forefront of contemporary formal design, often composing in short sections based on single themes, and growing the music organically into larger structures. Many of Persichetti's compositions were for piano (he was a virtuoso pianist), and he produced a wealth of vocal and choral music, but he is perhaps most known for his unsurpassed contribution to the American concert wind band repertoire. Highly regarded as a teacher, Persichetti both started and ended his 1961 *Twentieth-Century Harmony* text with the following lines, expressing the attitude toward composition he earnestly sought to impress upon his students:

> Any tone can succeed any other tone, any tone can sound simultaneously with any other tone or tones, and any group of tones can be followed by any other group of tones, just as any degree of tension or nuance can occur in any medium under any kind of stress or duration. Successful projection will depend upon the contextual and formal conditions that prevail, and upon the skill and the soul of the composer.[11]

In a 1980 interview with Jane LePage, Richter commented about her teachers: "Unlike so many composition teachers, they did not try to turn me into weak carbon copies of themselves but helped me learn how to make my own musical ideas into finished pieces."[12]

Under Persichetti's tutelage, Richter composed the exhilarating three-movement *Sonata for Clarinet and Piano* (1948), a work with frequent metric changes and an exciting rhythmic palette of irregular rhythms and cross-rhythms. She was beginning to find her distinct voice as both composer and innovator, utilizing rhythmic motives as important structural elements in the work. The frequent contrasts between *staccato* and *legato* articulation, careful use of rests with occasional "extra" rests, and call-and-response patterns between the two instruments generate excitement and help define the rhythmic motives, which are metrically transformed from eighth notes to triplet eighths to sixteenths to thirty-second notes. In the piano part, cross-hands triplet chords and alternation of chords from the outer limits to the inner registers create a dramatic physical performance.

Example 8.3. *Sonata for Clarinet and Piano*, mm. 1–8[13]

It's an incredible piece for the age when I wrote it—I don't know, it just came out of nowhere. I found my rhythmic excitement, and harmony, everything. And I just started pouring it out, I didn't think about it.

In 1949, while still a student, Richter completed a song cycle for voice and piano entitled *Transmutation*, a setting of eight texts by various Chinese poets, translated by Henry H. Hart.[14] Sensitive to their symbolic meanings, Richter exquisitely captures the mood of the texts with her music, and the piece, which was a great success, foreshadowed the composer's lifelong affinity toward composing for the voice.[15] Both *Transmutation* and the *Sonata for Clarinet and Piano* were performed on the Composers' Forum series in New York City to much acclaim, garnering positive reviews in both the *New York Times* and the *Herald Tribune*; therefore, at the tender age of twenty-four, as the youngest composer ever presented on these concerts, Richter was already establishing herself as a compositional force, a fact deservedly noted by Australian composer and critic Peggy Glanville-Hicks at the time:

> Miss Richter's evolution should be allowed to follow its own inner nature, avoiding formula or systems as much as possible. The most valuable of her musical attributes are an original sense of rhythm, a sense of drama in choice of materials and, above all, an ability to make her own forms grow from the very nature of her materials and ideas. This is the very essence of composition.[16]

In her last years at Juilliard, Richter composed her first dance score, a work entitled *All Desire Is Sad* (1949), which was performed at the Juilliard concert hall. *All Desire Is Sad* foreshadowed Richter's increasing involvement with the world of modern dance. After graduating in 1951, she quickly earned recognition when MGM commissioned and issued a series of records of her music, and several American choreographers began commissioning her dance pieces. Leaving the conservatory behind, Richter turned to face the unbounded future for which she had been so well prepared.

During the 1950s, Richter composed increasingly complex works. Her large-scale pieces from this time include *Concerto for Piano and Violas, Cellos and Basses* (*Piano Concerto no. 1*); *Lament*, for string orchestra; *Aria and Toccata*, for viola and string orchestra; *Variations on a Sarabande*, for orchestra; *Melodrama*, for two pianos; and *Sonata for Piano*.

The demands of nurturing a budding career were coupled with the everyday joys and challenges of a traditional personal life; in 1953, Richter married Alan Skelly (who later became the chairman of the Philosophy Department at C. W. Post College, Long Island) and had two children with him: a son, Michael, in 1955, and a daughter, Maureen, in 1957.[17] In keeping with the times, Marga became the primary day-to-day caregiver for the children (while continuing her composing), and Alan's career provided financial security for the family. It was during this time that Richter learned her mother was suffering from terminal cancer. As a Christian Scientist, her mother rarely spoke about illnesses, and so when Richter went to visit (with five-month-old Michael), there was no discussion of the disease that threatened her mother's life, and all surface emotions were held in check, even as Richter flew back to New York, knowing she had seen her mother for the last time. But she would find her expression of sorrow through composing her *Lament* (1956) for string orchestra. Fate would dictate that the very day she wrote the last notes of *Lament*, she received the phone call saying her mother had died. When the piece was subsequently performed by a chamber orchestra in Philadelphia, conducted by William Smith (associate conductor of the Philadelphia Chamber Orchestra), Richter's family and friends came out for the performance, and catharsis.[18]

The MGM orchestra recorded the work in 1956 with Izler Solomon conducting. A second recording of *Lament*, conducted by Carolann Martin, was released on compact disc in 1987 by Leonarda Records, and music critic Kenneth Lafave hailed it as "a major work, looking for its rightful place in the repertoire."[19] The anguished eleven-minute *Lament* maintains its powerful sense of pathos through the continual transformation of the primary melodic material in many different modal contexts. Beginning in a slow triple-simple meter, the music, which finds itself primarily in E Phrygian with added chromaticism, gradually ebbs and flows with regard to both tempo and modality, snaking a path through G-sharp Phrygian and G Phrygian before winding down to a conclusion in E Dorian. A chromatic ostinato unifies the piece as the main melody is altered, and the mournfulness is enhanced with frequent, hollow perfect fifth harmonies.

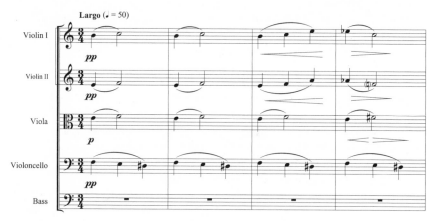

Example 8.4a. *Lament,* mm. 1–4, melody in second violin[20]

Example 8.4b. *Lament,* mm. 133–136, melody in second violin and viola

Lament was written in 1956 as my mother was dying; it is dedicated to her (she died the day I completed the score). It is built on a single quasi-modal theme, surrounded by sometimes dissonant counterpoint and ostinati. Growing slowly through a multiplicity of almost obsessive repetitions (which one conductor characterized as "mono-maniacal"), it reaches an intense climax, then subsides to a quiet ending.[21]

Although Richter was never very interested in teaching, she did inspire many younger composers, including composer Dianne Goolkasian Rahbee, who, while a student at Juilliard herself, was hired as a daytime caregiver for Richter's children in the late 1950s. Rahbee's recollections address motherhood, working as a composer, and music:

Marga was an inspiration and wonderful role model for me. She was a composer of great accomplishment, a devoted wife and mother, and was able to manage it all! This is no easy feat, as I later found out in my own life. I would arrive at her apartment each day at 8:00 a.m. and babysit for three or four hours while she was in the music room composing. I remember her working on only one measure sometimes for the entire three hours! She would endlessly repeat chords and phrases, each time making various modifications until she was completely satisfied with the results. It was really hard work and very intense. Sometimes when I babysat in the evening, when the children were sleeping, I listened to some of her records but was astonished when I found so few. Her collection consisted almost exclusively of Bach and the Beethoven string quartets. When I asked her if she had more recordings, she said, "What else do I need?!" I always remembered that statement. . . . For my birthday, she gave me a recording of the Swingle Singers singing various keyboard music of Bach. I was surprised at her flexibility in accepting this arrangement of Bach's music. It opened my mind to new and freer ways of thinking.[22]

In the early 1960s, while Richter balanced professional life with raising her children, she continued to produce several new chamber and piano works, more modest in scale and somewhat Webern-like, but never systematized by compositional methodology: *Darkening of the Light*, for viola; *Suite*, for violin and piano; *Eight Pieces*, for piano; and *Fragments*, for piano. She also composed short pieces for chorus: *Psalm 91*, *Three Christmas Songs*, and *Seek Him*.

An important acknowledgment of the power of her craft came with the Harkness Ballet commission of *Abyss* (1964), a modern ballet score after the Leonid Andreyev story of the same name. The Harkness Ballet premiered the work in Cannes in 1965 and continued to perform it in Europe, North Africa, Asia, and North and South America. Quickly rising as one of Richter's most sought-after scores, the Joffrey and Boston Ballet companies soon adopted the work, and Roland Johnson conducted an adapted orchestral version with the Madison Symphony. The remarkable success of *Abyss* led to a second Harkness Ballet commission for Richter: *Bird of Yearning*, in 1967.

In the 1970s and 1980s, as her children became more independent, Richter increased the number and size of her works substantially, producing numerous large-scale orchestral and chamber works. She received significant performances by prominent orchestras, such as the London Philharmonic, the Minnesota Orchestra, the Milwaukee Symphony Orchestra, the Atlanta Symphony Orchestra, the Civic Orchestra of Chicago, the Tucson Symphony, and the Buffalo Philharmonic Orchestra. Richter's music also began to attract outstanding solo performers, including Daniel Heifetz, Natalie Hinderas, and David Wells. In 1975, Richter received a publishing contract with Carl Fischer Inc. and helped found both the League of Women Composers and the Long Island Composers Alliance (LICA).

> *When we have enough music by women to make a study of the question, we may find that women are able to express emotion in a different way. I also feel it may turn out that we construct music differently when we are being ourselves and not following male models—not worse or better, just differently. To put it simply, I don't think men can write music like women—nor vice versa. After all, I am a woman, I express what I am; therefore, it will be different from what a man will express—or any other woman.*[23]

It was also during this decade that Richter composed her largest and most ambitious work to date, the superlative *Landscapes of the Mind*, which is a series of three pieces: a concerto for piano with orchestra, a work for violin and piano, and a piano trio. While the three works share musical material and a similarity of mood, each is inimitable enough to stand alone, and each of the three pieces received multiple performances and was met with decidedly favorable reviews. *Landscapes of the Mind I* (the piano concerto) infuses Eastern influences into its Western structure, creating a captivating collagelike sonoral result. The work was initially inspired by two Georgia O'Keeffe paintings Richter saw in a 1968 issue of *Life Magazine*: *Sky Above Clouds II* and *Pelvis I*. It requires full orchestra (without trombones or tubas) plus electric guitar, electric bass, electric tamboura or sitar, tom-toms, and Indian drums. The final ten-minute section uses the classical Indian *raga Marva*— C–C#–E–F#–A–B–C—against a continuous drone on the tonic C. The music slowly accelerates (sometimes through metric modulation) and exploits the dyadic dissonance created between C-sharp or F-sharp and the C-natural drone.

Example 8.5. *Landscapes of the Mind,* I, mm. 451–452[24]

Landscapes served as inspiration for two of Richter's most important works for orchestra: the symphonic poems *Blackberry Vines and Winter Fruit* (1976) and *Out of Shadows and Solitude* (1985). *Blackberry Vines and Winter Fruit* was inspired by the Vermont winter landscape and lines by Thoreau; *Out of Shadows and Solitude* was inspired by a documentary featuring the flight of a condor over the Andes Mountains of Peru.

Another work inspired by landscape imagery is the one-movement *Spectral Chimes/Enshrouded Hills* (1978–1980), stimulated by Richter's reading of Thomas Hardy's *Tess of the D'Urbervilles*. Loosely based on sonata form, Richter places three quintets (woodwind, brass, and string) against the orchestra, allowing for a panoptic range of textures. Reviewer and composer Mark Lehman writes, "The resulting work is a remarkable synthesis of complex scoring, rigorous structural integrity, and deeply-felt emotion that—like Thomas Hardy's doomed protagonists and desolate landscapes—encompasses impassioned defiance, granitic strength, evocative mystery, forlorn majesty, and, ultimately, stoic resignation."[25]

Melodic contour, rather than any formula for tonality or serialization, is the fundamental element in my music. The continuous line from the beginning to the end of each piece is what governs the form. Each new piece is a new experience for me. Most of the thematic relationships occur subconsciously, spontaneously as I play through the piece and allow, coerce, new material to develop. This can be a painfully slow process, but when I try to develop new sections by consciously manipulating themes and chords and rhythms, I invariably destroy the work. I have to

*throw out these constructions and go back to my own system—allowing the music
to come from its own mysterious source.*[26]

Notwithstanding the broad scope of her orchestral repertoire, Richter
has always composed at the piano, and she has composed much music specifically for that instrument. *Sonata for Piano, Remembrances,* and
Requiem are her major works for the keyboard, representing a panoply
of variegated harmonies, textures, and emotions. The *Sonata* is sharply
dissonant; *Remembrances* is gentle and wistful. Originally intended for
guitar, *Requiem* leans toward the improvisational in nature and purveys
an intense cathartic effect to the listener; "It was written in response to a
deeply-felt personal loss," says Richter, "and became a plea for the ultimate repose of all departed souls."[27]

After her husband's death in 1988, the general direction of Richter's music began to subtly shift from the dissonant toward the consonant, a move
evidenced by the short choral cycle entitled *Into My Heart* (1990), a work
dedicated to her late spouse.[28] The tonal nature of *Into My Heart* provides
striking contrast to the far more discordant earlier choral works, such as *To
Whom?* (1980), a setting of an erotically charged text by Virginia Woolf.[29]

To speak to Marga Richter's compositional style is to embrace the
changeling nature of the composer herself. Chance, choice, and life circumstance have lent a certain malleability to her writing, exposing Richter
as a stylistic chameleon. The fundamental ingredients found within her
scores evolve and change with time, adapting and reshaping themselves.

*I like the rhythmic and harmonic strength in Bach, and perhaps the formal architecture
of Beethoven. And I have to admit I especially like Bartók and Shostakovich. The sound
of minor sevenths and ninths that I heard from Shostakovich's works was a theme I had
been using a lot—the same notes, but a different rhythm. Bartók—I like his rhythms,
especially in* Music for Strings, Percussion, and Celesta *(1936) and* Mikrokosmos
*(1926–1937). I also like Hovhaness's modal and oriental harmony, with the religious
tonal dissonance in* St. Vartan Symphony *(1951). I admire Stravinsky's rhythmic
division and metrical displacement in* Symphony of Psalms *(1930).*[30]

Richter has always enjoyed word play and wit, and in 1991 she composed an explicitly humorous piece entitled *Quantum Quirks of a Quick
Quaint Quark.* This offbeat orchestral creation exploits the extremes of
instruments, such as contrabassoon and piccolo, while incorporating frequent meter changes, syncopation, and rapid juxtaposition of modified
stylized genres, including a 5/4 waltz, a boogie-woogie, and a fandango.
Furthermore, in an intriguing usage of *self*-quotation, Richter utilizes additional material from two of her early dance scores, *All Desire Is Sad* and
The Wanderers. Quantum Quirks was premiered by Marin Alsop, conducting the Long Island Philharmonic, in 1992.

Example 8.6. *Quantum Quirks of a Quick Quaint Quark*, mm. 1–7

Variation technique is another of Richter's familiar traits, but she rarely adheres to any rigid orthodoxy; rather, Richter embraces variation simply as a means for perpetual transformation and development of her melodic ideas. She paired her interest in variation technique along with a preexisting general affinity toward antiphonal structures in a large-scale *hommage* entitled *Variations and Interludes on Themes from Monteverdi and Bach* (1992). The primary theme for the twelve variations in this triple concerto for violin, cello, piano, and large orchestra is the "Prologue" from Monteverdi's *Orfeo*. In addition, nine iterations of the final chorale from *Orfeo* are interspersed among the individual variations. Other source materials include an improvisation on J. S. Bach's C-major Prelude from *The Well-Tempered Clavier, Volume I*; a variation of the *Dies Irae*; and a recurring four-chord harmonic progression, used as bridge material. Richter designed the piece in the form of a grand rhapsodic fantasy, with an introduction, variations, interludes, a triple cadenza followed by cadenzas for each of the individual soloists, and a coda. Initially, Richter effectively captures the spirit of the Baroque sound with a concertino approach, setting the presentation of Monteverdi's theme for the string soloists and harp. Her creative transformation of the theme quickly evolves into a contemporary sound.

Example 8.7. *Variations and Interludes on Themes from Monteverdi and Bach,* theme, mm. 15–22

For much of her career, Richter was a bit reluctant to compose an opera, wary of the difficulties often found in securing performances; nevertheless, in 1996 (at age seventy) she finished her first, a one-act chamber opera named *Riders to the Sea*, with a libretto by John Millington Synge.[31] Some forty years after reading Synge's work, Richter traveled to the Aran Islands in 1989 in an attempt to absorb the atmosphere of the tragic play (in which a woman and her two daughters must accept the loss of a husband and five sons who have all drowned at sea). She began her compositional process for the opera by working out rhythmic inflection for the text and researching Irish folk song until she felt surefooted enough to capture its essence within her own dissonant musical style, which is certainly suitable for such mournful subject matter.

Example 8.8. *Riders to the Sea*, mm. 475–483

Richter's music for *Riders to the Sea* immerses the listener into the Irish *mise-en-scène* with apt instrumentation, including Celtic harp, pennywhistle or flute, bodhran (Irish drum), free-bass concert accordion, and string quintet. Because the opera was scheduled to be performed by

Opera Millenium in 1996, Richter spent the entire summer of 1995 at her vacation home in Vermont laboring to prepare a complete piano score.[32] The project fell through (due to unforeseeable financial difficulties) before the premiere, but fortunately for the composer the piece had already captured the interest of soprano Julie Nord, who at the time was performing a concert series in New York City. Nord sang various segments of the opera in a series of showcase concerts, and *Riders to the Sea* was finally given its successful premiere at St. Mark's Episcopal Church in New York in December 2002.

For Marga Richter, music has always been about connecting with other people. Her compositions either allow her to share responses to images that intrigue or delight her, or they are dedicated to people with whom she is bonded, reflecting some aspect of their personalities in musing tones. I once asked her if her music was spiritual, and she responded that she thought the word was overused; nonetheless, when she refers to the act of composing and what the works mean to her, she often talks of feeling compelled to compose in response to feelings of awe. And though her music is often dissonant and anguished, the composer openly and reverently speaks of its elemental beauty. Richter unabashedly delights in virtually every dimension of life, with no intention of *rallentando*; she simply wants to write music as long as she is able.

A CONVERSATION WITH MARGA RICHTER

Having spoken now and then with Marga Richter since 2002, when I was completing a study of her choral music, I have grown accustomed to, and quite fond of, her wonderfully feisty nature. I first visited her New England home in February of 2005, when she graciously invited me to stay for a few days, just a short walk from the Huntington Bay. Her house was certainly reflective of an artistic personality—the colorful abstract paintings on the walls were done by Richter herself; a Steinway grand piano occupied much of the living room, along with stereo equipment; and five playable and decorative oxygen-tank bells were hung on one wall. In other rooms of the house, numerous shelves of manuscripts lined the walls; some were drafts, revisions, or variants of final copies. In addition to the many scores, she has an extensive collection of recordings of her own works, as well as literature by diverse authors. I have returned there on several occasions since that time, have continued to speak with her on the phone and through e-mail, and have met her in Manhattan for performances of her works. I have enjoyed accompanying Richter on her late-afternoon walks, sharing kitchen duties as we do some light cooking, and listening to her music together. During my visits, I recorded many of our conversations; the following is extracted from those fascinating discussions.—Sharon Mirchandani

MIRCHANDANI: Tell me about your earliest musical training and experiences.

RICHTER: The earliest I was told about—I don't remember it; I was three—was a time when my sister was taking piano lessons and practicing (I was sitting on the floor with my dolls), and when she'd play a wrong note or hesitate, I'd sing out the proper note. And that's when they said, "Let's take a look at this kid." So I started piano lessons when I was four or five (real piano lessons) with Mary Dillingham; she was probably sixty or seventy when I started—she seemed like a very old lady. What she taught me was how to play musically; she did everything kind of by ear, by demonstration—which in a sense is why I don't sight-read music very well. There was always a shape to the line; it wasn't just, "Put your fingers down here and there." My second teacher was named Irene Hellner; she was just the opposite. She was all for the right fingering and, you know, "Do it exactly the way it's supposed to be done," and there wasn't much music to it. My mother gave her lessons for free, and she gave me lessons for free. They became like best friends, so this Irene was like our aunt after a while. This was probably the reason I came to New York when I did. I think my family decided that I really should have a better teacher, but how are you going to tell your best friend she's not good enough to teach your daughter? So, when the opportunity came to go to New York, we took it.

MIRCHANDANI: Did you start Juilliard at that time?

RICHTER: No, this Irene Hellner had studied with a person named Countess Morsztyn, who came to Minneapolis every summer and gave master classes; and so I happened to go to one—I won a contest one year when I was fourteen or fifteen. I had a few lessons with this countess, and then she came back the next year, and I studied with her again. I think she might have said, "Why don't you come to New York?" So my family decided to do it. I took my last year of high school in the summer and got my diploma. I wasn't eighteen yet. It was 1943. And the whole family moved to New York—this was the extraordinary thing. We had to sell the house and my father's business in the local newspaper; my parents didn't think I should go alone. I think about that every little while, because to me, at the time, it didn't seem so extraordinary. I think I lived all my life with blinders on, just thinking about the music and what I was doing.

MIRCHANDANI: You've had a lot of exposure to Bach through Rosalyn Tureck at Juilliard, and you quoted Bach in some of your compositions. He sounds like a favorite composer?

RICHTER: He's one of my, you know—sometimes when people say if you were going to be on a desert island, which composer would you take? Of course I love Beethoven, but I think you could just listen to Bach forever.

MIRCHANDANI: Do you know why Bach has such a strong appeal for you?

RICHTER: No, do you? [Laughs] It's just so gorgeous. I think it's the harmonies and the rhythm. It's the rhythm. You probably noticed in my music—I hope you noticed—that rhythm is the thing. It's different from just about anybody—not anybody, but most people.

MIRCHANDANI: Rhythm and color and pacing, I think.

RICHTER: And shape. And a "getting to where you're going" kind of thing. But that constant motion—I mean, when I listen to my music, it's embarrassing. People say, "Stop moving like that." So, probably that's why I took to Tureck's teaching.

MIRCHANDANI: After studying piano with Tureck, you studied composition with William Bergsma and Vincent Persichetti. What was that like?

RICHTER: It was good, because William Bergsma made me feel like a composer, but he wasn't specific. He would just get excited about everything. And we actually had group lessons. I think there were two or three of us at once. We went through music, and we tried to write. The stuff I wrote that year was pretty much terrible. But then, Persichetti was a very good teacher. I think he's the person who encouraged my natural bent to have the music arrive somewhere. He was very big on having it go someplace, make some sense out of it. The only thing he didn't do was teach me anything about orchestration, which I'm sort of surprised at, because he was good at that. I had to learn that later, way later. Actually, I got to take orchestration lessons from Mrs. Harkness's orchestrator; his name was Danny Hollingsworth. He taught me more about orchestration in six weeks than I ever learned anywhere else. And she paid for this.

MIRCHANDANI: Was being a "woman composer" ever an issue for you?

RICHTER: No, I didn't think anything of it; I thought it was wonderful. I was unique. And then in 1975, when we started the League of Women Composers, we found out there were hundreds of us, each in our little house thinking we were the only one. In one sense, it was a good thing to get out and meet these other women, but in another sense it was kind of deflating. Oh, God!

MIRCHANDANI: Not special anymore?

RICHTER: Right, exactly.

MIRCHANDANI: When you compose, do you have any specific goals in mind or anything you're trying to achieve? Does it vary with the piece? Do you have any kind of consistent thing that you're striving for from work to work?

RICHTER: Not usually. If it's for a song, or a dance, or something where you have more going on with it, you have to fit a time frame or be very practical. Or when you write with words—when the words are finished, you're finished. But if I'm writing an abstract piece, it seems like—well, you just go in where you're going to work, and a switch goes on. Something happens then, and then you can turn it off again. Ned Rorem has said this happens to him. I used to do that all the time—I still do it—it's a very strange thing. When I had my children, and they were young, they'd have to go to school, and as soon as they got on that bus, I'd come home and turn on the composer switch, and as soon as they'd come home, I'd turn it off. Things I suppose keep percolating while you're living, and then the next day you go to back to work, and you get onto a different plane—you become a different person in a sense.

MIRCHANDANI: What do you think about more systematic approaches to composition, such as serialism? Set theoretical approaches?

RICHTER: I think they're not for me, and I'd like to be a little bit stronger and say I don't think they're for anybody, but people seem to like that sort of music. I don't like the effect. I don't like the result. It just doesn't make any sense to me.

MIRCHANDANI: What's your actual compositional process like? Is it completely intuitive?

RICHTER: Yes.

MIRCHANDANI: But you must have some kind of organizational plan behind your pieces. Do you create rough drafts? Or sketches?

RICHTER: No, none of the above—except for *Quantum Quirks of a Quick Quaint Quark*. When I did the orchestration, I used a chart to figure out who was going to do what. As far as notes, in 1979, I discovered the tape recorder for composition. I would turn it on, and then I would just improvise. And that was so great because you didn't have to keep stopping to remember what you wrote. How I ever wrote pieces before that—like the *Piano Sonata*, which sounds like it goes from beginning to end; every time I'd write five or six measures, I'd have to stop and write it down before I forgot it. And then I would play from the beginning. I think one reason my music has this "undertow" feeling is because I always start at the beginning, every day, and play the whole thing through to where I am. So it's never just tagged on. In fact, during the close of the day, if I get stuck, I just play through it, so it always feels like whatever happens next *has* to happen next. But I'm not thinking; it's just coming. The few times when I've tried to map something out, I'm never as satisfied. Even variations and things, I don't like to think about which one would come next. One time, for *Eight Pieces for Piano*, I just lay them on the floor and moved them around like chess pieces until I was satisfied with the order.

MIRCHANDANI: I know you have made changes in your earlier works over the years. Is that because you are a perfectionist?

RICHTER: Of course. Sometimes when you write a piece, you're not quite satisfied with it. If there's a performance and you have it played, then you change it afterward. On one occasion, with the *First Concerto* [for piano, violas, cellos, and basses], I changed the ending once because I thought it was sort of corny. Arthur Cohn at Carl Fisher said you should never go that far back and change a piece, because you're a different person now and you're going to ruin it. And he was right, so I think when I finally put that piece on the computer, I'll go back to the original ending. And I did the same with *Abyss*—I changed the very end a couple of times for the ballet score. And the *Toccata*—that's the *Aria and Toccata*—I don't think that's better either.

MIRCHANDANI: You were not changing it because of differences in dance choreography?

RICHTER: No, no, no. In fact, funny you should ask. When it was performed in New York, I finally got to see it and hear it. I didn't like the ending, and after it was done like three times, I went back to the orchestra pit and changed some of the notes at the end. When I told the conductor I was changing the ending, he said, "We can't do that," and I said, "Yes you can." And they did. It was just completely a different rhythm, and it worked for the dance. But I don't think for the concert piece it's the best ending. But if it's a recent piece, and I just decide there is something better, I'll change it.

MIRCHANDANI: Does that mean you are never satisfied with the final product?

RICHTER: Sometimes I think, "This didn't make its point; what's wrong with the harmony here? It's okay, but is it really the best way?" The end of *Fandango*—I've changed the chords there in the last ten bars—I must have played that over five thousand times, because there was just something that didn't suit me. I had two different possibilities, and they had different meanings to me. My husband used to say, "All colors are great; pick one and put it on the wall. It doesn't matter. Or it matters, but, this would be good, and that would be good." You have two things you like, and you're thinking, "Now which is really the one that makes this feel satisfying to me?" And I just go over and over and over it. And now unfortunately the best [recorded] performance I have [of *Fandango*] has the first version, and it's not right. So, yes, I guess I am a perfectionist.

MIRCHANDANI: It's interesting about "All colors look nice"—it could be good this way, or it could be good that way. Do you feel there's one right answer for your scores?

RICHTER: That's the thing, I'm sure that there's one that is better. And you can't have two. If you say perfectionist, you might think in terms of scoring or something, but I'm thinking in terms of meaning. You've got to find the right thing, and sometimes it's elusive. Sometimes when

I improvise I get something that's really great, but I didn't get it on tape, and I can't find it again. Even with *Requiem*—I kept changing that too, to get just the right number of things going the right places, over and over. I think I have it right, now.

MIRCHANDANI: I know you taught piano students. Was this important to you artistically or did you feel like it was a distraction?

RICHTER: It was important to me financially. I mean, I enjoyed it, but I didn't feel it was my calling.

MIRCHANDANI: Do you think you benefited from it? Did it help you ever with your composition?

RICHTER: No. I wrote some teaching pieces, but that was probably a good idea for the students, really.

MIRCHANDANI: If you could have done without it, you would have been happy to not teach piano?

RICHTER: Yes. I'm perfectly happy now and I have no students.

MIRCHANDANI: Did you ever want to teach composition?

RICHTER: Never.

MIRCHANDANI: So you don't feel you missed out on something.

RICHTER: Not at all. I feel lucky to have ducked that responsibility.

MIRCHANDANI: Where do you think your inspiration comes from?

RICHTER: It seems to come from the ether. It seems to be something that—here I am talking to you, making jokes, sitting here and being silly, and then, when you leave, if I were going to go in and write a new piece, it just is a whole different thing. It comes from inside someplace, or outside.

MIRCHANDANI: Can you control it? Can you turn it on and off?

RICHTER: Well, that's what I do when I'm working, especially when I had kids. The minute they got on the school bus, I'd turn it on, and when they got off, I'd turn it off.

MIRCHANDANI: So you don't ever have trouble getting inspired?

RICHTER: No, not yet.

MIRCHANDANI: You've never set aside time to compose and had "composer's block" or something?

RICHTER: Never, never. It's amazing.

MIRCHANDANI: Oh, that's great.

RICHTER: I just start to play the piano, and something just happens, and away we go. So far.

MIRCHANDANI: So far! [laughs] That's a pretty good track record.

RICHTER: Not bad. About seventy years' worth.

MIRCHANDANI: Your son was trained as a classical pianist and works in classical music today. If you had a child today, would you encourage them to study classical music?

RICHTER: I wouldn't discourage them. I would certainly give them the opportunity. I mean, Michael insisted—he was two years old—"Teach me to play the piano." He seemed to have been born to play the piano. There was no stopping that.

MIRCHANDANI: Did you try to teach him to compose?

RICHTER: No. He tried to write a couple pieces—it wasn't him, and that's good, because I wouldn't want to compete with my own kids, or have them competing with me or whatever.

MIRCHANDANI: But again, if you had a child today, do you think piano training would be the best?

RICHTER: You don't tell them what to play; they tell you.

MIRCHANDANI: So you would wait for the child to ask?

RICHTER: You'd certainly start piano, because I have a piano and I know how to teach piano. But my daughter didn't like to play the piano. She had lessons, and she could do it, but no, she wanted to play stringed instruments—violin and cello, sitar, guitar.

MIRCHANDANI: So you didn't feel like you controlled what they did; it was a matter of exposing them, and then they chose.

RICHTER: Right. They choose to do this, to do that.

MIRCHANDANI: And if they didn't want to do any music, then?

RICHTER: That's fine, too. I wouldn't force them into it, but I wouldn't prevent it just because it's a hard life. I think it's a great life. You know, even if you just end up teaching piano up the street somewhere, if that's what you like to do, do it.

MIRCHANDANI: What do you think makes your music distinctive?

RICHTER: I think what sets my music apart from a lot of music that I hear is that I'm very conscious of where the downbeats are, and a lot of music just goes along and you don't know where you are because it doesn't seem to have any sense to it as far as an overrhythm.

MIRCHANDANI: You want the audience to feel where those downbeats are.

RICHTER: Yes.

MIRCHANDANI: When you use an ostinato passage, do you think that listeners should hear them as hypnotic or mesmerizing?

RICHTER: No. I think I use it a lot to set off something else. I'm just too lazy to make a change, so I just do it and then put things over it that are interesting.

MIRCHANDANI: It sets up a background for melodic changes somewhere else?

RICHTER: Yes. It's sort of a palette. I put the color on the canvas and paint on top of it. It functions like a foundation.

MIRCHANDANI: What do you think about the current state of art music?

RICHTER: [laughs] Lousy! The current state of music is a different question than the state of the music business. I thought you were asking about other people's music, what kind of music people are writing today.

MIRCHANDANI: Well, that would also be interesting.

RICHTER: Yes. And that I think is . . . kind of boring. But it's not the fault of the music. I mean, shall we get into this?

MIRCHANDANI: Yes. The music of today's composers—how would you regard it? Is there any you admire? What do you not like about it? You told me you went to a recent concert where you didn't like the compositions.

RICHTER: Well, obviously you have millions of people writing music. And you take any epoch—what did we end up with?—about five or six people that seem to last. And that's not necessarily valid because there were probably a lot of people that got lost in the shuffle who were good. But there has to be a whole lot of people who aren't that good. Anybody can write music. But it takes something special to create a piece that makes any sense. You know, I think with all of the machines people are using today and all of the sampling, they don't even have to orchestrate.

MIRCHANDANI: When you say "something special," is that more training, or something you're born with?

RICHTER: I think you have to be born with it. I think that's the whole business. And I think if you try to learn it from the outside, "Oh, here's how you do this . . ."—you know, it's like painting. Everybody paints, and yet some paintings seem to have something that really stands out, and other things are just a painting. Everybody at school does art work, and it's all very nice. But for some reason, we pick certain ones that seem to have something extra. Take poetry—everybody can write a poem. But it has to have that extra something. And that's in short supply.

MIRCHANDANI: What's the something?

RICHTER: I don't know. That's why I think so much music gets played, because people don't know right off. My son's always saying, "You don't like that piece, but you only heard it once. You have to hear it three times." And I say that to people about my music: "Listen to it again," you know? But I have a feeling that if something doesn't grab me—something—the first time around, it's not going to. Do you ever drive down the road and you hear a piece you don't know and suddenly you find you're really listening to it, and you pull over to find out what the hell the piece was?

MIRCHANDANI: That's how I found your music, actually. I heard it in the car and thought, ooh, who composed that? That's really interesting.

RICHTER: Right! [laughs]

MIRCHANDANI: Do you feel you have to work at it?

RICHTER: No. I have to work at shaping it. But things just come to me when I go to write a new piece. I could start off with an A-minor chord, and suddenly there's some note in there that's just—nobody else could think of using. And then I grab on to that and go on from there.

MIRCHANDANI: It's very aural.

RICHTER: Yes.

MIRCHANDANI: You don't think of it as intellectual.

RICHTER: Not at all. That's what I think is wrong with most music. It comes from the outside. You know, everybody can build a house, but some houses look like hell, and other houses are great. Everybody's using the same wood and the same blocks, and they follow the patterns and they put it up, and there's no imagination to it. There's nothing that suddenly makes your heart race or stop or skip a beat or hold your breath.

MIRCHANDANI: Do you think it's good that you went to Juilliard and have the training that you have?

RICHTER: I think I was lucky. I was lucky with the two teachers that I had that fostered what we wanted to do. I said before I don't think Bergsma was a good teacher because he didn't really teach me anything—but he made me feel like I was a composer and let me do what I wanted.

MIRCHANDANI: He didn't force a particular approach to composition on you.

RICHTER: Right, and the same with Persichetti. I mean, he tried to kind of inch you along, but his whole thing was the same thing that I like to do. "Where are you going with this? It has to go somewhere. Has to get there." And his music does that, but I just didn't like his colors. But when you think of Persichetti's students—they're so different, which is great. Philip Glass, Steve Reich, Jack Druckman, Paul Overton, myself—I mean, we're all different. So either he didn't teach anybody anything, or he let everybody develop what they had. He let you just find the shapes of the thing that made some sense.

MIRCHANDANI: What *do* you think about the business side of music today?

RICHTER: I think as far as new music goes, a lot of people are still trying—the Philharmonic is trying to do new pieces. The trouble is they're going to do new pieces by new composers, and they're not going to find me. They'd better find me somewhere along the line! [laughs] I keep hoping somebody's going to come along and I'm going to get another break, because basically my life has been a matter of accidents.

MIRCHANDANI: What do you mean by that—an accident? Chance?

RICHTER: Well, I think it's what most people experience in their lives. You have to be lucky to be at the right place at the right time. And then some people also have the gift of self-promotion. I've tried that, and I thought my gift was working for a while, but . . . . So I'm just going to have to wait for the next tap on the shoulder that's going to happen accidentally, I think. I've come to terms with that. I don't worry about it anymore; I just do my thing. I mean, you came along, look at that!

MIRCHANDANI: Yes.

RICHTER: And this book may open up a whole new door to me. In which case, it will be because you were listening to the radio one day.

ANALYSIS: *QHANRI (SNOW MOUNTAIN):*
TIBETAN VARIATIONS FOR CELLO AND PIANO (1988)

In the spring of 1986 I visited Tibet. It was an overwhelming experience; the feeling of being in another world was all pervasive. I decided to write a piece about these feelings.

In 1988, at age sixty-two, Marga Richter composed *Qhanri (Snow Mountain): Tibetan Variations for Cello and Piano*. She revised the piece for publication in 1994 and recorded it with cellist David Wells. The work is in free variation form (a form in which the composer seems to revel more than any established formal "norm"), consisting of a theme with twenty-one variations. The twenty-two sections are designed as a collection of three larger subsections separated by scherzi.

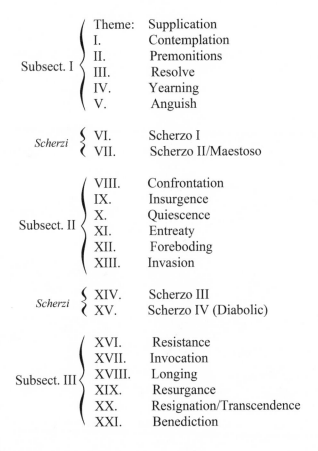

	Theme:	Supplication
	I.	Contemplation
	II.	Premonitions
Subsect. I	III.	Resolve
	IV.	Yearning
	V.	Anguish
Scherzi	VI.	Scherzo I
	VII.	Scherzo II/Maestoso
	VIII.	Confrontation
	IX.	Insurgence
	X.	Quiescence
Subsect. II	XI.	Entreaty
	XII.	Foreboding
	XIII.	Invasion
Scherzi	XIV.	Scherzo III
	XV.	Scherzo IV (Diabolic)
	XVI.	Resistance
	XVII.	Invocation
Subsect. III	XVIII.	Longing
	XIX.	Resurgance
	XX.	Resignation/Transcendence
	XXI.	Benediction

Figure 8.1.

With its wealth of changing meters and moods, a heightened sense of drama is the work's predominant feature. Tempos fluctuate suddenly and wildly, lavish chromaticism envelops functional harmony, and though the piece is monothematic, Richter freely spins her theme through countless permutations so as to render it, at times, virtually unrecognizable. The myriad ways in which the composer achieves her end goals of musical freedom, while at the same time remaining true to her overall vision of variation technique, merits closer investigation.

Richter reports that the theme for *Qhanri* was written during an early-morning drive through the Lhasa Valley, "as the heavy pre-dawn fog slowly lifted, showing first the rich dark brown color of the lower mountains, then gradually clearing to reveal the snowy peaks in all their primordial grandeur, set off against the glowing azure sky."[33] The muted, melancholy F-minor theme is fifteen measures long, in mixed triple and duple meter.

Example 8.9.   *Qhanri*, theme, mm. 1–15[34]

The theme's fifteen measures are divided into three phrases. The first phrase, marked by alternation between large leaps and falling scale patterns, is repeated in harmonics as phrase two. The third phrase, then, functions as codetta, commenting on the theme's opening gestures. The entirety of the theme is written in the cello's higher register, requiring some care on the part of the performer to intone Richter's inspiring mountain vision (see figure 8.2).

Figure 8.2. The original chant source material

Outside the Jokhang Temple I had recorded a chanting monk. When I subsequently heard a similar refrain sung by young novices at the nearby Drepung Monastery, I decided to use it as thematic material, although not as the opening theme, for the variations. My chromatic alterations of the original diatonic (but melismatically embellished) chant are an expression of what I perceived to be a deep sadness underlying the cheerful demeanor of the Tibetan people.

The aural journey through *Qhanri* is a dramatic one, with its constantly changing tempos, mixed meters, and colorful titles for the variations like "Confrontation" or "Resurgence." These titles (perhaps surprisingly) came after the piece was finished, as Richter revisited her original thoughts and feelings about the music. Not only do the labels seem suitable to the expressive qualities of the variations, but they also help unify *Qhanri* interpretively as a spiritual work. For instance, the theme and its opening variation, respectively labeled "Supplication" and "Contemplation," along with variation 10, "Quiescence"; variation 17, "Invocation"; and the final variations, labeled "Resignation/Transcendence" and "Benediction," suggest a quasi-religious or spiritual interpretation of the work as a whole. The majority of the remaining variations bear more romantic titles, such as "Yearning," "Anguish," and "Longing." These variations typically feature elongated, tense, unresolved melodies.

The most cohesive element of the piece is motivic economy and developmental practice. Every important idea is in some way traceable back to the theme, and as Richter's motives develop gradually throughout the work, the music unfolds in a seemingly constant state of flux and continuous evolution. Seven primary motives are central to *Qhanri*; for purposes of identification, they are presented in figure 8.3, labeled as motives *a* through *g*:

(continued)

Figure 8.3.

Figure 8.3. (*continued*)

Richter's encompassing vision for *Qhanri* is that the variations are to be free elaborations upon her theme, each featuring a specific rhythm, figuration, or interval. Their respective lengths are freely asymmetrical, ranging anywhere from thirteen measures (variation I) to seventy-eight measures (variation IX). Many of the variations emphasize an F tonal center through repetition or ostinato, though some lean toward C or C-sharp. Several lack a tonal center altogether, instead emphasizing rhythmic or intervallic manipulation.

The first variation illustrates a few of the more interesting traits of Richter's approach to the piece. Primarily scored for the piano alone, this variation consists of repeated chromatic figurations on each beat, mostly mirroring each other in the separate hands. This is the first appearance of motive *a*, in which rhythmic suppleness is created by morphing groups of four sixteenth notes into quintuplets.

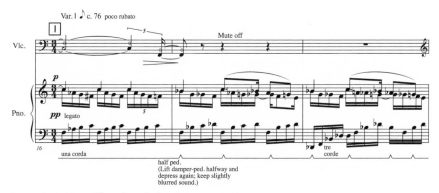

Example 8.10.   *Qhanri*, variation I, mm. 16–18

The theme is laid upon this scaffold, with only some of the note durations altered. Although the variation is chromatic in nature, the listener still perceives it as F minor, making quick, darting moves to B minor and E diminished sonorities. The variation's climactic moment, at measure 25, is marked by the first occurrence of the Tibetan chant motive (motive *b*). The motive, chromatically altered, descends in the cello, interrupting the established piano pattern.

Example 8.11.   *Qhanri*, variation I, mm. 24–25

This is just the first of many iterations; Richter uses numerous variants of motive *b* as secondary thematic material throughout the piece. Her initial versions, like the one seen above, are disguised through chromaticism. Two notable instances are shown in examples 8.12a and 8.12b.

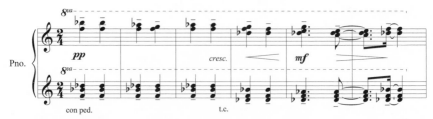

Example 8.12a. *Qhanri*, motive *b* in variation II, mm. 30–35, piano

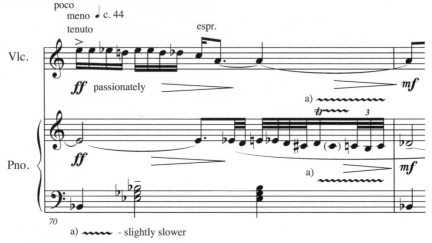

Example 8.12b. *Qhanri*, motive *b* in variation IV, m. 70

Toward the end of the work, the chant motive becomes more diatonic, sometimes suggesting the Lydian mode; other times, it is supported by a major triad, creating a more optimistic atmosphere. The combination of this secondary material derived from the Tibetan chant with Richter's original theme (and its variants) creates a myriad of aural and interpretive relationships—relationships the composer readily exploits to heighten the emotional impact of the music.

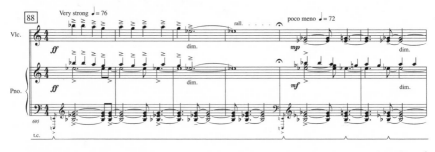

(continued)

Example 8.13. *Qhanri*, motive *b* in variation XX, mm. 695–706

Example 8.13. (*continued*)

Variations IV and V introduce another two of Richter's important motives for *Qhanri*. Variation IV ("Yearning") is the first to have little trace of the theme itself; its primary focus is to continue an evolutionary process Richter initiated in the previous section. As variation III ("Resolve") draws to a close, Richter begins to employ the tritone as a replacement for the perfect fourths and fifths of its source material, effectively expanding her harmonic palette for the rest of the work.

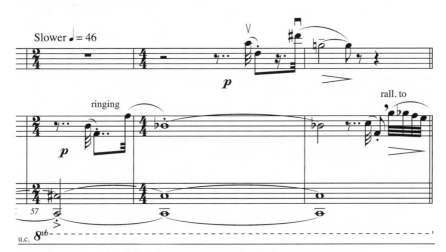

Example 8.14. *Qhanri,* last three measures of variation III, mm. 57–59

This leads directly into measure 61, where the cello launches variation IV with motive *c*.

Throughout this variation, both instruments perform turning and twisting trills, in stark contrast to what came before. These types of evolutionary passages are central to Richter's style and are prevalent throughout the work.

Closely related to variation IV, variation V ("Anguish") continues to shift the perfect intervals from the theme and its earlier variations to

Example 8.15.   *Qhanri*, variation IV, mm. 60–63

prevalent tritones, minor seconds, and minor ninths. After the opening section of the theme has been presented (with its new chromatic sheen) in the cello, the piano takes over the texture and ushers in motive *d*.

Example 8.16.   *Qhanri*, variation V, mm. 81–83

The second phrase of the theme then begins in the cello, now consisting almost solely of tritones and minor ninths. These gestures repeat, highly fragmented, with no distinct correlation with the ordering of events in the theme. All of this shifting is birthed from motive *c* of the previous variation.

Another important *Qhanri* motive makes its initial appearance in variations VIII through IX. The variation opens with a series of arpeggios in both instruments, in which the top note forms the contour of the theme and the bottom note emphasizes the C pedal point from the previous variation. The arpeggios utilize many of the intervals that have been heretofore prevalent (minor ninths, tritones, perfect fourths and fifths, minor thirds, and minor seconds), creating a harmonic sound consistent with the rest of the work. But the arpeggio pattern is abruptly interrupted at measure 244 by motive *g*.

Example 8.17. *Qhanri*, variation IX, mm. 244–247

Richter injects motive *g* into many different situations within *Qhanri*, often developing or disguising it in some way. Later in variation IX, she intertwines motives *g* and *b* together, illuminating (and also masking) both.

Example 8.18. *Qhanri*, variation IX, mm. 276–282

In variations XI through XIII, Richter seeks to create another mesmerizing dramatic effect with a lengthy bass ostinato set in a plodding 5/4 meter. While the ostinato takes on several forms throughout these three variations, it usually contains a diminished triad embedded in an octave, with a pattern reminiscent of motive *a*. It is pitted against a treble ostinato, which is typically chromatic in nature, circular in contour, and in contrary motion to the bass. Motive *c* is presented (in rhythmic augmentation) in the cello, while a ghostly recalling of motive *b* haunts the piano (see examples 8.19a–b).

As it pushes into variation XIII, the ostinato accelerates and crescendos, building to a *fortississimo* climax in a new 3/2 meter. This variation marks the culmination of the ostinato figure, the climactic moment of variation XIII, and arguably the climax of the entire work (see example 8.20).

Example 8.19a.   *Qhanri*, variation XI, mm. 331–334

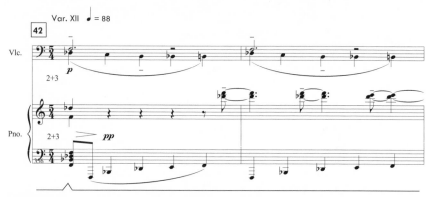

Example 8.19b.   *Qhanri*, variation XII, mm. 356–357

Example 8.20.   *Qhanri*, variation XIII, mm. 397–398

The cello also adds various tremolos and arpeggios, as the ostinato slowly evolves and changes. Eventually it succumbs to syncopation, which serves to propel the section forward toward the climax. After that, the figure slowly dies away.

In variations XVII and XVIII, fragments of the ostinato from variations XI through XIII (but in altered form) help create a similar effect to that of variation IX, revealing the intertwining as a distinct characteristic of

Richter's writing in *Qhanri*. Here she whimsically alternates and develops a variety of the ideas and themes presented earlier in the piece, choosing to fulfill dramatic purposes over systematic presentation. The opening measures of variation XVII are drawn from the opening measures of variation I, developing motive *a*, but these quickly evolve into a passage taken from the end of the first phrase of the theme, presented in unison by both instruments. Motive *b* also makes an appearance here, juxtaposed with altered, elongated versions of *d* and *g*.

Example 8.21. *Qhanri*, variation XVII, mm. 559–573

As the music moves into variation XIX ("Resurgence"), Richter begins to feature a long D pedal point (an idea drawn from variation VIII) that builds to a dramatic climax before subsiding again. A virtuosic cello cadenza initiates the variation, with material taken from the first phrase of the theme. After the piano joins the texture, the same phrase is presented and repeated in both instruments at various pitch levels (G, F, and B♭ are all tonal centers), with increasing chromaticism, dynamics levels, and tempi. By the time the variation reaches its climax, the pedal point in the cello has been virtually reduced to noise.

Example 8.22. *Qhanri*, variation XIX, mm. 656–661

The passage does not resolve but *dissolves* into a diminished fifth A-E♭ over D as the next variation begins.

Richter ends the work with "Benediction," where the theme is presented in its entirety in the cello, returned to its home key. This is accompanied at first by B-flat-minor block chords in the piano, and then by the cascading quintuplets of motive *a*.

Example 8.23.   *Qhanri*, variation XXI, mm. 719–720

Four of the variations in *Qhanri* (variations VI, VII, XIV, and XV), are set apart with the labels scherzo I, II, III, and IV, respectively. These variations feature lively rhythmic play, syncopation, and dialogue between the two instruments. The scherzi serve as dividing points in a symmetrical structure, but they also seem to provide a sense of relief from the relative intensity of the variations that immediately precede them, creating a satisfying contrast to what has come before.

The first of these scherzi, variation VI, is only loosely associated with the theme, instead employing the chant (motive *b*) as its basis. The melody is played in the right hand of the piano while the left hand accompanies with broken B-flat-minor chords in irregular rhythms. The cello sporadically interrupts with the striking motive *e*.

(*continued*)

Example 8.24.   *Qhanri*, variation VI, mm. 102–112

Example 8.24. (*continued*)

Variation VII ("Confrontation") establishes motive *f* from figure 8.3. This rhythmically punctuated pedal point in the cello alternates triplets and sixteenth notes in such a way as to produce an unsettled, strange sensation for the listener. The theme is rather well defined melodically, but it is again chromatically altered in many places.

Example 8.25. *Qhanri*, **variation VII, mm. 194–200**

In variations XIV and XV, Richter uses rests and dotted rhythms to provide a jazzy feel. Variation XIV opens with a lightly bouncing figure played by the cello alone, loosely based on the opening figure of the theme. The piano enters at measure 427 with the actual theme, but in the guise of figures the cello has just introduced.

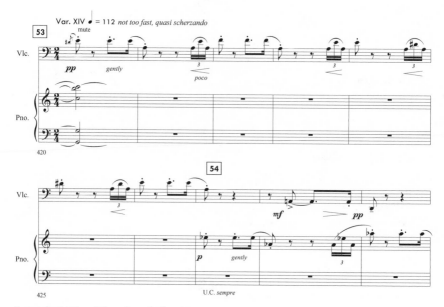

Example 8.26. *Qhanri,* variation XIV, mm. 420–429

The cello continues to interrupt the piano with scalar passages in opposite directions, sometimes making small references to motive *d.*

Variation XV continues the same idea, but differs in that here the cello takes over the theme and adds a bit of harshness to it. The theme in this presentation has lost any tonal bearing from the last, mixing perfect intervals with tritones, minor ninths, and major sevenths. The piano interrupts the cello in a reversal of roles from the previous variation, but this time with arpeggio patterns harkening back to variation IX.

(continued)

Example 8.27. *Qhanri,* variation XV, mm. 452–460

Example 8.27. (*continued*)

Richter's creative utilization of these four variations as scherzi in *Qhanri* is reflective of her compositional approach as a whole. When she employs an established formal structure, she inevitably twists it to suit her own aesthetic goals. She accomplishes this with the insertion of extra or contrasting sections, unexpected phrase lengths, and interesting juxtapositions. These elements bring to many of her works a fantasia-like form and improvisatory feel. At the same time, Richter's works are highly unified by their melodic material. In *Qhanri*, the theme and variations, the Jokhang Temple source chant, and an array of convincing motives and their combinations in the scherzo sections coalesce into a well-crafted, intensely emotional *tour de force* that is satisfying for performers and audiences alike.

CODA

Marga Richter, now in her eighties, is vigorously active and in good health.[35] She continues to receive commissions for her works, mostly for soloists and chamber ensembles. Particularly notable is a major chamber work composed in 2006, *Fandango Fantasy* for piano, clarinet, violin, and cello. This exciting work, commissioned by the Concert Artists Guild of New York, received an excellent premiere performance by the Antares Piano-Clarinet Quartet in February 2007 at Park Avenue United Methodist Church in Manhattan. In 2009, Richter decided to compose a work in memory of her father, having earlier dedicated *Lament* to her mother. She had received a commission to compose a string trio, and so she created the poignant *Threnody* to fulfill that commission.

When Richter is not composing, she is busy organizing performances and recordings of her pieces, and inputting her earlier manuscripts into digital format using the Sibelius notation program. She maintains strong relationships with numerous professional colleagues and several very close lifelong friends, and she also enjoys visiting with her children and their families whenever possible.

NOTES

1. Marga Richter, liner notes to *Snow Mountain: A Spiritual Trilogy*, compact disc, Leonarda LE 337, 1994. Photograph used by permission, Lenny Marks.

2. Inez Chandler's last professional performance was as a soloist in an "all-Wagner" program with the Minneapolis Symphony Orchestra and Eugene Ormandy in 1934.

3. Unless otherwise cited, all quotes and personal information are from interviews and conversations between Marga Richter and Sharon Mirchandani held between February 2005 and August 2007, and are used with permission by Marga Richter.

4. Excerpt used by permission, Carl Fischer Music Inc. Other composers who have set "Jabberwocky" include John Duke, Lee Hoiby, Deems Taylor, and Susan Botti.

5. Excerpt used by permission, Shrewsbury Press.

6. For the complete anecdote, see Jane Weiner LePage, *Women Composers, Conductors, and Musicians of the Twentieth Century: Selected Biographies* (Metuchen, NJ: Scarecrow Press, 1980), 211.

7. In the summers, Richter also attended the Juilliard Summer School (which dissolved in 1952).

8. The composer William Schumann had just become the president of the Juilliard School in July of 1945.

9. Marga Richter, cited in LePage, *Women Composers*, 212.

10. At the time, the master's was the highest degree offered in composition (Ellen Taaffe Zwilich was the first female composer to receive a doctorate from Juilliard, in 1975); Jacob Druckman, Hall Overton, and Hugh Aitken were among Richter's fellow students. You Ju Lee, "Marga Richter: A Biographical Sketch and Study of Her Piano Works with Emphasis on Sonata for Piano" (D.M.A. diss., University of Georgia, 2000), 6.

11. Vincent Persichetti, *Twentieth-Century Harmony* (New York: Norton, 1961), 13, 277.

12. Marga Richter, cited in LePage, *Women Composers*, 212.

13. Excerpt used by permission, Carl Fischer Music Inc.

14. The songs, in order, are as follows: (1) "Twilight" (Ch'en Yün); (2) "The Orchid" (Liu Sung); (3) "Change" (Hsaio Kang); (4) "Desolation" (Chang Chi); (5) "On Seeing a Red Cockatoo on the Road to Mount Shang" (Po Chü I); (6) "Sleeplessness" (anonymous); (7) "A Song of Ch'ang An" (anonymous); (8) "Transmutation" (anonymous).

15. Richter's interest in Chinese poetry resurfaced in 1953, when she set two more songs, "The Hermit" and "Fishing Picture."

16. *New York Herald Tribune*, "Composers Forum," February 4, 1951; cited in LePage, *Women Composers*, 213; and Lee, "Marga Richter," 7. The performers were clarinetist Herbert Tishman, singer Phyllis Goodmund, and pianist Marga Richter.

17. Michael Skelly is now on the piano faculty at Columbia University; Maureen, a nurse, has studied sitar in India.

18. Marga Richter, videotaped interview by Frances Harmeyer, July 9, 1975, interview no. 51 a–e, transcript, *Oral History of American Music*, Yale University, New Haven, CT, pp. 88–89.

19. *Kansas City Star*, July 31, 1988, 4D; cited in Lee, "Marga Richter," 9. Richter's *Lament* has been performed by Stanislaw Skrowaczewski and the Minnesota Orchestra; the National Gallery Orchestra in Washington, D.C.; the Maracaibo Symphony in Venezuela; and Sheldon Morgenstern with the Eastern Music Festival Philharmonic in Greensboro, North Carolina.

20. Excerpts from *Lament* reproduced with the permission of Broude Brothers Limited.

21. Marga Richter, liner notes to *Journeys: Orchestral Works by American Women*, compact disc, Leonarda LE 327, 1987.

22. Dianne Goolkasian Rahbee, letter to Michael Slayton, 2007. I'd like to thank Michael Slayton for sharing this with me.

23. Marga Richter, cited in LePage, *Women Composers*, 223.

24. Excerpt used by permission, Carl Fischer Music Inc.

25. Mark Lehman, liner notes to *Modern American Classics*, Vol. 3, compact disc, MMC 2066, 1998, 2.

26. Marga Richter, cited in LePage, *Women Composers*, 223.

27. Marga Richter, CD liner notes to *Snow Mountain: A Spiritual Trilogy*, Leonarda LE 337, 1994.

28. *Into My Heart* features texts by Robert Frost, A. E. Housman, R. Glenn Martin, Cathleen Schurr, Maureen Skelly, and Walt Whitman.

29. See Sharon Mirchandani, "The Choral Music of Marga Richter," *Choral Journal*, May 2003, 9–17.

30. Marga Richter, interview with You Ju Lee, April 2, 1999, cited in Lee, "Marga Richter," 6.

31. Synge's text had been previously set by Ralph Vaughn Williams in his opera by the same title, *Riders to the Sea*.

32. At this time, Angela Malleck was the director of Opera Millenium.

33. Marga Richter, liner notes to *Snow Mountain: A Spiritual Trilogy*, compact disc, Leonarda LE 337, 1994.

34. In measures 7 through 15, harmonics, the touch points of which are indicated by the diamond-shaped note heads, create sounding notes two octaves higher than the regular note heads notated in the score.

35. The photo here is of Marga Richter with the author; used by permission, Sharon Mirchandani.

APPENDIX A: LIST OF WORKS

Opera/Stage

All Desire Is Sad (1949)—chamber orchestra, dance score for Juilliard
The Wanderers (1952)—chamber orchestra, dance score for choreographer James Waring
Johnny Got His Gun (1952)—chamber orchestra, dance score for choreographer Irving Burton
Miracles (1953)—two pianos and percussion, dance score for choreographer Alec Rubin
Abyss (1964)—one-act ballet for orchestra; choreography by Stuart Hodes
Bird of Yearning (1967)—one-act ballet for orchestra; choreography by Stuart Hodes; also concert version for small orchestra (28 players) and piano
Riders to the Sea (1995–1996)—one-act chamber opera; libretto by John Millington Synge; for soprano, mezzo-soprano, alto, tenor, 5 or more mixed voices, flute (+ piccolo, tin whistle), Celtic harp/harp, accordion, tubular bells (+ bodhran), 2 violins, viola, 2 celli; published by Carl Fischer; also version with string orchestra instead of 5 strings

Orchestra

Concerto for Piano and Violas, Cellos and Basses (Piano Concerto no. 1) (1955)—published by Carl Fischer (rental)

Lament (1956)—string orchestra
Aria and Toccata (1957)—viola and string orchestra; also version for viola and piano
Variations on a Sarabande (1959)—published by Carl Fischer (rental)
Eight Pieces for Orchestra (1961)—large orchestra (version of piano work); published by Carl Fischer (rental)
Bird of Yearning (1967)—small orchestra (28 players) (version of ballet); published by Carl Fischer (rental)
Landscapes of the Mind I (Piano Concerto no. 2) (1968–1974)—piano, large orchestra; published by Carl Fischer, 1979
Fragments (1978)—(version of piano work); published by Carl Fischer (rental)
Country Auction (1976)—symphonic band; published by Carl Fischer, 1977
Blackberry Vines and Winter Fruit (1976)—published by Carl Fischer, 1980
Spectral Chimes/Enshrouded Hills (1978–1980)—3 quintets (flute, oboe, clarinet, French horn, bassoon; French horn, 2 trumpets, trombone, tuba; string quartet, double bass), orchestra, 1978–1980; published by Carl Fischer, 1981
Düsseldorf Concerto (1981–1982)—flute, harp, viola, small orchestra (timpani, percussion, strings) (also chamber version); published by Carl Fischer (rental)
Out of Shadows and Solitude (1985)—large orchestra; published by Carl Fischer (rental)
Quantum Quirks of a Quick Quaint Quark (1991)—published by Carl Fischer (rental)
Variations and Interludes on Themes from Monteverdi and Bach (1992)—(concerto) violin, cello, piano, large orchestra; published by Carl Fischer (rental)
Kyrie (2004)—string orchestra

Chamber Music

One for Two and Two for Three (1947, revised 1974)—3 trombones
Sonata (1948)—clarinet, piano
Aria and Toccata (1957)—viola, piano (version of orchestral work)
String Quartet no. 2 (1958)
Ricercare (1958)—string quartet, brass quartet (French horn, 2 trumpets, tuba), band; published by Carl Fischer
Darkening of the Light (1961)—viola; also version for cello, 1976; published by Carl Fischer (facsimile)
Suite for violin and piano (1964)—published by Carl Fischer, 1964/2000
Landscapes of the Mind II (1971)—violin, piano; published by Carl Fischer, 1979
Pastorale (1975)—2 oboes
Landscapes of the Mind III (1979)—violin, cello, piano; published by Carl Fischer
Sonora (1981)—2 A-clarinets, piano
Düsseldorf Concerto (1981–1982)—flute, harp, viola, ensemble (timpani, percussion, string quartet, double bass) (version of orchestral work)
Exequy (1983)—oboe, clarinet, cello, piano (version of piano work)
Seacliff Variations (1984)—violin, viola, cello, piano; published by Carl Fischer
Obsessions (1986)—trombone
Qhanri (Snow Mountain): Tibetan Variations (1988)—cello, piano; published by Carl Fischer

Elegy (1994)—flute/violin, guitar/piano, cello ad libitum
Air (2003)—oboe, bassoon; also version for piano
Kyrie (2004)—string quintet
Bye-Bye Bake Shoppe (2005)—string quartet and narrator
Divers (Diverse) Divertimento (2005)—flute, oboe (English horn), guitar
Not Your Grandmother's Four-Hand Piece (2006)—piano four-hands
Trio (2006)—alto sax, baritone horn, and piano
Fandango Fantasy (2006)—piano, clarinet, violin, and cello
Serenade (2007)—flute, percussion, and harp
Two Pieces for Two Violins (2008)
Threnody (2009)—string trio

Choral

Relations (1951)—cantata; text by Gerd Stern; SATB and orchestra
Three Songs of Madness and Death (1955)—text by John Webster; SATB
Psalm 91 (1962)—SATB; published by Elkan-Vogel, 1963
Three Christmas Songs (1964)—texts by Eugene Field, Isaac Watts, and Phillips
    Brooks; SSAA (children's or female chorus), 2 flutes/piano; published by
    Broude Brothers, 1992
Seek Him (1965)—text from the Book of Amos; SATB
To Whom? (1980)—Text by Virginia Woolf; SATB
Do Not Press My Hands (1981)—Text by Gabriela Mistral; SSATTB
Three Songs on Poems of Emily Dickinson (1982)—SSAA; published by G. Schirmer,
    1984 (out of print)
Into My Heart (1990)—texts by Robert Frost, A. E. Housman, R. Glenn Martin,
    Cathleen Schurr, Maureen Skelly, and Walt Whitman; SATB, oboe, French horn,
    2 trumpets, trombone, baritone horn, tuba, violin, timpani, percussion; also ver-
    sion for SATB, piano four-hands

Vocal

Jabberwocky (1941)—text by Lewis Carroll; speaker, piano
Lullaby (1941)—for Mary Howell Brinkman on birth of her son (melody only)
Four Songs ("Alone," "Midnight," "When I Am Not With You," and "Peace")
    (1942–1944)—texts respectively by Marga Richter, James Russell Lowell, Sara
    Teasdale, and Marga Richter
Transmutation (1949)—(song cycle) texts by Chinese poets (Ch'en Yün, Liu Sung,
    Hsaio Kang, Chang Chi, Po Chü I, and anonymous), translated by Henry
    Hersch Hart; soprano, piano
Into What Unknown Chamber (1950, rev. 1983)—text by Phyllis Roberts; medium
    voice, piano
Two Chinese Songs: "The Hermit" and "Fishing Picture" (1953)—texts by Chinese
    poets (Li Hai-Ku and Ta Chung-Kunkuang), translated by Amy Lowell; so-
    prano, piano
She at His Funeral (1954)—text by Thomas Hardy; soprano, piano
Lament for Art O'Leary (1984)—text by Eileen O'Leary; soprano, piano; published
    by Carl Fischer

Sieben Lieder (1985)—text by Francisco Tanzer; voice, piano
Sarah Do Not Mourn Me Dead (1995)—text by Sullivan Ballou; medium voice, piano
Erin Odyssey (2000)—text by the composer; medium voice, piano
Testament (2001)—text by Anne Morrow Lindbergh; alto, English horn, piano
Dew-drops on a Lotus Leaf (2002)—(song cycle) text by Ryokan, translated by Jakob
   Fischer; countertenor/alto, string quartet/piano
Goat Songs (2006)—(song cycle) text by Marcia Slatkin; medium voice, piano
Sonnet 128 and *Sonnet 71* (2007)—text by William Shakespeare; medium voice,
   piano
"Wild Moon" (2009)—text by Phyllis Latimer; alto/countertenor and piano

Keyboard

PIANO: TEACHING PIECES (EASY)

Short Suite no. 1 for Young Pianists (1949)
Short Suite no. 2 for Young Pianists (1954)
Hugh's Piece (1970)
Elephants and Violets (1970)
For Something That Had Gone Before (1970)

PIANO: INTERMEDIATE

Nocturne for Sara Lee (1953)—published by Carl Fischer
A Farewell (1962)
Two Piano Pieces: "The Lost People" and "The Dancers" (1968)—published by Carl
   Fischer
Bits and Snatches (1970)—(requires metal drum)
Regrets (2005)
Homage J. S. Bach (2007)

PIANO: ADVANCED/DIFFICULT

Ballet of the Pixilated Penguins (1944)
March Berserk (1945)
Dream Andante (1945)
Sonata for Piano (1954)—published by Carl Fischer, 1980
Melodrama (1956, rev. 1958)—two pianos
Eight Pieces for Piano (1961)—also version for orchestra; published by Carl Fischer
   (facsimile)
Fragments (1963)—also version for orchestra; published by Carl Fischer (facsimile)
Variations on a Theme by Latimer (1964)—piano four-hands
Short Prelude in Baroque Style (1974)—(version of harpsichord work)
Bird of Yearning (1976)—(version of ballet)
Remembrances (1977)—published by Elkan-Vogel, 1979
Requiem (1978)—published by Carl Fischer (facsimile)
Exequy (1980)—also version for oboe, clarinet, cello, and piano
Prelude for Piano (In Memoriam) (1993)—published by Carl Fischer

Quantum Quirks of a Quick Quaint Quark no. 3 (1993)
Air (2003)—(version of chamber work)
Three Improvisations (2004)
Four Miniatures: Hommage J. S. Bach , March Berserk (not same as earlier), Valse Melancolique, Toccatina (2008)

ORGAN

Variations on a Theme by Neithart von Reuenthal (1974)—published by Carl Fischer (facsimile)
Quantum Quirks of a Quick Quaint Quark no. 2 (1992)—published by Vivace Press

HARPSICHORD

Soundings (1965)—published by Carl Fischer (facsimile)
Short Prelude in Baroque Style (1974)—also version for piano

APPENDIX B: DISCOGRAPHY

Blackberry Vines and Winter Fruit. Harold Farberman/London Philharmonic. Leonarda LE 331. "The London Philharmonic Celebrates American Composers." 1990.
Exequy. Nanette Kaplan Solomon, piano. Leonarda LE 334, 1994. "Character Sketches: Solo Piano Works by 7 American Women."
Fragments. Nanette Kaplan Solomon, piano. Leonarda LE 334. "Character Sketches: Solo Piano Works by 7 American Women." 1994.
Lament. Carolann Martin/Bournemouth Sinfonietta. Leonarda LE 327. "Journeys: Orchestral Works by American Women." 1987.
Landscapes of the Mind II. David Wells, cello; Marga Richter, piano; Daniel Heifetz, violin; Michael Skelly, piano. Leonarda LE 337. "Snow Mountain: A Spiritual Trilogy." 1994.
Out of Shadows and Solitude. Gerard Schwarz/Seattle Symphony Orchestra. MMC 2118. 2003.
Qhanri. David Wells, cello; Marga Richter, piano; Daniel Heifetz, violin; Michael Skelly, piano. Leonarda LE 337. "Snow Mountain: A Spiritual Trilogy." 1994.
Quantum Quirks of a Quick Quaint Quark. Gerard Schwarz/Czech Radio Symphony Orchestra. MMC 2066. "Modern American Classics, Volume 3." 1998.
Quantum Quirks of a Quick Quaint Quark no. 2. Barbara Harbach, organ. Gasparo GSCD 294.
Requiem. David Wells, cello; Marga Richter, piano; Daniel Heifetz, violin; Michael Skelly, piano. Leonarda LE 337. "Snow Mountain: A Spiritual Trilogy." 1994.
Seacliff Variations. Sea Cliff Chamber Players. Musical Heritage Society MHS 5512563L.
Spectral Chimes/Enshrouded Hills. Gerard Schwarz/Czech Radio Symphony Orchestra. MMC 2066. "Modern American Classics, Vol. 3." 1998.

String Quartet no. 2. Meridian String Quartet. Capstone CPS-8692. "Diverse Light." 2001.

Variations and Interludes on Themes from Monteverdi and Bach. Renata Knific, violin; Pamela Frame, cello; Robert Weirich, piano; Joel Suben/Polish Radio National Symphony Orchestra. Leonarda LE 351, 2004. "Orchestral Excursions."

Privately-held Taped Performances

Do Not Press My Hands. Western Wind.
Into My Heart. Georgia State University, with piano four-hands. New Amsterdam Singers, with Chamber Ensemble.
Psalm 91. Nassau Community College Choir.
Seek Him. Nassau Community College Choir.
Three Songs of Madness and Death. Occasional Singers.
To Whom? New Calliope Singers.

SOURCES

Ammer, Christine. *Unsung: A History of Women in American Music.* 2nd ed. Portland, OR: Amadeus Press, 2001.

Fürst-Heidtmann, Monika. "Komponieren als emotionale Notwendigkeit: Ein Porträt der Amerikanischen Komponistin Marga Richter" (Composing as Emotional Necessity: A Portrait of American Composer Marga Richter). *Neuland* (Germany) 4 (1983/1984): 268–276.

Hinson, Maurice. *Guide to the Pianist's Repertoire.* 3rd ed. Bloomington: Indiana University Press, 2000.

Jezic, Diane. *Women Composers: The Lost Tradition Found.* 2nd ed. Prepared by Elizabeth Wood. New York: Feminist Press at the City University of New York, 1994.

Lee, You Ju. "Marga Richter: A Biographical Sketch and Study of Her Piano Works with Emphasis on Sonata for Piano." D.M.A. diss., University of Georgia, 2000.

LePage, Jane Weiner. *Women Composers, Conductors, and Musicians of the Twentieth Century: Selected Biographies.* Metuchen, NJ: Scarecrow Press, 1980.

Mirchandani, Sharon. "The Choral Music of Marga Richter." *Choral Journal,* May 2003, 9–17.

Olmstead, Andrea. *Juilliard: A History.* Urbana: University of Illinois Press, 1999.

Persichetti, Vincent. *Twentieth Century Harmony.* New York: Norton, 1961.

Rosen, Judith. "Richter, Marga." In *New Grove Dictionary of Women Composers,* 389–390.

Taylor, Vivian. "Richter, Marga." In *Women and Music in America since 1900, an Encyclopedia.* Vol. 2, 570–571. Edited by Kristine H. Burns. Westport, CT: Greenwood Press, 2002.

Van Gelder, L. "For a Composer, a Week of Special Note." *New York Times,* April 9, 1978.

Judith Lochhead

JUDITH SHATIN

I think of my musical imagination as a semi-permeable membrane, like the plasma membrane that surrounds the cells of all living creatures. While not open to all, I am open to many experiences of the world as musical phenomena, including current events of virtually any sort.[1]

Judith Shatin is a composer whose music intertwines multiple strands. Her deep fascination with timbre led to pioneering work in electronic and digital media, while she continued to augment her acoustic palette. Shatin's professional career began in the late 1970s, and over the last thirty years, the inclusivity of her sound sources and the range of her work has continually expanded. The high regard for Shatin's compositional work is marked by numerous awards, fellowships, and commissions, including four National Endowment for the Arts fellowships; residencies at Bellagio, the McDowell Colony, the Virginia Center for the Arts, and Yaddo; and commissions from groups such as the National Symphony, Kronos Quartet, and the newEar Ensemble. Additionally, three compact discs have been released that present Shatin's music exclusively: *Dreamtigers*, *Piping the Earth*, and *Tower of the Eight Winds*. Shatin's music is published primarily by Wendigo Music, as well as by Arsis Press, C. F. Peters, Colla Voce, E. C. Schirmer, and Hal Leonard.

In her early years, Shatin lived in the northeast region of the United States. Born in 1949 in Boston, Massachusetts, she moved with her family to Seagate, then to Albany, New York, and eventually to South Orange, New Jersey. While not a predominant factor of family life, music was an important part of Shatin's upbringing. At the college level, Shatin chose to major in music at Douglass College, the sister school to Rutgers University, and eventually chose composition as a primary musical focus.[2] Further formal education took Shatin to the Juilliard School and Princeton University for graduate degrees in composition, while summer programs at the Aspen Music Festival and Tanglewood provided summer opportunities for apprenticeship. During these years, Shatin had the opportunity to study with a number of composers, including Milton Babbitt, Paul Lansky, Otto Luening, Robert Moevs, J. K. Randall, and Gunther Schuller. In describing her work with them, she is always careful to point out the breadth of their teaching. More than just the technical issues of notation and craft, compositional learning for Shatin included a broad spectrum of critical thought as the context for music making.

Now herself a teacher of renown, Shatin currently holds the William R. Kennan Jr. Professorship in the McIntire Department of Music at the University of Virginia, where she has been on faculty since 1979. She teaches a wide array of classes, ranging from music composition and theory to songwriting and computer music, and also serves as the director of the Virginia Center for Computer Music, which she founded in 1987–1988. While the phrase "academic composer" is often used pejoratively, the intellectual environment afforded by Shatin's involvement in a university community has enriched and enlivened her process in tangible ways. As an engaged academic musical citizen, she has been provided opportunities to assume important leadership roles within several of the groups with which she has been affiliated. She served as chair of the Department of Music at the University of Virginia from 1995 until 2002 and as president of American Women Composers Inc. from 1989 to 1993.[3] Additionally, Shatin has served as a juror for organizations such as the National Endowment for the Arts, the Rome Prize, and the Eleventh Composition Competition of the Fribourg International Festival of Sacred Music. She has also served on the boards of the American Composers Alliance, the League/ISCM, and the International Alliance for Women in Music.

The university setting of Shatin's life and work as a composer is far from any simplistic notion of the "ivory tower" as a place that encourages social hermits. Throughout her career, and indeed her life, Shatin has fervently absorbed ideas from the world around her, including areas such as the sciences, psychology, social theory, and religion. As sparks to inspiration, these ideas serve not simply as elements to infuse into her music, but rather as formative essentials. Unlike others who might respond to such ideas through verbal or visual media, Shatin has absorbed them into her sonoral landscape. Through sound, she responds to the problems and joys of contemporary life. Composing is not a means for her to tap into some separate realm of transcendent and arcane expression, but a way of articulating the particularities of living in a world of other people, other cultures, and other living creatures—a world that is both social and natural. There is nothing extramusical for Shatin: music is an *inclusionary* activity. The academy as the site for such music making affords many opportunities for intellectual and creative exchange, and through its various pathways links the composer directly to the world.

> *The action of musical imagination on a personal level is certainly not static, and I am aware that over the years my listening has changed. Now I am more aware of a continuous feedback loop between composing and listening. For instance, my recent piece,* For the Birds, *for amplified cello and electronic playback, utilizes calls from birds in the Yellowstone National Park region. After having composed that piece, I find that I listen to bird calls differently. Now when geese fly overhead I find myself tracking the pitches. So, it works both ways—hearing the world leads to music, and music leads to the world. They are mutually informative.*

In Shatin's music, the pathways into the world are most clearly present in two works: *COAL*, a folk oratorio, and *Singing the Blue Ridge*, a piece for mezzo, baritone, orchestra, and electronics. Premiered in 1994, *COAL* is scored for chorus; Appalachian band (hammered dulcimer, fiddle, banjo, guitar, two singers); electronics; and synthesizer. The composition of the piece included study of various business, social, environmental and health issues pursuant to the coal-mining industry in West Virginia. Supported by a grant from the Lila Wallace–Reader's Digest Arts Partners Program and in conjunction with Shepherd College (Shepherdstown, West Virginia), *COAL* gives sonic expression to the lives of people residing in that region. A central part of the compositional process for Shatin was working with and learning from regional citizens, among them miners, business owners, musicians, local historians, political leaders, and union leaders. As a piece of musical art, *COAL* acts as a portrait of the coal-mining community of West Virginia while at the same time providing sounding expression to a broad range of social and environmental issues facing citizens in the Appalachian region (see example 9.1).

Singing the Blue Ridge has a similar sort of correlation to a region of the eastern seaboard of the United States. The work was commissioned as part of a project of the Wintergreen Performing Arts, based in Nelson County, Virginia, and was sponsored by the Animating Democracy Initiative of Americans for the Arts. Comprising part of the Preserving the Rural Soundscapes project, the piece and several other related activities encouraged people in the community to engage with the sounds of their environment and to participate in civic dialogue regarding regional growth during a period of intense development. In addition to creating the work and overseeing its performance, Shatin taught classes to schoolchildren, met with environmentalists from the community, and took

Example 9.1. COAL, mm. 8–15

people on sound walks.[4] The piece itself incorporates the calls of animals indigenous to the region: frogs, deer, otters, raccoons, wolves, peepers, and toads, among others. The four movements set poems created for the piece by poet Barbara Goldberg, with the poetry addressing issues of human and animal interactions (see example 9.2).

> *The calls are themselves entrancing in their intrinsic musicality, and I found it fascinating to choreograph the interaction of musical voices and instruments with the animal calls. Their interaction allows us not only to hear the music of the natural world but also to hear the natural world in the constructed sounds we have bracketed as music. I hope the musicality of the animal sounds and their interactions with the music of humans will draw attention to the animals themselves. In particular, I hope this piece will encourage people to think more about the animals they live among, and that this experience will change some behaviors toward them.*

Both *Singing the Blue Ridge* and *COAL* exemplify an expanded role for the composer in contemporary life: as an active member of a community, both large and small, who encourages response and thought through the sounds of music. While it is clear that Shatin's music is not political in the sense of Luigi Nono's, Cornelius Cardew's, or Christian Wolff's,

Example 9.2. *Singing the Blue Ridge,* **opening**

it definitely takes a stance; her music consistently engages listeners in a dialogue about issues important to our time and beyond.

Redefinition of the term *academic composer* has not been an explicit goal for Shatin, but it has been enabled by a variety of factors, most notably her personality, intellect, and cultural awareness. This redefinition can be traced directly to her teaching and mentoring. Shatin teaches the usual array of courses for undergraduate and graduate students, but she incorporates the process of teaching as a way to reframe traditional topics, using music to approach the world in a new way. For instance, during the summer of 2007, while teaching on Semester at Sea in Latin America, she introduced basic music theory through a focus on musics of the region. This required Shatin to learn a repertoire new to her, to cast her teaching around it, and to introduce students to concepts through the study of music not regularly addressed in standard curricula in the United States.

The musical imagination can also be affected by music itself. I love listening to a large variety of music, some of which I come across through my teaching. In order to maximize the variety of music I encounter, I often teach courses that expand my base of musical knowledge. I am also teaching a course during this voyage on soundscape composition, and I have been in touch with a number of fascinating electroacoustic composers from Chile. These preparations for teaching not only broaden my own musical knowledge, but also affect my musical imagination.

Mentoring young composers and musicians is of primary concern to Shatin. More than just providing career support for young composers, mentoring for Shatin includes fostering a sense of community and generating interest in musical creation and performance as a form of cultural exchange. She readily takes advantage of the "academic" composer's unique opportunity to focus attention on music in the concert tradition while also creating a forum for musical exchange and dialogue. Thus, she uses both the resources and the intellectual-artistic environment of the university to foster a vital musical community.

I encourage my students to find performances of their music and help create opportunities for that to happen. But my active mentoring entails a lot of other activities. These include suggesting places where students can send their music, such as festivals, competitions, and the like; introducing students to composers and performers; involving student participation in choosing composers to invite to grounds and creating ways for them to meet and interact with them; hosting social events at my home with visiting composers and performers; and creating recital opportunities and inviting well-known groups to perform student works.

Over the course of her thirty-year career as a professional composer, Judith Shatin has written a large number of diverse pieces, from solo works to larger orchestral, choral, electroacoustic, and digital pieces. Here I organize my discussion of the music by themes that may be traced through Shatin's work list. This approach to the music, as opposed to a chronological account, allows continuities and diversities to come into focus.

Timbre as a material presence of sound has been an enduring compositional concern for Shatin. This focus on sound is distinct from the Cageian notion of "sound as sound," in the sense that Shatin takes great authorial care to shape her sonorities and to give specific timbres a primary structural role in her music. For instance, the 1990 orchestral work *Piping the Earth* begins with a minute-long (the first thirteen measures) "rumbling up" of sound from the orchestra. Low and long-held tones by the basses, tuba, and timpani are gradually joined by the lower strings (whose players silently finger quick rhythms), short percussive jabs from the bassoons, and occasional flashes of color from the upper winds and upper strings. An increasing dynamic builds until after about one minute (measure fourteen) a sudden burst of musical energy fills the sonic landscape. The timbral shaping of this opening musical gesture is a microcosm of the pervasive idea of the whole.

Example 9.3. *Piping the Earth*, mm. 13–15, strings and percussion

Shatin's concern for timbral shaping is also a motivating factor in her collaborations with performers. Working with specific players on the sound capabilities of their instruments has been a lifelong interest for Shatin, as a careful reading of her work dedications can attest. One interesting manifestation of her focus on performers as individuals is the recent development of multiple versions of pieces for different instruments. For instance, there are a number of versions of *Penelope's Song*—for viola, violin, cello, clarinet, and soprano saxophone—sparked by performers' requests.

Another sign of her interest in timbral shaping is Shatin's frequent use of electronic sound. The role of electronically generated or manipulated sounds has become increasingly important in Shatin's work since she founded the Virginia Center for Computer Music in 1987–1988, but her attraction to the timbral resources of electroacoustic music harks back to her introduction to the Buchla synthesizer at the 1971 Aspen Music Festival. As a medium of musical thought, electronically created or manipulated sounds offer a sonic plasticity and a working immediacy not possible in the traditional compositional mode. Within Shatin's works, electronic sound either serves as one of the timbral strands, as in *Sea of Reeds*, *Kairos*, or *Elijah's Chariot*, or it constitutes the entirety of the piece, as in *Civil War Memories* or *Glimmerings*.

> *Michael Chaikovsky, who taught at the Aspen Festival, introduced me to the Buchla synthesizer in 1971. During the following year in New York, he enabled me to continue working in this medium, and I was fascinated by it. I had had some experience with classical studio technique at Rutgers, but never enjoyed splicing tape! Working with the Buchla facilitated a much more immediate approach to sound.*

Shatin's concern for sound as a material presence is a governing compositional principle. We may also observe a number of themes that point not only to Shatin's compositional personality, but also to her position as an attentive citizen of the world. The themes that I have detected follow:

- Literary narrative frame
- The natural world and its processes—sounds, colors, creatures
- Specific places or events
- Sound images
- Judaism

These thematic categories do not take account of every work in Shatin's oeuvre, but they do provide a way to focus her compositional profile. I will exemplify each theme with a brief discussion of some representative works. Some pieces may be understood to exemplify more than one theme.

Literary Narrative Frame

Dreamtigers, a 1996 work for flute and guitar, takes as its point of departure the prose poem of Jorge Luis Borges of the same title. Borges's work, published in Spanish in 1960, explores the often fluid and ephemeral distinctions between the "real" and the "dream" worlds. Borges tells of remembering tigers in his youth and how he attempts to conjure them up in dreams of the present. Shatin's piece explores the often ephemeral distinctions between memory and presence by musical processes that "curl back on themselves and ultimately evaporate,"[5] while carefully chosen extended techniques create a sense of departure from the everyday to the dream world.

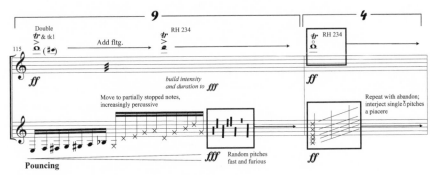

Example 9.4. *Dreamtigers*, mm. 115–116

Werther, a 1984 work for flute, clarinet, violin, cello, and piano, takes the Romantic "striving for the unobtainable" in Goethe's 1774 novel, *The Sorrows of Young Werther*, as its premise.[6] It holds close to the narrative, linking specific instruments to particular characters or ideas in Goethe's novel. Over the course of the piece, the instrumental interactions and the specific motivic presentations tell the story of conflict, impatience, anguish, and tragedy. Pianist Gayle Martin Henry described the opening bars as a "cry into the void,"[7] with its piercing opening chord, repetition of the scream, and the rhythmic quickening of the piano chords (see example 9.5).

The Natural World and Its Processes—Sounds, Colors, Creatures

The before-mentioned 1990 orchestral composition *Piping the Earth* takes its title from a text by the Chinese writer Chuang Tzu (also transliterated as *Zhuangzi*), who most likely lived in the fourth century BCE. The phrase "piping the earth" in Chuang Tzu's text takes account of the diverse sounds created by the wind as it moves through and around various physical places. Shatin's piece explores how a constant harmonic configuration creates diverse sounding effects as it is transformed rhythmically, timbrally, and texturally. This provides just one example of how Shatin interacts with the natural world in her music (see example 9.6).

Example 9.5. *Werther,* mm. 1–6

52

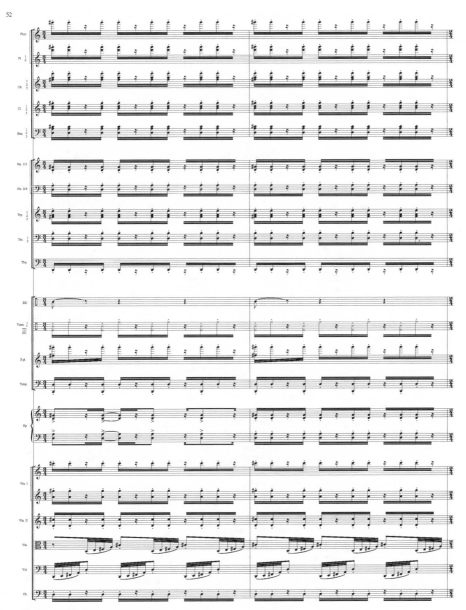

Example 9.6.   *Piping the Earth,* p. 52

For the Birds is a 2005 piece for amplified cello and electronics. The electronic part consists of recorded, often processed bird calls indigenous to the Yellowstone region of the western United States. Shatin uses these sounds to generate new musical phenomena. The interaction of the cello with the bird sounds musically enacts a joining of the human with that of the animal world, suggesting a respectful and harmonious interaction as an ideal.

Example 9.7.   *For the Birds*, 0:15–1:10

Specific Places or Events

Scored for oboe and two percussionists, the 2006 work *Time to Burn* responds to the violence that has been present in our world culture over the last decade, and especially since 2001. Present for some directly and for others through images and sounds, the wars in Iraq, Afghanistan, and the Middle East, and the constant instances of terrorism throughout the world have become a regular part of daily life. *Time to Burn* responds to that violence, linking it to historical eras of ethnic and religious violence such as "the 'burning time' of the Inquisition or the burning of witches."[8]

Example 9.8. *Time to Burn*, mm. 222–230

The 1992 work for amplified piano and percussion, *1492*, marks the five-hundredth anniversary of a tumultuous year that included "Columbus's voyage to the New World, the expulsion of the Jews from Spain, and the invasion of France by Henry VII."[9] The composer inscribes this date into its rhythmic structure by using the numbers 1, 4, 9, and 2 as values for durations and time signatures, and into the intervallic structure using the numbers to determine intervallic sequences.

Example 9.9.   *1492,* mm. 1–14

Sound Image

Some of Shatin's music produces a "sounding image" of something that we would typically see, and in doing so, it conjures up a virtual visual experience of that thing. *Penelope's Song* demonstrates this effect well, as does *Cherry Blossom and a Wrapped Thing: After Hokusai,* a 2004 work for amplified clarinet and electronics that responds to a print of the same title by the Japanese artist Hokusai (1760–1849). This piece, while preserving the intense stillness of the print, supplements that sense of static presence with subtle sounds, perhaps of insects which hover and define the place of the blossom (see example 9.10).

The sense of a virtual, sonically induced visuality also occurs in the 1992 string orchestra work *Stringing the Bow.* This piece plays off the imagery of the string players' arm movements and of the arcing movement of an arrow after being released from the archer's bow. The music organizes around the trajectory of an arrow in flight—the energetic release, the suspended height of the arc, and the final descent and loss of energy (see example 9.11).

Judaism

Shatin's Jewish heritage emerges through the stories of the Old Testament that serve as a background narrative or suggest places of religious significance. These works are not religious in the sense that they espouse a belief or serve a ritual function; rather, the stories and places provide opportunities for reflection on ideas and issues that have cur-

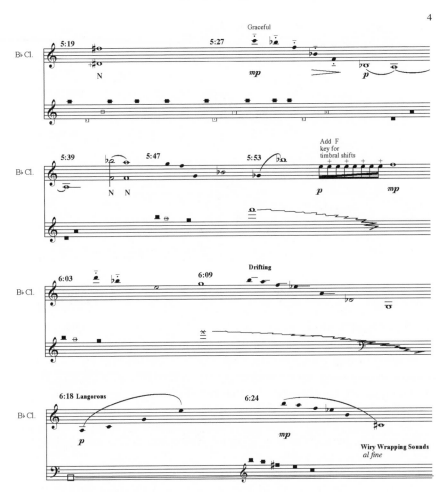

Example 9.10. *Cherry Blossom and a Wrapped Thing,* 5:19–ca. 6:24

rent cultural relevance. *Elijah's Chariot,* for string quartet and electronics from 1996, musically depicts the story of the prophet Elijah. Swept up to heaven on a chariot of fire, Elijah is the focus of many stories in Jewish lore. Shatin inscribes the story into the work by incorporating a recorded and manipulated sound of the shofar, symbolically calling Elijah to heaven, and the folk song *Eliahu HaNavi,* a song which often closes the Jewish sabbath (see example 9.12).

The 1986 piano trio *View from Mt. Nebo* weaves together cultural myths from both the Jewish tradition and the United States of the mid-twentieth century. The same Mt. Nebo, the mountaintop from which Moses looked to the Promised Land, serves also to define a goal of freedom in Martin Luther

Example 9.11. *Stringing the Bow,* mm. 488–497

King's "I Have a Dream" speech from 1963. The work has three movements: the first tells of the struggle of the journey to the Promised Land, the second a "meditation of faith," and the third a "radiant acceptance of fate"[10] (see example 9.13).

Through illumination of these five thematic elements, Shatin is further revealed as a person who puts much forethought into her artistic creations. Ties among literature, nature, and faith resonate through her sound world with clear conviction. It is this conviction that has shaped

Example 9.12. *Elijah's Chariot*, mm. 233–257

her not only as one of America's preeminent composers, but also as a leading figure among women in music. Shatin's dedication, for instance, to the activities of the International Alliance of Women in Music and its recognition of the practical need to provide opportunities, encouragement, and networking for present and emerging women composers is

Example 9.13. *View from Mount Nebo*, mm. 161–170

noteworthy. And while Shatin is aware of ways that she has been categorized as a "woman composer" and of the subtle and diverse ways that
cultural attitudes can marginalize one's work, she does not claim these as
impediments. If anything, she has used those cultural attitudes as a call
to action. The assumption of difference in the context of contemporary
identity politics can have a narrowing effect that shuts off imagination
and possibility; recognizing this, Judith Shatin has utilized difference to
positive effect in the creation of exceptional music that is diverse, imaginative, communicative, and of the world.

A CONVERSATION WITH JUDITH SHATIN

*In the winter and spring of 2007, Judith Shatin and I communicated in various
ways—e-mail and in-person meetings in New York City—during the lead-up to
the formal interview in April. While I had been acquainted with Judith's music
over the years, I spent those winter and spring months getting to know many*

more of her pieces and the contexts in which she composed them. My sense of Judith's music—music of great beauty and integrity—was affirmed by the person I came to know during that time. Indeed, one of my great pleasures as a scholar of contemporary musical practices has been the opportunity to deepen my knowledge of musical works through knowledge of the person. I was particularly impressed with how Shatin's music engages the larger social and intellectual issues of our time and how as sounding presence the music informs the circumstances of life at the turn of the millennium.—Judith Lochhead

LOCHHEAD: How do you conceive your musical imagination, and what are the kinds of things, activities, people, or ideas that affect it?

SHATIN: This has to do with my idea of the composer's mind as a semi-permeable membrane. For instance, in the summer of 2006 I was commissioned to write a piece for oboe and two percussionists. I was working intensively that summer and was acutely aware of the war in the Middle East and of the horrific events in Darfur. So I decided to compose a piece called *Time to Burn*, which is infused with frustration and anger. In this case, specific world events passed through the membrane of my imagination and were transformed into music. But this "membrane" is involved even in the specific physical details of my workspace. My office, for example, faces the Jeffersonian lawn and rotunda of the academic village at the University of Virginia. From the physical experience of this vista, with its frequent changes of weather and the myriad activities on the lawn, the idea came for a film. I had met the Boston filmmaker Robert Arnold in Bellagio, and as his films often entail time-lapse photography, I interested him in the project. We have collected hundreds of thousands of images of the rotunda, and I have collected and processed a variety of sounds from within and around it. Additionally, I interviewed a wide range of people about their experiences of the rotunda as a physical and historical presence, including students, the president of the university, and architectural historians. The music for the film will include the aural sound print of the rotunda, voices drawn from the interviews, and musical transformations of both. While the work has grown and flowered into a project encompassing the worlds of sight, sound, and memory, it began from the simple experience of viewing the world from my office and having that experience stimulate my imagination.

LOCHHEAD: These projects suggest that we rethink the often negative notion of the "academic composer." Far from being shut up in the ivory tower, the academic composer today has great opportunities to explore and learn a wide range of music in the broader context of the learning community.

SHATIN: Absolutely. When I taught a new course on songwriting, for instance, preparation for the class led me to encounter a huge variety of music I would not have otherwise, some of which I found fascinating. I'm always on the lookout for new music and intrigued by what other composers are doing. I have recently become acquainted with the music of the Estonian composer Veljo Tormis, whose music is fabulous.[11] And in the domain of soundscape music, which has been of long interest to me personally, I much admire the music of Hildegard Westerkamp,[12] as well as my colleague Matthew Burtner's electroacoustic music.

LOCHHEAD: And these are things which might influence your imagination?

SHATIN: Yes, though my musical imagination has likewise been affected by my study of perception in the field of neo-Gestalt psychology. I am interested in how we perceive the organization of patterns, and especially what we do with ambiguous ones. This is not a new interest for me. While in high school, I read the work of Gestalt psychologists like Kurt Koffka and Wolfgang Köhler on issues of perception. My husband, Michael Kubovy,[13] is a cognitive psychologist whose primary fields are auditory and visual perception—questions of perceptual organization. Michael's work, as well as that of other cognitive psychologists, continues to raise the question, "What can we perceive?" This general question and the broader questions about perception explored within cognitive psychology have piqued my musical imagination.

LOCHHEAD: What kinds of memories of musical imagination do you have from your youth?

SHATIN: I grew up in a family that was not particularly musically inclined; both of my parents were scientists. My mother, seven months pregnant with me when she defended her dissertation, was a bacteriologist, and my father a clinical psychologist. When I was quite young, we did get a piano that I gravitated to. When my father asked if I would like lessons, I immediately said yes. In my early schooling at PS16 in Albany, New York, I was involved in a wide variety of music-making activities. We learned recorder in music class, and I played flute in the school band, in addition to studying piano. Later, when we moved to South Orange, New Jersey, I played in the orchestra, sang in the chorus, and also did some solo playing.

LOCHHEAD: And what opportunities for hearing music were afforded to you?

SHATIN: I didn't attend many concerts, nor did I listen to a lot of recordings before high school. It wasn't until college and after that I became an avid concertgoer.

LOCHHEAD: Do you have any particular aural memories from your youth?

SHATIN: Well, I remember being sensitive to the sounds around me. Oh, and I have a strong memory of our dog, a German shepherd named Psi, who looked just like Rin Tin Tin. I have a clear aural image of his bark, as well as other sounds he made.

LOCHHEAD: Has your sense of musical imagination changed or been transformed over the course of your career?

SHATIN: Since I began to work professionally as a composer, there have been two major changes that have affected my musical imagination. First, the opportunities to hear music from diverse parts of the world have increased greatly. Second, the advent of digital sound has greatly affected how people listen and how composers work. Even the category of composer has been transformed by the possibilities afforded by digital sound, such that often the activities of composers intermingle with those of sound artists. In fact, one could say that these creative categories are becoming less and less distinct. For me, the working procedures have changed in ways that sometimes lead me to think of the creative activity involved in digital music as musical fabrication.

LOCHHEAD: In your compositional work, how do you negotiate the relation between sound and idea?

SHATIN: The relation between sound and the ideas it projects has changed dramatically over time. I think of sound and idea as mutually informing one another and have always used the timbral specificity of sound to articulate and shape musical form. It seems artificial to think of idea apart from its sonic projection—to think of an idea as something on which you can hang a sound. Not all composers are interested in sound per se, in the sensuality of sound and the psychological feel of it. But for me, sound and idea are inextricably intertwined.

LOCHHEAD: This focus on the materiality of sound raises the question of embodiment more generally. How do current concepts of embodiment figure into your compositional work?

SHATIN: I think of embodiment in several ways. There is a sense in which composing is a way of inscribing oneself in sound. Unlike other composers who want to take themselves out of the composition, I am interested in placing myself right in the thick of it. Ultimately, it is not possible to remove oneself from a composition because all you can do is negotiate where the choice points are that go into the piece. So, in a very real sense, there is an embodied relation between myself and each of my compositions.

LOCHHEAD: And so you would say your emotions are tied up in the sounds you create?

SHATIN: Yes, I also think of music as embodying dynamic emotional states. As an aesthetic position, this statement is, of course, fraught with questions: do those states reside *in* the music, or do listeners necessarily hear the same emotional states that the composer identifies? But from my perspective as a composer, the situation is clear: I feel the emotional embodiment of music. The differences in the ways that listeners hear the emotional states of music is a given, but these differences do not invalidate the role that emotional embodiment plays in my compositional process. The music carries a kind of physical trace of embodied emotional states; or, to use a concept from art, the facture of the music includes a trace of emotional embodiment.

LOCHHEAD: At what point in your life did you decide to become a composer? What led up to that decision?

SHATIN: The decision involved a process, not a single moment. I had done some composing before college, but my interest increased dramatically after my return from spending my junior year at Hebrew University in Jerusalem. While there, with the typical European split between university and conservatory, it was quite difficult to study music. I was glad for the opportunity to study political science, psychology, and other areas, but I really missed music. Then, when I returned to Douglass College, I had the opportunity to study with Robert Moevs, a wonderful composer at Rutgers. I also had excellent theory teachers at Douglass, including Robert Lincoln and James Scott. The return to intense musical study made me realize how much it mattered to me. And though there was a strong expectation that my senior project be a piano recital, I made a counterproposal for a composition recital. The proposal was accepted, but I was told that I would have to arrange for performers and rehearsals—which I did. This was the first composition recital in the history of the department! [Only one of those pieces, a setting of verses from the Book of Ruth, remains in Shatin's work list.] But it was actually my experience at the Aspen Music Festival after graduating from college that was most spellbinding.

LOCHHEAD: Can you talk about that?

SHATIN: Sure. I attended Aspen the summer after graduating college. I loved the wonderful master classes and concerts given by performers such as Jan DeGaetani. I also had opportunities to encounter many first-rank composers, among them Iannis Xenakis, George Crumb, and Jacob Druckman. The opportunity to create acoustic music and hear it performed by fine and enthusiastic musicians at Aspen also enhanced my growing interest in composition. I think in particular of such musicians as violist Rosemary Glyde, pianist Gayle Martin Henry, and soprano Katharine Soroka. These collaborative connections were central to my early compositional development. It is not enough to have a place to study and compose; productive learning occurs when composers work intensively with musicians and hear the results. These were not only outstanding musicians; they were also terrifically enthusiastic about new music! It was the collaborative work with performers at Aspen and the encounters with such fantastic contemporary music that most affected my decision to continue as a composer.

LOCHHEAD: Did you ever have doubts about becoming a composer?

SHATIN: No, there were no doubts as such. I didn't know enough to have them! What I am most aware of now, though, are the frustrations of being a composer of concert music in this current cultural climate. Within the academy, the rise of the study of popular music has in effect devalued and further marginalized contemporary concert music. This effect, while perhaps not intended, has resulted in part from a false dichotomy between high and low art. There is captivating music to be found in many genres, but the distinctions of "high" and "low" often serve as labels which discourage people from listening. The characterization of concert music as "elite" sets most people up to assume they cannot understand and enjoy the music. And even further, for those who do listen to concert music, the "new music" category often carries a negative connotation. This obsession with the labeling of musical genres often has the effect of channeling listening behavior into rather narrow hearways. I also think that this labeling intersects with the current climate of identity politics in North America in ways that amplify this narrowing effect. If, when I was growing up, I thought that I could only listen to and care about music of my ethnic and gender group, my musical world would have been very constricted and impoverished. In fact, most of the music I care about would never have been a part of my experience.

LOCHHEAD: What led you to the teachers you sought out as a composer in your apprentice years?

SHATIN: I sought out Milton Babbitt because of the depth of his thinking about music. I had heard him lecture and then was able to work with him while studying for my master's degree at the Juilliard School. I took a course with him on the music of Schoenberg and Stravinsky and found particularly appealing not only his insights into the music but also his ability to articulate ideas. He is a virtuoso thinker and speaker. At Juilliard, I also sought out the composer Hal Overton, whose work I admired. Unfortunately, he became ill and died not long after I started working with him. After Overton died, Otto Luening stepped in. While this was unplanned, I really enjoyed studying with him. He was very open, had excellent ideas, and we worked well together. After completing my degree at Juilliard, I decided to attend Princeton to continue studying with Babbitt. The practice there was to study with all of the composition teachers, and for me, J. K. Randall turned out to be an absolutely terrific teacher. So, some of my most positive experiences with teachers were in a certain sense accidental.

LOCHHEAD: What kind of impact did your teachers have on your musical creativity?

SHATIN: My teachers affected my creativity in diverse ways. While my music is obviously different from Milton Babbitt's, the depth of his thinking influenced me greatly. I have also been affected by composers with whom I did not study directly, such as John Cage. Many of my musical ideas exemplify a kind of thinking about music that would not have been possible without Cage. For instance, my piano trio *Ignoto Numine* [1986] grapples with traditional notions of form. The piece ends with the instruments virtually screaming—and I decided, having dreamt it, to add the voices of the players screaming as well. So, while I did not get this directly from Cage, his expansion of the idea of what constitutes music certainly affected my openness to this choice.

LOCHHEAD: So, in the case of both Babbitt and Cage, the influences were more about compositional imagination and matters of process rather than about specific techniques.

SHATIN: Yes, that is true, although my studies with Babbitt led me to explore serial techniques much more thoroughly. In general I avoided teachers who were more "guru-like," who insisted that students follow their lead. I had good early training in counterpoint, harmony, orchestration, and analysis, and I continued to work on those on my own. In addition, while studying at Juilliard, I also studied Schenkerian analysis with composer Tom James. At the time, no one at Juilliard touched that, and I was curious about it. This study made me much more aware of large-scale connections and how to make them clear. As a young composer, I was interested in broad issues of musical design and of ways of thinking about music. So, while work in lessons did include some technical issues, conceptual issues were more crucial at that point.

LOCHHEAD: And how do you conceive of your role as a teacher of young composers?

SHATIN: I offer questions and suggestions to enable students to focus more clearly on their ideas. We focus on both matters of technique, often through analysis of music by other people, and broader compositional issues. And I try to get students to think about what motivates their musical choices and about how the music unfolds. Often students have interesting initial ideas but then struggle with their temporal unfolding. Now I'm in the wonderful position of working with sophisticated composition students in our new Ph.D. program in composition and computing technologies at the University of Virginia. I help students refine their ideas and suggest other music, as well as readings, in a variety of fields that I believe will be important for them. I also suggest music that I think will be relevant for them to study, ranging from Feldman to Lachenmann, from Hovda to Saariaho, among many others.

LOCHHEAD: What kind of role does or should a composer play in contemporary society? Are there issues specific to the late twentieth and early twenty-first centuries that affect the kind of roles that you have or might assume?

SHATIN: One important role composers can take in contemporary society is that of community partner. They can help create projects that involve a whole community—no matter how one conceives of community. I have had the pleasure of being involved in two such projects. The first was called Coal: A Blueprint for Understanding Twentieth Century Music and involved a two-year retrospective of my music in Shepherdstown, West Virginia. Centered at Shepherd College, with sponsorship from the Lila Wallace–Reader's Digest Arts Partners Project, the project was conceived and organized by the terrific pianist Mary Kathleen Ernst, then on the faculty at Shepherd College. It involved four week-long residencies, each focused on a different aspect of my music. All of them involved outreach activities, as well as master classes and performances. Perhaps most meaningful was the fourth residency, for which I composed my folk oratorio, *COAL* (1992–1994). I spent two years researching the topic and worked with a variety of community partners in Shepherdstown, including the Rotary Club, classes at the college, the Masterworks Chorale (a local amateur chorus), the Labor Law Center, and many others. I traveled the state, working in archives in Bluefield and Morgantown, and met with miners, mine owners, and leaders of the mine unions. I also harvested sounds in Eaglesnest coal mine in Twilight, West Virginia. The premiere of the piece included a preconcert panel discussion, including myself and then-president of the United Mine Workers of America, Richard Trumka. People from all around the community came, including a number of miners and others in the industry, as well as many locals. Overall, the experience was incredibly satisfying, and one in which the aesthetic experience of music was integrated with the everyday life of the community. While I still relish the idea of creating what one might call self-contained music, I loved working with people from the community and creating a work that had a special meaning for them.

LOCHHEAD: And the second project?

SHATIN: The other project was called Preserving the Rural Soundscape, a project organized by Wintergreen Performing Arts with sponsorship from Americans for the Arts Animating Democracy Initiative.[14] The goal of the project was to stimulate arts-based civic dialogue about issues of development in Nelson County, Virginia. I interacted with community groups and local governance, discussing the effects of development on our sonic environment. We engaged people in the community through several types of activities. I led several sound walks, encouraging people to focus on the sounds of their environment. Also, people were given cassette recorders and invited to record sounds around them that were important to them; these sounds were then posted at a website for others to hear. I met with various environmental groups and also gave classes for schoolchildren. For them, I composed a short waltz with bird songs and asked them to identify what birds they heard. They were really excited by the task of identifying the different birds because these are sounds that are an everyday part of their sonic world. It turned out to be an effective way to engage children through sound and music. These two projects demonstrate that creating music about something that matters to a community in their immediate world, and with their participation, offers an important role for composers.

LOCHHEAD: What draws you to the use of electronically generated or manipulated sounds?

SHATIN: My interest in electronically generated sound arises in part from my focus on timbre and sound more generally. But the process of making sounds electronically has also been important for my musical creativity. I find great joy in the transformation of sound through electronic manipulation. There is a kind of magic in the transformation happening right before your very ears. Sound in this context becomes an aurally plastic medium. I am also interested in the science of sound manipulation. Understanding the science of sound and its electronic manipulation opens up new ways of thinking about music.

LOCHHEAD: Have you faced any particular challenges as a woman using electronic technologies as a composer?

SHATIN: When I was in graduate school, there were few women doing electronic music. But Paul Lansky was very supportive, and I got a lot of support from other students, such as Michael Dellaira. And while the working conditions were more like a boys' club, there was no malevolence at all on the part of my male colleagues. But the opportunities for sharing information were not easy because of the boys' club atmosphere. At the University of Virginia, where I created the Virginia Center for Computer Music, the working environment has been strong and supportive. Additionally, my colleagues, such as Matthew Burtner, Ted Coffey, and technical director David Topper, as well as former colleagues John Gibson and Alison Warren, and systems engineer Pete Yadlowsky, have all been very collegial, and I have learned a lot from them.

LOCHHEAD: Would you say that your sense of the working relation between composer and performers has changed over the years? If so, what motivated those changes?

SHATIN: I think that my relationships with performers have become increasingly collaborative. I have had many excellent experiences working with performers since those years at Aspen. In the early 1980s, I participated in the composer-choreography program at the American Dance Festival where the E.A.R. Unit was in residence. We were asked to create four pieces in a month, one with each of the four choreographers, and to create music for the E.A.R. Unit. In particular, I worked with clarinetist James Rohrig, cellist Erika Duke, flutist Dorothy Stone, and percussionist Daniel Kennedy. While the experience of working with performers for such an extended period of time is a bit unusual, I have been lucky in having performers available for such exchanges, sometimes through the Music Department at the University of Virginia. For instance, I worked extensively with the Monticello Trio when they were in residence. And more recently I have collaborated with oboist Scott Perry and percussionists I-Jen Fang and Mike Schutz on the piece *Time to Burn*, working out various oboe multiphonics and percussion techniques. I've also had the privilege of working with many other performers: the clarinetist F. Gerard Errante, flutist Patricia Spencer, cellist Madeline Shapiro, and soprano saxophonist Susan Fancher, to name a few. I find the process of spending time with them and experimenting with sounds extremely valuable. I learn so much from these performers because they are virtuosos in the timbral worlds of their instruments. But no matter how much I think I know and they think they know, together we always seem to discover new possibilities. So, collaboration has become increasingly important for me.

LOCHHEAD: And so for you performance is about collaboration?

SHATIN: Yes, I think of performance as collaboration in a fundamental sense. I decided to make this overt in a 1995 piece for piano, *Chai Variations on Eliahu HaNavi*. In Jewish mysticism, *chai* stands for the number eighteen, so I composed a set of eighteen variations on the folksong *Eliahu HaNavi*. I left the ordering of the variations to the performer. Since there are eighteen possible orderings of the movement, one could not possibly play them all. I've been very interested to see what trajectory different performers choose.

LOCHHEAD: The category of "woman composer" is certainly still a marked one in Western concert music in the early years of the twenty-first century. Has being so categorized been problematic for you? Or have you seen it as in some ways liberating?

SHATIN: Well, one particular activity related to being a woman and a composer was a particularly gratifying one. From 1989 to 1993, I served as president of American Women Composers Inc. As president, I met many outstanding women who were composers and performers, many more than I would have met otherwise. And through these contacts, many new opportunities emerged, and I became much more aware of the productivity of women in both fields. I also saw that the range of music created by women was very broad and that it was impossible to generalize about particular qualities that suggest essential differences between music created by women and men. We were able, during that period, to create an annual recording award for music by a woman, and we also continued and further developed an annual program at the National Museum of Women in the Arts in Washington, D.C. The goal was, and remains, the mainstreaming of music by women. But for that to happen, the larger community needs to be made aware of it.

LOCHHEAD: Are you aware of yourself as a woman composer when you teach aspiring students?

SHATIN: I am not aware of it directly—only reflectively. That is, I am aware of "woman composer" as a category in terms of how people talk about me, perceive me, and behave toward me. While there have been some negative experiences over the years, they have mostly been fleeting. I do, however, still remember well an experience when I arrived at Tanglewood as a fellow in composition. In casual conversation with some of my colleagues, I said I was there to study composition. The response was, "Ooh, a lady composer." So, while I do not think of myself as a woman composer, it is true that others perceive one in gendered terms.

LOCHHEAD: Do you have any specific or special concerns when you teach or mentor young composers who are women or girls?

SHATIN: I am not aware of any significant differences in the way I teach and mentor young composers who are female. This is largely because I treat each student as a unique individual and tailor my approach accordingly. If anything, I have noticed that some young women need more encouragement to promote their music, but this does not apply to all of them. I wish we had more female applicants to our Composition and Computing Technologies program, and hope this will build over time.

LOCHHEAD: Are there things you've wanted to do as a composer but haven't yet had opportunity?

SHATIN: I would like to expand my work in multimedia and musical theater/opera. I have not yet composed a large-scale musical theater piece, and if I find the right situation, I will. I have composed a chamber opera, *Follies and Fancies*, based on Molière's *Les précieuses ridicules*, commissioned by the Ash Lawn Opera. While that one was a period piece, in keeping with its setting, I would like to return to that genre on a larger scale and without those constraints. Creating music for film also interests me. I have had some experience in this area—first, for Kevin J. Everson's film *Cinnamon*. For that music, I created a soundtrack built from the sounds of the racing cars that were almost a constant in the film. I also collaborated with videographer Kathy Aoki on *Grito del Corazón*, a piece commissioned by the Barcelona New Music Ensemble for a program called Painting Music. Each piece had a video inspired by an artist, and I chose Goya and his *Black Paintings*. Kathy and I sent materials back and forth during the compositional process. And she and her colleague, animator Marco Marquez, have created a video for my piece *Penelope's Song*. In this instance, the music was finished first, and what I love is how the video dances with the music yet creates its own visual rhythms.

LOCHHEAD: Ambitious! Anything else?

SHATIN: Well, in my electroacoustic music—I have not yet composed for electric ensemble, though I have plans to do so with the Cassatt Quartet. I also plan to create more music for amplified ensembles with interactive electronics, such as my *Spring Tides*, commissioned and premiered by the Da Capo Chamber Players.

LOCHHEAD: As we look to the future of music making in the United States, what kinds of challenges do you foresee? And what kinds of musical opportunities would be your ideal?

SHATIN: I think that identity politics is playing an increasing role in what cultural products people consume, as does the powerful anti-intellectual attitude that is so strong in the United States. What I hope is that the kinds of educational outreach that have been undertaken by community groups and ensembles, as well as music in the schools, can help young people discover the deep pleasures of many kinds of music, including classical and contemporary music based on its traditions. In my own case, had it not been for early experiences singing in the school chorus and playing in band and orchestra, it is not clear at what point I would have had the opportunity to expand my musical awareness. Of course at this point we are overloaded with all kinds of music. All the more important that guidance and active participation are available, and that people are not limited to the music most closely associated with their basic cultural groups. When one considers what has been achieved with *El Sistema*,[15] it is clear that educating students with music is hugely important, and making sure that students have this available is something we should all push for in the political arena.

LOCHHEAD: What projects do you see in your future?

SHATIN: This coming year I plan to study percussion with I-Jen Fang, a marvelous percussionist on faculty at the University of Virginia. I have worked closely with her in developing percussion pieces, especially *Time to Burn*, which she and another colleague commissioned. I am excited to learn more from the performance angle. Some years ago I studied conga drumming with another outstanding local player, Robert Jospé. It was fascinating to see how difficult it was to develop even basic chops, and how much fun!

ANALYSIS: *PENELOPE'S SONG* (2003, REV. 2005)

Judith Shatin's stunning electroacoustic work, *Penelope's Song*, currently exists in five closely related versions, each of which comprises an electronic part and a solo instrument: amplified violin, viola, cello, clarinet, or soprano saxophone. Here we will focus on the version for cello, but all of them take as a narrative reference the story of Penelope as told in Homer's

Odyssey. Penelope, the Queen of Ithaca and wife of Odysseus, stays at home in wait for her husband to return from war. Odysseus is away for nearly thirty years, and during this time Penelope, always believing that he will return, discourages suitors with various excuses. Once, she claims she can take no suitors until she finishes weaving a shroud for Odysseus's father, Laertes. But in order to prolong the process, she unravels at night what she has woven during the day. Penelope's weaving stands as a sign of her courage and steadfast belief.

Shatin's piece takes Penelope's story as its premise, valorizing her heroic and often unacknowledged actions. It inscribes Penelope's weaving in the electronic part by sampling the sound of wooden looms used by the weaver Jan Russell as a sound source. The recorded samples are sonically shaped through digital processing.[16]

This analysis considers overall formal design, including motivic and rhythmic organization, and concludes with a summary of pitch design and its coordination with formal articulations. For the purposes of formal discussion, we will reference the form map of *Penelope's Song* depicted in figure 9.1.

Form Map for *Penelope's Song*, version for amplified Cello and Electronics

Section I: Weaving and Spinning

Sub-Sections	Weaving 1	"Dancing" 2	"Spinning" 3	"Defiant" 4	Memory and Dissolution 5
Time	0:00	:41	1:31	2:37	3:04
Cello	WS1-5	WS6	WS1	WS7	WS2r
Loom	Weaving	Weaving	Spinning--crescendo	Spinning/Chords--fade	Quiet spinning
	Cue 1				

Section II: Reverie

Sub-Sections	"Dreaming" 1	"Wistful" 2	"Distant" 3	Despair 4	Ominous "Yearning" 5
Time	3:59	4:19	4:47	5:12	5:44
Cello	RE1	RE2	RE2	RE3	RE2
Loom	"Low rumble"	"Wind"	"Low Hum"	"Gong-like sounds"	"Humming Sounds"
	Cue 2				

Section III: After Reverie--Weaving and Spinning

Sub-Sections	Hesitant--"singing" 1	Gathering Momentum 2	Weaving 3	Dancing 4	"Determined" 5	"Triumph" 6
Time	6:52	7:19	7:33	7:58	8:15	8:48
Cello	AR1	AR2	We1	AR3	WS2i/We2	WS2i'
Loom	Bobbin Rattle	Cont .to Weaving	Weaving	Weaving	Weaving	Weaving
	Cue					

Approx. Length of Sections	Motive Key
———	WS=Weaving 1-7
I=4 min	r-retrograde i-inversion
	RE=Reverie 1-3
II=3 min	AR=After Reverie 1-3
	See Figure For details
III=2 min	

Figure 9.1.

This map is based on the performance by cellist Maxine Neuman on April 9, 2007, at the Leonard Nimoy Thalia Recital Hall at Symphony Space in New York City. The map constitutes my own analytical interpretation of the formal design of *Penelope's Song*, illustrating major sectional articulations as well as shorter subsections. We may see that the piece has two significant articulations, creating three large sections of decreasing length: four to three to two minutes approximately. The first section, "Weaving and Spinning," establishes the defiant determination of Penelope's project, with music that embodies her actions of weaving and spinning. The middle section enacts a reverie of remembering and desire, which at one point turns to despair. And, in the final section, Penelope's resolve is renewed through a transformed recurrence of music from the opening, the work ending with a rising gesture of triumph.

Figure 9.1 employs descriptive terms that are taken either from performance indications in the score or from my own sense of musical affect (performance indications are indicated in quotation marks). The lines separating columns in each section indicate the relative degree of continuity between the subsections. The dotted lines indicate a greater degree of continuity, solid lines a stronger sense of ending and beginning between subsections. Both sections I and III have continuity between all subsections, but in section II there is an internal articulation before the "Despair" subsection. This strong articulation in the middle serves to fragment the section, enhancing its dreamlike qualities and drawing attention to the despondency Penelope must overcome. The "Time" row shows the timings from Shapiro's performance.[17] The "Cello" row indicates motives occurring at the beginning of each subsection, and the "Loom" row provides a general description of the electronic part.

The Loom descriptors are taken directly from Shatin's cues for the cellist in the score.[18] While the descriptions indicate the timbres and textures of the electronic part only in general terms, they do show that the middle section has a sound profile distinct from the outer sections, affirming the overall sectional design.

The Cello row indicates motives that begin each of the subsections of the piece. I have labeled three distinct categories of motives corresponding to the three sections, but there is a strong family resemblance among all of the motives in the piece. As Figure 9.2a indicates, the pitch organization of *Penelope's Song* is built around two tetrachord types. These are 0236 and 0147, each used in prime and inversional form.[19]

Figure 9.2b demonstrates the way in which two transpositions of 0236 may be combined with a form of 0147 to form the aggregate. All of the motives of the work are fashioned from particular intervallic projections of these two tetrachord types in conjunction with a distinct rhythmic profile.

a) Two Tetrachord Types

Name	pc set	Initial transposition	Label
Penelope	0236	G A Bb C#	P^0
Loom	0147	B C D# F#	L^0

b) Two Initial Aggregates

Aggregate A:	P^0: G A Bb C#	P^7: D E F G#	L^0: B C D# F#
Aggregate B:	PI^0: Eb F# G A	PI^5: Ab B C D	LI^0: Bb Db E F

Figure 9.2.

Shatin introduces these two important set classes early in the piece. Set class 4-12 begins work, presented at transposition level seven. 4-18 makes its first appearance about a minute later, at transposition level eleven.

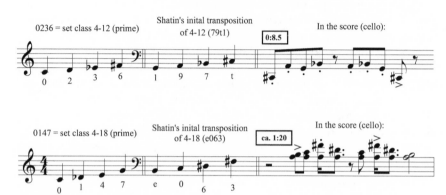

Example 9.14. *Penelope's Song,* set classes 4-12 and 4-18 and their initial transpositions

Figure 9.3 lists the distinct motives for *Penelope's Song.* The motives of each section are labeled according to the section of their first occurrence and then numbered chronologically. For instance, motives of section I are labeled as "Weaving and Spinning," abbreviated as *WS*, and then assigned a number chronologically. With the exception of the initial "Weaving" subsection, figure 9.3 does not show all the motives of each subsection but only the motives that mark formal beginnings.

Section/ Sub-section	Motive	Normal Order	Ordered PCs	Successive Pitch Intervals
Weaving and Spinning				
Weaving	WS1	G A Bb C#	C# A G Bb	+8 -2 +3
	WS2	D E F G#	G# E F D	-4 1 -3
	WS3	D E F G#	E F D G#	+1 -3 6
	WS4	B C D# F#	B C F# D#	-11 6 -3
	WS2inv	Eb F# G A	Eb G F# A	+4 -1 +3
	WS5	G A Bb Db	G Db Bb A	+6 -3 +11
	WS2rgd	D E F G#	D F E G#	+3 -1 +4
Dancing	WS6	D E F G#	E/G# D/F	8 9 : -2 -3
Defiant	WS7	G A Bb D	G A Bb D	+2 +1 +6
Reverie				
Dreaming	RE1	C# Bb B G	G Bb B C#	+3 -11 +14
Wistful	RE2	E F# G Bb	Bb F# G E	+8 +1 +9
Despair	RE3	NA	Abb G F## G#	- - +
After Reverie				
Hesitant	AR1	Db E F G	E F Db G	+1 -4 +6
Gathering	AR2	Bb C C# E	C# E Bb C	+3 +6 +2
Dancing	AR3	D E F G#	D G# F E	+6 -3 -1

Figure 9.3.

The columns of figure 9.3 delineate the section and subsection associated with the motive, normal order of the tetrachord, the ordered pitch classes of the motive, and the successive pitch intervals ("+" indicating a rising interval and "–" a descending interval). This figure illustrates two distinct features of Shatin's formal design for *Penelope's Song*. First, there is a strong family resemblance among all the motives deriving from their generation in two tetrachord types. This resemblance serves to inscribe the spinning narrative of Penelope's story within the musical design of the piece, since the "spinning out" of the tetrachords through motivic projection serves to weave together a consistent harmonic fabric. Further, the motivic design shows that the contrasting middle section utilizes motives with larger or smaller pitch trajectories. For instance, RE2 comprises three relatively large rising intervals and RE3 quarter tones. These motivic distinctions serve to set apart the reverie character of the middle section.

The motivic designations for the cello in the form map of figure 9.1 show several significant things about the formal design of *Penelope's Song*. First, the opening "Weaving" subsection presents five distinct motivic projections of the two tetrachords in a relatively short amount of time, establishing the opening as expository. The second section, "Reverie," does not concretely rely on any of the motives of the first section, but the concluding section does serve as a transformed recollection of the opening. These formal delineations are confirmed by the distinctions and recurrences of the Loom sounds of the electronic part.

Overall, the three-part form in conjunction with the spinning out character of motivic design musically depicts the narrative of Penelope's resolve and triumph. The "Weaving and Spinning" section creates a sonic image of Penelope's determined weaving, the "Reverie" recounts the dreams and doubts of her inner thoughts, and the "After Reverie" replays her weaving as triumphant achievement.

Pitch Organization

As previously mentioned, the music of *Penelope's Song* is organized primarily by two tetrachord types, or pc sets, that recur throughout the piece. And several times during the work, a particular combination of tetrachords articulates the aggregate. Figure 9.2 shows the tetrachordal units in a labeling scheme I have devised to take account of their formal functions. Figure 9.2a demarcates the two tetrachord types, 0236 and 0147, which I call Penelope (P) and Loom (L). The figure also shows that I take the initial transposition of these tetrachords as the "0" form. Figure 9.2b shows the two initial aggregates that occur in the first subsection of the piece. Aggregate A consists of P^0, P^7. and L^0. Aggregate B is formed from the inversional form of the P and L tetrachords: PI^0, PI^5, and LI^0.[20] Motives are fashioned from both the prime and inversional forms of the tetrachords.[21]

Example 9.15a. *Penelope's Song,* "Aggregate A," P^0, P^7, and L^0 combined

Example 9.15b. *Penelope's Song,* "Aggregate B," PI^0, PI^7, and LI^0 combined

But while aggregate articulation certainly occurs in *Penelope's Song,* it is not a prevailing compositional feature. More importantly, the tetrachords establish small melodic-harmonic units, not a specific pitch class ordering; as discussed above, motives are fashioned from a specific pitch ordering of a tetrachord. Pitch groupings are often organized around four-note configurations, assuring the aural presence of the tetrachords as harmonic identities in *Penelope's Song.*

Three sorts of overall pitch design operate in this piece. Either repetition of a limited number of related tetrachords serves to shape a harmonically homogeneous passage; several diverse tetrachords are chained together, creating a harmonically active passage; or articulations of the aggregate play a role in short-term formal processes. Figure 9.4 lists tetrachord occurrences in the piece both by page number and system and by place in the form. Aggregate completion occurs most frequently in the first section and especially in the first, expository subsection.

Page	System	Tetrachords and other information on pitch	Place in Form	
			Sec.	Sub-sec
1	1-2	P^0, P^7, L^0=aggregate A	I	1
	3	PI^0, PI^5, LI^0(no e)= aggregate B; PI^0, PI^5, LI^0(no e)=aggregate B; P^0		1
	4	P^0—P^7		1--2
	5	P^7		2
2	1	P^7		2
	2	(end P^7); L^0; (0369); (0248); PI^3; LI^{10}		2
	3	P^0		3
	4	P^0, P^7, L^0=aggregate A		3
	5	P^0		3
	6	P^0, P^7, L^0=aggregate A		3
3	1	P^0		3
	2	P^0		3
	3	P^0		3
	4	P^0		3
	5	P^0—P^0		3--4
	6	P^0		4
4	1	P^0—P^0		4--5
	2	P^0		5
	3	P^0—PI^4	II	1
	4	PI^6(incomplete)—P^9; P^7—P^1		1—2--3
	5	P^8; (024)—Quarter-tone		3--4
	6	Quarter-tone—P^6; (0123)		4--5
5	1	(4210); P^4; L^9; (01)		5
	2	(01)—PI^{10}	III	1
	3	PI^{10}—P^3		1—2
	4	P^3; P^0—P^{11}		2—3
	5	P^9; P^4, P^{11}, L^4=aggregate A; P^3		3
	6	P^2; P^{10}		3
6	1	P^{10}—P^7		3—4
	2	P^7; PI^{11} and P^1 alternate		4
	3	PI^{11} and P^1 alternate		4
	4	PI^{11} and P^1 alternate—PI^{11}; P^1; LI^1; L^{11}; (0369)		5
	5	P^1; PI^{11}; LI^1; L^{11}		5
	6	PI^{11}; L^{11}; P^1; PI^{11}; P^1 (inc)		5
7	1	PI^{11}		5
	2	PI^{11}		6
	3	PI^{11}→D Major Triad		6

Figure 9.4.

As figure 9.4 indicates, section I is restricted to the tetrachords first articulated in aggregates A and B, with particular emphasis on P^0. The one exception occurs at the end of subsection 2 when two symmetrical tetrachords occur, 0369 and 0248, followed by two new versions of PI and LI.[22]

Example 9.16. *Penelope's Song,* symmetrical tetrachords in section I, subsection 2

Section II, "Reverie," has more harmonic diversity, articulating several different transpositions of P and PI, and includes a passage of quarter tones. Section III presents some new transpositions but toward its end settles into a regular alternation of P^1, PI^{11}, and to a lesser extent L^{11} and LI^1. The formal and harmonic significance of these alternations are discussed below.

In order to demonstrate in more detail aspects of pitch design in *Penelope's Song,* let us focus on three passages: the expository presentations of the Penelope and Loom tetrachords and their aggregate formations in section I, the sense of ungrounded harmonic and motivic design in section II, and the triumphal conclusion of the work in section III.

Example 9.17 cites the opening four systems of *Penelope's Song.* The annotations above the cello part show the occurrences of the three tetrachords comprising aggregate A which is completed at the end of system two. The tetrachords comprising aggregate B occur twice with no pc repetitions at the beginning of system three. The first tetrachord, P^0, completes the initial "Weaving" subsection, and P^7 begins the second "Dancing" subsection (see example 9.17).

While not a controlling principle in this opening section, aggregate completion serves a partial articulatory function, marking off phrase units. More important for pitch organization is the cycling of pitches within the two tetrachord types in both the prime and inversional forms, in conjunction with the presentation of distinct motives, shown in figure 9.3 as WS1-5.

The middle "Reverie" section depends on the effects of motivic and harmonic ungroundedness and discontinuity for its particular role in narrative design. Example 9.18 cites systems three (end) through six of page four. The passage presents in relatively quick succession a sequence of distinct tetrachords: PI^4, PI^6, P^9, P^7, P^1, and P^8. The quick turnover ungrounds the harmony, a dreamy effect enhanced by the quarter-tone passage that follows. The motivic construction of the passage further enhances this reverie and its ensuing despair by means of the larger and smaller intervals and the discontinuity between subsections three and four of section II (see example 9.18).

Penelope's Song

Example 9.17. *Penelope's song*, section I, 0:00–0:41

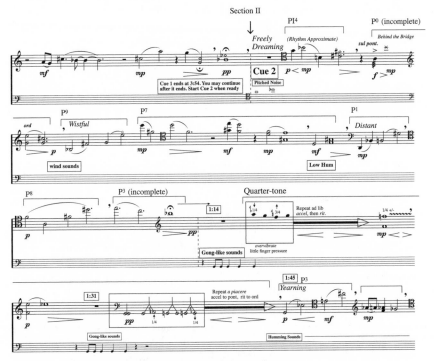

Example 9.18. *Penelope's Song*, tetrachords in section II

As mentioned earlier, the concluding two subsections of *Penelope's Song* consist largely of an alternation of P^1 and PI^{11} and L^{11} and L^1 (see figure 9.4). The consistency of harmonic units determined by the Penelope and Loom tetrachords along with downbeat-oriented and fast rhythms underscore Penelope's triumphal determination at the conclusion of the piece. The particular tetrachord choices Shatin makes here help to further assure this harmonic consistency in the pitch domain. Figure 9.5, which cites the pitch classes of the four dominant tetrachords, shows that both Penelope tetrachords share a D-G♯ frame, and both Loom tetrachords share a B-D-F trichord.

Set-Type	PI^{11}	P^1
PCs in normal order	D F F♯ Ab	G♯ Bb B D
Set-Type	LI^1	L^{11}
PCs in normal order	B D F F♯	Bb B D F

Figure 9.5.

Further, PI^{11} and LI^1 share a D-F-F♯ trichord, and P^1 and L^{11} share a B♭-B-D trichord. The common tones between tetrachords help to propel a forward momentum that underscores Penelope's determination. And, in a sly turn to the triumphal, Shatin ends the work with a D-major sonority that emerges seamlessly from the PI^{11} and LI^1 tetrachords.

Example 9.19. *Penelope's Song,* **ending**

Shatin's *Penelope's Song* musically embodies the narrative of determination and triumph of its heroine, the often forgotten character of the Ulysses story. As discussed above, pitch and motivic structure realize an overall formal design that recounts Penelope's determined weaving, subsequent despair, and finial triumph. The electronic part, which also plays an integral role in formal design, adds another dimension to musical meaning, owing to its physical tracing of the loom. The timbral and rhythmic character of the loom samples and their digital transformations sonically suggest the physicality of weaving and spinning—both their repetitiveness and goal-oriented practicality. Embedding the physicality of weaving into the totality of the musical design, the electronic part is much more than a timbral novelty. Rather, it deepens the sense of embodied action that is crucial to Penelope's story in all of its aspects—determination, despair, and triumph.

CODA

Judith Shatin remains active as both composer and educator. In addition to her work at the University of Virginia, Shatin will be in residence during the summer of 2010 at two festivals: California Summer Music, at Sonoma State University, and Wintergreen Performing Arts, in Virginia's Blue Ridge Mountains.[23] Concerts at each of these festivals will include performances of Shatin's music. Since the time of our interview and discussions, several pieces have been completed and premiered, and several new commissions have come along. If the purpose of a coda is to bring things to a close, this one will surely fail—Judith Shatin is squarely focused on the future.

Rotunda, her collaboration with filmmaker Robert Arnold based on images and sounds collected over the course of a year, was completed in 2009 and shown at the University of Virginia's Art Museum as part of the exhibit *Thomas Jefferson's Academical Village: The Creation of an Architectural Masterpiece. Spring Tides,* for amplified flute, clarinet, violin, cello, and piano and interactive electronics, was commissioned and premiered by the Da Capo players on June 2, 2009, and was also performed on Juilliard's *Beyond the Machine* concerts in 2010. *Spring Tides* is also scheduled for the Bowdoin Festival on their 2010 summer series. Another new piece, *Jefferson in His Own Words,* for orchestra and narrator, was premiered on March 12, 2010, by the Illinois Symphony, Karen Deal conducting. Additional performances are scheduled by the other co-commissioners, including the Charlottesville and University Symphony Orchestra and the Richmond and Virginia symphonies.

A new CD of Shatin's music, *Tower of the Eight Winds*, was released by Innova Records (770) in 2010, with performances by the Borup-Ernst duo. It includes *Icarus*, *Penelope's Song* (version for violin), *Tower of the Eight Winds*, *Widdershins*, and *Fledermaus Fantasy*. *Penelope's Song*, performed by Susan Fancher in the version for soprano sax and electronic playback, was also recently released on Innova Records (736). In addition, *Cherry Blossom and a Wrapped Thing: After Hokusai*, for amplified clarinet and electronics, performed by F. Gerard Errante, has just been released on Aucourant Records (AUREC 1001), and *Ockeghem Variations*, for wind quintet plus piano, will also be released in 2010 by the Dutch Hexagon Ensemble.

Shatin has a variety of compositional projects in the works. These include a solo piano piece, *Chanting to Paradise*, commissioned for Gayle Martin Henry. This piece uses lines from poems by Emily Dickinson, a favorite of both Henry and Shatin, as titles for each of five movements. For the 2010–2011 season, the Peninsula Women's Chorus and Scottish Voices have both commissioned works for women's voices. And for the 2011–2012 season, Shatin will fulfill her recently awarded Fromm Commission with a new piece for amplified string quartet and electronics for the Cassatt Quartet.

For Judith Shatin, the future is full and promising. Her music and expertise are much in demand, and we should expect to hear a rich offering of new music as she remains at the forefront of artistic activity in the United States.

NOTES

1. Unless otherwise cited, all quotations and personal information are from direct correspondence between the author and composer. All quotes are used with permission of the composer. Photo used by permission, Peter Schaaf.

2. Shatin was the first student to give a composition recital for her senior project at Douglass College.

3. In 1995, American Women Composers Inc. merged with the International Congress for Women in Music and the International League of Women Composers to form the International Alliance for Women in Music.

4. Sound walks were a focus of the World Soundscape Project, and the term is defined in Barry Truax, *The Handbook for Acoustic Ecology* (Vancouver, BC: A.R.C. Publications, 1978). Shatin took people on walks to focus on the sounds in the area.

5. From Judith Shatin's program notes for *Dreamtigers*.

6. From Judith Shatin's program notes for *Werther*.

7. Personal communication with the composer.

8. From Judith Shatin's program notes for *Time to Burn*.
9. From Judith Shatin's program notes for *1492*.
10. From Judith Shatin's program notes for *View from Mount Nebo*.
11. See www.emic.kul.ee/InglE/composers/Tormis,%20Veljo.htm.
12. See www.sfu.ca/~westerka.
13. See http://people.virginia.edu/~mk9y.
14. See www.artsusa.org.
15. *El Sistema* is the publicly funded music education program in Venezuela officially known as *Fundación del Estado para el Sistema Nacional de las Orquestas Juveniles e Infantiles de Venezuela*. This music educational system, founded in 1975 by José Antonio Abreu, came into the international spotlight within recent years.
16. Shatin reports in her program notes that the electronic transformations are made with RTcmix, running under Linux. The electronic part consists of three parts, which can be cued individually in order to assure coordination with the live instrumentalist.
17. While Neuman's performance is not publicly available, it does provide a good general sense of proportions. The timings here should be understood as representing a single performance, not some ideal performance.
18. In those few instances when no descriptors are given, I have extrapolated from the prior occurrences of the Loom music.
19. I discuss pitch organization in more detail below. Discussion of motivic design necessarily entails a consideration of the underlying pitch organization, albeit a brief one.
20. Note that aggregate B is missing pc4 (E-natural)
21. I have chosen to label the "⁰" form of inversions by their first occurrence, not with respect to the prime form. This choice better reflects how the tetrachords function in the piece.
22. While not versions of the Penelope and Loom tetrachords, these symmetrical sets serve a transitional function.
23. Photo is from Judith Shatin's trip into Eagle's Nest Mine in Twilight, West Virginia, to harvest sounds for the COAL project. Used by permission, Judith Shatin.

APPENDIX A: LIST OF WORKS

[*Unless otherwise noted, music is published by Wendigo Music and can be ordered through* www.judithshatin.com]

Opera/Stage

Follies and Fancies (1981)—soprano, mezzo, tenor, baritone, bass; piano
Follies and Fancies (1982)—soprano, mezzo, tenor, baritone, bass; flute, bassoon, violin, cello, harpsichord

Orchestra

Arche (1978)—viola and orchestra
Aura (1981)—full orchestra

The Passion of St. Cecilia (1983–1984)—piano concerto
Ruah (1985)—concerto for flute and chamber orchestra
Piping the Earth (1990)—large orchestra
Stringing the Bow (1991)—string orchestra
Glyph (2000)—solo viola, string orchestra and piano
Singing the Blue Ridge (2002)—mezzo, baritone, orchestra, electronics from indigenous wild animal calls
Songs of War and Peace (2008)—chorus and chamber orchestra
Jefferson, in His Own Words (2010)—narrator and orchestra

Band

Commonwealth Salute (1986)—concert band

Choral

'Tis a Gift to be Simple (1984)—chorus; published by Arsis Press
We Bring You Peace (1990)—chorus; published by E. C. Schirmer
Hark My Love (1991)—chorus and piano
We Hold These Truths (1992)—chorus, brass quintet, timpani
Beetles, Monsters and Roses (ClickBeetle, Someone, I Am Rose, The Wendigo) (1993)—four songs for SSA and electronic playback; published by Colla Voce Music Inc.
COAL (1993–1994)—chorus, Appalachian band (banjo, fiddle, guitar, hammered dulcimer, 2 Appalachian singers), synthesizer and electronic playback
Adonai Ro'i (1995)—chorus
Adonai Ro'i (1996)—chorus and string orchestra
Nun, Gimel, Hei, Shin (1996)—chorus (three-part); published by Colla Voce Music Inc.
Songs of War and Peace (1998)—4 songs for chorus (SATB) and piano
Eseret Makot (1998)—chorus (three-part) (passover round), plus flute, cello, piano
Shapirt Y'fehfiah (2000)—SSA
Alleluia (2001)—SATB; published by E. C. Schirmer
Amulet (2004)—SSA
Opinion Is Power (2004)—SATB
The Jabberwocky (2006)—TTBB; published by E. C. Schirmer
Why the Caged Bird Sings (2007)—SATB, piano; published by E. C. Schirmer
Avadim Hayinu (Once We Were Slaves) (2008)—chorus (three-part passover round)

Chamber Music

Psalm 100 (1973)—tenor or soprano and piano
When the Moon of Wildflowers Is Full (1975)—flute/cello
Quatrain (1978)—violin, viola, clarinet, bass clarinet
Wind Songs (1980)—wind quintet
Lost Angels (1980)—trumpet, bassoon, piano
Gazebo Music (1981)—flute and cello; published by Arsis Press
Study in Black (1981)—flute and percussion; published by Arsis Press

Akhmatova Songs (1982)—mezzo, flute, clarinet, violin, cello, and piano
Werther (1983)—mezzo, flute, clarinet, violin, cello, and piano
Icarus (1983)—violin and piano
Glyph (1984)—solo viola, string quartet, and piano
Monument in Brass (1986)—brass quintet fanfare
View from Mt. Nebo (1986)—piano trio
Ignoto Numine (1986)—piano trio
Wedding Song (1987)—soprano and English horn (or alto flute, clarinet, or viola)
Marvelous Pursuits (1987)—vocal quartet and piano 4-hands
Gabriel's Wing (1989)—flute and piano
Secret Ground (1990)—flute, clarinet, violin, and cello
1492 (1992)—piano and percussion
Sister Thou Wast Mild and Lovely (1994)—soprano and viola (or clarinet)
Ruah (1994)—flute/piano version
The Janus Quartet (1994)—string quartet
Hearing the Call (1995)—2 trumpets and 2 snare drums
Dreamtigers (1996)—flute and guitar
Spin (1997)—flute, clarinet, bassoon, violin, viola, cello
Fantasia Sobre el Flamenco (1998)—brass quintet
Houdini, Memories of a Conjurer (1999)—cello, piano, percussion
Calling (2000)—cello, piano, percussion
Ockeghem Variations (2000)—wind quintet and piano
Run (2001)—piano quartet
Fledermaus Fantasy (2003)—version for solo violin + viola, cello, contrabass, piano
Ki Koleich Arev (2004)—soprano, flute, piano
Three Summers' Heat (2005)—version for soprano, flute, viola, harp
Clave (2005)—flute, clarinet, tenor sax, violin, viola, percussion, piano
Teruah (2006)—shofar, 2 trumpets, 2 trombones, 3 horns, timpani
Time to Burn (2006)—oboe and 2 percussion
Glyph (2007)—version for solo clarinet, string quartet, and piano
Akhmatova Songs (2008)—version for dramatic soprano or mezzo and piano
Tower of the Eight Winds (2008)—violin and piano

Solo

Entreat Me Not (from the Book of Ruth) (1971, rev. 1977)—voice
Limericks (1974)—flute
Scirocco (1981)—piano
Sursum Corda (1981)—cello
Bagatelle (1982)—piano
Widdershins (1983)—piano; published by Arsis Press
L'étude du Cœur (1983, rev. 1987)—viola; published by Edition Peters
Assembly Line #1 (1985)—oboe
Fasting Heart (1987)—flute
Carreño (1987)—pianist/mezzo
Meridians (1988)—clarinet
Round 3 (1989)—trombone

Chai Variations on Eliahu HaNavi (1995)—piano
Baruch HaBa (1995)—voice (versions for male or female)
Coursing Through the Still Green (1995)—Flute; Subito Music, *The American Flute Fantasy on St. Cecilia* (1996)—piano
Penelope's Dream (2006)—cello

Electroacoustic

Hearing Things (1989)—amplified violin, MIDI keyboard, computer running HMSL, and electronic instruments
Three Summers' Heat (1989–1990)—mezzo or soprano and electronic playback
Hosech Al P'ney HaTehom (*Darkness in the Face of the Deep*) (1990)—electronic playback (realized at Stanford's Center for Research in Music and Acoustics, CCRMA)
Kairos (1991)—amplified flute, Mac computer running HMSL, VP-70 voice processor, and Quadraverb; rescored in 2007 for amplified flute and Max-MSP, with the assistance of composer Troy Rogers
Beetles, Monsters and Roses (*ClickBeetle, Someone, I Am Rose, The Wendigo*) (1993)—four songs for SSA and electronic playback; published by Colla Voce
Elijah's Chariot (1995)—amplified string quartet and electronic playback
Grito del Corazón (2001–2010)—version 1: flute, violin, cello, keyboards; additional versions for various chamber and solo combinations
Penelope's Song (2003, rev. 2005)—amplified viola, electronic playback
Tree Music (2003)—interactive installation (not available)
Glimmerings (2003)—electronic playback
Cherry Blossom and Wrapped Thing: After Hokusai (2004, rev. 2006)—clarinet and eight-channel or stereo electronics
Penelope's Loom (2004)—electronic playback
Civil War Memories (2005)—electronic playback
For the Birds (2005)—amplified cello and electronic playback
Penelope's Song (2005)—versions for clarinet + electronics and violin + electronics
Penelope's Song (2006)—version for cello and electronic playback
Penelope's Song (2007)—version for soprano sax + electronic playback
Housemade Music (2007)—electronic playback
Spring Tides (2009)—amplified flute, clarinet, violin, cello, piano + interactive electronics

Multimedia

Cinnamon (2007)—film by Kevin J. Everson, music by Judith Shatin
Rotunda (2009)—film with video by Robert Arnold, music by Judith Shatin

APPENDIX B: DISCOGRAPHY

1492. Hugh Minton, piano; Mike Parola, percussion. New World Records 80559-2. "Bending the Light." 1994, 1999.

Adonai Roi. Judith Clurman and the New York Concert Singers. New World Records 80504-2. "Divine Grandeur." 1996, 1997.

Akhmatova Songs. Lucy Shelton, soprano; Da Capo Chamber Players. Innova Recordings 613. "Dreamtigers." 2004.

Aura. Richmond Symphony. Opus One 125 (analog disc). "Premiere Recordings." 1984.

Cherry Blossom and a Wrapped Thing: After Hokusai. F. Gerard Errante, clarinet. Aucourant Records AUREC 1001. 2010.

Dreamtigers. William DeVito, guitar; Patricia Spencer, flute. Innova Recordings 613. "Dreamtigers." 2004.

Fantasía sobre el flamenco. St. Mary's Brass. Sonora Publications SO22591CD. "Hearing the Call." 1999.

Fasting Heart. Neuma B00000VXI. "Narcissus and Kairos." 1995, 1997.

Fledermaus Fantasy. Borup-Ernst Duo. Innova Recordings 770. "Tower of the Eight Winds." 2010.

Gazebo Music. Andre Emilianoff, cello; Patricia Spencer, flute. Innova Recordings 613. "Dreamtigers." 2009.

Glimmerings. Capstone CPS 8744. 2004.

Hearing the Call. St. Mary's Brass. Sonora Publications SO 22591CD. "Hearing the Call." 1999.

Housemade Music. JKR Pass3. Open Space 21. 2007.

Icarus. Borup-Ernst Duo. Innova Recordings 770. "Tower of the Eight Winds." 2010.

Ignoto Numine. Monticello Trio. Composers Recordings Inc. CRI CD 583. Now available through New World Records. "Monticello Trio." 1990.

Kairos. Patricia Spencer, flute. Neuma B00000VXI. "Narcissus and Kairos." 1995, 1997.

Nun, Gimel, Hei, Shin. New London Children's Chorus; Ronald Corp, conductor. Naxos 8.559410. "A Hanukkah Celebration." 1992, 2003.

Ockeghem Variations. Hexagon Ensemble. In press, 2010.

The Passion of St. Cecilia. Gayle Martin Henry, pianist; Joel Suben, conductor; Moravian Philharmonic. Capstone CPS 8727. "Piping the Earth." 2003.

Penelope's Song (soprano saxophone version). Susan Fancher, soprano sax. Innova Recordings 736. 2009.

Penelope's Song (violin version). Hasse Borup, violin. Innova Recordings 770. "Tower of the Eight Winds." 2010.

Piping the Earth. Joel Suben, conductor; Moravian Philharmonic. Capstone CPS 8727. "Piping the Earth." 2003.

Ruah. Renee Siebert, flute; Robert Black, conductor; Prism Chamber Orchestra. Composers Recordings Inc. CRI CD 605. 1991.

Ruah. Renee Siebert, flute; Robert Black, conductor; Prism Chamber Orchestra. Capstone CPS 8727. "Piping the Earth." 2003.

Sea of Reeds. F. Gerard Errante, clarinet. Centaur CRC 2454. "Music from the Virginia Center for Computer Music." 1998, 1999.

Secret Ground. Da Capo Chamber Players. Innova Recordings 613. "Dreamtigers." 2004.

Spin. North/South Ensemble. North/South Recordings NSR 1046. 2007.

Stringing the Bow. Joel Suben and the Moravian Philharmonic. Capstone CPS 8727. "Piping the Earth." 2003.

Three Summers' Heat. Susan Narucki, Soprano. Centaur CRC 2454. "Music from the Virginia Center for Computer Music." 1998, 1999.
Tower of the Eight Winds. Borup-Ernsto Duo. Innova Recordings 770. "Tower of the Eight Winds." 2010.
The Wendigo (for treble chorus and electronics). San Francisco Girls Chorus. SFGC 9601. "I Never Saw Another Butterfly." 1996.
Werther. Da Capo Chamber Players. Innova Recordings 613. "Dreamtigers." 2004.
Widdershins. Mary Kathleen Ernst. Innova Recordings 770. "Tower of the Eight Winds." 2010.
Wind Songs. Clarion Wind Quintet. Opus One 87. "Wind Songs." 1983, 1984.

SOURCES

"Judith Shatin: A Conversation with the Publisher," *New Music Connoisseur* 12, no. 4 (2004): 5–7.
Edwards, J. Michelle. "Judith Shatin: Talking Music." *International Alliance for Women in Music Journal* 10, no. 2 (2004): 1–7.
Shatin, Judith. Composer website. www.judithshatin.com.

INDEX

1492 (Shatin), 417–18

Abanico, 282
Abyss (Richter), 365–66, 376
ACA. *See* American Composers
　Alliance
academic, 65, 111–12, 117, 119–20, 192,
　209–10, 230, 300, 303, 305, 327, 406,
　409–10, 423, 443
Ácana (Léon), 254
acciaccatura, 263–65
acoustic, 120, 194, 206, 211, 222, 329,
　405, 426
Adagio (McTee), 328, 334–35, 339, 350
Adagio for Strings (Barber), 335
Adams, John, 324
Africa/African, 87, 130, 195, 251, 256,
　258–59, 279, 365
Afro-Cuban, 256, 258–59, 272, 279–82,
　285n30, 285n33, 285n34
ageism, 29
aggregate, 7, 338–39, 435, 437–40
Agnus Dei (McTee), 335
aikido, 88, 90, 121
Albany Symphony Orchestra (New
　York), 94
Alber, Brian, 308, 352n13
alborada, 109
Albright, William, 90
aleatoric/aleatory, 27, 57, 60–62, 67, 73,
　79, 92, 104, 120, 126
ALIAS ensemble, 133
All Desire Is Sad (Richter), 363, 368
Alsop, Marin, 368
American Academy in Rome, 54, 255

American Academy of Arts and
　Letters, 54, 142, 255
American Composers Alliance (ACA),
　414
American Composers Orchestra, 54,
　254
American Composers' Forum, 192
American Organist Guild, 229
American Society of Composers,
　Authors and Publishers (ASCAP),
　94, 101, 142, 148, 255
American String Teachers Association,
　313
American Symphony Orchestra
　League, 163, 192
American Women Composers Inc.,
　406, 431
An American in Peru (Frank), 102
An American Triptych(Austin), 19
An die Nachgeborenen(Austin), 5
Andean/Andes, 88, 90, 92–94, 96, 100,
　103–6, 112–13, 119–24, 131–32, 367
Andreyev, Leonid, 365
Animating Democracy Initiative of
　Americans for the Arts, 407
Anne of Cleves, 213, 222–25
Antares Piano-Clarinet Quartet, 395
Aoki, Kathy, 432
Argentina, 91
Argento, Dominic, 204, 212
Arguedas, José Maria, 90, 93
Aria and Toccata (Richter), 363, 376
Arnold, Robert, 423, 443
Arsis Press, 405
Arthur Murray Dance Studio, 332

451

INDEX OF MUSICAL WORKS BY COMPOSER

*Names in **boldface** indicate the nine female composers highlighted in this collection.*

ABOUT THE EDITOR
AND CONTRIBUTORS

EDITOR

Michael K. Slayton is associate professor and chair of the Department of Music Composition and Theory at Vanderbilt University's Blair School of Music in Nashville, Tennessee. His music is regularly programmed in the United States and abroad, most recently in Leipzig, Droyssig, and Weimar, Germany; Paris, Tours, and Marquette-lez-Lille, France; Brussels, Belgium; Johannesburg and Potchefstroom, South Africa; London, UK; and New York, NY. In recent years, he has contributed articles for the *Journal of the International Alliance for Women in Music*, presented scholarly papers on the music of Elizabeth R. Austin, and been invited to serve as a forum panelist to discuss issues facing women in contemporary composition. Slayton is a member of the American Composers' Alliance, Society of Composers Inc., the College Music Society, Connecticut Composers Inc., and Broadcast Music Inc.

CONTRIBUTORS

Carson Cooman is an American composer with a large catalog of music in many forms; his work has been performed on all six inhabited continents. Cooman's music appears on over twenty-five recordings, including ten complete CDs on the Naxos, Albany, Artek, and Zimbel labels. Cooman's primary composition studies have been with Bernard Rands, Judith Weir, Alan Fletcher, and James Willey, and he holds degrees from Harvard University and the Carnegie Mellon School of Music. As an active concert organist, Cooman specializes exclusively in the performance of new music. Over 130 new works have been composed for him by composers from around the world, and his performances of the work of contemporary composers can be heard on a number of CD recordings. Cooman's musicological writing has focused primarily on living American and Australian composers, and he has written articles and reviews for a number of international publications. Cooman serves as an active consultant on music business matters to composers and performing organizations. For more information, visit www.carsoncooman.com.

Deborah Hayes, musicologist, is a professor emerita and former associate dean for graduate studies in the College of Music, University of Colorado at Boulder. Her publications include studies of the theoretical writings of J.-P. Rameau and new editions of the music of several late-eighteenth-century European composers, including Marie-Emmanuelle Bayon Louis (1746–1825) and Francesca LeBrun (1756–1790). Hayes was an associate editor of *Women and Music in America Since 1900: An Encyclopedia* (2002), to which she contributed many entries on gender issues. She has written bio-bibliographies of Peggy Glanville-Hicks (1912–1990) and Peter Sculthorpe (1929–), and she is completing a book about the life and works of Ruth Shaw Wylie (1916–1989).

Donald McKinney is the wind ensemble conductor at Interlochen Arts Academy, where he guides the band program, coaches chamber music, and instructs conducting students. From 2004 to 2007, he was associate conductor of ensembles at Duquesne University's Mary Pappert School of Music, during which time he served as the assistant to violinist and conductor Sidney Harth, teaching courses in undergraduate conducting. McKinney has published articles in volumes 5, 6, and 7 of *Teaching Music through Performance in Band*, a project which led to his performing and recording with the North Texas Wind Symphony. Further, he has participated in numerous conducting symposiums, including New England Conservatory, University of North Texas, University of Minnesota, and the Conductors Institute of South Carolina. In the summer of 2010, he will begin conducting at Interlochen Arts Camp. McKinney received the D.M.A. in conducting from the University of Michigan in 2010; his primary conducting teachers have been Michael Haithcock, Jack Stamp, and Robert Cameron. He has completed additional study with H. Robert Reynolds and Frank Battisti.

Tina Milhorn Stallard maintains an active career as a soprano soloist, chamber musician, researcher, and teacher. She has sung with Opera Omaha, Central City Opera, Opera Theatre of Lucca (Italy), Cincinnati Opera, Kentucky Opera, Cincinnati Chamber Orchestra, Lexington Philharmonic Orchestra, Johnson City Symphony, Louisville Orchestra, South Carolina Philharmonic Orchestra, and Bowling Green Western Symphony. As part of the cultural prelude to the 2008 Summer Olympics, she performed the soprano solos in Vivaldi's *Gloria* with the Shanghai Philharmonic Orchestra and members of the Beijing National Ballet Orchestra. A frequent recitalist, Stallard has presented programs in Puerto Rico, Hawaii, New York, Indiana, Texas, Florida, Louisiana, Georgia, Tennessee, and throughout South Carolina. In 2010, she joined the faculty of the Varna (Bulgaria) Music Academy. Stallard also serves as a clinician and researcher, with special interests in the music of living American composers and voice pedagogy. She holds the doctor of musical arts degree from the University of Cincinnati College Conservatory of Music and is an alumnus of the University of Kentucky (Haggin Fellow) and Belmont University. She is a member of the voice faculty at the University of South Carolina, where she teaches applied voice and vocal pedagogy.

James Spinazzola is associate professor of music and director of instrumental activities at the University of Indianapolis, where his responsibilities include the direction of the Symphonic Wind Ensemble and Chamber Orchestra, and the instruction of courses in conducting and woodwind pedagogy. He also serves as conductor of the New World Youth Philharmonic and as music director of the Indianapolis Youth Wind Ensemble. He frequently appears as a guest clinician and has conducted local, regional, and all-state ensembles in eight states. Spinazzola's publications include articles in *Teaching Music through Performance in Band* (GIA) and a wind ensemble transcription of John Adams's *Lollapalooza* (Boosey & Hawkes). His arrangements and compositions have been performed throughout the world, at conferences of the College Band Directors National Association and the Percussive Arts Society, and by the Nashville Ballet. Also active as a saxophonist, he has recorded a compact disc for the Mark Custom label. Spinazzola holds degrees from Duquesne University (B.S.), the University of Colorado (M.M.), and Louisiana State University (D.M.A.).

Sharon Mirchandani is associate professor of music history and theory at Westminster Choir College of Rider University. She received her bachelor of music degree in piano performance (with a pedagogy emphasis) from Bowling Green State University, master of music degrees in both music history and piano accompanying and chamber music from Temple University, and her Ph.D. in musicology from Rutgers, the State University of New Jersey. She has presented research papers at the annual meeting of the American Musicological Society, the annual meeting of the Society for American Music (formerly the Sonneck Society), the American Musicological Society GNYC chapter meeting, and a College Music Society workshop. She has also served as a panelist at conferences of the College Music Society and the Mid-Atlantic Women's Studies Association, as a board member of the International Alliance for Women in Music, and on the AMS Committee on the History of the Society. Mirchandani's publications include articles in *Notes, Historical Anthology of Music by Women, Choral Journal, Women and Music in America Since 1900: An Encyclopedia, The Hymn,* and *Journal for the International Alliance for Women in Music.* She is currently working on a biography of American composer Marga Richter.

Judith Lochhead, Stony Brook University, is a theorist and musicologist whose work focuses on the most recent musical practices in North America and Europe. Utilizing concepts and methodologies from post-phenomenological and poststructuralist thought, she develops modes of thinking about recent music that address the uniquely defining features of this repertoire. Her work distinguishes between the conceptions of musical structure and meaning that derive from the differing perspectives of performers, listeners, and composers. Some recent articles include "Refiguring the Modernist Program for Hearing: Steve Reich and George Rochberg" (2004), "Visualizing the Musical Object" (2006), "'How Does it Work?': Challenges to Analytic Explanation" (2006), and "The Sublime, the Ineffable, and Other Dangerous Aesthetics" (2008). With Joseph Auner, Lochhead coedited *Postmodern Music/Postmodern Thought* (Routledge 2001). She is currently completing a book on the analysis of recent music entitled *Reconceiving Structure: Recent Music/Music Analysis*.